THE EUROPEAN UNION IN INTERNATIONAL ORGANISATIONS AND GLOBAL GOVERNANCE

The European Union is a key participant in international organisations with its involvement taking different forms, ranging from full membership to mere observer. Moreover, there is also not only one status of observer, but different ones depending on the constituent charters of the organisations. This book provides a comprehensive overview of the participation of the EU in five international organisations: the UN, the ILO, the WTO, the WHO and the WIPO. It identifies its role and influence in diverse areas of global governance, such as foreign policy, peace, human rights, social rights, trade, health and intellectual property.

EU and international experts, diplomats and scholars have contributed to this book to give an overview of the different aspects linked to the participation of the EU in these organisations and to the coordination that takes place internally with its Member States. They also examine the EU's actual influence in the various areas and its contribution to global governance. The combination of these two dimensions allows the work to identify the strengths and weaknesses of the participation of the EU in these five international organisations.

The book provides valuable insights for scholars and policymakers, and is useful for representatives of other international organisations and civil society actors.

Volume 56 in the Series Modern Studies in European Law

Modern Studies in European Law
Recent titles in this series:

EU Environmental Law, Governance and Decision-Making
Maria Lee

Shaping the Single European Market in the Field of Foreign Direct Investment
Philip Strik

Nationalism and Private Law in Europe
Guido Comparato

EU Asylum Procedures and the Right to an Effective Remedy
Marcelle Reneman

The EU Accession to the ECHR
Edited by Vasiliki Kosta, Nikos Skoutaris and Vassilis P Tzevelekos

The European Court of Justice and External Relations: Constitutional Challenges
Edited by Marise Cremona and Anne Thies

A Critique of Codification
Leone Niglia

Protecting Vulnerable Groups: The European Human Rights Framework
Edited by Francesca Ippolito and Sara Iglesias Sanchez

EU International Relations Law Second Edition
Panos Koutrakos

Fundamental Rights in the EU: A Matter for Two Courts
Edited by Sonia Morano-Foadi and Lucy Vickers

What Form of Government for the European Union and the Eurozone?
Federico Fabbrini, Ernst Hirsch Ballin and Han Somsen

The UK and European Human Rights: A Strained Relationship?
Edited by Katja S Ziegler, Elizabeth Wicks and Loveday Hodson

For the complete list of titles in this series, see the
'Modern Studies in European Law' link at
www.hartpub.co.uk/books/series.asp

The European Union in International Organisations and Global Governance

Recent Developments

Edited by
Christine Kaddous

·HART·
PUBLISHING
OXFORD AND PORTLAND, OREGON
2017

Hart Publishing
An imprint of Bloomsbury Publishing Plc

Hart Publishing Ltd
Kemp House
Chawley Park
Cumnor Hill
Oxford OX2 9PH
UK

Bloomsbury Publishing Plc
50 Bedford Square
London
WC1B 3DP
UK

www.hartpub.co.uk
www.bloomsbury.com

Published in North America (US and Canada) by
Hart Publishing
c/o International Specialized Book Services
920 NE 58th Avenue, Suite 300
Portland, OR 97213-3786
USA

www.isbs.com

HART PUBLISHING, the Hart/Stag logo, BLOOMSBURY and the Diana logo are trademarks of Bloomsbury Publishing Plc

First published in hardback, 2015
Paperback edition, 2017

British Library Cataloguing-in-Publication Data
A catalogue record for this book is available from the British Library.

ISBN: PB: 978-1-50991-837-9
HB: 978-1-84946-700-1

Typeset by Compuscript Ltd, Shannon
Printed and bound in Great Britain by
Lightning Source UK Ltd

Preface

The contributions brought together in this book are based on the reports presented at the Conference 'The European Union in International Organisations and Global Governance', organised in Geneva on the occasion of the 50th Anniversary of the Centre d'études juridiques européennes (CEJE), which was awarded the label of 'Centre d'excellence Jean Monnet' by the European Commission in 2014.

This book provides a comprehensive overview of the participation of the European Union in five international organisations, selected not only because of their presence in Geneva, but also because of the variety of forms of EU participation they allow (such as observer or full member). The selection comprises the United Nations (UN), the International Labour Organization (ILO), the World Trade Organization (WTO), the World Health Organization (WHO) and the World Intellectual Property Organization (WIPO).

The main purpose of the book is to discuss the interaction between the European Union and these international organisations and it focuses on the Union's position in global governance. However, this interaction, as will be shown, depends deeply on the allocation of powers between the Union and its Member States in the fields of activity of the international organisations under examination.

The originality of the book lies in the fact that it brings together contributions by European Union and international relations experts, diplomats, policy makers and scholars, providing a variety of analyses of the legal, political and economic aspects linked to the participation of the Union in these international organisations. The contributions consider the coordination that has to take place internally between the Union and the Member States on the one hand, and try to evaluate the Union's influence and contribution to global governance on the other. The addition of these different dimensions allows us to define the strengths and weaknesses of EU participation in the five selected international organisations.

The Lisbon Treaty has been in force for five years and it is now possible to reflect on the way the Union and its Member States apply the provisions on external action in relation to the participation in international organisations and on the role played by the European External Action Service (EEAS). Taking into account these changes and the practice which has been developed on the basis of the Treaty on the European Union (TEU) and the Treaty on the Functioning of the European Union (TFEU), the Introduction addresses the general question of how to explain the ever greater participation of the European Union in international organisations today, despite the numerous challenges it has to face internally and externally in relation to that participation. Should this phenomenon be considered the result of a functional necessity or is it a general aspiration of the Union to participate in most international fora which contribute to global governance? Christine Kaddous first discusses the principles applicable to EU external representation taking into account the very latest developments in the matter. The author considers the main foundations for the Union to participate in such international organisations and analyses the recent challenges the Union has to face, in particular the establishment of EU positions to be held in international organisations. The conclusive part assesses the main reasons for the ever greater participation of the Union to international fora and determines the essential needs to better strengthen its position and role within international organisations.

Part I of the book covers the participation of the European Union in the United Nations (UN). Mariangela Zappia introduces the issues related to this participation from a European Union perspective and brings her invaluable experience as Head of the EU Delegation to the UN and other international organisations in Geneva. The contribution makes an appraisal of the practical changes in the EU representation brought by the establishment of the EEAS and by the adoption in 2011 of the UN General Assembly Resolution on the participation of the Union in the UN. Markus Schmidt brings the United Nations' perspective to the discussion and provides a valuable analysis of the European Union's position in the UN Human Rights Programme and the UN Human Rights Council, in UN Humanitarian Affairs and in the International Strategy for Disaster Reduction as well as in the UN Economic Commission for Europe. The contribution of Jan Wouters, Anna-Luise Chané, Jed Odermatt and Thomas Ramopoulos deals with the legal and political issues of EU representation in the UN system in general, with a particular examination of the difficulties in UN bodies such as the FAO, IAEA and UNESCO. The authors of this last and rich contribution consider that despite the existence of the Barroso–Ashton Strategy of December 2012 there is for the time being no convincing strategy to improve the EU's status in the UN system.

The contributions of Part II offer an analysis of the participation of the European Union in the International Labour Organization (ILO). Marco Ferri examines the coordination between the European Union and its Member States with that organisation, of which the Union is not a member, although it has significant competences in the field of social policy. As a Counsellor at the EU Delegation in Geneva, the author brings a valuable appraisal of the practical issues raised in the coordination between the Union and the Member States in the technical, policy and political activities within the ILO. The second contribution, written by Geneviève Pons-Deladrière, Director of the Legal Service of the ILO, analyses the European Union's participation and cooperation in ILO institutions and activities from an ILO perspective, highlighting the convergence in the objectives of the two organisations and their common agenda on employment and social affairs as well as on the promotion notably of 'decent work' in global multilateral fora, which should bring better interaction and reciprocal influence.

Part III of the book is devoted to the participation of the European Union in the World Trade Organization (WTO). Detlev Brauns and Tomas Baert consider that the EU's representation to the WTO remains special and of a *sui generis* nature, in particular compared to the other international organisations located in Geneva.

The external representation through a single voice remained unchanged pre- and post-Lisbon, but at the same time new issues and litigations arose in relation to the legal basis for the negotiator role of the Commission. Janos Volkai, Counsellor at the Legal Affairs Division of the WTO, gives a WTO perspective in pointing out specific and classical issues, such as membership, budget, right to speak, decision making, WTO dispute settlement, schedules, EU enlargements and Treaty-making powers, bringing to light some oft-forgotten elements. Frank Hoffmeister wonders very interestingly whether the participation of the Union in the WTO could be a model for the EU's status in other international organisations. He answers the question affirmatively, but draws attention to the fact that the success of the EU in the WTO is due to a number of factors he enumerates, but which should be checked before exploring a potential transposition of the model to other international organisations.

The fourth Part of the book contains an analysis of the participation of the European Union in the World Health Organization (WHO). This Part opens with a paper by Lourdes Chamorro on the coordination between the Union and the Member States from a European Union perspective. The author considers that while the EU holds an observer status, its participation at the different levels and within the various settings and processes of the WHO has been recently widely developed and recognised. Gian Luca Burci addresses the issue of the interactions and collaboration between the Union and the WHO from a governance and policy perspective. He stresses that the increase of EU competence in areas directly or indirectly related to global health will bring progress in the impact of the Union on the work of the WHO and the next step might be the conclusion of a general agreement on the EU's participation in the WHO's governance. Ilona Kickbusch, Stephen A Matlin, Samantha Battams and Albrecht Jahn explore the important topic of the European Union's role and potential in research and innovation for global health, which is fundamental to the objectives of Europe 2020. This very enriching contribution analyses the challenges the Union has to face and proposes recommendations and strategies in the field of global health.

Part V refers to the participation of the European Union in the World Intellectual Property Organization (WIPO). Jean-Christophe Galloux assesses this participation as being of a cloudy complexity. The EU legal situation in the WIPO is no less complex than in any other international organisation. However, intellectual property is a disparate set of rights fundamentally rooted in the principle of territoriality, subject to different international regimes, and constantly changing. The author regrets that the Union still appears in that field as a minor player. More coherence between national and EU intellectual property rights should be developed and more solidarity on the part of the Member States would contribute to the success of the Union within the WIPO.

Part VI contains a contribution by Ernst-Ulrich Petersmann, which opens a new perspective with respect to the other contributions to the book. The idea is to take into consideration the various forms of EU participation in international organisations in order to determine the 'criteria' that should allow an evaluation of the normative power of the Union in multilevel governance of public goods. The contribution focuses on methodological pluralism (lawyers, economists, and political scientists) before considering that there is a need for interdisciplinary clarification of the 'principles of justice' underlying UN and WTO law. Briefly formulated, the author states that the rule of law should be protected at national and international levels of governance and that the Union should take the lead in the matter for the benefit of citizens and their human right to a social and international order in which the rights and freedoms set forth in Article 28 of the Universal Declaration of Human Rights of 1948 can be fully realised.

The book contains a variety of perspectives on the participation of the European Union in international organisations. The contributions obviously do not all come to the same conclusions but the differences help to build up the complex picture of this ever greater participation of the Union in international fora. The key word is certainly not 'simplicity', but it is also not 'cacophony' but rather 'complexity' due to the hybrid nature of the European Union and to the distribution of competences between itself and the Member States on the one hand, and to the constituent charters of the international organisations to which the Union participates on the other.

As appears from the contributions and to take two clear examples, the role of the European Union within international organisations may be major, as in the WTO, or minor, as in the WIPO. However, progress is being made in the UN, the ILO and the WHO as reflected in the individual contributions. Clearly the legal, political and economic influence of the European Union within international organisations is improving day by day.

Acknowledgements

The editor is grateful to the *Centre d'études juridiques européennes*, the Faculty of Law, the University of Geneva and Union Bancaire Privée, UBP SA, for their financial support for the Geneva conference at which most papers included in this volume were presented. I would also like to thank the *Fonds général* of the University of Geneva for its financial support, which made possible the publication of this book. I am grateful to the staff of the *Centre d'études juridiques européennes*, in particular Sandy Kirsch, for their help in the preparation of the above event and of the present volume.

Christine Kaddous

Contents

List of Contributors

Tomas Baert

Tomas Baert is an official at the Directorate-General for Trade of the European Commission, which he joined in 2005. From 2010 to 2014, he worked as a first secretary at the Permanent Mission of the European Union to the World Trade Organization (WTO) in Geneva, where he was responsible for intellectual property rights, WTO rules negotiations and competition policy. Prior to joining the EU Mission in Geneva, from 2008 to 2010 he worked in DG Trade as the coordinator for EU investment policy, responsible for managing the transition towards exclusive competence on foreign direct investment. From 2007 to 2010, he was the EU's negotiator on investment and services trade in the EU–India free trade negotiations. Between 2005 and 2007 he dealt with various EU–China and EU–US trade dossiers in the area of services trade and investment, including the setting up of the EU–US investment dialogue.

Prior to joining the European Commission, from 2002 to 2005 he worked for the US multinational corporation DuPont as an EU government affairs representative. In 2001, he was a researcher at the International Trade Policy Unit of the London School of Economics where he researched the emergence of regulatory barriers to trade in goods and services. He holds an MSc from the London School of Economics (LSE), United Kingdom, and an MA from the Catholic University of Leuven (KUL), Belgium. He also spent a term as an exchange student at the Graduate Institute of International and Development Studies in Geneva, Switzerland.

Samantha Battams

Associate Professor Samantha Battams is Program Director of Public Health at Torrens University, Australia and Senior Lecturer at the Southgate Institute of Health, Society and Equity at Flinders University, South Australia. Previously she was Course Director for the Global Health: An Interdisciplinary Overview course at the University of Geneva. She also works as an independent consultant on global and public health matters.

Recently she was Visiting Fellow at the Graduate Institute of International and Development Studies (Global Health Programme), Geneva, and Senior Researcher for the National Centre for Education and Training on Addiction, Flinders University.

Her research interests include mental health, alcohol and other drugs, the social determinants of health and governance for health and policy processes. Other research interests include social housing, NCD policy and strategy, inter-sectoral policy and action, user/carer involvement in policy and services, human rights and health, and community and social history.

She has a PhD in public health policy from Flinders University, where she worked in teaching and research in the Discipline of Public Health and National Centre for Education and Training on Addiction (2003–2010). She also has a BA (Hons) (Sociology, University of Tasmania), BA (Psychology, Sociology) and Graduate Certificate in Health Service Management (Flinders).

Prior to moving to academia, she worked in the health and community services sectors in Australia in policy development, advocacy and project management for 10 years, and also served on government panels and boards in South Australia. From 2005 to 2010, she was a Panel Assessor (community/industry) on the District Court of South Australia hearing appeals made under the Guardianship and Mental Health Acts (Governor appointed). Samantha has also undertaken consultancy work on NCD strategy, primary health care models, health promotion for people with disabilities, mental health promotion and family carer policy.

Detlev Brauns

Detlev Brauns is the Deputy Permanent Representative of the EU to the World Trade Organization (WTO). From 2006 to 2011 he was the Alternative Permanent Representative to the WTO at the German Permanent Mission in Geneva; he chaired the Committee for Regional Trade Agreements from 2008 to 2010. Between 2001 and 2006 he was a Head of Unit responsible for Trade Policy at the German Federal Ministry of Economics and Technology in Berlin. In his earlier assignments he served as a Deputy Head of Unit for Transatlantic Relations at the Economics Ministry (1999–2001), as Economic and Commercial Counsellor at the German Embassy in Bangkok (1995–1999) and as a Desk Officer for EU–ACP relations, again at the Economics Ministry in Bonn (1992–1995). He holds law degrees from Germany, a Maîtrise en Droit from the University of Aix-en-Provence and a postgraduate Diploma of Public Administration from the Ecole Nationale d'Administration (ENA) in Paris (France).

Gian Luca Burci

Professor Gian Luca Burci is Legal Counsel of the World Health Organization (WHO), a position he has held since 2005. Prior to that appointment, he was Senior Legal Officer in the WHO between 1998 and 2005, legal officer in the Office of the Legal Counsel from 1989 to 1998, and legal officer in the International Atomic Energy Agency between 1988 and 1989. He has been Adjunct Professor of international law at the Graduate Institute for International and Development Studies in Geneva since 2010 and is Director of the Joint LLM in Global Health Law and International Institutions co-organised by the Graduate Institute and the Georgetown University School of Law. His research interests focus on the law of international immunities, the law and governance of international organisations, global health law and governance, and the role of the Security Council. He is currently on the editorial board of the *International Organization Law Review*. He is the co-author of *World Health Organization* (2004) and of a large number of articles and book chapters, most recently on the responsibility of international organisations and public–private partnerships. An Italian national, he holds a doctorate in law from the University of Genoa.

Lourdes Chamorro

Lourdes Chamorro joined the European External Action Service in 2011 and since then has been working in the area of Health at the European Union Delegation in Geneva. Her work mainly focuses on the coordination and representation of the EU and its Member States at health-related processes in Geneva, notably at the World Health Organization. She also works on other processes such as the Global Fund to fight Aids, tuberculosis and malaria, and the 'right to health' at the Human Rights Council.

Previously, she worked at the European Commission in Luxembourg and Brussels in the areas of Health and Research & Development. She has been closely involved in the negotiations of the Framework Convention on Tobacco Control (FCTC) since the very early phases in 2001 and accompanied the process as an EU negotiator until its fifth Conference of the Parties held in Seoul in November 2012. She also supported and joined the European Anti-fraud Office in the negotiations of the Protocol on illicit trade in tobacco products.

She is a medical doctor by training and a specialist in public health. She is also a civil servant in the Spanish administration and she served as Deputy Director-General in the Ministry of Health in charge of the HIV/AIDS Programme.

Anna-Luise Chané

Anna-Luise Chané is a Research Fellow and PhD candidate in Law at the Leuven Centre for Global Governance Studies and at the Institute for International Law, University of Leuven (KU Leuven). Her research focuses on the relationship between multilateral organisations, in particular the United Nations and the EU, on the EU and human rights, and on judicial dialogue in international human rights law. She is a researcher on the large-scale FP7 project 'Fostering Human Rights Among European Policies' (FRAME). Anna-Luise studied law at the University of Cologne and KU Leuven and passed her First and Second Juridical State Examination with distinction. She holds a Master of Laws degree from Harvard Law School, where she was an ERP Scholar of the German Ministry of Economy and Technology and the German National Academic Foundation.

Marco Ferri

Marco Ferri has been Minister Counsellor at the European Union Delegation in Geneva since 2011. He is the head of the Health and Social Section. Before joining the Delegation he spent his entire career at the European Commission, where he dealt with a wide range of external relations and enlargement issues: the United Nations, China, the United States and Canada as well as the Western Balkans. He was the European Commission lead negotiator for the United Nations Convention on the Rights of Persons with Disabilities (2003–2007). In 2005 he negotiated the first EU–China Memorandum of Understanding on social issues. He graduated in Political Science from the University of Milan. He holds a Master's in Diplomacy from ISPI, the Italian Institute for International Political Studies.

Jean-Christophe Galloux

Professor Jean-Christophe Galloux is a graduate of the University of Burgundy (LLM in private law, 1983), of the European University Institute of Florence (LLM in European and comparative law, 1987) and the University of Bordeaux (Doctorat d'Etat en droit: PhD Summa cum laude, 1988). He became professor at the University of Reims in 1991 (National professor examination: agrégation, 1991). He was elected as professor of law at the University of Paris, Panthéon-Assas (Paris II) in 2000, where he holds the Chair in industrial property.

He also teaches intellectual property law and competition law at the International Centre for Intellectual Property Law (CEIPI) in Strasbourg and is the President of the IP research Institute of Paris (IRPI). He has been visiting professor in these subjects at the universities of Montreal (Canada), Casablanca (Morocco), Moscow (MGU), Saint Petersburg State University, Bahrein, Budapest (ELTE), Munich (LMU and Max-Planck Institute), Tokyo (Toddaï) etc.

He is the author of more than 250 publications in intellectual property law, competition law, and pharmaceutical and biotechnology law. He is a member of the Board of *Revue Trimestrielle de Droit Commercial* since 2000 (Dalloz editor) and is the co-founder of the new legal review *Propriétés Intellectuelles* (Thomson editor). He has published several books, including *Droit de la propriété industrielle* (Dalloz, Paris, 2003 and *Les biotechnologies en débat: pour une démocratie scientifique* (Balland, Paris, 2002). He also co-authored (with Professor Jacques Azema) *Droit de la propriété industrielle* (Dalloz, Paris, 2012), which is the leading academic book in this field.

He has been an adviser to the European Commission, UNESCO and OECD for IP matters and a member of the European Ethic Committee for the European Federation of Biotech Industries (EUROPABIO) in Brussels (1999–2003). He was recently elected a member of the National Academy of Pharmacy. He practises IP as a litigator and arbitrator.

Frank Hoffmeister

Frank Hoffmeister holds a PhD from the University of Heidelberg (1998) and served as academic assistant at the Walter Hallstein Institute for European Constitutional Law from 1998 until 2001. He then joined the European Commission where he worked first in the Cyprus Unit in DG Enlargement before becoming a member of the Commission Legal Service (external relations and institutional team). From 2010 to 2014 he acted as Deputy Head of Cabinet of the EU Trade Commissioner De Gucht. He teaches international economic law at the Free University of Brussels and has written extensively on EU and international law matters. Most recently, he edited (together with PJ Kuijper, J Wouters, G Debaere and T Ramodopoulos) *The Law of EU External Relations, Cases, Materials and Commentary on the EU as an International Legal Actor* (Oxford, OUP, 2013).

Albrecht Jahn

Professor Albrecht Jahn MD, PhD, MSc Community Health, MSc Biol, is a specialist in obstetrics and gynaecology, infectious diseases, and public health. After several years of clinical work in Germany, Kenya and Tanzania, he joined the Institute of Tropical Hygiene at Heidelberg University as senior lecturer and researcher. His research work comprises the assessment of systems and specific interventions to improve maternal, perinatal and child health, as well as infectious diseases control with a focus on assessing and improving the access and quality of services in the context of the Millennium Development Goals. He worked with the European Union's Directorate General for Research as Scientific Officer from 2004 to 2010 on international public health and health systems as well as reproductive health and neglected infectious diseases with respect to project management, research policy development, as well as communication with the scientific community, the WHO, and other stakeholders.

In September 2010 he joined the Institute of Public Health at Heidelberg University, focusing on global health policies. He is the leader of the German Society for Tropical Medicine and International Health's working group on Global Health and consultant to the German Government on Global Health issues. He is also a member of the WHO's Consultative expert working group on research and development: financing and coordination (CEWG), which is tasked with proposing innovative financing mechanisms for global public health to the World Health Assembly.

Christine Kaddous

Christine Kaddous is Professor of European Law at the University of Geneva, Jean Monnet Chair *ad personam*, and Director of the Centre d'études juridiques européennes, Jean Monnet Centre of Excellence at the same University. Her academic interests and activities cover many different areas of European Union law, including external relations, the internal market—in particular the free movement of persons and services—judicial protection and relations between the European Union and Switzerland. She is author and editor of many books on European Union law. Among her recent publications are: *Die Zusammenarbeit zwischen der EU und der Schweiz* (2014), *The European Union's Common Values and National Identities: Convergence or Contradiction?* (2014), *European Union Participation in International Financial Organizations* (2014), *Loyauté du commerce et défense des intérêts des Etats membres et de l'Union européenne* (2013), *The Significance of 'Precedent' in the Bilateral Agreements between Switzerland and the European Union* (2012), *Le rôle de la Cour de justice dans l'interprétation de l'accord d'association CEE-Turquie* (2012), and *Les compétences de l'Union européenne en matière d'énergie après Lisbonne* (2011).

Ilona Kickbusch

Professor Ilona Kickbusch is recognised throughout the world for her contribution to health promotion and global health. She is currently adjunct professor at the Graduate Institute of International and Development Studies, Geneva and director of the Global Health Programme. She advises organisations, government agencies and the private sector on policies and strategies to promote health at the national, European and international level. She has published widely and is a member of a number of advisory boards in both the academic and the health policy arena. Professor Kickbusch has received many awards and served as the Adelaide Thinker in Residence at the invitation of the Premier of South Australia. She has launched a think tank initiative 'Global Health Europe: A Platform for European Engagement in Global Health' and the 'Consortium for Global Health Diplomacy'. Her key areas of interest are global health governance, global health diplomacy, health in all policies, the health society and health literacy. She has had a distinguished career with the World Health Organization, at both the regional and global level, where she initiated the Ottawa Charter for Health Promotion and a range of 'settings projects' including Healthy Cities. From 1998 to 2003 she worked at Yale University as head of the global health division, where she contributed to shaping the field of global health and headed a major Fulbright programme. She is a political scientist with a PhD from the University of Konstanz, Germany.

Stephen A Matlin
Stephen Matlin, PhD, DSc, is a former Executive Director of the Global Forum for Health Research (GFHR), promoting health research for the needs of low-and middle-income countries. He worked in academia for over 20 years, researching, teaching and consulting in medicinal, biological and analytical chemistry, collaborating with the Special Programmes in human reproduction and tropical diseases at the World Health Organization and the International Organization for Chemical Sciences in Development (IOCD). In 1995 he left academia to work full time in international development, holding senior positions in the Commonwealth Secretariat and UK Department for International Development, before joining GFHR.

Professor Matlin has served as Kelvin Lecturer of the British Association for the Advancement of Science; President of the British Association for International and Comparative Education; Vice-President of the Royal Institution of Great Britain; Vice-President and Chair of the Commonwealth Association of Science, Technology and Mathematics Educators; and Senior Research Fellow at Oxford University. He has served on the governing bodies of the Alliance for Health Policy and Systems Research, the Child Health and Nutrition Research Initiative and the Initiative for Cardiovascular Health in Developing Countries. He currently serves on the board of IOCD and the Steering Committee of the Netherlands Global Programme in Health Policy and Health Systems Research; he is also an Adjunct Professor at the Institute of Global Health Innovation, Imperial College London. He was a co-founder and co-chair of Global Health Europe. He has published more than 250 papers, articles, reviews and book chapters.

He has experience working with governmental, inter-governmental and non-governmental agencies in areas including policy and strategy development, capacity strengthening, advocacy, facilitation and consensus building, priority setting and resource tracking.

Jed Odermatt
Jed Odermatt is Research Fellow and PhD Candidate at the Leuven Centre for Global Governance Studies—Institute for International Law, KU Leuven.

Ernst-Ulrich Petersmann

Ernst-Ulrich Petersmann is emeritus professor of international and European law at the European University Institute at Florence (Italy) and former professor of European law at the University of Geneva and its Graduate Institute for International Studies. For more than 35 years, he combined working as legal advisor in German, GATT and WTO institutions, as representative of Germany in European and UN institutions, and as secretary, member or chairman of numerous GATT/WTO dispute settlement panels with an academic career and teaching at numerous universities in Germany, Switzerland, Italy, North America, Africa and Asia. He has published some 30 books and more than 280 articles on topical legal issues of European and international law.

Geneviève Pons-Deladrière

Honorary Director of the European Commission and Former Legal Adviser of the ILO, Geneviève Pons-Deladrière is a graduate of the French National School of Administration (ENA) and holds degrees in both Law, from the University of Pantheon-Sorbonne (Paris, France) and Political Sciences, from the Institute of Political Sciences (Paris, France).

She entered the French Administrative Courts in 1982. She joined the Legal Service of the European Commission in 1989 and the Cabinet of Jacques Delors, President of the European Commission (EC), in 1991. She was responsible for ensuring that EU law was applied throughout all Member States and, in this capacity, chaired the Commission's infringements committee. In 1995, she joined the Directorate-General for Enterprise and Industry where she held several management positions. In 2008 she joined the Impact Assessment Board of the Commission and, in 2010, became Head of the Simplification Unit, part of the Commission's Smart Regulation agenda to simplify European legislation. She was appointed Honorary Director of the European Commission in 2011 and Legal Adviser of the ILO in 2013.

Thomas Ramopoulos

Thomas Ramopoulos currently works as an official in the European Commission (DG AGRI).

Markus Schmidt

Dr Markus Schmidt is currently the senior legal adviser to the United Nations Office at Geneva. He worked previously with the Office of the UN High Commissioner for Human Rights, where he served, inter alia, as secretary of the Human Rights Committee and chief of the Petitions Unit. He holds law degrees from the University of Bonn and the College of Europe as well as an MA and a PhD in International Relations from Oxford University.

János Volkai

Following his university studies in Budapest, Hungary, János Volkai obtained a PhD in European law at the European University Institute of Florence, Italy. Before joining the WTO Secretariat, he worked at the European Commission and the OECD on competition issues.

Upon joining the WTO Secretariat in 2002, he spent three years at the Intellectual Property Division working on competition and government procurement. In 2006, he moved to the Legal Affairs Division of the WTO Secretariat, where he has been servicing WTO dispute panels, assisting the DSU negotiations, and providing legal advice on depositary and other legal matters to Members and Secretariat colleagues.

Jan Wouters

Jan Wouters is Professor of International Law and International Organizations, Jean Monnet Chair *ad personam* 'EU and Global Governance' and Director of the Leuven Centre for Global Governance Studies—the Institute for International Law at the University of Leuven, Belgium. He is also Visiting Professor at Sciences Po Paris, at the University of Barcelona and on the European Master's Degree in Human Rights and Democratisation in Venice. He is President of the Flemish Foreign Affairs Council, which advises the Flemish Government, and of the United Nations Association Flanders. He is member of the Royal Flemish Academy of Belgium for Sciences and Arts and practises law as Of Counsel at Linklaters, Brussels. He studied law and philosophy in Antwerp and at Yale University (LLM 1990), was a Visiting Researcher at Harvard Law School and obtained his PhD at the University of Leuven (1996). He taught at the Universities of Antwerp and Maastricht, was Visiting Professor at Liège and Kyushu University and Référendaire at the European Court of Justice (1991–1994).

He is editor of the International Encyclopedia of Intergovernmental Organizations, Vice-Director of the *Revue belge de droit international* and editorial board member of ten international journals. He has published widely on international, EU, corporate and financial law (over 500 publications including 46 books and 85 journal articles). Among his recent publications are: *The EU's Role in Global Governance: the Legal Dimension* (2013), *The European Union and Multilateral Governance* (2012), *International Prosecutors* (2012), *Informal International Lawmaking* (2012), *Private Standards and Global Governance* (2012), *China, the European Union and Global Governance* (2012), *Upgrading the EU's Role as Global Actor* (2011), and *Accountability for Human Rights Violations by International Organizations* (2010).

Mariangela Zappia

In May 2011, Mariangela Zappia took office as Head of the European Union Delegation to the UN and other international organisations in Geneva. She is a high-ranking Italian diplomat with 28 years' experience. She has been Minister Plenipotentiary at the Mission of Italy to the UN and other international organisations in Geneva, and coordinated major events under the Italian Presidency of the G8 in 2009. She was Head of the Mediterranean, Middle East and Balkans Department at the Ministry of Foreign Affairs in Rome, and held various positions in New York, Brussels, Rome, and Dakar. She has a Master's degree in Political Science and International Relations from the University of Florence and a Postgraduate degree in Diplomatic and International Relations.

List of Abbreviations

ACTA	Agreement on Counterfeiting
ARVs	anti-retroviral drugs
ASEAN	Association of South East Asian Nations
ASPHER	Association of Schools of Public Health in the European Region
CAC	Codex Alimentarius Commission
CAP	common agricultural policy
CARICOM	Caribbean Community
CAS	Committee on the Application of Standards
CEWG	Consultative Expert Working Group on Research and Development
CFSP	Common Foreign and Security Policy
CGIAR	Consultative Group on International Agricultural Research
CITES	Convention on International Trade in Endangered Species of Wild Fauna and Flora
CJEU	EU Court of Justice
COHOM	Council Working Party on Human Rights
CONUN	Council Working Party on UN Affairs
COREPER	Committee of Permanent Representatives
CSR	corporate social responsibility
DEVCO	Directorate General on Development
DG SANCO	Directorate General on research and health and consumers
EBRD	European Bank for Reconstruction and Development
EC	European Community
ECDC	European Centre for Disease Prevention and Control
ECHO	European Commission Humanitarian Aid Office
ECHR	European Convention on Human Rights
ECJ	European Court of Justice
ECtHR	European Court of Human Rights

EDCTP	European and Developing Countries Clinical Trial Partnership
EEA	European Economic Area
EEAS	European External Action Service
EEC	European Economic Community
EESC	European Economic and Social Committee
EFTA	European Free Trade Area
EMSA	European Maritime Safety Agency
EU	European Union
Euratom	European Atomic Energy Community
FAFA	Financial and Administrative Framework Agreement
FAO	Food and Agriculture Organization
FAO Communication	The 2013 Commission Communication on 'The role of the European Union in the Food and Agriculture Organisation after the Treaty of Lisbon'
FCTC	Framework Convention on Tobacco Control
GATT	General Agreement on Tariffs and Trade
GPA	Government Procurement Agreement
HICs	high-income countries
HRC	Human Rights Council
HRL	human rights law
IAEA	International Atomic Energy Agency
ICAO	International Civil Aviation Organization
ICSID	International Center for the Settlement of Investment Disputes
IEL	international economic law
IFAD	International Fund for Agricultural Development
ILC	International Law Commission
ILO	International Labour Organization
IMEC	Industrialized Market Economy Countries
IMF	International Monetary Fund
IMO	International Maritime Organization
INSC	Instrument for Nuclear Safety Cooperation
INTA	International Trade Committee

ISDR	International Strategy for Disaster Reduction
ISPS Code	International Ship and Port Facility Security Code
ITFoM	IT Future of Medicine
LICs	low-income countries
LMICs	low- and middle-income countries
MAP	Monitoring and Assessing Progress on Decent Work
MDGs	Millennium development goals
MERCOSUR	Mercado Común del Sur
MFN	most favoured nation
MoU	Memorandum of Understanding
NCDs	non-communicable diseases
OCHA	Office for the Coordination of Humanitarian Affairs
OECD	Organisation for Economic Co-operation and Development
OIE	*Organisation internationale des épizooties*
OIV	International Organisation of Vine and Wine
OSCE	Organisation for Security and Co-operation in Europe
OTIF	Intergovernmental Organisation for International Carriage by Rail
PCIJ	Permanent Court of International Justice
PGs	public goods
PHG	Public Health Genomics
QOL	quality of life
REIO	regional economic integration organisation
SICAs	Specific International Cooperation Actions
SMEs	Small- and medium-size enterprises
SOLAS Convention	Convention for the Safety of Life at Sea
TEC	EC Treaty
TEU	Treaty on European Union
TFEU	Treaty on the Functioning of the European Union
TPC	Trade Policy Committee
TRIPS	trade-related aspects of intellectual property rights
TVET	Technical and Vocational Education and Training

UN	United Nations
UNASUR	Union of South American Nations
UNCTAD	United Nations Conference on Trade and Development
UNDP	United Nations Development Programme
UNECE	UN Economic Commission for Europe
UNESCO	United Nations Educational, Scientific and Cultural Organization
UNGA	United Nations General Assembly
UNSG	UN Secretary-General
UPR	universal periodic review
VCLT	Vienna Convention on the Law of Treaties
WEOG	Western European and Others Group
WFP	World Food Programme
WHO	World Health Organization
WIPO	World Intellectual Property Organization
WTO	World Trade Organization

1

Introduction: The European Union in International Organisations—Functional Necessity or General Aspiration?

CHRISTINE KADDOUS

THE EUROPEAN UNION (EU) is today the largest exporter of goods in the world and the world leader in trade in services. The euro, adopted by 19 of the 28 Member States, has become the world's second currency. Economically, the EU may be considered a global actor. But has this economic success allowed an increase in the role and influence of the EU within international organisations?

For decades, the European Community, and later the Union, developed relationships with various international organisations and became parties, usually with the Member States, to a large number of international agreements which created international organisations. This development was also promoted by the reaffirmation, in 2003, by the European Council of the concept of 'effective multilateralism', which is considered central to the external action of the EU.[1] At the core of the realisation of this concept was the participation of the Union in the United Nations, but also in other diverse international fora.

The increasing participation of the EU within international organisations occurred on the basis of the Union's capacity to exercise rights in international legal transactions and enter into obligations over the whole field of the Treaties' objectives.[2] The well-established case law on the external competence of the Union

[1] Revised version of the Presidency Conclusions of the Brussels European Council (12 and 13 December 2003), of 5 February 2004, para 91.

[2] In recent years, the EU's role as a global actor has become the centre of interest of many scholars. See notably Enzo Cannizzaro (ed), *The European Union as an Actor in International Relations*, (The Hague, Kluwer, 2002); Marisa Cremona, *The Union as a Global Actor: Roles, Models and Identity* (2004) *CML Rev* 553–73; Panos Koutrakos, *EU International Relations Law* (Oxford, Hart Publishing, 2006); Charlotte Bretherton and John Vogler, *The European Union as Global Actor* (New York, Routledge, 2006); Christopher Hill and Michael Smith (eds), *International Relations and the European Union* (Oxford, Oxford University Press, 2011); Bart von Vooren, Steven Blockmans and Jan Wouters (eds), *The EU's Role in Global Governance* (Oxford, Oxford University Press, 2013).

played a central role in this evolution.[3] The Union concluded a large number of international agreements with third countries and international organisations. The entry into force of the Lisbon Treaty reinforced this trend. The capacity to participate in international organisations was stressed in Article 21(1) of the Treaty on the European Union (TEU), which provides that the Union seeks 'to develop relations and build partnerships with third countries and international, regional or global organisations'. It is worth noting that whereas the provision distinguishes between two levels of organisation, regional and global, no clear consequences seem to follow from this broad distinction in practice. According to Article 21(2) TEU, the Union shall work for a high degree of cooperation in all fields of international relations in order to promote an 'international system based on stronger multilateral cooperation and good global governance'.

Given these various elements, the EU has become an active member on the international scene, not only as far as international representation is concerned, but also in the conclusion of international agreements and in its participation in multiple international fora.

The EU is a full member of a large number of international organisations. The best known are the World Trade Organization (WTO) and the Food and Agriculture Organization (FAO). Apart from these two famous examples the Union is a member of organisations active in diverse fields, such as Eurocontrol, the European Bank for Reconstruction and Development (EBRD), the Codex Alimentarius Commission (CAC), the Hague Conference on Private International Law, the Energy Community, the Intergovernmental Organisation for International Carriage by Rail (OTIF) as well as of regional fisheries organisations.[4] However, the EU is not a member of the United Nations (UN) or of any of the major UN organisations (except the FAO). It is not, for example, a member of the International Labour Organization (ILO), nor of the International Monetary Fund (IMF) or the World Bank.[5] Therefore, it participates in many international organisations through an observer status, the precise design of which depends on the text of the constituent charter of the organisation. For example, it enjoys 'observer status' at the United Nations Educational, Scientific and Cultural Organization (UNESCO),

[3] ECJ, Case 22/70 *Commission v Council* [1971] ECR 263; ECJ, Joined Cases 3, 4 and 6/76 *Kramer* [1976], ECR 1279; *Opinion 1/76* [1977] ECR 741, and the subsequent case law.

[4] Communication from the Commission to the Council and the European Parliament Community—Participation in Regional Fisheries Organisations (RFOs), COM (1999) 613 final.

[5] See notably Lorenzo Bini Smaghi, 'A Single EU Seat in the International Monetary Fund?' in Knud Erik Joergensen (ed), *The European Union and International Organizations* (London and New York, Routledge, 2009) 64; Alan Hervé, *The Participation of the European Union in Global Economic Governance Fora* (2012) *European Law Journal* 143; Jan Wouters, Steven Sterkx, Tim Corthaut, *The International Financial Crisis, Global financial Governance and the European Union*, Working Paper No 5 (Leuven, Leuven Centre for Global Governance Studies, 2010); Jean-Victor Louis, 'L'Union européenne et la régulation de la finance international' in Muriel Le Barbier-Le Bris (ed), *L'Union européenne et la gouvernance mondiale* (Brussels, Bruylant, 2012); Christine Kaddous, 'European Union Participation in International Financial Organizations' in Inge Govaere and Sara Poli (ed), *EU Management of Global Emergencies*, Studies in EU External Relations (Leiden Boston, Brill book series, 2014) 277–95.

'enhanced observer status' at the General Assembly of the United Nations, and a 'special position' within the Organisation for Economic Co-operation and Development (OECD), which may be considered very close to full membership.[6]

In this context, one of the issues to be addressed, taking into account the changes brought about by the Lisbon Treaty and the establishment of the European External Action Service (EEAS) as well as the practice which has been developed on the basis of the new Treaties, relates to the question of how to explain today the ever greater participation of the EU in international organisations, despite the numerous challenges it has to face internally and externally in relation to this participation. Is this phenomenon the result of a functional necessity, or is it a general aspiration of the Union to participate in most international fora which are contributing to global governance?

In order to answer these questions, this chapter analyses the principles applicable to the external representation of the EU taking into account the very latest developments in the matter (I), the foundations for the Union to participate in international organisations (II), as well as the challenges it faces because of such participation (III). The conclusion assesses the main reasons for the ever greater participation of the Union in international fora and determines the essential needs to better strengthen its position and role within international organisations (IV).

I. PRINCIPLES APPLICABLE TO THE EXTERNAL REPRESENTATION OF THE EUROPEAN UNION

Originally the issue of external representation was dealt with in the *Costa v ENEL* case. Referring to the creation of the European Economic Community, its institutions and its own personality, the Court of Justice recognised the Community's capacity of representation on the international scene.[7] This capacity of external representation is reflected today particularly in the exercise of the 'right of legation'[8] and in the ability of the EU to participate in international organisations with the status of full member or observer.

The very foundation of EU external representation lies within the recognition of its legal personality, which is explicit since the entry into force of the Lisbon Treaty (Article 47 TEU). Under the previous Treaties, the situation was different. The European Community had legal personality explicitly conferred by Article 281 TEC, while the Union had a de facto legal personality, resulting from the practice

[6] See notably Knud E Joergensen and Ramses A Wessel, 'The Position of the European Union in (Other) International Organizations: Confronting Legal and Political Approaches' in Panos Koutrakos (ed), *European Foreign Policy. Legal and Political Perspectives* (Edward Elgar Publishing, 2011) 261–86, 269; Piet Eeckhout, *EU External Relations Law* (Oxford, Oxford University Press, 2011) 222–31.

[7] ECJ, Case 6/64 *Costa v ENEL* [1964] ECR 1141, 1159.

[8] The right of legation is the right of the EU to receive diplomatic missions from third states. It also covers the right to send diplomatic missions to third states. The Union has no diplomatic missions as such but operates with a network of 139 EU Delegations in the world.

that has developed in relation to the previous Articles 24 and 38 TEU, which raised no objection from the Member States as was attested notably by the signature with the United States in 2003 of international agreements in the fields of extradition and legal assistance,[9] and that with Switzerland in 2004 of an international agreement permitting the association of this third country to the Schengen area.[10]

Recognised first de facto and conferred explicitly since 2009, the legal personality of the EU allowed the development of relationships with international organisations. The express conferral of the legal personality in Article 47 TEU was a consequence of the decision to merge the Union and the European Community into one single entity. This change constituted a major innovation brought by the Lisbon Treaty in favour of a better identification of the Union on the international scene.[11] It also had the advantage of putting an end to the confusion concerning the co-existence of the Union and the European Community and the respective competences of each in the field of external relations.

The merging of the Union and the Community into one single entity increased legibility and clarity in the relations with third countries and international organisations, which today have as partner one general representative: the EU,[12] if one leaves aside the Euratom Community, which disposes of competences linked to the field of atomic energy. However, it should not be forgotten that, despite the improvements brought about by having a 'single partner', the Union is composed of Member States which may themselves be parties to international organisations along with the Union. This joint participation raises complex and very interesting issues which will be dealt with below.[13] In fact, the EU sometimes participates alone in an international organisation; sometimes it participates together with its Member States; and sometimes it does not participate at all, and only the Member States are parties. These different scenarios depend on various central factors, among which the distribution of competences between the EU and the Member States and the possibility for the Union to participate as such in the organisation as a 'regional economic international organisation' (REIO).[14]

[9] Agreement on extradition between the European Union and the United States of America, OJ L181, 19.7.2003, 27; Agreement on mutual legal assistance between the European Union and the United States of America, OJ L181, 19.7.2003, 34.

[10] Agreement between the European Union, the European Community and the Swiss Confederation on the Swiss Confederation's association with the implementation, application and development of the Schengen acquis, OJ L53, 27.2.2008, 52.

[11] The legal personality of the EU was also provided for expressly in the Treaty establishing a Constitution for Europe in Art I-7. See notably the contribution of Jean-Claude Gautron in Laurence Burgorgue-Larsen, Anne Levade, Fabrice Picod, *Traité établissant une Constitution pour l'Europe. Commentaire article par article*, Vol 1 (Brussels, Bruylant, 2007) 117; and Johannes Christian Wichard in Christian Calliess and Matthias Ruffert, *Verfassung der Europäischen Union* (München, Beck, 2006) 141.

[12] Except the European Atomic Energy Community, which survived the entry into force of the Lisbon Treaty.

[13] See section III.

[14] See our developments below, under section II.

It must also be stressed that the provisions set out in the Treaties on EU external representation are still complex, despite the simplifications brought about by the Lisbon Treaty. In matters other than the Common Foreign and Security Policy (CFSP), the representation is entrusted to the European Commission, the rotating Presidency, the EU Delegations and the Member States depending on the division of competences between the Union and the Member States. In principle, where the competence is exclusive, the European Commission represents the Union. Where the competence is shared, the rotating Presidency and the Commission participate in the representation of the Union. Where a national competence is at stake, the Member States may negotiate separately or decide to designate a person to represent them.

In CFSP matters, the representation of the Union is shared between the President of the European Council, the High Representative, the EU Delegations and the Member States.[15] Article 15(6) TEU provides that the President of the European Council shall, at his or her level and in that capacity, ensure the external representation of the Union on issues concerning CFSP, without prejudice to the powers of the High Representative. In parallel, Article 27(2) TEU provides that the High Representative shall represent the Union for matters relating to the CFSP, shall conduct political dialogue with third parties on the Union's behalf and shall express the 'Union's position in international organisations', the whole with the assistance of the EEAS. The role of the Member States in CFSP matters is dealt with in Declaration No 13, which recalls that the adoption of the provisions in the TFEU covering this policy, including the creation of the office of High Representative and the establishment of an EEAS, does not affect the responsibilities of the Member States, as they existed, for the formulation and conduct of their foreign policy nor of their national representation in third countries and international organisations.[16]

The external representation provisions in these CFSP matters gave rise to divergences of interpretation with regard to the distribution of competences between the Union and the Member States, which generated problems in practice. The difficulties occurred in 2011 after the adoption by the General Assembly of the United Nations of the Resolution on the participation of the EU in the work of the organisation with an enhanced observer status.[17] The United Kingdom blocked several statements that had to be delivered by the EU within the

[15] On the High Representative, see notably C Kaddous, 'Role and Position of the High Representative of the Union for Foreign Affairs and Security Policy under the Lisbon Treaty' in Stefan Griller and Jacques Ziller (eds), *The Lisbon Treaty. EU Constitutionalism without a Constitution Treaty?* (Berlin, Springer Verlag, 2008) 205–23.

[16] Declaration 13 annexed to the final act of the intergovernmental conference which adopted the Treaty of Lisbon, signed on 13 December 2007.

[17] Resolution A/65/PV.88 of 3 May 2011, Doc A/RES/65/276, see Annex II in this volume.

United Nations,[18] the reason being a disagreement as to who should deliver the statements. The UK Delegation to the United Nations considered that these statements were to be made by representatives of the Union 'on behalf of the European Union and its Member States' and not on behalf of the EU alone. This divergence of interpretation of the Treaties provisions and the blocking by a Member State created a true crisis in the external representation of the Union. Ultimately a compromise has been found, the main lines of which are included in a document which has been adopted by the Council of the European Union in October 2011, named 'EU Statements in multilateral organisations—General Arrangements'.[19]

This document recalls that the Lisbon Treaty enables the Union to achieve coherent, comprehensive and unified external representation. It refers to the close and sincere cooperation provided for in the Treaties between the Member States and the Union and takes over the principles laid down in the relevant case law of the Court of Justice. The document stresses that the preparation of statements relating to the sensitive area of competences of the Union and its Member States should 'remain internal and consensual', introducing thereby a kind of disconnection between what happens internally within the Union and what is expressed externally at the international level.[20]

It results from the Arrangements that the Union can only make a statement in the cases where it is competent and where there is a position which has been agreed in accordance with the relevant Treaty provisions.[21]

The Member States and the EU actors, defined in the document as being the President of the European Council, the Commission, the High Representative and European Delegations, have to coordinate their action in international organisations to the fullest extent possible as set out in the Treaties. Moreover, it is added that EU representation is to be exercised from behind a EU nameplate unless prevented by the rules of procedure of the forum in question.[22]

Consequently, the unity of representation is guaranteed to the extent that the Member States seek to ensure and promote possibilities for the EU actors to deliver statements on behalf of the Union. The Member States may complement statements made on behalf of the Union whilst respecting the principle of sincere cooperation.[23]

[18] Julian Borger, 'EU Anger over British stance on UN Statements', *The Guardian*, 20 October 2011, states: 'The other 26 member states objected, arguing that the UK was using a technicality to stop the EU mission from functioning properly and to prevent the EU from speaking in one voice on important issues even when all the members were in full agreement'; see www.theguardian.com/world/2011/oct/20/uk-eu-un-statements-wording.

[19] Council of the European Union, *EU Statements in Multilateral Organisations—General Arrangements*, Document 16901/11, 24 October 2011, see Annex I in this volume.

[20] ibid, para 2.

[21] ibid, para 3.

[22] ibid, para 3.

[23] This last duty led Joris Larik and Andres Delgado Casteleiro to write an article entitled 'The Duty to Remain Silent: Limitless Loyalty in EU External Relations' (2011) *EL Rev* (2011) 524–41.

These Arrangements are intended to be applied broadly unless more specific practical arrangements such as those at the WTO, at the FAO and in burden sharing exist for coordination and/or representation.[24] Despite the fact that they do not deal with the core and sensitive issue of the distribution of competences which should be determined internally and consensually, they bring helpful, concrete rules on the external representation of the Union and allow the determination of 'who' is going to represent 'the Union', once the internal question on competences is agreed upon. In that sense, the document presents the advantage of regulating the daily business life of the Union and its Member States within international organisations. This is already a progress that can be welcomed, even if the expectations were higher.[25]

To take briefly another example of Union participation within an international organisation, the WTO gives a completely different picture of the external representation. First, the above-mentioned Arrangements of 2011 do not apply to the WTO. Second, the Union is a full member of the organisation along with its Member States. According to Article 17(1) TEU, the European Commission represents the Union in the area of trade. At the level of Heads of State this role falls to the Commission President and at the level of Ministers to the EU to the Trade Commissioner. The EU ambassador accredited to the WTO is (like all EU ambassadors) an official of the EEAS, but receives instructions from the Commission headquarters. It is only where a WTO matter is not covered by a EU competence but by a national competence that the situation would be legally different. In such instances, Member States may choose whether they wish to express themselves individually or entrust the Presidency of the Council to speak on their behalf.[26]

As a result of the foregoing, the application of Union representation rules depends largely on the distribution of competences between the Union and its Member States in a specific area of the external action.

II. THE FOUNDATIONS FOR THE UNION TO PARTICIPATE IN INTERNATIONAL ORGANISATIONS

The foundations of such participation are dual. They relate first to the conferral and distribution of competences between the Union and the Member States (A), and second to the statute of the international organisation at stake and the various forms of EU participation (B).

[24] ibid, para 3.

[25] In the same sense, see Bart van Vooren and Ramses A Wessel, *EU External Relations Law, Text, Cases and Materials* (Cambridge, Cambridge University Press, 2014) 261.

[26] On the participation of the Union within the WTO, see Frank Hoffmeister, Chapter 9, this volume; see also Peiter Jan Kuijper, Jan Wouters, Frank Hoffmeister, Geert De Baere and Thomas Ramopoulos, *The Law of EU External Relations. Cases, Materials and Commentary on the EU as an International Legal Actor* (Oxford, Oxford University Press, 2013) 373.

A. Conferral and Distribution of Competences Between the Union and the Member States

There are no general provisions in the treaties regulating the EU's participation in international organisations.[27] However, some helpful indications are to be found in specific provisions. Article 216 TFEU empowers the Union to conclude international agreements with third countries or international organisations. Article 220 and 221 TFEU constitute a new title since the entry into force of the Lisbon Treaty and relate to the Union's relations with international organisations, third countries and Union Delegations.

By virtue of Article 220 TFEU, the Union shall establish all appropriate forms of cooperation with the organs of the United Nations and its specialised agencies, the Council of Europe, the Organisation for Security and Co-operation in Europe (OSCE) and the OECD.[28] It shall also maintain such relations as are appropriate with other international organisations. The High Representative shall be instructed to implement this provision. On the other hand, Article 221 provides that Union Delegations in third countries and at international organisations shall represent the Union. These are placed under the authority of the High Representative and they act in close cooperation with Member States' diplomatic and consular missions.[29] In addition, other provisions of the TFEU deal with cooperation at the international level with respect to specific fields, such as the environment (Article 191 TFEU), space (Article 189 TFEU), development cooperation (Article 211 TFEU), and economic, financial and technical cooperation (Article 212 TFEU).

All these provisions, as well as their predecessors under the TEC, do not expressly provide for the Union's membership of an international organisation.[30] It is through case law that the Union's capacity to participate as such in international organisations has been recognised. In *Opinion 1/76*, it was considered that the Community was not only entitled to enter into contractual relations with a third country but also had the power, while observing the provisions of the Treaty, to cooperate with that country in setting up an appropriate organism such as

[27] Jorn Sack, 'The European Community's Membership of International Organisations' (1995 *CML Rev* 1227); Christine Kaddous, *Le droit des relations extérieures dans la jurisprudence de la Cour de justice* (Collection des Dossiers de droit européen, No 6 (Basle, Helbing, 1998) 135; Catherine Flaesch-Mougin, 'Les relations avec les organisations internationales et la participation à celles-ci' in *Commentaire J Mégret* (Bruxelles, Etudes européennes, 2005) chapter 6; Inge Govaere, Jeroen Capiau and An Vermeersch, 'In-Between Seats: The Participation of the European Union in International Organisations' (2006) *European Foreign Affairs Review* 155; Frank Hoffmeister, 'Outsider or Frontrunner? Recent Developments under International and European Law on the Status of the European Union in International Organisations and Treaty Bodies' (2007) *CML Rev* 41.

[28] Those provisions are not different in substance from the former articles of the EC Treaty, see Arts 229–31 TEC.

[29] Art 221(1) and (2) TFEU.

[30] See Kaddous, *Le droit des relations extérieures*, above n 27, 135.

the public international institution which was proposed to be established.[31] This principle of participation was later implicitly confirmed in *Opinion 1/94*[32] when the Court recognised the competence of the European Communities to create the WTO with the other members of the organisation.

Once the basic principle of Union participation in international organisations has been acquired, the debates have focused on the distribution of competences between the Union and the Member States in order to determine 'who' of them will be empowered to participate in a specific international organisation. According to the Treaties and case law, the EU participates alone in an international organisation where it enjoys exclusive competence. It participates jointly with the Member States where the competence is not exclusive.

In cases of non-exclusive competences, and as to the relationship between the Union on one hand and the Member States on the other, the duty of cooperation plays a central role. The Court of Justice had the opportunity in *Ruling 1/78*,[33] and later in *Opinions 2/91*[34] and *1/94*,[35] to assert that this duty of cooperation between the European institutions and the Member States results from the requirement of unity in the international representation of the Community, today the EU. It applies both in the process of negotiation and conclusion of an international agreement or convention as well as in the fulfilment of the obligations entered into.

However, the participation of the EU in international organisations depends also on one element which is not a matter of EU law. The constituent treaty of the international organisation at stake should allow membership for RIEOs, otherwise only the Member States of the Union will be able to take part in the said organisation. Consequently, the statute of the international organisation determines whether the Union shall participate and, if so, in which form.

[31] *Opinion 1/76, Draft Agreement establishing a European Laying-up fund for inland waterway vessels* [1977] ECR 741, para 5.

[32] *Opinion 1/94, Competence of the Community to conclude the WTO agreements* [1994] ECR I-5267.

[33] ECJ, *Ruling 1/78* [1978] ECR 2151, paras 34–36.

[34] ECJ, *Opinion 2/91, Convention No 170 of the International Labour Organization concerning safety in the use of chemicals at work* [1993] ECR I-1061, para 36: '[...] when it appears that the subject-matter of an agreement or contract falls in part within the competence of the Community and in part within that of the Member States, it is important to ensure that there is a close association between the institutions of the Community and the Member States both in the process of negotiation and conclusion and in the fulfilment of the obligations entered into. This duty of cooperation, to which attention was drawn in the context of the EAEC Treaty, must also apply in the context of the EEC Treaty since it results from the requirement of unity in the international representation of the Community.'

[35] ECJ, *Opinion 1/94*, above note 34, para 108: '[...] where it is apparent that the subject-matter of an agreement or convention falls in part within the competence of the Community and in part within that of the Member States, it is essential to ensure close cooperation between the Member States and the Community institutions, both in the process of negotiation and conclusion and in the fulfilment of the commitments entered into. That obligation to cooperate flows from the requirement of unity in the international representation of the Community.'

B. Forms of European Union Participation in International Organisations

The participation of the Union in international organisations may take different forms, varying from the status of observer (1) to that of full membership (2). In addition, there is also more than one type of observer status, the differences depending on the constituent charters of the organisations, which may in some cases allow for more active participation of the Union and consequently greatly reduce the differences between members and non-members.[36]

i. Observer Status

When the EU has very limited powers in the field of the organisation's activities, or when the statute establishing the international organisation at stake does not allow full membership and/or the EU Member States oppose this last status, the Union may nevertheless be eligible for an observer status.

The rights and obligations of the observer are determined in each case by reference to the constituent charter of the organisation. Usually, observers enjoy the right to access to meetings, the right to speak, the right to take part in the discussions and the right to obtain official documentation. Nevertheless, the status of observer does not give the right to vote.

The EU is not member of the United Nations or any of the major United Nations organisations, except the FAO. It has held, as mentioned above, an 'enhanced observer' status at the UN General Assembly since 2011.[37] The participating rights of the EU at the United Nations allow its representatives to present the Union's agreed common positions, to make interventions, present proposals and circulate EU communications as official documents.[38] Whereas all the Member States of the Union participate in the United Nations General Assembly, only few of them participate in the Security Council. The EU as such is not represented at this organisation. However, Article 34 TEU empowers the Member States which are also members of the UN Security Council to concert and keep the other Member States and the High Representative fully informed. They are required, in the execution of their functions, to defend the positions and interests of the Union, without prejudice to their responsibilities under the provisions of the UN Charter. The same provision also provides that when the Union has defined a position on a subject which is on the UN Security Council agenda, those Member States which sit on the Security Council shall request that the High Representative be invited to present the Union's position.

[36] See Hoffmeister, 'Outsider or Frontrunner?', above n 27.

[37] A/RES/65/276, Resolution adopted by the General Assembly on 3 May 2011, *Participation of the European Union in the work of the United Nations*, see Annex II in this volume.

[38] On the participation of the EU in the UN, see the contributions of Mariangela Zappia; Markus Schmidt; and Jan Wouters et al, Chapters 2, 3 and 4, this volume.

The ILO presents the particularity that the EU, although it does have competences in the field of social policy, is not member of the organisation, because the ILO constitution does not allow for EU membership.[39] The complex distribution of competences between the Union and its Member States in the ILO was addressed in *Opinion 2/91*.[40] The Union also has observer status at the World Health Organization (WHO)[41] and the World Intellectual Property Organization (WIPO).[42]

On the other hand, EU claims to full membership status in international organisations have faced many obstacles.

ii. Full Membership

The status of full participation of the Union in international organisations has raised difficulties, the most important of which are institutional and political. At the institutional level, the fact that the constituent charters of international organisations generally reserve membership status to the States alone implies that the participation of the EU cannot be achieved without modification of these acts.

The political obstacle, still present today, lies in the fact that Member States of the Union are not necessarily in favour of abandoning their role in international fora and allowing the EU to take over their rights and powers. The Member States are often prepared to accept that the Union joins the 'club', but not that it replaces them.

If the constituent charter of the organisation allows the EU to be a member and if its participation is joint with the Member States, the situation becomes complex within both the Union and the international organisation itself, in particular with regard to the issue of which—the Union or the Member States—may exercise the rights attached to membership.[43]

It is not only the Member States which are opposed to the granting of membership to the Union in international organisations. Third states have in the past invoked the legally imprecise nature of the EU and the issues related to its international responsibility. In particular, they questioned wrongly the Union's ability to compel its Member States to respect the commitments made by it at the

[39] On the participation of the EU in the ILO, see the contributions of Marco Ferri and Geneviève Pons-Deladrière, Chapters 5 and 6, this volume.

[40] ECJ, *Opinion 2/91, Convention No 170 of the International Labour Organisation concerning safety in the use of chemicals at work* [1993] ECR I-1061.

[41] On the conditions of this participation as well as the evaluation of the role of the Union in the WHO, see the contributions of Lourdes Chamorro; Gian Luca Burci; and Ilona Kickbusch et al, Chapters 10, 11 and 12, this volume.

[42] On the participation of the EU in the WIPO, see the contribution of Jean-Christophe Galloux, Chapter 13, this volume.

[43] For an illustration of this difficulty, see ECJ, Case C-25/94 *Commission v Council* [1996] ECR I-1469 and our developments below under section III.

international level.[44] They also highlighted the danger of setting precedents, the risk of encouraging the formation of blocs within the organisation by the accession of the EU (making the decision more difficult), and the problems related to the simultaneous membership of the Union and its Member States to the same international organisation. This resistance of third states is still present today.

Despite these objections, internally and externally, the EU was granted the status of full membership of many organisations,[45] the most famous and successful example being the WTO.

The status of full membership puts the EU on an equal footing with the Member States of the organisation. The Union thus mainly acquires the right to vote, the right to make proposals and the right to speak.

The difficulties raised by the EU's participation lie in the fact that, most often, it is not involved alone in the organisation, but alongside its Member States. This joint participation is explained by the division of competences between the Union and the Member States.[46] Very often, there is a 'mixity' situation, based on the fact that many competences are shared between the Union and the Member States.

Joint membership raises a number of important issues, particularly in relation to the decision-making process and voting rights. For example, how many votes could be provided for the EU in the internal rules of the organisation? How would, and could, these rights be exercised? Two possible models may be envisaged. The voting rights may be exercised alternatively by the Union or by its Member States, or these rights may be cumulated, allowing the Union to add its vote to those of the Member States. The cumulative vote is opposed by the other members of the organisation, considering this modality as an expression of a new kind of over-representation of the Union and its Member States within the organisation.

The alternative way of exercising voting rights requires a definition of the cases in which the Union votes and those in which the Member States vote,[47] based presumably on a clear delineation of the powers between the EU and the Member States in the fields of the organisation's activities.

In 1995 the European Communities became one of the founding members, along with their Member States, of the WTO. At the time of membership negotiations, one of the problems that had to be solved was how to regulate the voting

[44] The existence of infringement procedure of Arts 258–260 TFEU proves that this is not true. Furthermore, the case law demonstrates that the Commission does not hesitate to bring the matter before the ECJ when it considers that a Member State has failed to comply with commitments made by the EU on the international scene. ECJ, Case C-61/94 *Commission v Germany* [1996] ECR I-3989, para 41.

[45] To be precise one may indeed distinguish two kinds of participation as a member. The first gives the EU the possibility of acceding to an international organisation, as such, an organisation that has an independent existence with a developed structure. The second type occurs in the case of an international agreement on a specific subject, creating a kind of organisational structure between the parties, in order to implement its provisions.

[46] See our developments above under section II, A.

[47] See, eg, the FAO.

rights within the WTO, because the Communities could have been perceived by third states as additional members of the organisation. The solution was the alternative vote.[48] Today, when the Union votes, it gets the number of votes equal to the number of its Member States that are members of the WTO. It must nevertheless be stressed that the voting rules exceptionally apply within the WTO, due to the fact that decisions are generally taken through consensus by the members.

Since the entry into force of the Lisbon Treaty, common commercial policy falls within the exclusive competence of the Union and covers not only trade in goods, but also trade in services, trade-related intellectual property rights and foreign direct investment. As a consequence of this exclusivity, the European Commission enjoys the responsibility of conducting trade negotiations and of representing the Union in international fora. The Member States seem to have accepted the leading role of the Union in the WTO, even if new issues on the negotiator position of the Commission arise between the protagonists.[49]

In the international organisations to which the Union participates as a full member or as an observer, along with the Member States, the issue of coordination is fundamental and constitutes one of the main challenges the Union has to face.

III. CHALLENGES LINKED TO THE PARTICIPATION OF THE UNION IN INTERNATIONAL ORGANISATIONS

Different scenarios of Union participation are possible. The Union may be a full member along with the Member States. This implies the existence of a shared competence which results in a joint participation of the Union and the Member States to the same international organisation. However, very often the Union does have competences in the field of activity of the international organisation, but the constituent charter of the said organisation does not allow for the Union's membership. In this precise legal situation, only the Member States participate in the international organisation, either all of them or, depending on the organisation, only some of them.[50] In addition, in these two last hypotheses the Union may or may not have an observer status.

Practice has revealed two main challenges linked to the participation of the Union in international organisations. The first relates to the coordination between the Union and the Member States (A) and the second deals with the establishment of positions to be adopted by the Union in an international organisation (B).

[48] Art IX of the WTO Agreement.

[49] On the participation of the Union in the WTO, see the contributions of Detlev Brauns and Thomas Baert; Janos Volkai; and Frank Hoffmeister, Chapters 7, 8 and 9, this volume. See, on the very last point mentioned, the contribution of Detlev Brauns and Thomas Baert, Chapter 7 (I, D), this volume.

[50] ECJ, Case C-399/12 *Germany v Council* (OIV), EU:C:2014:2258.

A. Coordination Between the Union and the Member States in International Organisations

The issue of coordination in cases of shared competences in the field of external relations arose early in the case law of the Court of Justice. In Ruling 1/78, it was pointed out that when it appears that the subject-matter of an agreement or a contract falls under the category of shared competences, it is important to ensure that a close cooperation between the institutions and the Member States takes place both in the process of negotiation and conclusion and in the fulfilment of the obligations entered into. That obligation to cooperate flows from the requirement of unity in the international representation.[51]

In the subsequent case law, in *Opinions 2/91*[52] and *1/94*,[53] the duty of close cooperation between the Member States and the institutions was examined in relation to participation in the ILO and the WTO, which present different legal situations. In the ILO, only the Member States participate in the international organisation, whereas the European Communities became contracting parties of the WTO, along with the Member States, after *Opinion 1/94* was rendered. It follows from the case law that the principle of cooperation applies whether the Union is a member of the international organisation or not. From that point, two lines of case law have been developed: the first concerning situations where the Union and the Member States participate in the international organisation: WTO (*Opinion 1/94*) and FAO (*Commission v Council*[54]); the second covering situations where only the Member States are members of the international organisation or parties to the international agreement: ILO (*Opinion 2/91*), IMO (*Commission v Greece*[55]) and the PFOS case (*Commission v Sweden*[56]). These two lines of case law are examined below.

In the 1996 *Commission v Council* case, the Court of Justice had to deal with the joint participation of the Union and the Member States in the FAO. The main issue at stake related to the internal Arrangement between the Council and the

[51] ECJ, *Ruling 1/78* [1978] ECR 2151, paras 34–36. On the duty of co-operation, see notably Christophe Hillion, 'Mixity and Coherence in EU External Relations: the Significance of the "Duty of Cooperation"' in Christophe Hillion and Panos Koutrakos, *Mixed Agreements Revisited* (Oxford, Hart Publishing, 2010) 87–115; Marise Cremona, 'Defending the Community Interest: The Duties of Cooperation and Compliance' in Marise Cremona and Bruno de Witte, *EU Foreign Relations Law—Constitutional Fundamentals* (Oxford, Hart Publishing, 2008) 125–69; Eleftheria Neframi, 'The Duty of Loyalty: Rethinking its Scope through its Application in the Field of EU External Relations' (2010) *CML Rev* 323–59.

[52] ECJ, *Opinion 2/91, Convention No 170 of the International Labour Organisation concerning safety in the use of chemicals at work* [1993] ECR I-1061, para 36.

[53] ECJ, *Opinion 1/94, Competence of the Community to conclude the WTO agreements* [1994] ECR I-5267, para 108.

[54] ECJ, Case C-25/94 *Commission v Council* [1996] ECR I-1469.

[55] ECJ, Case C-45/07 *Commission v Greece* [2009] ECR I-701.

[56] ECJ, Case C-246/07 *Commission v Sweden* [2010] ECR I-3317. The case relates to the Stockholm Convention on Persistent Organic Pollutants.

Commission on the right to vote in the said organisation.[57] The two institutions had concluded an internal Arrangement for the preparation of FAO meetings, interventions and voting rights. *In casu*, the Commission brought an action for annulment of the decision of the Fisheries Council giving the Member States the right to vote in the FAO on the adoption of the Agreement to Promote Compliance with International Conservation and Management Measures by Fishing Vessels on the High Seas.

Pursuant to the FAO Constitution, the European Community made a declaration, at the time of its acceptance within the international organisation (1991), specifying that it had exclusive competence in, inter alia, all matters concerning fisheries aimed at protecting fishing grounds and conserving the biological resources of the sea. As regards the rights attaching to membership, the General Rules of the FAO provide for a system of alternative exercise as between the Member Organisation and its own Member States, as follows: 'Before any meeting of the Organization the Member Organization or its Member States shall indicate which, as between the Member Organization and its Member States, has competence … and which, as between the Member Organization and its Member States, shall exercise the right to vote in respect of each particular agenda item. In cases where an agenda item covers both matters in respect of which competence has been transferred to the Member Organization and matters which lie within the competence of its Member States, both the Member Organization and its Member States may participate in the discussions. In such cases the meeting, in arriving at its decisions, shall take into account only the intervention of the party which has the right to vote.'[58]

In the case of the adoption of the agreement within the FAO, the Commission proposed to the Council that the 'shared competence formula' provided for in the internal Arrangement concluded in 1991 between the Commission and the Council should apply.[59] It nonetheless proposed a vote by the European Community, since the thrust of the agreement fell within the area of conservation of fishery resources, for which the Community had competence. Whilst the Commission and the Member States acknowledged that this was a matter for shared competence, they disagreed over the question of the right to vote.

[57] ECJ, Case C-25/94 *Commission v Council* [1996] ECR I-1469.

[58] ECJ, Case C-25/94 *Commission v Council* [1996] ECR I-1469, paras 3 and 4.

[59] ECJ, Case C-25/94 *Commission v Council* [1996] ECR I-1469, paras 9 and 10. The Arrangement sets up a co-ordination procedure to decide on the exercise of responsibilities or on statements on a particular point. Sections 1.12 and 1.13 of the Arrangement provide:

> 1.12
> In the absence of an agreement between the Commission and the Member States … the matter will be decided according to the procedure provided for in the Treaty and the agreed practice. In the absence of agreement on this basis, the matter will be referred to the Permanent Representatives Committee [Coreper].
>
> 1.13
> Decisions referred to in 1.12 are without prejudice to the respective competences of the Community and its Member States.

Thus, on the one hand, the Commission proposed to the Member States the adoption of a draft agreement prepared within the FAO. On the other hand, the Council confirmed an earlier decision of the Committee of Permanent Representatives (COREPER), under which it was not the Commission but the Member States who should vote in the FAO Conference concerning the adoption of the envisaged agreement. After a thorough examination, the Court of Justice held that the Council had violated one of the aspects of the international Arrangement and therefore its decision had to be annulled.

Clearly, the joint participation in an international organisation requires coordination between the Union and the Member States and respect of the principle of sincere cooperation, enshrined in Article 4(3) TEU. According to this provision, the EU and the Member States shall, in full mutual respect, assist each other in carrying out tasks which flow from the Treaties.[60] This principle shall also cause the Member States to refrain from taking any measure which could jeopardise the attainment of the EU's objectives.

The other line of case law has been well illustrated in the IMO and the PFOS cases, rendered in 2009 and 2010, which cover the situation where only the Member States are allowed to participate in the international organisation or international conference.[61]

The relevant provisions of the rules on statements and voting in FAO meetings are in Section 2. Sections 2.1–2.3 stipulate as follows:

2.1
Where an agenda item deals with matters of exclusive Community competence, the Commission shall speak and vote for the Community.

2.2
Where an agenda item deals with matters of national competence, Member States shall speak and vote.

2.3
Where an agenda item deals with matters containing elements both of national and of Community competence, the aim will be to achieve a common position by consensus. If a common position can be achieved:

— the Presidency shall express the common position when the thrust of the issue lies in an area outside the exclusive competence of the Community. Member States and the Commission may speak to support and/or to add to the Presidency statement. Member States will vote in accordance with the common position;
— the Commission shall express the common position when the thrust of the issue lies in an area within the exclusive competence of the Community. Member States may speak to support and/or add to the Commission's statement. The Commission will vote in accordance with the common position.

[60] Art 4(3) also provides that: 'The Member States shall take any appropriate measure, general or particular, to ensure fulfilment of the obligations arising out of the treaties or resulting from the acts of the institutions of the Union. The Member States shall facilitate the achievement of the Union's tasks and refrain from any measure which could jeopardise the attainment of the Union's objectives.'

[61] ECJ, Case C-45/07 *Commission v Greece* (IMO) [2009] ECR I-701; ECJ, Case C-246/07 *Commission v Sweden* [2010] ECR I-3317.

In *Commission v Greece*, the main issue was to determine whether Greece, a member of the International Maritime Organization (IMO), was entitled to submit a proposal to the IMO, on its behalf, in an area covered by Union law.[62] The European Commission argued that, since the adoption of the Regulation which integrated into Union law provisions of the SOLAS Convention and the ISPS Code,[63] the Union had enjoyed exclusive competence to assume international obligations in the area covered by that Regulation. For the Commission, the Union alone was competent to ensure that the standards on the subject are properly applied at Union level and to discuss with other IMO Contracting Parties the correct implementation of subsequent developments in those standards. Therefore, in its opinion, the Member States no longer had competence to submit to the IMO national positions on matters falling within the exclusive competence of the Union, unless expressly authorised to do so by the Union.[64] Given these elements, the Commission alleged a violation by Greece of Article 4(3) TEU as well as of the provisions of the Treaty on common transport policy, in formulating a proposal within the IMO which might have 'affected' the Regulation in the meaning of the ERTA judgement.[65]

Following the Commission, the Court held that Greece took an initiative which could have led to the adoption by the IMO of rules likely to affect the provisions of the Regulation. In those circumstances, such behaviour had to be considered as constituting an infringement of the obligations under Article 4(3) as well as under the provisions of the Treaty on common transport policy.[66]

It follows from the case law that the duty of cooperation entails many commitments; it may require from the Member States positive actions, but also abstentions, in order to achieve the Treaties' objectives. The cooperation duty appears to govern not only the situation where both the Union and the Member States participate in the international organisation, but also that where only the Member States are members of the organisation, provided that the latter is active in areas which fall under the Union's competence. It does not matter whether the competence is exclusive (IMO case) or shared (PFOS case).[67] The duty has to be respected in the whole field of external action.[68]

[62] ECJ, Case C-45/07 *Commission v Greece* [2009] ECR I-701.

[63] The Convention for the Safety of Life at Sea (SOLAS Convention) and the International Ship and Port Facility Security Code (ISPS Code).

[64] ECJ, Case C-45/07, *Commission v Greece* [2009] ECR I-701, para 14.

[65] ibid, paras 16–20.

[66] ibid, paras 21–23.

[67] In *Commission v Sweden* (PFOS), the issue was similar to the one in the IMO case. A Member State brought its own proposal at the international level in a situation where a common position or a strategy of the Union was deemed to have been established, see ECJ, Case C-246/07 *Commission v Sweden* [2010] ECR I-3317, para 77.

[68] ECJ, *Opinion 2/91* [1993] ECR I-1061, para 10; ECJ, *Opinion 1/03* [2006] ECR I-1145, para 119. See also the subsequent case law: Case C-459/03 *Commission v Ireland* [2006] ECR I-4635, para 174; Case C-246/07 *Commission v Sweden* [2010] ECR I-3317, para 69.

Therefore, coordination between the EU and the Member States, as well as respect for sincere cooperation, are fundamental for ensuring effective representation and participation of the Union in international organisations, whether the Union as such is a member of the organisation or not.

It is worth noting that Union participation in international organisations constantly raises new challenges. One of these concerns the establishment of Union positions to be held within an international organisation or a body created by an international agreement.

B. Establishment of Positions to be Adopted on the Union's Behalf within an International Organisation

The establishment of Union positions was discussed twice in the case law of the Court in relation first to the legality of the decision taken (*Commission v Council*)[69] and second to the conditions to be fulfilled by the Union under Article 218(9) TFEU in order to take such a position (*Germany v Council*).[70]

In *Commission v Council*, the legality of the Council decision establishing the position to be adopted on behalf of the European Community with regard to certain proposals submitted at a Conference of the parties to the CITES Convention has been challenged because the contested decision had been adopted without any mention of its legal basis. The failure to indicate any legal basis has not been regarded as a purely formal defect and the decision has been annulled.[71]

The more recent case, in which the judgment was rendered in 2014, gave the Court of Justice the opportunity to provide clarifications on the preparation of positions to be adopted by the Union in international organisations, whose issue is at the core of our concerns in the present contribution. In *Germany v Council*,[72] the Member State brought an action against the Council challenging the decision adopted pursuant to Article 218(9) TFEU establishing the position to be adopted on behalf of the EU with regard to specific resolutions to be voted in the framework of the International Organisation of Vine and Wine (OIV).[73] According to Germany, Article 218(9) TFEU was not the correct legal basis for the adoption of the contested decision, given that the provision only applies for the adoption

[69] ECJ, Case C-370/07 *Commission v Council* (CITES) [2009] ECR I-8917. CITES is the Convention on International Trade in Endangered Species of Wild Fauna and Flora.

[70] ECJ, Case C-399/12 *Germany v Council* (OIV), EU:C:2014:2258.

[71] ECJ, Case C-370/07 *Commission v Council* (CITES) [2009] ECR I-8917, paras 61 and 62. However, the effects of the contested decision have been maintained on grounds of legal certainty, para 66.

[72] ECJ, Case C-399/12 *Germany v Council* (OIV), EU:C:2014:2258. For a comment before the judgment has been rendered in the case, see Inge Govaere, 'Novel Issues Pertaining to EU Member States Membership of Other International Organizations: The OIV Case' in *The European Union in the World. Essays in Honour of Marc Maresceau* (Leiden/Boston, Martinus Nijhoff, 2013) 225–43.

[73] Council Document No 11436 adopted on 18 June 2012 at the 3176th Council meeting, Agriculture and Fisheries, see Press Release 11179/12, 16.

of Union positions in bodies, set up by international agreements, of which the Union is a member. It held, therefore, that the said provision could not be applied in relation to the representation of the Member States in bodies of international organisations in which only the Member States participate by virtue of separate international treaties.[74] Furthermore, the German Government and the Member States which intervened in its support claimed that Article 218(9) TFEU covers only 'acts having legal effects', which are meant to be acts of international law being binding on the EU.[75] For Germany and its supporters the OIV's recommendations did not fall within this category of acts referred to in Article 218(9).[76]

For its part, the Council, supported by the European Commission, contended first that Article 218(9) TFEU was applicable to the establishment of positions to be adopted on the Union's behalf in an organisation, such as the OIV, which has been set up by an international agreement concluded by the Member States and which was called upon to adopt acts having legal effects, if the area in question fell within the competence of the EU.[77] According to the two institutions, Article 218(9) TFEU requires only that acts which the international body was called upon to adopt must have effects in the EU legal order, but it is not necessary for those acts to produce effects in the international legal order.[78] Consequently, they held that the international recommendations relating to oenological practices and methods of analysis, which were at stake, although non-binding, produced legal effects within the EU through the provisions of Union law which enforced them.[79]

The judgment in this case was highly awaited because of the challenges it brings for the Union and the Member States in relation to the participation in an international organisation in which only some of the Member States are members. The Court first noticed that Article 218(9) TFEU was making reference to a body set up by 'an agreement', but did not specify whether the EU had to be a party to that agreement. Similarly, the reference in that provision to the positions to be adopted 'on the Union's behalf' did not mean that the EU had to have been a party to the agreement which set up the international body in question. Consequently, the Court held that nothing in the wording of the Treaty provision prevented the Union from adopting a decision establishing a position to be adopted on its behalf in a body set up by an international agreement to which it was not a party.[80]

[74] Germany, supported by the Czech Republic, Luxembourg, Hungary, the Netherlands, Austria, the Slovak Republic and the United Kingdom, claimed that Art 218(9) TFEU was not applicable in the context of an international agreement which, like the OIV Agreement, had been concluded by the Member States and not by the EU. ECJ, Case C-399/12 *Germany v Council* (OIV), EU:C:2014:2258, para 29.

[75] ECJ, Case C-399/12 *Germany v Council* (OIV), EU:C:2014:2258, paras 35 and 36.

[76] Art 218(9) TFEU reads as follows: 'The Council, on a proposal from the Commission or the High Representative of the Union for Foreign Affairs and Security Policy, shall adopt a decision suspending application of an agreement and establishing the positions to be adopted on the Union's behalf in a body set up by an agreement, when that body is called upon to adopt acts having legal effects, with the exception of acts supplementing or amending the institutional framework of the agreement.'

[77] ECJ, Case C-399/12 *Germany v Council* (OIV), EU:C:2014:2258, para 38.

[78] ECJ, Case C-399/12 *Germany v Council* (OIV), EU:C:2014:2258, para 44.

[79] ECJ, Case C-399/12 *Germany v Council* (OIV), EU:C:2014:2258, paras 45 and 46.

[80] ECJ, Case C-399/12 *Germany v Council* (OIV), EU:C:2014:2258, paras 49 and 50.

In addition, the Court stressed that the case concerned matters relating to the common agricultural policy and, more specifically, the common organisation of the wine markets, an area which was regulated for the most part by Union legislature in the exercise of its competence under Article 43 TFEU. It stated that where an area of law falls within a competence of the EU, such as the one at stake in the case, the fact that the EU did not take part in the international agreement in question does not prevent it from exercising that competence by establishing, through its institutions, a position to be adopted on its behalf in the body set up by that agreement, in particular through the Member States which are party to that agreement acting jointly in its interest.[81] Consequently, the fact that the EU was not a party to the OIV Agreement did not prevent it from applying Article 218(9) TFEU.

As to the other main argument brought by Germany, the Court checked whether the recommendations to be adopted by the OIV constituted 'acts having legal effects' for the purposes of Article 218(9). It appeared from the proceedings that the Commission 'bases itself' on the OIV's recommendations when it authorises oenological practices. This means that those recommendations are taken into consideration for the purposes of drawing up rules of Union law. It followed that the recommendations, which related to new oenological practices, methods of analysis for determining the composition of products of the wine sector, were capable of decisively influencing the content of the legislation adopted by the Union legislature in the area of the common organisation of the wine markets.[82] On this basis, the Court concluded that the recommendations, in particular by reason of their incorporation into Union law by virtue of specific provisions of secondary legislation in that specific field, had legal effects in that area for the purposes of Article 218(9) TFEU and that the Union, while not a party to the OIV Agreement, was entitled to establish a position to be adopted on its behalf with regard to those recommendations, in view of their direct impact on the EU's *acquis* in that area.[83]

It follows from this important judgment that Article 218(9) TFEU applies for the establishment of positions to be adopted by the Union in an international organisation whether or not the Union as such participates in the international organisation concerned. The possibility of an 'action' by the Union in an international organisation is therefore not prevented by the fact that it is not itself a member of the said organisation.[84] Furthermore, the fact that only some of the Member States are members of the international organisation has no impact on their obligation to respect, present and defend the common position adopted by the Union and act jointly in the interest of the latter. The determining factor is the existence of a Union competence in the area concerned. There is nothing really

[81] ECJ, Case C-399/12 *Germany v Council* (OIV), EU:C:2014:2258, paras 51 and 52. See also Case C-45/07 *Commission v Greece* [2009] ECR I-701, paras 30 and 31; *Opinion 2/91* [1993] ECR I-1061, para 5.

[82] ECJ, Case C-399/12 *Germany v Council* (OIV), EU:C:2014:2258, para 63.

[83] ibid, para 64.

[84] In the same sense see Inge Govaere, 'Novel Issues', above note 72, 225–43, 227.

new in the duties which must be met by the Member States in such a legal situation. In CFSP matters, Article 34 TEU provides expressly that in international organisations where not all the Member States participate, those which do take part shall uphold the Union's positions. Furthermore, the Member States which are also members of the UN Security Council will defend the positions and the interests of the Union. The judgment in the *Germany v Council* case actually presented no real surprise on the question of the consequences for the Member States parties to an international organisation. Only the question of the application of Article 218(9) TFEU had a specific legal interest. In the absence of a general provision governing all issues raised in connection with the participation of the Union in international organisations, the Court rightly gave an extensive interpretation of the Treaty provision in order to cover the situation where the Union is a member of the international organisation as well as that where it is not provided that it has competence in the field of activity of the said organisation. In doing so, the Court participates in increasing legal certainty in the preparation of positions to be adopted on the Union's behalf within an international organisation or a body set up by an international agreement.

IV. IS THE EVER GREATER PARTICIPATION OF THE UNION IN INTERNATIONAL ORGANISATIONS THE RESULT OF A FUNCTIONAL NECESSITY OR A GENERAL ASPIRATION?

Taking into account the diverse challenges the Union has to face internally in its relationship with the Member States, and externally in its relationship with the other members of an international organisation, it must be acknowledged that such participation is a complex matter. However, this complexity did not prevent the ever greater participation of the Union in international fora.

The increase in this participation of the Union is the result of many factors: the new architecture of the EU's external action under the Lisbon Treaty, the replacement of the dual personality (Community and Union) by a single one which improved the identification of the Union internationally, the process of conferring more competences—very strong ones and very diverse ones—to the EU entailed a larger scope of activities on the international scene, the establishment of the EEAS, the better identification of the role of each of the European actors (the President of the European Council, the Commission, the High Representative, EU Delegations, Member States, etc) allowed a more effective representation of the Union, the reaffirmation of the 'effective multilateralism' concept by the EU as a central element of its external action, and last but not least the contribution of case law on the coordination between the Union and the Member States as well as on the duty of sincere cooperation which clarified the obligations to be respected by the Member States as to Union participation within international organisations.

This ever greater participation of the Union is clearly an inexorable process. But it is also an aspiration to weigh heavily on the international scene, to weigh as heavily as or heavier than the most important partner of the EU in a globalised world. Functional necessity and aspiration are both essential elements in the foundation of the participation of the Union in international organisations. In order to have an impact on the international organisations to which the Union is party alone or with the Member States or to which the Union is not party but only the Member States, it has to act in the most 'united manner'. It is clearly not in acting in a disorderly manner that the individual Member States will have influence, but united within the Union, that they will exercise more influence on the international scene. Reciprocally the influence of the work of international organisations on EU law has no longer to be demonstrated (recently the OIV case). This interaction between the EU and other international organisations definitely contributes to a better global governance.

Part I

The European Union in the United Nations

2

The United Nations: A European Union Perspective

MARIANGELA ZAPPIA

THE OBJECTIVE OF this chapter is to present the overall approach of the European Union (EU) to the United Nations (UN) and its specialised organisations. Merit goes to the *Centre d'études juridiques européennes* for having set up a full day of reflection on the role of the EU in several international bodies in Geneva, selecting with the International Labour Organization (ILO), the World Health Organization (WHO) and the World Intellectual Property Organization (WIPO) bodies that are truly relevant for the EU.

After a brief historic review the chapter will look at the changes introduced by the Lisbon Treaty for the European Union's external representation, in particular concerning the work in multilateral fora, the UN General Assembly Resolution on the participation of the European Union in the United Nations in 2011 and the working methods established in the Geneva context.

I. INTRODUCTION

Looking at the UN in the Geneva context is particularly relevant in light of Geneva's international history as the birthplace of today's UN system. While the history of the European construction is shorter, the ideals at the foundation of the United Nations and the EU are the same. As with the UN, the European project is fundamentally a peace and reconciliation project. Industrial and economic integration, which stood at the beginning of the European integration project, mainly served the political objective of rendering another war on the European continent impossible. This was explicitly recognised when the EU was awarded the Nobel Peace Prize in 2012. As the President of the European Commission, José Manuel Barroso, said in his speech on Europe in Frankfurt on 5 November 2013: 'Europe is the most impressive creation in the history of international relations. No other political construction to date has proven to be a better way of organising life to lessen the barbarity in the world.'[1]

[1] José Manuel Durao Barroso, President of the European Commission, Erste Frankfurter Europa-Rede, Paulskirche, 5 November 2013.

In line with the UN Charter, which explicitly encourages the constitution of regional organisations, the EU is fundamentally a community of values. The history of Europe is one of reconciliation and reunification founded on strong values. This is why the EU can also claim to set an example or serve as a model for the inspiration of others. It is not about imposing a model—far from that—but European history bears all the different phases: changing alliances, confrontation, some of the worst wars in history with the use of chemical weapons in World War I and barbarity affecting the civilian population at large. From there, Europeans have reached the conclusion that they want to build a different model and never go back again. This is why the EU today gives strong political and economic support to other regional organisations such as the African Union, the Association of South East Asian Nations (ASEAN) and regional organisations in Latin America.

II. THE OVERALL FRAMEWORK OF UN–EU COOPERATION

The EU's commitment to effective multilateralism—with the UN at its core—is a central element of the EU's external action. This commitment is enshrined in the EU Treaties (Article 21(1) TEU). A solid and fruitful cooperation has developed between the UN and the EU for many years. The EU is the single largest financial contributor to the UN system, in all areas: contributions to the regular budget make up almost 40 per cent, contributions to peace-keeping operations more than 40 per cent and contributions to UN funds and programmes about half of the total contributions. The EU and its Member States are also the world's largest donors to official development assistance, contributing 55.6 per cent of global development aid. The European Commission alone spent €1.3 billion in humanitarian assistance in 2012. It ranges among the top five donors to the Office for the Coordination of Humanitarian Affairs (OCHA).

Shaping the policies with regard to the UN and setting them into a longer-term perspective, the EU has adopted mid-term priorities for the years 2012–2015.[2] These are complemented by the definition, on an annual basis, of the EU's priorities for the UN General Assembly. The EU's medium-term priorities are organised around the three key pillars of the UN: peace and security, sustainable development and human rights. They are very much interlinked, as there cannot be sustainable development without peace and security, and without development and poverty eradication there will be no sustainable peace. In addition, human rights, the promotion of democracy and the rule of law are cross-cutting issues for the European Union that run as silver threads throughout the EU action at the UN.

[2] The European Union medium-term priorities at the United Nations (2012–15), document 9820/1/12 REV 1, 23 May 2012.

A. The European Union Becoming a Real Actor on the International Scene

The cooperation between the EU and the UN has been further strengthened with the entry into force of the Lisbon Treaty in 2009. The EU[3] has become a real actor in the international context, alongside the EU Member States, working jointly with them, as well as speaking and acting on behalf of them. The examples of Catherine Ashton, the EU High Representative for Foreign Affairs and Security Policy, presiding over the Iran nuclear talks, or the Serbia-Kosovo dialogue, also facilitated by the EU, or the reintegration of Myanmar/Burma into the international community, are just a few of the most visible examples of the EU taking responsibility on the international scene, where the EU is recognised for its mediation role but beyond that as a deal-maker.

Looking back at the history of EU–UN relations since the predecessor of the EU, the European Communities, became an observer at the UN in 1974, things have changed dramatically. It is now a completely different set-up. The EU today has 28 Member States. While this number, compared to the 193 Member States of the UN, seems small, in reality this already constitutes a very solid and strong regional bloc in the UN—the most consolidated, steady and cohesive in the whole UN. The EU intervenes in all areas, ranging from environmental, to development, labour, telecommunications, humanitarian, disarmament, human rights and highly political issues; as indeed since 2011 the EU speaks in the general debates in the UN Security Council on the Middle East Peace Process, Afghanistan, Syria and the Democratic Republic of Congo, to cite just a few examples.

B. The Lisbon Treaty and the UN General Assembly Resolution on the Participation of the EU in the UN

This change is due to the internal advancement of the EU with the entry into force of the Lisbon Treaty. The Lisbon Treaty conferred the responsibilities previously held by the country holding the rotating Presidency on the EU itself. Notably, it conferred the external representation to the European institutions, that is, to the President of the European Council, the EU High Representative for Foreign Affairs and Security Policy, the European Commission, and also the 141 EU Delegations of the EU in the world and their Heads of Delegation.

Subsequent to the changes introduced by the Lisbon Treaty, the EU had to find ways to reflect these changes in its external action, notably within the international fora, where the observer status only provided the EU institutions with limited rights compared to the rights of the Member States. An important step forward

[3] When we speak about the EU, we mean the EU as an entity, comprising the EU Member States and the European institutions.

was the adoption in May 2011 by the UN General Assembly (UNGA) of the Resolution on the participation of the European Union in the work of the United Nations (UNGA/65/276).[4] The Resolution considerably enhanced the EU's participation in the UNGA and its committees, where the EU can be registered in the list of speakers alongside major regional groups. The Resolution allows EU representatives to present common positions, have EU communications circulated directly, present proposals or amendments and make interventions during sessions and exercise the right of reply. The EU as such is also invited to participate in the general debate of the General Assembly among the States. The President of the European Council, Herman Van Rompuy, did so again in September 2013. However, the EU still sits among the observers. It does not have the right to vote—which is reserved for Member States—and it cannot introduce or co-sponsor resolutions.

The UNGA Resolution on the participation of the European Union in the United Nations applies to the UNGA and its committees and made the situation in New York clearer. The picture becomes more blurred, however, when looking at the situation in Geneva, as the Resolution does not apply *mutatis mutandis* to all the other UN bodies, not to mention the situation in international organisations completely outside of the UN system such as the International Migration Organization. In these cases, the rules of procedure of each organisation frame and determine to what extent an EU representative or the EU Delegation can represent a position agreed by the 28 EU Member States, or the means through which the EU view can be expressed.

III. EU WORKING METHODS IN GENEVA FOLLOWING THE ENTRY INTO FORCE OF THE LISBON TREATY

Just three years have passed since the Lisbon arrangements started to be put into practice. This became possible through the formation in 2011 of the European External Action Service (EEAS), a sort of diplomatic service of the EU, to which 141 Delegations worldwide belong, including the Permanent Representation to the UN in Geneva. Three years is a very short period. During this time a lot of ground has already been covered, in particular considering the fact that the international environment in Geneva is very different from that in New York, dominated as it is by the UNGA and its organs. In Geneva, the Permanent Delegation of the European Union covers a whole range of issues, a lot of them not being issues of foreign policy under the competence of the EEAS, to which the EU Delegation formally belongs, but issues dealt with by the services of the European Commission and for a large part issues with shared competences between the EU and its Member States. The issue of the status of the EU in the international organisations and the

[4] Resolution 65/276 on Strengthening of the United Nations System: Participation of the European Union in the work of the United Nations, see Annex II in this volume.

issue of the competences thus complicated the application of the arrangements of the Lisbon Treaty on external representation. While a lot of ground has been covered, this is still a work in progress.

A. The EU Delegation at the Centre of the EU Coordination

As in all EU Delegations, the tasks previously held by the country holding the rotating Presidency have been taken over by the EU Delegation. This required a total change of mindset by the EU staff but also by the EU Member States. In practice it means that the EU Delegation is convening, setting the agenda and chairing all EU meetings. There are weekly meetings of the EU Heads of Mission, where all the issues on the Geneva international agenda are discussed. The EU Heads of Mission under the chairmanship of the EU Head of Delegation also hold regular dialogue meetings with the UN Heads of Agencies to discuss more strategically the agency's work programme and the preparation of major meetings. In addition, there are numerous EU meetings at expert level. Expert groups exists in the areas of human rights, health, the United Nations Conference on Trade and Development (UNCTAD), WIPO, disarmament, humanitarian and migration affairs as well as labour and social issues. They convene throughout the year and more frequently before and during major meetings, to coordinate and agree the EU positions then presented in the international fora. All these meetings are made up of experts based in Geneva. As an example, in the field of human rights alone, the EU Delegation holds around 100 coordination meetings each year. This intense coordination work has strengthened the EU cohesiveness in the UN Human Rights Council enormously and allowed the EU to present common positions and speak on basically every issue debated in the Human Rights Council, also providing the EU with a stronger role overall in the shaping of international human rights policy.

B. Developing Practical Working Mechanisms Together with the Member States

The additional tasks conferred by the Lisbon Treaty have put a huge strain on the EU Delegation. Previously, the Presidency had been preparing its six-month chairmanship for a long time and built up staff in the run-up to the Presidency term. Now the EU Delegation has to ensure a sort of continuous Presidency. It was thus inevitable that it would come up with working methods which ensure the continuous involvement and interest of the EU Member States (that is, developing their ownership and making the EU work more and more as a team, as in most cases they are the members of the international organisations whereas the EU is just an observer) and at the same time ensure the smooth running of an ever-increasing workload. This is where the system of burden sharing with the EU Member States comes in. Burden sharing has worked well for the EU. It allows making good use of the combined resources and it has contributed to the EU making a bigger impact in the international bodies. It also helps to ensure coherence between national initiatives and EU strategic priorities.

There is also now better and more strategic forward planning and priority setting of the work within the EU in Geneva, both at expert level and at the level of Heads of Mission. The strategic planning has greatly enhanced the effectiveness of the EU. In addition, these annual priorities are discussed with the relevant working groups in Brussels, notably the Council Working Parties on Human Rights (COHOM) and on UN affairs (CONUN). The objective is to be an effective player while ensuring overall coherence of EU action across the different areas and organisations.

IV. OUTLOOK AND CONCLUSION

Looking at the future with the review of the EEAS that took place in 2013, one thing is for sure: the strength of the Lisbon Treaty and of the EEAS lies in its comprehensive approach. As the High Representative Catherine Ashton put it in her speech before the European Parliament in June 2013 when she presented the review of the EEAS:[5] 'our strength lies in our ability to respond to a crisis in a wide-ranging way. Two and a half years after the establishment of the EEAS, we can say that we have a modern and operational service that is there to deliver EU foreign policy.' The Lisbon Treaty makes the EU a unique foreign policy partner that can combine diplomacy with development aid, rule of law support, military and civilian operations. Its strength also lies in providing the 'critical mass'. Collectively the EU can achieve what the EU Member States individually cannot do. The success of the EEAS rests on its unique capacity to bring together all the EU institutions and contributions, to maximise influence. One of the key tasks of the EEAS—and indeed of the Delegation in Geneva—is to provide a clear and authoritative lead in building consensus between the EU Member States on strategies and priorities. However, in situations where there is an absence of political will or of agreement amongst the Member States there are limits to what the EU can deliver.

To end with the words of EU High Representative Catherine Ashton before the EU Heads of Delegation at their annual meeting in September 2013: 'We do not have some of the hard power that some of our individual countries or other nations or organisations have. We do not have many of the tools of others. What we have is an amazing combination of things. We have history where we can point to the fact that practically every situation the world is now facing, the EU and its Member States have faced. We have had war, dictatorship and oppression.

[5] EU High Representative for Foreign Affairs and Security Policy and Vice President of the European Commission on EEAS Review, European Parliament, Strasbourg, 12 June 2013.

We have new democracies and mature democracies. We have seen human rights grow. We have had economic growth and we had recessions. But we stand together as a union of 28 countries determined in our common values and our common approach and wanting not to interfere but to lead and show that there is a way of doing this that we know and understand and can offer to other people.'

In spite of all the challenges that the implementation of the Lisbon Treaty still faces, the EU, as the UN, is learning fast how to 'deliver as one'.

3

The Position of the European Union in the United Nations: A United Nations Perspective

MARKUS SCHMIDT*

THE POSITION OF the European Union (EU) in the United Nations (UN) has developed very significantly over the last 40 years, ever since it became an observer member at the UN in 1974. When the author of this chapter joined the UN human rights programme in 1987, it was difficult, if not impossible, to identify an 'EU position' on emerging human rights issues. Today, the EU is among the most, if not *the* most, active non-State entity in the UN human rights programme and consistently coordinates the position of all the 28 Member States, thereby allowing it speak with one voice on many, but not on all, issues.

The predecessor of the EU was the first non-State entity to be given observer status by the UN General Assembly in October 1974; this gave the European Economic Community a number of specific participation rights, especially in the context of the work of the UN Economic and Social Council. Over the years, EU participatory rights in the UN have increased significantly, and after the adoption of the Lisbon Treaty, the EU was granted enhanced observer status by General Assembly Resolution 65/276 of 3 May 2011. Under the enhanced observer formula, the EU may speak in debates among representatives of Member States and regional groups, submit proposals and draft amendments, exercise the right of reply, and circulate documents. It may not, however, exercise voting rights, nor do EU representatives have the right to raise points of order.[1]

The UN continues to welcome the active engagement of the EU in its activities and programmes, and both former Secretary-General Kofi Annan and Secretary-General Ban Ki-moon have referred to the UN's partnership with the EU as one that deserves praise and emulation. It is therefore not surprising that several UN

* Opinions expressed in this chapter are personal and do not reflect the position of the United Nations Organization. The author gratefully acknowledges research assistance from Ms Yusra Suedi and Ms Emma Scott, interns in the legal liaison office of the UN Office at Geneva.

[1] See Document A/65/856 (1 June 2011), paras 11 and 12.

entities have set up liaison or regional offices in Brussels, the principal seat of the European Union.[2]

In addition, the EU, as the only non-State entity, is a party in its own right to more than 50 multilateral treaties adopted under UN auspices, such as the environmental conventions implemented under the auspices of the UN Economic Commission for Europe or the UN Framework Convention on Climate Change. It is a full member of the Food and Agricultural Organization and the World Trade Organization. It has also secured a special status of 'full participant' in a number of important UN Conferences, such as the Rio and Kyoto summits on climate change.

The EU and its Member States are the single largest contributor to the UN budget. The 28 EU Member States fund roughly 39 per cent of the UN's regular budget, a little more than 40 per cent of the current UN peacekeeping operations and roughly half of all UN Member States' contributions to the activities of UN funds and programmes. The EU Commission alone provides more than $1.35 billion in support of UN external aid programmes and projects.

EU financial contributions to UN development, humanitarian, disaster risk reduction and other aid activities are governed by the Financial and Administrative Framework Agreement concluded between the EU and the UN in April 2003. It applies to all contribution-specific agreements signed between both organisations after 29 April 2003. The Financial and Administrative Framework Agreement must be implemented through contract templates or 'contribution-specific agreements'. Two sets of templates have been prepared: the first concerns humanitarian aid as managed by the Commission's Humanitarian Aid Office, the second concerns all other types of cooperation.

Financial and Administrative Framework Agreements are meant to be 'results-based' and focus on 'actions' to be implemented by the UN. Where possible, EU–UN cooperation takes the form of actions, the performance of which requires the pooling of resources from several donors, and where it is not reasonably possible to assign the share contributed by each donor to each type of expenditure. In such cases of 'multi-donor actions', the UN may manage EU contributions in accordance with its own rules and regulations, based on the understanding that they are compatible with internationally accepted standards concerning accounting, audit, control and procurement procedures.[3]

Financial and Administrative Framework Agreements tend to be very complex, and the administrative services of many UN entities tend to view reporting requirements under such Agreements as very demanding. In fact, many UN entities for whom the EU is an important donor face a dilemma: on one hand, they are not keen to bite the hand that feeds them. On the other hand, they consider that the 'verification missions', which are similar to auditing procedures

[2] See, eg, Seventh annual Partnership Report 'Saving and Improving Lives: Partnership between the United Nations and the European Union in 2011', at www.unbrussels.org/report2012.

[3] Financial and Administrative Framework Agreement of 29 April 2003, Preamble, para 4.

and in fact regarded by a number of UN entities as such, used by the EU under Financial and Administrative Framework Agreements to monitor the use of its financial contributions are very if not excessively intrusive, and some UN entities have sought to fend off or to contest planned EU verification missions under such Agreements.

On the other hand, such 'verification missions' are fairly predictable, as the competent EU office regularly sends a list of completed, current or planned verification missions to the Office of the UN Controller.[4] One should also keep in mind the original purpose of the Financial and Administrative Framework Agreement: to facilitate the pursuit of common UN–EU objectives and achieve common results, for example in the field of human rights, humanitarian aid or disaster-reduction activities. One might add that arguably, the resistance of some UN entities to verification missions under Financial and Administrative Framework Agreements stems from a perception that the EU tends to perform mere input–output performance verification, not substantive or results-based performance verification.

The EU today works with all UN bodies, specialised agencies and programmes across a broad range of UN activities, spanning from development policy and peace building to humanitarian assistance, disaster risk reduction, environment and sustainable energy, human rights and humanitarian law.

The EU coordinates voting of its Member States in the UN General Assembly's six main committees and other bodies and agencies (such as the UN Economic and Social Council). More than 1,000 internal EU coordination meetings are held every year in New York, Geneva and Vienna to help develop a common EU stance in relation to the above subjects.[5] The permanent representatives of the 28 EU Member States meet every Tuesday morning at the EU's mission to the UN in New York with a view to agreeing on a common policy.[6]

Prior to the start of the annual session of the UN General Assembly (UNGA), the Council of the EU will in general determine the EU priorities for the next UNGA. Article 19 of the EU Treaty further stipulates that those EU States also members of the UN Security Council will consult each other and keep all the other Member States informed. Without prejudice to their responsibilities under the UN Charter, those EU States with a permanent seat on the Security Council—the United Kingdom (UK) and France—shall endeavour to foster the interests of the EU when fulfilling their duties.

Since the inception of the EU's Common Foreign and Security Policy, the cohesion of EU voting has risen from roughly 86 per cent in 1991/1992 to 97 per cent in 1998/1999, and it has remained at roughly that level since. The quest for more

[4] See table of 'European Commission verification missions to the United Nations, indicative planning 2013—Update', addressed to the UN Controller, 21 October 2013 (on file with the author).

[5] See UN Regional Information Center for Western Europe, 'How the European Union and the UN cooperate' (2007).

[6] See *Der Spiegel Online*, 26 August 2013, at www.spiegel.de/international/world/secretar-nsa-documents-show-how-the-us-spies-on-europe.

cohesion and consensus was dented in 2011, when the UK blocked more than 70 EU statements before various UN committees. Arguably, this dispute was primarily over terminology: the statements were to be read 'on behalf of the EU', rather than 'the EU and its Member States', as insisted on by the UK, whose actions were widely interpreted as intended to slow down the perceived drift towards a common EU foreign policy.[7]

Inasmuch as political cooperation is concerned, the UN Department of Political Affairs regularly supports the Secretary-General in convening high-level consultations with EU representatives to achieve coordination and mutual understanding on operational imperatives and broader strategic issues facing the UN and its partners. The Department of Political Affairs also encourages and facilitates regular 'desk to desk' dialogues, to review and improve channels of cooperation. In practice, desk to desk exchanges take place between the External Relations Directorate of the EU Commission and its UN counterparts. Country or thematic desks of both organisations regularly discuss their respective policy approaches with a view to ensuring complementarity of each other's action. One example is the close interaction between the UN Department of Political Affairs and the EU in relation to the situation in Kosovo, where the EU has been responsible for 'Pillar IV' of the UN Interim Mission in Kosovo on reconstruction and development.[8]

I. THE EU IN THE UN HUMAN RIGHTS PROGRAMME AND THE UN HUMAN RIGHTS COUNCIL

The EU's endeavour to adopt common positions in respect of the promotion and protection of human rights by the UN is a long-standing one. The ministerial statement on human rights of 21 July 1986 may be seen as a basis for a nascent EU human rights policy. It affirms that 'the promotion of economic, social and cultural rights as well as of civil and political rights is of primordial importance for the attainment of human dignity … neither the absence of economic and social development, nor particular convictions or ideologies, may serve as a justification for the denial of civil and political rights.'[9] Today, the EU and the UN are universally considered as having a mutually reinforcing relationship in the area of human rights: the EU needs the UN to 'export' its human rights and democracy values and norms, whereas the UN needs the support of the EU in its human rights bodies to help uphold and reinforce universal human rights norms and objectives.

[7] Julian Borger, 'EU anger over British stance on UN statements', *The Guardian*, 20 October 2011, at www.guardian.co.uk/world/2011/oct./20/uk-eu-un-statements-wording.

[8] For a general overview, see Alexandra Novosseloff, *EU–UN Cooperation in Peacekeeping: Challenges and Prospects*, Global Governance Institute, GGI Analysis 4/2012.

[9] See Markus Schmidt, 'The EC Approach to the Protection of Human Rights' (1994) 61/62 *Nordic Journal of International Law* 229–32, at 229. For a general survey, see Philip Alston (ed), *The EU and Human Rights* (Oxford, Oxford University Press, 2000).

The EU has been instrumental in the establishment of the UN Human Rights Council. It may be interesting to note that EU Member states were far from unanimous in their opinion on the composition, membership and mandate(s) of the Council during the negotiations that preceded the adoption of General Assembly Resolution 60/251 of 15 March 2006, which created the Council. In particular, EU countries agreed to a re-allocation of Council seats among the UN regional groups which largely benefited the African and Asian groups and resulted in a lower number of Council seats being allocated to the Western European and Others Group, which in turn arguably weakened the political leverage that this regional group subsequently was able to exercise in the Council.[10]

This said, the EU has supported the activities of the Council since the inception in 2006 of its Universal Periodic Review mechanism, the development of the special procedures system, as well as the recent review of Council mechanisms. It seeks to advance coordinated positions, proposals and draft resolutions to the largest possible extent. Prior to, during and after all regular and special sessions of the Council, EU Member States convene coordination meetings[11] to ensure that a common position may be presented not only in the Council plenary but also in the process of negotiating Council resolutions (Article 34 Treaty on European Union (TEU)). Similar mechanisms are in place in the Third Committee of the General Assembly, which deals with human rights issues. When resolutions are put to a vote in the Human Rights Council, an EU Member State also a member of the Council may explain the vote on behalf of other EU Members of the Council (and, by extension, on behalf of other EU Member States).

Despite all these efforts at coordination, several setbacks continue to bedevil the EU's foreign policy in relation to human rights. During the annual meetings of the Third Committee of the General Assembly, developing country delegations used to quip that 'the stronger the EU statement, the more likely that the EU will either abstain or unravel'.[12] Lack of EU cohesion frequently is equated with lack of effectiveness, or vice versa—'if the EU is united they cannot be defeated'.[13]

A solid coordination mechanism does not necessarily translate into a strong show when it comes to voting. The EU has on occasion failed to lobby effectively on certain resolutions or has taken a moderate stand simply to allow consensus to be reached, thus prompting some to criticise its passive approach to addressing

[10] See Markus Schmidt, 'United Nations' in Daniel Moeckli, Sangeeta Shah and Sandesh Sivakumaran (eds), *International Human Rights Law* (Oxford, Oxford University Press, 2010) 391–432, at 394, 398.

[11] See Sudeshna Basu, 'The European Union in the Human Rights Council' in Jan Wouters (ed), *The European Union and Multilateral Governance—Assessing EU Participation in UN Human Rights and Environmental Fora* (London, Palgrave, 2012) 86–102, at 90.

[12] Hadewych Hazelzet, 'The EU's Human Rights Policy in the UN: An Example of Effective Multilateralism?' in Jan Wouters (ed), *The United Nations and the European Union: An Ever Stronger Partnership* (The Hague, Asser Press, 2006) 183.

[13] Katie Verlin Laatikainen and Karen Smith, 'Introduction—the EU at the United Nations: Leader, Partner or Failure?' in KV Laatikainen and K Smith (eds), *The European Union at the United Nations: Intersecting Multilateralisms* (London, Palgrave, 2006) 1–23, at 16.

human rights violations in the Council.[14] An example would be the failure to renew the special procedures mandate for the Democratic Republic of the Congo in 2009, in relation to which the EU declared 'that it was joining the consensus but was disappointed to see the mandate of the Independent Expert go'.[15] Also in 2009, EU Members of the Council found it difficult to collect the required 16 endorsements from other Council members to convene a special session on alleged massive human rights abuses in Sri Lanka. When the special session was eventually held, its outcome was considered disappointing for many and considered too mild by Western observers. This suggests that Council members, and above all those from the EU, must not only be able to secure the necessary votes for the convening of a special session of the Council but also have a suitable strategy in place to secure the acceptance of their proposed draft resolution.[16] It is argued here that the EU has learned from the experience with the Democratic Republic of the Congo mandate and the special session on Sri Lanka—where the EU nowadays calls for or sponsors the convening of a special session of the Council, this will be accompanied by a coordinated draft resolution, the acceptance of which has been assessed as likely.

That the EU still sometimes struggles to articulate a coherent approach to human rights is exemplified by its role in the Syrian conflict. In a statement before the UNGA on 29 July 2013, the EU called for an end to the deteriorating situation in Syria and the serious human rights abuses, including war crimes, that had been identified by the Council's Independent International Commission of Inquiry on Syria.[17] To display a common stand on documented human rights abuses in Syria in a UN forum is one thing—to agree on how best to deal with the situation on the ground is another. Thus, the economic sanctions against the Syrian regime adopted by the EU in May 2013 were thrown into disarray after France and the UK forced a lifting of the EU arms embargo.[18] The vast majority of EU states opposed this move, but finally assented to preserve a semblance of unity. Disagreements over how to respond to the civil war in Syria have exposed deep divisions within the EU, and it is not accordingly surprising that the EU's role in efforts to convene a second UN Conference on Syria in January 2014 was relatively limited.

In its political and human rights dialogue with third countries (including the People's Republic of China), the EU regularly raises the issue of cooperation with the Council's special procedures mandate holders and with the UN human rights treaty bodies and the follow-up to their recommendations and concluding observations.The High Commissioner for Human Rights and the special rapporteurs of the Human Rights Council have been invited to brief the Political and Security Committee of the EU. The EU and its Member States have taken a very proactive

[14] Basu, 'The European Union', above n 11, at 91.

[15] Basu, above n 11, at 91.

[16] See Schmidt, 'United Nations', above n 10, at 397.

[17] At www.eu-un.europa.eu/articles/en/article_13837_en.htm.

[18] *The Guardian*, 28 May 2013, 'UK forces EU to lift embargo on Syria rebel arms' at www.theguardian.com/world/may/28/uk-forced-eu-embargo-syria-rebel-arms.

part in UN human rights standard-setting activities,[19] for example in negotiations on a UN Convention on Enforced or Involuntary Disappearances or on the Optional Protocol to the Convention on the Rights of the Child instituting a complaints mechanism under the Convention. Arguably, the adoption of a number of recent UN human rights instruments would not have been possible without the strong support of the EU and its Member States.

II. THE ROLE OF THE EU IN UN HUMANITARIAN AFFAIRS AND IN THE INTERNATIONAL STRATEGY FOR DISASTER REDUCTION (ISDR)

Collectively, the EU and its Member States are the largest provider of humanitarian assistance worldwide. The Commission's Humanitarian Aid Office (ECHO) plays a crucial role by providing relief supplies and services through intermediary organisations in crisis regions. Some €700–800 million are made available each year, and roughly a third of this sum goes to UN humanitarian programmes, such as the Office for the Coordination of Humanitarian Affairs (OCHA).[20]

However, this financial clout is not necessarily matched by a comparable political EU impact on international humanitarian action in UN fora because of the relatively fragmented character of European humanitarian aid. Within UN fora, there tend to be distinctive humanitarian aid policies of the Commission, via ECHO, and of all EU Member States. Put succinctly, there simply is no agreement on a common EU stand in relation to humanitarian aid administered by UN entities, and there are no regular EU coordination meetings convened to seek to formulate a common EU position on UN humanitarian action and programmes.

Some EU countries with large humanitarian aid budgets (such as the UK or Sweden) simply do not wish to surrender control over their budgets to the EU (or to other EU States). They also have the administrative, logistical and substantive expertise to implement large-scale humanitarian aid projects which smaller EU countries do not have. Smaller EU countries or those with smaller humanitarian aid budgets (such as Belgium and Luxembourg, but also France and Germany) would like to push for a better EU integration of humanitarian aid programmes at the UN level. For smaller EU countries, it might indeed make sense to give their humanitarian budget to the multilateral system (whether the EU or the UN). The European Council's Committee on Humanitarian Aid and Food Aid, which is chaired by the country which holds the EU Presidency, is meant to foster an enhanced and common EU position in relation to delivery of humanitarian aid—but thus far with limited results.

In relation to the work of OCHA, for example, because the EU contribution is split into individual grants (ECHO plus the Member States), the possibility of

[19] See Hazelzet, 'The EU's Human Rights Policy in the UN', above n 12, at 187.

[20] UN Regional Information Center for Western Europe, 'How the EU and the UN cooperate', above, n 5.

EU influence on OCHA's activities and programmes, or those of other important humanitarian aid actors such as the World Food Programme or UNICEF, is smaller when compared to that of the United States. In addition, the lack of vertical coherence may work to the detriment of the efficiency of the overall EU humanitarian aid effort, which in the eyes of some is characterised by either duplication of efforts or by gaps in the coverage of humanitarian needs. A 2006 evaluation of humanitarian aid mandated by EU Member States concluded that there were no common actions, no common procedures and no common visibility, and that most countries acted without reference to the other players.[21]

The EU is an essential partner in the implementation of the Hyogo Framework of Action, adopted by the UN in 2005 to explain, describe and detail the work that is required from all different sectors and actors to reduce disaster losses. The EU has become the first donor to activities and programmes of the ISDR. It has developed disaster risk reduction policy guidance for all of its Member States through a number of instruments, and it played a critical role in generating and stimulating EU Member States' contributions to the 'Sendai Framework for Disaster Risk Reduction 2015–2030', adopted by the UN World Conference on Disaster Risk Reduction held in Sendai (Japan) in March 2015. In addition—and this can be seen as being complementary to UN efforts in the area—the EU also pushes for disaster risk reduction action in its bilateral and multilateral activities. EU internal procedures on disaster risk reduction tend to be very cross-cutting, which results in a number of EU entities and directorates being very engaged with the ISDR in disaster risk reduction activities.[22] For the 67th UNGA, the EU had identified more effective integration of disaster risk reduction and transition to recovery into UN development and humanitarian aid policies and programming as a priority.[23]

III. THE ROLE OF THE EU IN THE UN ECONOMIC COMMISSION FOR EUROPE

At the level of UN activities in Geneva, the EU plays both an active yet at the same time somewhat ambiguous role in relation to the work of the UN Economic Commission for Europe (UNECE), whose activities are focused primarily on environmental issues, sustainable energy, transport, trade and economic cooperation and integration.

The EU actively supports the activities of the UNECE Committee on Environmental Policy and the 'Environment for Europe' process. During the 2013 review of the 2005 reform package for UNECE, both the EU and its Member States supported the continuation of the environment sub-programme within UNECE.

[21] See Helen Versluys, 'Coherence of EU external action: the case of humanitarian aid', paper presented at the 10th Biennial EUSA Conference, Montreal, 17–19 May 2007.

[22] Communication to the author by staff member of the ISDR, 30 July 2013.

[23] See 'EU priorities for the 67th General Assembly', at www.eu-un.europa.eu/articles/articleslist_s115_en.

EU support includes both in-kind contributions (hosting meetings and events, providing experts and expertise, seconding associate experts) and financial contributions to trust funds set up under the environment sub-programme. EU delegates regularly participate in annual and special sessions of the Committee on Environmental Policy, and the European Environment Agency actively engages with the Committee on Environmental Policy in relation to work on environmental monitoring, assessment and reporting. The European Environment Agency also participates in UNECE's Environmental Performance Review Programme, and has provided in-kind contributions to the Environmental Performance Reviews of Albania, Moldova, Croatia and Morocco. The EU has actively supported the Environment for Europe process since its inception in 1991, a process which focuses on supporting countries in Eastern and South-Eastern Europe, the Caucasus and Central Asia in their efforts to raise environmental standards and comply with their international commitments.[24]

The EU is supportive of UNECE's activities related to the implementation of the Industrial Accidents Convention. It conducts a number of programmes that are supportive of activities under the Convention, such as activities concerning the implementation of the EU's Seveso II Directive and the work on evaluation of safety reports in several Balkan states which are candidates for EU accession. Another good example of cooperation is the current discussion on the possible amendment of Annex I of the Convention to harmonise it with Annex I of the EU's forthcoming Seveso III Directive, related to the transition to a globally harmonised system of classification and labelling of chemicals in the EU region.[25]

Similarly, the EU is supportive of activities under the Convention on the Protection and Use of Trans-boundary Watercourses and International Lakes (the so-called Water Convention), as can be seen by numerous EU-funded grants for trans-boundary water resources management projects in the Eastern European, Caucasus and Central Asian regions. The Convention has contributed to, and is acknowledged by, key EU legislation on water resources management, as well as the EU Water Framework Directive of 2000. It has also contributed to many of the agreements governing EU trans-boundary river basins and the creation of joint bodies and commissions for such basins. The EU Water Initiative's National Policy Dialogues for Integrated Water Resources Management and Water and Sanitation is jointly implemented by the Organisation for Economic Co-operation and Development and by the UNECE in Eastern European countries, the Caucasus and countries of Central Asia. The EU has provided long-term funding for the National Policy Dialogues.[26]

The EU is a party to the Convention on Long-Range Transboundary Air Pollution and to the majority of protocols to it, along with all the Member States. Interesting voting issues may arise if, on particular issues, both the EU and its

[24] Communication to author by staff member of the UNECE, 1 November 2013.

[25] ibid, 18 October 2013.

[26] ibid, 21 October 2013.

Member States seek to exercise the right to vote concurrently. The issue arose in 2013 in the context of the interpretation of the provisions and rules of procedure of the above Convention. Pursuant to Article 14(1) of the Convention, it is open for signature by Member States of the UNECE and by regional integration organisations. The EU and all 28 Member States are parties to the Convention. The right of regional economic integration organisations to vote is regulated by the rules of procedure of the Executive Body of the Convention. Thus, rule 29(7) stipulates that '[e]xcept as provided for in paragraph 8 of this rule, each Party shall have one vote'. Paragraph 8 then provides that '[r]egional organizations, in matters within their competence, shall exercise their right to vote with a number of votes equal to the number of their member states which are parties to the Convention'. It follows that Article 14(2) of the Convention and rule 29, paragraph 8, of the rules of procedure make it clear that the EU and its Member States may not exercise their rights concurrently, including the right to vote. The rationale is to avoid a situation where votes already cast by Member States of the EU are counted twice if the EU votes concurrently. Whether a certain issue falls within the competence of the EU should be determined by the EU itself, and if it indeed does, the EU would need to ensure that its Member States do not vote concurrently.[27]

During recent negotiations on the revision of some of the protocols to the Convention, the EU acted in a coordinated manner, and its position was presented by the EU Presidency, speaking on behalf of all EU Members. In December 2012, the EU Commission's Environment Directorate signed a contribution agreement with the UNECE, to provide funding for a post for several years to support capacity-building activities under the Convention in Eastern Europe, the Caucasus and Central Asia.[28]

In other areas of UNECE's activities, the EU position is more multi-faceted and, some would say, more problematic. In the area of energy, the Lisbon Treaty introduces some notable changes, including a dedicated chapter on energy, that arguably affect the energy politics between the EU and its Member States, including in relation to EU external representation of Member States in international fora.[29] Within UNECE, the EU delegation in Geneva has, in the recent past, tabled a series of procedural challenges in the Committee on Sustainable Energy, UNECE's intergovernmental body responsible for promoting international cooperation in the field of energy. These challenges have tended to focus on procedural points and not on the substance of UNECE energy activities, but they have made the implementation of UNECE sustainable energy programmes more difficult. Backstage bureaucratic politics and delays or stalemate in the implementation of some projects have been the result of these challenges, as well as procedural skirmishes

[27] Advice provided to the Secretariat of the Convention by the UN Office of Legal Affairs, 10 April 2013.

[28] Communication to author by staff member of the UNECE, 18 October 2013.

[29] See analysis by Jan Frederik Braun, 'EU Energy Policy under the Treaty of Lisbon Rules—between a new policy and business as usual', EPIN Working Paper No 31, February 2011.

between the EU delegation and other, non EU, delegations to the UNECE, to the extent that some within UNECE are tempted to argue that the common position of the 28 EU Members would be better achieved if the EU let its Member States present their own national position.

During 2013, in the context of further debates in the Executive Committee of UNECE about review of structural reform, the EU delegation argued that further meetings of two sectoral committees of UNECE, the Committee on Trade and the Committee on Economic Cooperation and Integration, could not take place without a further explicit decision of the Executive Committee. This position, which was not shared by the UNECE Secretariat nor for that matter by a number of EU Member States, prompted a request for legal advice from a number of EU States, and the position of the EU delegation was ultimately disavowed by a legal opinion from the UN Office of Legal Affairs.[30] Arguably, the current position of the EU within UNECE is not necessarily a faithful reflection of the common position of its Member States.

IV. CONCLUSION

The cohesion of the EU action in various UN fora has risen remarkably over the past 15–20 years, and this cohesion has not been affected by continuous EU enlargement over this period. For some UN programmes (development, disaster reduction), the EU is the biggest donor and/or provider of funds; for others (human rights in particular), the EU has become the most important catalyst for UN standard-setting activities.

Consistent efforts at coordinating the position of EU Member States in UN fora have strengthened the political clout that the EU is able to wield in many UN entities and fora. However, the foreign policy considerations of larger EU Member States can and sometimes do pose a threat to the coherence and the consistency of the 'EU position' in the UN, as political discord among EU States in relation to a number of sensitive human rights issues debated in the Human Rights Council or in relation to the current conflict in Syria have shown. Conversely, the position of the EU does not necessarily reflect that of all of its Member States, as the recent example of the EU procedural challenges to several of the programmes and activities of the UN Economic Commission for Europe has shown.

[30] Legal Opinion of the UN Office of Legal Affairs, dated 6 November 2013, addressed to the Chairperson of the Executive Committee of the UNECE. This legal opinion has been challenged in turn by the EU as being one-sided and factually incomplete.

4

Improving the European Union's Status in the United Nations and the UN System: An Objective Without a Strategy?

JAN WOUTERS, ANNA-LUISE CHANÉ,
JED ODERMATT AND THOMAS RAMOPOULOS*

I. INTRODUCTION: THE UN AS A POLITICAL PRIORITY OF THE UNION

THE LISBON TREATY emphasises the commitment of the European Union (EU) to multilateralism, stating that the EU 'shall seek to develop relations and build partnerships with ... international, regional or global organisations' and to 'promote multilateral solutions to common problems, in particular in the framework of the United Nations' (Article 21(1) Treaty on European Union (TEU)). Moreover, one of the objectives of the EU's external action is to 'promote an international system based on stronger multilateral cooperation and good global governance' (Article 21(2)(h) TEU). The EU itself being one of the most advanced forms of multilateral cooperation among states, it is quite understandable that it would be committed to 'a stronger international society, well-functioning international institutions and a rule-based international order'.[1] The Union not only seeks to participate in this multilateral system, it actually aims to have a leading role in shaping it:

> At a global level, Europe must lead a renewal of the multilateral order. The UN stands at the apex of the international system. Everything the EU has done in the field of security has been linked to UN objectives. We have a unique moment to renew multilateralism, working with the United States and with our partners around the world.[2]

* The views expressed herein are purely personal.

[1] European Council, European Security Strategy: A Secure Europe in a Better World, 12 December 2003.

[2] Council of the European Union, Report on the Implementation of the European Security Strategy: Providing Security in a Changing World (S407/08, 11 December 2008) p 2. For a survey of scholarly

A key part of the EU's engagement in this multilateral order is its relationship with and participation in the United Nations (UN) bodies, specialised agencies, programmes, funds and related international organisations. In order to play a role in shaping and renewing the multilateral system, the EU should also have strong and effective voice within the UN and the UN system.

It is also clear from the Treaties that the UN is of major importance to the Union.[3] The UN tackles a number of issues that fall completely or predominantly within the competences of the Union. Furthermore, the UN is a cardinal example of an international organisation whose work affects a wide range of EU policies. Many of the EU's key foreign policy goals require some kind of engagement with the UN and the UN system. These include issues such as climate change policy, eradication of global poverty, humanitarian assistance and security issues such as Iran's nuclear aspirations and combating arms proliferation. Thus, achieving an effective representation of the Union in the UN and the UN system is in the interest of the EU, and is a significant political priority.

Despite being a priority, the cooperation of the EU with the UN encounters several stumbling blocks that at times hamper the EU's efforts to have a unified and effective presence within the organisation. One of the most contentious issues in this respect is the division of powers between the EU and its Member States, most notably with regard to the right to speak or the right to negotiate international agreements. These issues of external representation are aggravated by the variation of statuses that the EU has in the different UN fora. While there are several bodies in which only the EU Member States are represented, the EU has obtained observer status in most fora, was given enhanced participation rights in some, and was even granted the status of a member organisation in very few exceptional cases.[4] The type of status depends not only on the competences of the EU, but also on the institutional framework of the respective UN bodies, which is in turn contingent upon the political circumstances.[5] Consequently, the EU's status in UN fora does not necessarily correspond to its competences and priorities, thereby hindering its effective representation.

literature on the EU's commitment to multilateralism see R Kissack, 'The European Union and multilateralism' in KE Jørgensen and KV Laatikainen (eds), *Routledge Handbook on the European Union and International Institutions: Performance, Policy, Power* (London, Routledge, 2013) 405–15.

[3] Apart from the reference in Art 21(1) TEU, the UN or the UN Charter is referred to in 14 other instances in the EU Treaties: Art 3(5), Art 21(2)(c), Art 34(2), Art 42(1) and (7) TEU, 7th recital of the preamble of the TFEU, Art 208(2), Art 214(7), Art 220(1) TFEU, 3th and 8th recital preamble, as well as Art 1(b) Protocol No 10 on permanent structured cooperation, 3rd paragraph Declaration No 13 concerning CFSP, Declaration No 14 concerning CFSP.

[4] F Hoffmeister, 'Outsider or Frontrunner? Recent Developments under International and European Law on the Status of the European Union in International Organizations and Treaty Bodies' (2007) *CML Rev* 41–68.

[5] C Flaesch-Mougin, 'Le statut de la Communauté Européenne au sein des organisations internationales' in J-V Louis and M Dony (eds), *Commentaire J Mégret: Le Droit de la CE et de l'Union Européenne*, Vol 12 (Brussels, Editions de l'Université de Bruxelles, 2005) 369–97, 369 et seq; C Kaddous, 'European Union Participation in International Financial Organizations' in I Govaere and S Poli (eds), *EU Governance of Global Emergencies* (Leiden, Brill book series, Studies in EU External Relations, 2014) 277–95, 279–85.

In light of these shortcomings, European Commission President Barroso and Vice-President Ashton issued on 20 December 2012 a 'Strategy for the progressive improvement of the EU status in international organisations and other fora in line with the objectives of the Treaty of Lisbon' (Barroso–Ashton Strategy),[6] which contains a number of recommendations concerning EU representation in international organisations, including the UN framework. First, with regard to the EU's work in the UN General Assembly (UNGA), the Strategy recommends continued efforts to ensure the full implementation of UNGA Resolution 65/276 on the enhanced participation rights of the Union, as well as an evaluation of its possible extension to other UNGA subsidiary bodies. Second, with regard to other UN agencies and programmes, the Strategy makes a classification of the various situations, based on the potential for a status upgrade and on whether or not efforts are currently being undertaken. For each situation, recommendations and examples are provided, often indicating a number of priority organisations.

This chapter examines some of the legal and political issues that are at play as the EU attempts to enhance its cooperation with and representation in the UN and the UN system. Section II deals with general issues of EU external representation, which have recently played a major role in EU–UN relations. Section III analyses difficulties with regard to the practical implementation of UNGA Resolution 65/276 as well as the possibility to extend its application to UNGA subsidiary bodies, using the example of the Human Rights Council (HRC). Section IV takes a closer look at UN bodies that were identified as targets for closer cooperation in the Barroso–Ashton Strategy and where the EU could potentially pursue upgraded status, analysing both the EU's participation in the respective fora and the legal and political potential for improving the Union's status. Our analysis focuses on a series of UN bodies which illustrate the institutional diversity within the UN and the UN system—ranging from primary organs to subsidiary bodies, specialised agencies and independent organisations whose relationship with the UN is governed by special agreements—and the broad range of issue areas where the EU is involved internationally: human rights, food and agriculture, transport, security, science and culture. In addition to the UNGA and the HRC, the chapter examines the cases of the Food and Agriculture Organization (FAO), which is the only example of a UN specialised agency in which the EU holds membership status; the International Maritime Organization (IMO), a UN specialised agency in which the EU holds no status despite its prolific legislative and policy initiatives in maritime affairs; the International Atomic Energy Agency (IAEA), where the EU's external representation is complicated by the continuing existence of the European Atomic Energy Community (Euratom); and finally the United Nations Educational, Scientific and Cultural Organization (UNESCO), as an example of a UN specialised agency in a policy field of 'weak' EU powers but where the EU has nevertheless been granted an 'ad hoc' upgraded status for a specific purpose.

[6] Communication to the Commission from the President in Agreement with Vice-President Ashton—Strategy for the progressive improvement of the EU status in international organisations and other fora in line with the objectives of the Treaty of Lisbon, C(2012) 9420 final, 20 December 2012.

Thus, this chapter does not intend to give an exhaustive account of the UN bodies and organisations where the EU might pursue closer cooperation or an upgraded status; rather, it aims to illustrate the legal and political challenges that the Union encounters when it seeks to improve its status in the UN framework.

We argue that even after the entry into force of the Lisbon Treaty, which aimed to streamline the Union's external representation, the EU continues to struggle for more effective participation in the UN framework. The stumbling blocks are both internal—due to disagreements between the Union and its Member States—and external—in particular due to gaps between the EU's status in most UN bodies and its competences and priorities. Although aligning the Union's internal and external dimensions thus remains a focal point of the EU's engagement at the UN, this chapter aims to demonstrate that the Barroso–Ashton Strategy to achieve this goal lacks the required level of vision and precision, and is thus inadequate for guiding the EU's efforts towards assuming its desired leadership role at the UN level.

II. EU REPRESENTATION AT THE UN AFTER LISBON

The EU's representation in multilateral fora has long been a contentious issue. The Lisbon Treaty had intended to deal with some of the obstacles that plagued EU external relations. However, problems have persisted, and the EU's relationship with the UN has not been immune to this.[7] Much of this can be traced to the fact that the EU can be only a full member of some of these organisations and instruments and cannot be a full member of the UN in general.[8] It therefore must rely on and cooperate with the EU Member States, who are full members of the UN and of most UN specialised agencies.

In order to ensure unity in the international representation of the Union,[9] the Member States and the Union have the duty to cooperate closely in their activities

[7] S Gstöhl, 'EU Diplomacy After Lisbon: More Effective Multilateralism?' (2011) *Brown Journal of World Affairs* 181–91; N Hadeshian, 'European Union's External Relations: More Consistency?' (2010) *Yearbook of Polish European Studies* 107–27; N Helwig, 'EU Foreign Policy and the High Representative's Capability-Expectations Gap: A question of Political Will' (2013) *European Foreign Affairs Review* 235–54.

[8] Cf Art 4(1) UN Charter, which limits membership to states only. For literature examining the status and representation arrangements of the EU in different international organisations in accordance with the founding instrument of each organisation, see M Emerson, R Balfour, T Corthaut, J Wouters, PM Kaczynski and T Renard, *Upgrading the EU's Role as a Global Actor: Institutions, Law and the Restructuring of European Diplomacy* (Brussels, Centre for European Policy Studies, 2011); Hoffmeister, 'Outsider or Frontrunner?' above, n 4.

[9] On the 'requirement' or 'principle' of unity in the international representation of the EU see, inter alia, ECJ, Case 1/78 *IAEA* [1978] ECR 2151, paras 34–36; ECJ, *Opinion 2/91 ILO* [1993] ECR I-1061, para 38; ECJ, *Opinion 1/94 WTO* [1994] ECR I-5267, para 108; ECJ, Case C-25/94 *Commission v Council* [1996] ECR I-1469, para 48; ECJ, Case C-246/07 *Commission v Sweden* [2010] ECR I-3317, paras 73, 104.

at the UN level.[10] This entails among others that Member States must collectively submit a Union position, whenever a matter in a UN body in which the EU does not have member status falls in an area of exclusive EU competence.[11] Member States are not entitled to table unilateral proposals, even in areas of shared competences, when the Union has remained passive pursuant to a common strategy not to submit a proposal.[12]

An issue that has prominently manifested itself in the UN has been the question of in whose names statements are to be made. In particular, disagreement centred on the seemingly trivial issue of whether statements before the UN should be preceded by a short clause indicating if the statement was delivered 'on behalf of the EU', 'on behalf of the EU and its Member States', or 'on behalf of the Member States of the European Union'. In the second half of 2011, the United Kingdom blocked a significant number of EU statements in an ostensible attempt to safeguard its national competences in the field of shared competences,[13] thereby considerably impacting on the EU's external action.[14] The adoption of 'general arrangements' on EU statements in multilateral organisations by the Council on 24 October 2011[15] has ended the conflict for now, but these arrangements are far from offering

[10] The case law of the ECJ has so far not established complete clarity on the legal foundations of the duty of cooperation in the Union's external relations. While the ECJ has frequently held that the 'obligation to cooperate flows from the requirement of unity in the international representation of the Community' (see, eg, ECJ, *Opinion 1/94*, above, n 9, para 108; Case C-25/94, above, n 9, para 48; Case C-246/07, above, n 9, para 73), commentators interpret the recent judgments in Cases C-459/03, *Commission v Ireland* [2006] ECR I-4635 and C-246/07, above, n 9, to support the view that the Court derives the duty from the principle of sincere cooperation enshrined in Art 4(3) TEU. See C Hillion, 'Mixity and Coherence in EU External Relations: The Significance of the "Duty of Cooperation"' in C Hillion and P Koutrakos (eds), *Mixed Agreements Revisited: The EU and its Member States in the World* (Oxford, Hart Publishing, 2010) 87–115, 91–92; F Casolari, 'The principle of loyal co-operation: A "master key" for EU external representation?' in S Blockmans and RA Wessel (eds), *Principles and Practices of EU External Representation* (CLEER Working Papers 2012–15) 11–36; M Cremona, 'Case C-246/07 *Commission v Sweden* (PFOS), Judgment of the Court of Justice (Grand Chamber) of 20 April 2010, nyr' (2011) *CML Rev* 1639–66, 1650 et seq.

[11] ECJ, Case C-45/07 *Commission v Greece* [2009] ECR I-701, paras 14–38.

[12] ECJ, Case C-246/07 *Commission v Sweden* [2010] ECR I-3317, paras 69–105; G De Baere, '"O, Where is Faith? O, Where is Loyalty?" Some Thoughts on the Duty of Loyal Co-operation and the Union's External Environmental Competences in the light of the PFOS Case' (2011) *EL Rev* 405–19.

[13] T Vogel, 'Split Emerges over Remit of the EU's Diplomatic Service' (2011) *European Voice*, www.europeanvoice.com/article/imported/split-emerges-over-remit-of-the-eu-s-diplomatic-service/71168.aspx (16 February 2014); J Borger, 'EU Anger over British Stance on UN Statements' (2011) *The Guardian*, www.guardian.co.uk/world/2011/oct/20/uk-eu-un-statements-wording; S Barkowski and K Wiatr, 'External Representation of the European Union and Shared Competences—an Unsolved Puzzle' (2012) *Yearbook of Polish European Studies* 155–75, 166 et seq.

[14] European External Action Service, Report by the High Representative to the European Parliament, the Council and the Commission, 22 December 2011, point 17.

[15] Council of the European Union, EU Statements in Multilateral Organisations—General Arrangements, Doc No 15901/11, 24 October 2011 ('General Arrangements'). For a commentary see C Flaesch-Mougin, 'Représentation externe et compétences de l'Union européenne: quelques réflexions à propos des arrangements généraux du Conseil relatifs aux déclarations de l'UE dans les organisations multilatérales' in C Boutayeb (ed), *La Constitution, l'Europe et le droit—Mélanges en l'honneur de Jean-Claude Masclet* (Paris, Publications de l'Université Paris-Sorbonne, 2013) 571–92.

a permanent solution. Their provision that 'Member States agree on a case-by-case basis whether and how to coordinate and be represented externally'[16] immediately triggered criticism by the Commission[17] and risks creating confusion for third countries regarding the allocation of competences within the EU.[18]

Other disagreements with regard to the delivery of statements have focused on the use of nameplates. When the Commission proposed in 2013 that EU or common statements in the FAO should in the future only be delivered from behind the EU nameplate,[19] the United Kingdom disagreed, favouring the current practice according to which 'any Member State may intervene in support of an agreed EU statement from behind their national nameplate'.[20] It highlights the unease with which some Member States react whenever the EU advances into territory previously reserved to state actors, and illustrates their latent fear of competence creep.

The negotiation of international agreements is another case where similar problems arose with regard to representation in the post-Lisbon era, particularly in areas of shared competences.[21] In negotiations on a legally binding instrument on mercury, for example, the Commission held the view that it should be the negotiator on all Union competences, including shared ones, having to cooperate closely with the Member States. The Council, on the other hand, opted for a negotiating team comprising the Commission and the Presidency as a means to attain unity of representation. The current compromise foresees that the Commission will be the Union negotiator in areas where the Union has competence and has acted upon it, but that it will do so 'in consultation with a special committee of representatives of Member States, and in accordance with [specific] negotiating directives'.[22]

[16] ibid.

[17] Statement by the Commission to be entered into the minutes of the Council session endorsing the General Arrangements, Council of the European Union, EU Statements in Multilateral Organisations—General Arrangements, above, n 15.

[18] See further T Ramopoulos and J Odermatt, 'EU Diplomacy: Measuring Success in Light of the Post-Lisbon Institutional Framework' in A Boening et al (eds), *Global Power Europe*, Vol 1: Theoretical and Institutional Approaches to the EU's External Relations (Heidelberg, Springer, 2013) 19–35, 27 et seq.

[19] Communication from the Commission to the Council, The role of the European Union in the Food and Agriculture Organisation (FAO) after the Treaty of Lisbon: Updated Declaration of Competences and new arrangements between the Council and the Commission for the exercise of membership rights of the EU and its Member States (FAO Communication), COM(2013) 333 final, annex 2, p 13.

[20] United Kingdom, Department for International Development, Explanatory Memorandum on COM(2013) 333 final, Doc No 10368-13, 27 June 2013, para 17.

[21] See, eg, on the negotiations of a legally binding instrument on mercury T Corthaut and D Van Eeckhoutte, 'Legal Aspects of EU Participation in Global Environmental Governance under the UN Umbrella' in J Wouters et al (eds), *The European Union and Multilateral Governance* (Basingstoke, Palgrave Macmillan, 2012) 145–70; G De Baere, 'International Negotiations Post-Lisbon: A Case Study of the Union's External Environmental Policy' in K Koutrakos (ed), *The European Union's External Relations a Year After Lisbon* (CLEER Working Papers 2011–13) 97–112, www.asser.nl/upload/documents/772011_51358CLEER%20WP%202011-3%20-%20KOUTRAKOS.pdf. Similar disagreements were observed with regard to the negotiation of the Arms Trade Treaty, see Foreign & Commonwealth Office, Review of the Balance of Competences between the United Kingdom and the European Union: Foreign Policy, 22 July 2013, 40, www.gov.uk/government/uploads/system/uploads/attachment_data/file/227437/2901086_Foreign_Policy_acc.pdf, 38–39.

[22] Council Decision on the participation of the Union in negotiations on a legally binding instrument on mercury further to Decision 25/5 of the Governing Council of the United Nations Environment Programme (UNEP), Doc No 16632/10, 6 December 2010.

The EU has managed to overcome many of these representation issues, mostly due to the desire of the Member States and the EU institutions to work together to find practical arrangements. Nevertheless, the representation problems that were exhibited in the post-Lisbon period were never fully settled, and could possibly arise again in the future.

III. THE EU AT THE UNGA AND THE HRC: UNGA RESOLUTION 65/276 AND ITS AFTERMATH

The issues regarding EU representation discussed above are further aggravated by the incoherent picture of EU status at the level of the UN and the UN system. Across the wide range of UN bodies, the Union holds a variety of different legal statuses, ranging from no representation to full membership. As indicated above, the level of status depends not only on the competences of the EU but also on external factors, such as the institutional framework of the respective UN bodies and the political context.[23] This leads to the situation whereby the EU's status at UN bodies is not necessarily in line with its competences and priorities. Thus the EU frequently has very limited participation rights in those UN fora which are of high relevance for the effective exercise of its powers. Consequently, the Union has continuously pursued the objective of improving its representation at UN bodies.

One of the most prominent examples of such efforts is the 2011 upgrade of the EU's observer status at the UNGA. The Union had already been actively engaged at the UNGA for decades, ever since the European Economic Community (EEC) was invited to participate as an observer.[24] In light of the UNGA's high visibility and its rank as the premier forum to address the global community of states, it appeared to be the natural setting for the EU to seek an upgraded status.[25] Being one of the UN's primary organs, it was hoped that a status change in the UNGA would set a precedent for realigning the Union's participation rights in other UN bodies with its new internal institutional realities after the entry into force of the Lisbon Treaty. The Union aimed for an 'enhanced' observer status which would allow the EU, as far as possible, to be represented in the UNGA in its own right instead of through the Member State holding the rotating Council Presidency. Diplomatic efforts suffered a serious setback in September 2010 when a first draft resolution was met with opposition by third states and failed to be adopted.[26] It was only after increased outreach and substantive amendments that the UNGA adopted Resolution 65/276 on 3 May 2011 and saved the EU from a diplomatic

[23] Flaesch-Mougin, above, n 5; Kaddous, above, n 5.

[24] UNGA Res 3208 (XXIX) 1974, *Status of the European Economic Community in the General Assembly*, 11 October 1974.

[25] Cf G De Baere and E Paasivirta, 'Identity and Difference: The EU and the UN as Part of Each Other' in H de Waele and JJ Kuipers (eds), *The European Union's Emerging International Identity—Views from the Global Arena* (Leiden, Martinus Nijhoff, 2013) 21–42, 26.

[26] See M Emerson and J Wouters, 'The EU's Diplomatic Debacle at the UN: What else and what next?', Commentary, Centre for European Policy Studies, 1 October 2010.

debacle.[27] Still, the EU achieved far less than it had initially intended, as the final Resolution secured participation rights that were far lower than what had been proposed at the outset.

A. Practical Implementation

Even though UNGA Resolution 65/276 was eventually adopted with a large majority voting in favour, its implementation in practice presented new challenges. Based on lingering concerns of endangering the principle of sovereign equality of the UN's Member States and the intergovernmental character of the organisation, a number of States, most vocally the Caribbean Community (CARICOM) group, advocated a narrow interpretation of the Resolution. The disagreement centred in particular on the Union Delegation's right 'to be inscribed on the list of speakers among representatives of major groups, in order to make interventions'.[28] This had been interpreted by the UN Secretary-General (UNSG) to mean that the EU shall be inscribed 'in the order in which the European Union signified its desire to speak'.[29] In an interpretive declaration of UNGA Resolution 65/276 CARICOM stated that it did not share the UNSG's interpretation, expressing the view that the Union should not take 'priority over other major groups that are represented by a State Member of the United Nations'.[30] In order to maintain the clear hierarchy between States and observers, CARICOM concluded that 'in a speakers' list including multiple major groups, the European Union will not be able to speak prior to any major group represented by a full State Member of the United Nations'.[31]

The controversy had practical consequences when UNGA Resolution 65/276 was applied in the UNGA's 66th session. Speaking in the Third Committee, the representative of CARICOM reiterated its view, arguing that the UNSG's interpretation 'would appear to confer even more enhanced privileges to the European Union's observer'.[32] His view was shared by the representatives of Venezuela

[27] On the diplomatic saga involving the EU's upgraded status at the UNGA see E Brewer, 'The Participation of the European Union in the Work of the United Nations: Evolving to Reflect the New Realities of Regional Organizations' (2012) *International Organizations Law Review* 181–225; De Baere and Paasivirta, above, n 25; J Wouters, J Odermatt and T Ramopoulos, 'The Status of the European Union at the United Nations General Assembly' in I Govaere, E Lannon, P Van Elsuwege, S Adam (eds), *The European Union in the World: Liber Amicorum Professor Marc Maresceau* (Leiden, Brill Publishers, 2014) 211–23.

[28] UNGA Res 65/276, Participation of the European Union in the Work of the United Nations, 3 May 2011, annex Art 1(a).

[29] Note by the Secretary-General, Participation of the European Union in the Work of the United Nations, A/65/856, para 5.

[30] Letter dated 9 May 2011 from the Permanent Representative of the Bahamas to the United Nations addressed to the Secretary-General, A/65/834.

[31] ibid.

[32] UNGA Third Committee, 'As World Struggles with Economic Crisis, "Time Bomb" of Rising Social Inequality Could Tear Apart Moral Fabric of Societies, Third Committee Told', 3 October 2011, GA/SHC/4004.

and Nicaragua. Poland on the other hand rejected any unilateral interpretation of the 'crystal clear' text of the Resolution, while the United States stated that the EU Member States should be able to decide who would speak on their behalf.[33] In an attempt to resolve the disagreement, the Chair of the Third Committee launched open-ended consultations and, as an interim measure, decided to rotate the speaking order of the representatives of major groups in order to avoid setting a precedent.[34] Nevertheless, the dispute could not be settled, and escalated in a later meeting which had to be postponed when consensus on the list of speakers could not be obtained.[35] Subsequent consultations led to an additional hardening of the respective positions and the Chair's proposal that representatives of major groups could informally swap their places if they wanted to speak earlier, was met with hesitation.[36] A similar conflict erupted in the Fifth Committee, when the EU intended to take the floor after Argentina for the G77 and China, which initially resulted in having the EU speak after all regional groups.[37] Other Committees, however, established pragmatic solutions apparently without opposition, such as the Second Committee, where inscription of the major groups on the list of speakers was made on a 'first-come, first-served' basis.[38] For the time being, the issue appears to have been settled and the Union Delegation regularly speaks before other major groups represented by States. Yet, without a common understanding about the scope of UNGA Resolution 65/276, the disagreement about its accurate interpretation results in unequal application across the UNGA's Main Committees and may cause further discussions in the future.

Another conflict focused on the right to submit an explanation of vote. It was argued by some Member States that this right could only be exercised by those entities that had a right to vote, given that the two rights were inextricably linked.[39] It would thus fall again to the EU Member States to submit explanatory statements on behalf of the EU. In some cases the EU was granted the right to make a 'general statement' after the State Parties had delivered their explanations of vote; however, this practice has equally triggered criticism. When the UNGA President in a meeting on Resolution 65/281 gave the floor to the EU representative to make

[33] ibid.

[34] UNGA Third Committee, 'With Crises Disproportionately Affecting Most Vulnerable, World Community Must Ensure Economic, Social Rights Not Relegated to Second Tier, Committee Told', 26 October 2011, GA/SHC/4020.

[35] UNGA Third Committee, 'Landmark Election in Tunisia Superb Demonstration of UN Providing Advice, Support, while Fully Respecting National Leadership, Ownership Third Committee Told', 25 October 2011, GA/SHC/4019.

[36] UNGA Third Committee, GA/SHC/4020, above, n 34.

[37] Wouters, Odermatt and Ramopoulos, above, n 27, p 214; but see Brewer, above, n 27, p 208 et seq, who identified that the EU spoke before many major groups represented by states.

[38] Ad Hoc Working Group on General Assembly revitalization, Meeting devoted to the working methods of the Main Committees—briefing by the Chairs of the Main Committees, pursuant to operative paragraph 19 of GA Resolution 66/296: Statement by HE Ambassador George Talbot (Guyana), Chair of the Second Committee.

[39] UNGA, 'Five Years after Creation, General Assembly Maintains Human Rights Council as Subsidiary Body, Concluding Review of Work, Functioning', 17 June 2011, GA/11101.

a general statement, the representative of Saint Vincent and the Grenadines, supported by Venezuela, raised a point of order, arguing that the Union should not be granted the exclusive privilege to make a general statement, when the same right was denied to Member States, and reiterating the view that the EU 'would not be able to speak after the vote since it had no vote'.[40]

Other difficulties in the practical implementation of Resolution 65/276 stemmed from the EU's allocation of competences and its external relations architecture. This includes the above-mentioned disagreement between the United Kingdom and the Union on the question of in whose name statements ought to be delivered, and the often inconsistent external representation, either by the EU Delegation or by the Member State holding the rotating Council Presidency on its behalf.[41]

These hurdles prompted President Barroso and Vice-President Ashton to call for continued efforts to ensure the full implementation of the Resolution in their Strategy.[42] Nevertheless, despite certain setbacks, the overall application can be judged a success.[43] The Union Delegation has smoothly assumed its new responsibilities, EU representatives regularly address the plenary and the Committees, and Union communications are directly circulated as official documents. It is in this light that the President of the Commission and the HR/VP concluded in 2013: 'By now, the EU's enhanced participatory status in the work of UNGA, its committees and conferences, is broadly accepted at the UN; internal debates have largely subsided, although practical implementation requires permanent attention and vigilance by the EU Delegation in New York.'[44]

The EU's experience surrounding the 2011 upgrade at the UNGA not only demonstrates the challenges in seeking enhanced participation rights in the UN, it has been highly influential in shaping EU policy towards international organisations ever since. It is now clear that for the Union, securing upgraded status in international organisations is neither simple nor automatic, but requires a serious and careful diplomatic effort that takes into account the political sensitivities of third states, and even of the EU's own Member States. Moreover, this experience also makes clear that even once a higher status is reached, the EU may still have to fight for its place at the table to make sure the upgrade is given full effect. Consequently the Union has adopted a more cautious and deliberate approach to similar efforts in other international organisations, especially those in the UN system. Although UNGA Resolution 65/276 is touted as a diplomatic success, since 2011 there has been no comparable effort to replicate the EU's upgraded status in other international organisations or UN bodies.

[40] ibid.

[41] Brewer, above, n 27, p 209 et seq.

[42] Barroso–Ashton Strategy, above, n 6, p 4.

[43] PA Serrano de Haro, 'Participation of the EU in the work of the UN: General Assembly Resolution 65/276', CLEER Working Papers 2012–14, p 32.

[44] Note to the College of Commissioners from President Barroso and Vice-President Ashton on the implementation of the 'Strategy for the progressive improvement of the EU status in international organisations and other fora in line with the objectives of the Treaty of Lisbon, C(2012) 9420 final' (Information note), INFO(2013) 115, p 3.

B. Extension to the Human Rights Council

This does not mean, however, that the EU's ambitions to improve its status in the UN framework have been entirely crushed. As illustrated by the Strategy, Commission services and the EEAS are still evaluating and promoting options to remedy the perceived impediments for effective Union representation in UN bodies. Nevertheless, the Barroso–Ashton Strategy follows a significantly more cautious approach compared to similar EU communications dating from before the UNGA status upgrade. Written with a view to eventual EC membership of UN bodies, the Commission's 2003 Communication 'The European Union and the United Nations: The Choice of Multilateralism' boldly demanded that the EC 'should be given the possibility to participate fully in the work of UN bodies where matters of Community competence are concerned, and Member States should contribute effectively towards this',[45] and stated—referring to EC membership of the FAO[46] and the Codex Alimentarius—that '[t]his option should also be pursued for other relevant organisations that belong to the UN system'.[47] More than 10 years later, the Barroso–Ashton Strategy is far less ambitious. It avoids a clear commitment to any fixed negotiation goal and merely refers to the 'improvement of the EU status and its alignment with the objectives of the EU Treaties'.[48] For the time being, full participation of the EU in the UN framework as a member organisation seems to have been abandoned as the final aim, giving way to a strategy of piecemeal steps towards modest upgrades wherever these appear to be legally and politically feasible.

One of the ways forward recommended by the Barroso–Ashton Strategy is the application of Resolution 65/276 in UNGA subsidiary organs.[49] In particular, the Strategy recommends to focus, among others, on the HRC and to avoid 'reopening the resolution, under which [subsidiary bodies] are not explicitly covered'.[50]

The HRC, which in 2006 replaced the UN Commission on Human Rights,[51] is a body of 47 elected UN Member States, tasked with the promotion of human rights and fundamental freedoms. It addresses cases of human rights violations, provides recommendations, and monitors the fulfilment of each state's human rights obligations through the universal periodic review (UPR). As one of the foremost global human rights fora it is of significant importance for the Union's external action.[52]

[45] Communication from the Commission to the Council and the European Parliament—The European Union and the United Nations: The choice of multilateralism, COM(2003) 526 final, p 23.

[46] See for more detail below, IV.A.

[47] Communication from the Commission to the Council and the European Parliament, above, n 45, p 17.

[48] Barroso–Ashton Strategy, above, n 6, p 1.

[49] ibid, p 4.

[50] ibid.

[51] UNGA Res 60/251, Human Rights Council, 15 March 2006.

[52] Cf, eg, Council of the European Union, Council conclusions on EU priorities at the UN Human Rights Fora, Foreign Affairs Council meeting, 10 February 2014.

While fundamental rights have been enshrined in EU primary law since the Maastricht Treaty, and the Union adopted a non-binding Charter of Fundamental Rights in 2000, it is only with the entry into force of the Lisbon Treaty that the EU has reached the 'high point of its engagement with human rights'.[53] Not only does Article 6 TEU pave the way for the EU's accession to the European Convention on Human Rights and confer binding treaty force to the Charter of Fundamental Rights, Article 21 TEU defines human rights and fundamental freedoms as guiding principles and objectives of the EU's external action. Human rights are nowadays regarded as the 'silver thread running through all EU action both at home and abroad'.[54] In mid-2012 the EU appointed its first Special Representative for Human Rights,[55] and adopted a 'Strategic Framework and Action Plan on Human Rights and Democracy'[56] in which it 'underlines the leading role of the UN Human Rights Council in addressing urgent cases of human rights violations' and pledges to 'contribute vigorously to the effective functioning of the Council'.[57] More specifically, items 9(a) and 23(b) of the Action Plan single out the HRC as a forum for the EU to promote economic, social and cultural rights and the freedom of religion or belief. Furthermore, the promotion of human rights, democracy and the rule of law ranked consistently as one of the EU's priorities during UNGA sessions.[58]

The EU was a strong supporter for the establishment of the HRC since the idea first emerged in the 2004 sessions of the Commission on Human Rights, quickly endorsing the initiative for its establishment.[59] 'Welcom[ing] the presentation of a proposal reflecting the primacy of human rights by the creation of a Human Rights Council',[60] the EU actively lobbied for the realisation of its vision of the Council, which foresaw not only the creation of a standing body, possibly with the rank of a main organ of the UN, but whose membership should also be elected by a two-thirds majority of the UNGA and be smaller in numbers, admitting only those

[53] G de Búrca, 'The Road Not Taken: The European Union as a Global Human Rights Actor' (2011) *American Journal of International Law* 649–93, 649.

[54] European Commission/High Representative of the European Union for Foreign Affairs and Security Policy—Joint Communication to the European Parliament and the Council: Human rights and democracy at the heart of EU external action—Towards a more effective approach, COM(2011) 886 final.

[55] Council Decision appointing the European Union Special Representative for Human Rights, 2012/440/CFSP, 25 July 2012 (OJ 2012, L200/21).

[56] Council of the European Union, Human Rights and Democracy: EU Strategic Framework and EU Action Plan, Doc No 11855/12, 25 June 2012.

[57] ibid, p 8.

[58] See, eg, EU priorities since the 55th UNGA session, www.eu-un.europa.eu/articles/articleslist_s27_en.htm (18 February 2014).

[59] J Wouters, S Basu and N Bernaz, 'The Role of the European Union in the Human Rights Council', European Parliament, Directorate-General for External Policies, EXPO/B/DROI/2007/41, November 2008, p 6 et seq; for a more recent analysis, see J Wouters and K Meuwissen, 'The European Union at the UN Human Rights Council. Multilateral Human Rights Protection Coming of Age?' (2014) 2 *European Journal of Human Rights* 135–72.

[60] EU Presidency, Statement by the Representative of Luxembourg to the United Nations, Formal Plenary Session of the UN General Assembly, PRES05-032EN, 6 April 2005.

states which demonstrated genuine interest in the promotion of human rights.[61] Although the EU eventually had to compromise on many of its positions, it commented favourably on the final outcome and welcomed the HRC as an improvement over the Commission on Human Rights.[62] The Union has remained an active supporter of the HRC ever since, participating extensively in the 2009–2011 review process,[63] supporting special procedures and the Office of the High Commissioner for Human Rights, and proposing or supporting resolutions, in particular focusing on the freedom of religion or belief, the rights of the child, freedom of expression and country situations. Despite several recent successes,[64] the Union's impact at the HRC has often been described as marginal due to its inability, at least until recently, to forge cross-regional coalitions. This was caused by a lack of credibility in light of the Union's persistent 'double-standards problem', but also by its inflexible negotiation practice, defensive stance and insufficient outreach.[65]

Effective EU participation is among others hindered by its legal status in the HRC. Full membership is only open to UN Member States. The Union has observer status, meaning that it cannot vote or sponsor resolutions, and while it has the right to make interventions, it may not do so in the speaking slots for states.[66] The EU thus remains dependent on the representation by a Member State, in particular by the rotating Council Presidency. Even after the entry into force of the Lisbon Treaty, the Union's participation in the HRC is clogged by cumbersome internal coordination processes, which often focus on burden sharing rather than on substantive issues.[67] This heavy focus on the internal process often leaves insufficient time and resources to gather support for EU positions and to build successful coalitions. The necessary internal coordination also reduces the Union's flexibility during negotiations and with regard to new and unforeseen developments. Nevertheless, caution should be exercised to regard a status upgrade as a panacea that will solve all of the above-mentioned issues. On the contrary, the Union must avoid contributing to the persistent bloc dynamics in the Council.

[61] Wouters, Basu and Bernaz, above, n 59, p 10.

[62] UNGA, EU Explanation of vote on the draft resolution on the Human Rights Council (L48), Statement by Ambassador Gerhard Pfanzelter, Permanent Representative of Austria to the United Nations, on behalf of the European Union, 15 March 2006.

[63] UNGA Res 60/251, above, n 51, para 1, 16.

[64] See, eg, the initiative for the establishment of a new country mandate for Belarus, A/HRC/RES/20/13 of 16 July 2012.

[65] Wouters and Meuwissen, above, n 59; KE Smith, 'The European Union at the Human Rights Council: speaking with one voice but having little influence' (2010) *Journal of European Public Policy* 224–41. A salient and frequently cited example of EU 'failure' at the HRC includes the resolution terminating the expert mandate for the DR Congo where the EU joined the consensus although it had previously invested considerable diplomatic efforts for a renewal (HRC Resolution 7/20, Technical cooperation and advisory services in the Democratic Republic of the Congo, 27 March 2008), S Basu, 'The European Union in the Human Rights Council' in J Wouters, H Bruyninckx, S Basu and S Schunz (eds), *The European Union and Multilateral Governance: Assessing EU Participation in United Nations Human Rights and Environmental Fora* (Basingstoke, Palgrave Macmillan, 2012,) 86–102, 91 et seq.

[66] S Basu, above, n 65, p 90; Wouters and Meuwissen, above, n 59.

[67] Wouters and Meuwissen, above, n 59.

In parallel with efforts to improve its status in the Council, it should fully seize the possibilities offered by EU Member States participating in the Council, which can support the Union's message and bring invaluable expertise and third country networks.[68]

While there appear to be no plans to eventually aim for full EU membership of the HRC, the Barroso–Ashton Strategy considers the extension of Resolution 65/276 and thereby to grant the EU enhanced participation rights. This would permit the Union to participate in the work of the HRC 'in its own right', thus aligning its external representation with the requirements of Article 221 TFEU. However, the question remains whether it is legally and politically feasible to extend the application of Resolution 65/276 to the HRC. Adoption of the Resolution in the UNGA alone was not sufficient to modify the procedures of the HRC, given that the competence to decide on the granting of observer status and the modalities of participation rests with the HRC.[69] Participation of and consultation with observers in the HRC is governed by Rule 7(a) of its Rules of Procedure, which provides:

> The Council shall apply the rules of procedure established for committees of the General Assembly, as applicable, unless subsequently otherwise decided by the Assembly or the Council, and the participation of and consultation with observers, including States that are not members of the Council, the specialized agencies, other intergovernmental organizations and national human rights institutions, as well as non-governmental organizations, shall be based on arrangements, including Economic and Social Council resolution 1996/31 of 25 July 1996, and practices observed by the Commission on Human Rights, while ensuring the most effective contribution of these entities.

Enhanced participation rights for the Union would be within reach, if, first, Resolution 65/276 was part of the rules of procedure established for the UNGA committees and if, second, the UNGA and the HRC did not decide against its application. As to the first point, in a narrow reading the term 'rules of procedure' in Rule 7(a) of the HRC's Rules of Procedure might refer only to the UNGA's rules of procedure *sensu stricto*, which in Section XIII contain provisions for the proceedings in the committees.[70] A broader understanding of the term, however, would not depend on the formal status of a provision, but on its substance, thereby widening the scope to include resolutions which govern the procedure of the Assembly and its committees. This would also include the various resolutions granting participation rights to non-Member States and observers—matters on which the UNGA's rules of procedure *sensu stricto* are silent. Given that Resolution 65/276 contains 'modalities ... for the participation of the representatives of the European Union,

[68] ibid, p 19; Gstöhl, above, n 7, p 190.

[69] The HRC has made use of its competence to adopt its own rules of procedure, cf UNGA Res 60/251, above, n 51, para 11; HRC Resolution 5/1, Institution-building of the United Nations Human Rights Council, 18 June 2007; J Wouters, J Odermatt and T Ramopoulos, 'The Lisbon Treaty and the Status of the European Union in the International Arena: The May 2011 Upgrade at the UN General Assembly' (2011) *IEMed Mediterranean Yearbook* 166–70.

[70] UNGA, Rules of Procedure of the General Assembly, A/520/Rev 17, 2008.

in its capacity as observer, in the sessions and work of the General Assembly and its committees',[71] it can be regarded as forming part of the rules of procedure referred to in Rule 7(a) of the HRC's rules of procedure and would therefore find application in the HRC.

Second, however, the question remains as to whether the UNGA or the HRC 'subsequently [decided] otherwise'. Neither body adopted an explicit decision against the application of Resolution 65/276 in the HRC. They may have done so implicitly, though. At first glance, the sweeping title of the Resolution ('Participation of the European Union in the work of the United Nations') suggests a broad scope of application across the entire spectrum of UN bodies.[72] But it was clearly not the intention of the drafters to modify the EU's status in the UN framework in general, first because this would entail a restriction in those fora where the EU obtained full participant or membership status and thus even broader participation rights, second because the UNGA lacks the competence to set the rules of procedure for the various UN bodies and fora.[73] Instead, Resolution 65/276 limits its application to the 'sessions and work of the General Assembly and its committees and working groups, in international meetings and conferences convened under the auspices of the Assembly and in United Nations conferences'.[74] While this list is not explicitly declared to be exhaustive, it reveals a conscious inclusion of several subsidiary organs, namely committees and working groups, while other subsidiary bodies, such as boards, commissions, councils and panels, were omitted. It could therefore be argued that Resolution 65/276 implies a decision by the UNGA against its application in the HRC, in the terms of Rules 7(a) of the HRC's rules of procedure.

Independent of the legal aspects, the political feasibility of a status upgrade remains doubtful. Significant resistance, both externally and internally, against an enhanced EU status at the HRC has caused the current cautious approach of the Union. States, including the EU Member States, continue to regard human rights as a state prerogative and hesitate to accept 'that actors at the level of the EU … take over the role of state actors'.[75] The extension of Resolution 65/276 to the HRC therefore remains a rather distant possibility, which seems also reflected in the fact that it has completely disappeared in the 2013 information note on the implementation of the Barroso–Ashton Strategy.[76]

IV. THE STATUS OF THE EU IN THE WIDER UN SYSTEM

The EU has also pursued the objective of improving its representation at other UN agencies. In this regard the EU is faced with an important question: Which bodies

71 UNGA Res 65/276, above, n 28, para 2.
72 Wouters, Odermatt and Ramopoulos, above, n 69, p 5.
73 Cf Art 30 UN Charter (UNSC), Art 72 UN Charter (ECOSOC), Art 30(1) ICJ Statute (ICJ).
74 Above, n 71.
75 Wouters and Meuwissen, above, n 59, p 19.
76 Information note, above, n 44.

should it prioritise? The Barroso–Ashton Strategy proposes a set of criteria based on interest and prospect: status enhancement should be sought in those organisations that have both a 'strategic or economic interest' for the EU and/or 'impact on policy areas where the EU has important competences', and in which 'an upgrade appears realistic in the short to medium term'.[77] Regrettably, neither of those factors is explained in more detail. It thus remains unclear which criteria the Strategy applies to determine the feasibility of a status upgrade. Also, the interest criterion is by far too broad to allow for a workable prioritisation of Union efforts. There remain very few issues dealt with by the UN that are not of strategic or economic relevance to the EU or which do not impact on areas of important Union competences. This criterion, too, would have benefited from a more thorough definition in order to make the selection of priority organisations more transparent. The Barroso–Ashton Strategy's recommendation for resumed efforts with regard to the EU's participation in the FAO and for a status upgrade, among others, in the IMO and IAEA, therefore appears rather random. Furthermore, UNESCO, where the EU had been granted enhanced observer status for the negotiation of the Convention on the Protection and Promotion of the Diversity of Cultural Expressions, is not mentioned in the Barroso–Ashton Strategy. This raises questions, as will be demonstrated below, that this could serve as a precedent for a new approach of ad hoc upgraded EU participation for temporally restricted and closely defined purposes.

A. Food and Agriculture Organization

The FAO is among those organisations for which the Strategy instructs Commission services and the EEAS 'to sustain their efforts with a view to a positive outcome', given that 'efforts to upgrade the EU status or improve the position of the EU within the existing arrangements are underway and progress is being made'.[78] It thereby refers to the ongoing revision of the internal arrangements between the Commission and the Council. The 2013 Commission Communication on 'The role of the European Union in the Food and Agriculture Organisation after the Treaty of Lisbon' (FAO Communication)[79] foresees not only upgrades of the EU's status at the FAO, it also provides for more flexible internal coordination procedures and more robust external representation of the Union—thereby immediately prompting resistance on the side of EU Member States.

The FAO is the second oldest UN specialised agency, founded against the background of the Second World War, which had given rise to the idea that 'international cooperation between nation states and the international regulation and supervision of economic sectors with strategic significance … could act as

[77] Barroso–Ashton Strategy, above, n 6, p 3.
[78] ibid, p 2.
[79] FAO Communication, above, n 19.

safeguards against future conflicts'.[80] Tasked with eradicating hunger, combating poverty and promoting the sustainable use of natural resources, the FAO provides a network and forum of discussion for the dissemination of knowledge, expertise and up-to-date information.[81]

Agriculture is one of the core competences of the EU, and has been so since its earliest days, when the Treaty establishing the European Economic Community tasked the EEC with the creation of a common agricultural policy (CAP).[82] It encompasses a range of policy areas which overlap with the work of the FAO, in particular food safety, rural development and the environment. The importance of the CAP for the EU is clearly illustrated by its financial weight, which will—with a budget of €408.3 billion—amount to a 38 per cent share of the EU's overall budget in the years 2014–2020.[83] The work of the FAO additionally encompasses fisheries policies, for which the EU also shares competence with the Member States (Article 4(2)(d) TFEU).

The first contacts between the FAO and the Union coincided with the establishment of the EEC and the transferral of agriculture competences from domestic to Community level. While a first agreement between the EEC and the FAO had already been drafted in 1959, it was an exchange of letters between the President of the European Commission and the Director General of the FAO which in 1962 established principles of interaction between the two organisations.[84] The Commission participated as an observer in meetings of the FAO and obtained enhanced observer status in 1970. Still, its participation rights were deemed insufficient to effectively exercise its extensive competences.[85] The Commission deplored in particular its inability to table proposals and to fully participate in the policy making of the FAO and the work of its technical bodies.[86] As early as 1978 the Commission thus introduced its aim of EC accession to the FAO,[87] but it was only on 22 October 1990 that the

[80] F Schild, 'The Influence of the Food and Agriculture Organization (FAO) on the EU Legal Order' in RA Wessel and S Blockmans (eds), *Between Autonomy and Dependence: The EU Legal Order Under the Influence of International Organisations* (The Hague, Asser, 2013) 217–41, 224.

[81] J Maersk Pedersen, 'FAO-EU Cooperation: An Ever Stronger Partnership' in J Wouters, F Hoffmeister and T Ruys (eds), *The United Nations and the European Union: An Ever Stronger Partnership* (The Hague, Asser, 2006) 63–91, 63 et seq. On the crisis of the FAO and the role of the EU in the reform process see R Kissack, *Pursuing Effective Multilateralism: The European Union, International Organisations and the Politics of Decision Making* (Basingstoke, Palgrave Macmillan, 2010) 87–94.

[82] Art 3(d) 38–47 EEC Treaty.

[83] M Hall, EU ministers give farm policy final political seal, Euractiv, 2013, www.euractiv.com/cap/eu-ministers-give-farm-policy-fi-news-532383; note that the share of the CAP expenditure of the overall EU budget has significantly decreased since the 1980s, and still amounted to more than 60% of the Union's budget when the EC joined the FAO in 1991, see European Commission, CAP post-2013: Key graphs and figures, Graph 1: CAP expenditure in the total EU expenditure, 2014, http://ec.europa.eu/agriculture/cap-post-2013/graphs/graph1_en.pdf.

[84] For a historical overview see Schild, above, n 80, p 225 et seq.

[85] J Wouters, S de Jong, A Marx and P De Man, 'Study for the Assessment of the EU's Role in International Maritime Organisations, Final Report', April 2009, p 36.

[86] R Frid, 'The European Economic Community: A Member of a Specialized Agency of the United Nations' (1993) *European Journal of International Law* 239–55, 241.

[87] D Dormoy, 'Le statut de l'Union Européenne dans les organisations internationales' in D Dormoy (ed), *L'Union Européenne et les organisations internationales* (Brussels, Bruylant, 1997) 36–55, 39 et seq.

Council requested the opening of accession negotiations, which were launched on 7 February 1991.[88] Accession of the European Community (EC) as a full member was without precedent in the UN framework and required an amendment of the FAO constitution, to include a so-called 'regional economic integration organization' (REIO) clause. The negotiation process had to overcome concerns, both on the side of the EU Member States, which were reluctant to give up rights, and on the side of other FAO State Parties, which feared endangering the intergovernmental character of the UN by setting a precedent.[89] On 25 November 1991, however, the Council finally requested admission, which was accepted the next day by the FAO Conference.

Since then the EU has developed into the largest contributor of voluntary funding to the FAO.[90] Additional agreements have been concluded to align and strengthen the cooperation between both organisations. In 2004 the FAO and the EC adopted a strategic partnership agreement, to achieve more strategic cooperation in selected policy areas.[91] In June 2011 the EU concluded a 'Strategic Programmatic Framework on Food Security and Nutrition' with the three Rome-based agencies, the FAO, the World Food Programme (WFP) and the International Fund for Agricultural Development (IFAD), 'to harmonize and coordinate the implementation of … food security and humanitarian food assistance goals'.[92] Still, the role of the EU in the work of the FAO is evaluated controversially: while some detect a 'true partnership' between both organisations,[93] others posit that the FAO values the EU for its wallet, rather than for its policy cooperation.[94]

Although the EU has obtained the status of a Member Organisation[95] at the FAO, its effective representation continues to face serious challenges. These result first from the fact that, as a Member Organisation, the EU does not enjoy the same rights as Members: it may not hold office in the Conference, the Council and their subsidiary bodies,[96] it has no voting rights for elective places[97] or budget matters,[98] and no participation rights in the restricted committees[99] and the bodies dealing

[88] Frid, above, n 86, p 246.

[89] ibid, p 241 et seq.

[90] European Commission/FAO, 'FAO and EU join forces to fight hunger. Joint press release after the meeting of Commission President Barroso and FAO Director-General Graziano da Silva', IP/12/1090, 11 October 2012.

[91] European Commission/FAO, Memorandum of Understanding concerning the establishment of a Strategic Partnership between the Food and Agriculture Organization of the United Nations and the Commission of the European Communities in the field of development and humanitarian affairs, 13 September 2004.

[92] European Commission/Rome based United Nations Agencies, Statement of Intent: Programmatic Cooperation on Food Security and Nutrition, 27 June 2011.

[93] Maersk Pedersen, above, n 81, p 65.

[94] Schild, above, n 80, p 223.

[95] Art II(3) FAO Constitution.

[96] Art II(9) FAO Constitution; Rules XLIII(3), XLIV FAO General Rules.

[97] Rule XLV(2) FAO General Rules.

[98] Art XVIII(6) FAO Constitution.

[99] Programme Committee, Finance Committee, Committee on Constitutional and Legal Matters, Art II(9) FAO Constitution, Rule XLVI FAO General Rules.

with the internal working of the conference.[100] In its FAO Communication the Commission thus declared a need to address the limitations of the FAO Constitution in order to achieve coherence with the Lisbon Treaty and to achieve full and equal EU participation.[101] Given that any changes to the current modalities require a two- thirds majority in the biannual FAO Conference, the prospects of this initiative appear dim.

An additional complicating factor lies in the phenomenon of mixity. Since the EU acceded to the FAO as a Member Organisation alongside its Member States, speaking and voting rights have to be exercised on an alternative basis.[102] This causes a twofold problem of external transparency and internal coordination.

The former entails that the EU carries an additional burden of ensuring transparency vis-à-vis the FAO concerning its division of competences with the Member States. Under the FAO Constitution the EU was thus required to submit a declaration of competence in order to disclose its internal division of competences to the State Parties of the FAO,[103] and to notify the Director-General of any subsequent changes.[104] The EU's current declaration, however, still dates back to 1994, despite the significant reforms that have since been undertaken.[105] It was only with the 2013 FAO Communication that the Commission submitted an updated draft declaration to the Council, aiming to bring the present version in line with the provisions of the Lisbon Treaty.[106] The draft is currently under review.[107] It has already attracted criticism from the side of EU Member States, among others for not including 'any recognition of the extent to which the EU has not exercised its competence under shared competence areas'.[108] Furthermore, the FAO

[100] In particular: Credentials Committee, General Committee, Rule XLIII(2) FAO General Rules.

[101] FAO Communication, above, n 19, p 6; cf H de Waele, 'Name me your friends, and I will tell you who you are—The Union and the Member States in the global arena' in H de Waele and J Kuipers (eds), *The European Union's Emerging International Identity: Views from the Global Arena* (Leiden, Martinus Nijhoff, 2013), 239–56, p 242.

[102] Art II(8), (10) FAO Constitution; on the exercise of voting rights see J Heliskoski, 'Internal Struggle for International Presence: The Exercise of Voting Rights Within the FAO' in A Dashwood and C Hillion (eds), *The General Law of EC External Relations* (London, Sweet & Maxwell, 2000) 79–99.

[103] Art II(5) FAO Constitution.

[104] Art II(7) FAO Constitution.

[105] Council Decision of 25 November 1991, Declaration of Competence by the European Union in respect of matters covered by the constitution of the Food and Agriculture Organization of the United Nations (Pursuant to the General Rules of the Organization) (OJ 1991 C 238); updated by a letter sent on 4 October 1994 from the President of the Council to the Director-General of the FAO, cf Communication from the Commission to the Council on the notification of a change in the distribution of competence between the EC and its Member States pursuant to Article II(7) of the FAO Constitution, SEC 94 (437) final; cf Schild, above, n 80, p 226, fn 35. On the legal effects, the practice and effectiveness of declarations of competence see A Delgado Casteleiro, 'EU Declarations of Competence to Multilateral Agreements: A Useful Reference Base?' (2012) *European Foreign Affairs Review* 491–510.

[106] Draft Declaration of competences by the European Union in respect of matters covered by the Constitution of the Food and Agriculture Organisation of the United Nations (FAO), FAO Communication, above, n 19, Annex 1.

[107] Information note, above, n 44, p 3.

[108] United Kingdom, Department for International Development, Explanatory Memorandum on COM(2013) 333 final, Doc No 10368-13, 27 June 2013, para 3.

Constitution obliges the EU or its Member States to indicate before each meeting the division of competences for each agenda item and to declare which entity shall vote.[109] Given that this constitutes a significant additional burden, the Commission stated in its Communication that it considered 'the systematic submission of such an information note [to be] not required for meetings or specific agenda points thereof where either a vote is not envisaged or the division of competence between the EU and its Member States results directly from the present declaration of competence'.[110] This view appears questionable and has triggered criticism from the Member State side.[111] The General Rules of the FAO explicitly require an indication of competence 'before any meeting of the Organization'.[112] Also, the new Declaration of Competences, which adds little if any information to the provisions of the EU Treaties, is too vague to allow third states to determine by which competence a specific agenda item is covered.[113] This holds especially true for the area of shared competences, where up-to-date and tailored information notes can present the extent to which the Union has exercised its competences.

The biggest hurdle for effective EU participation at the FAO remains, however, the cumbersome internal coordination process between Member States and EU institutions. In order to facilitate the procedure, the Commission and Council agreed in the internal 'Arrangement Between the Council and the Commission Regarding Preparation for FAO Meetings and Statements and Voting' that the EU exercises speaking and voting rights if the issue falls in the area of its exclusive competence and that the EU Member State holding the rotating Council Presidency is competent in case of Member State competence.[114] If an issue falls both under EU and Member State competence, a common position should be sought, based on whether the 'thrust' of the issue falls exclusively in EU or Member State competence.[115] In case of disagreement the matter will be referred to the COREPER.[116] This Arrangement has not only failed to avoid legal disputes in the past,[117] it also has not sufficiently streamlined the cumbersome process in which statements by the EU or the EU and its Member States are negotiated and agreed upon. Time-consuming discussions of procedural issues leave insufficient

[109] Rule XLII(2) of the General Rules of the FAO.

[110] FAO Communication, above, n 19, annex 1, fn 4.

[111] United Kingdom, Explanatory Memorandum, above, n 108, para 4.

[112] Rule XLII(2) of the General Rules of the FAO.

[113] Cf J Heliskoski, 'EU Declarations of Competence and International Responsibility' in M Evans and P Koutrakos (eds), *The International Responsibility of the European Union: European and International Perspectives* (Oxford, Hart Publishing, 2013) 189–212.

[114] 'Arrangement concerning preparation for the meetings of the FAO as well as interventions and voting' (Arrangement), 18 December 1991, unpublished, reproduced in R Frid, *The Relations between the EC and International Organizations—Legal Theory and Practice* (The Hague, Kluwer, 1995) Annex VI, Art 2.1–2.2. The 1991 Arrangement was subsequently updated in 1992 and 1995.

[115] Arrangement, above, n 114, Art 2.3; Schild, above, n 80, p 228.

[116] Arrangement, above, n 114, Art 1.12.

[117] ECJ, Case C-25/94 *Commission v Council* [1996] ECR I-01469.

opportunity to focus on the substance, and weaken the EU's effective participation in the FAO. In an attempt to solve this problem, the Commission proposed a set of revised 'Arrangements between the Council and the Commission regarding the Exercise of Membership Rights of the European Union and its Member States in the Food and Agriculture Organisation',[118] in Annex 2 of its 2013 FAO Communication. According to the draft arrangements, full statements shall in the future only be prepared in exceptional cases, while the new default modus for EU positions in the FAO shall be the one of 'lines to take'.[119] Although this would ensure greater flexibility for the external representative of the Union, fears of 'unscripted interventions with which Member States do not fully agree' have already been voiced[120] and indeed the additional effort, which Member States might invest to 'ensure lines to take [are] sufficiently tightly drafted to reduce these risks'[121] might negate any hopes of a more efficient coordination process. This is strongly suggested by a recent incident at the FAO, when the Commission representative deviated from the exact wording of a statement, which had been previously agreed during the Coordination Working Party, omitting or exchanging words that had been particularly contentious.[122] Nineteen EU Member States subsequently issued a joint statement in which they expressed their deep regret about the incident and underlined that agreed statements should be fully respected.[123] A working method which accords a higher degree of flexibility to the Union representative might therefore fail to win the necessary support in the Council.

The example of the FAO shows that even though the Union obtained full membership status, its participation in the work of the organisation is still lagging behind.[124] This is not only due to the limitations which the FAO Constitution and the General Rules of Procedure impose on member organisations, but primarily results from EU internal procedures and quarrels. The Barroso–Ashton Strategy lists the FAO in the category of those international organisations where the prospects to improve the position of the Union are good, referring to the ongoing revision of the 1991 Arrangements between Council and Commission. In light of the above analysis, this evaluation of the Commission's FAO Communication might prove too optimistic. A two-thirds majority of the FAO Conference for the expansion of EU competences appears difficult to achieve, and EU Member States' fears of competence creep and loss of status might prevent the adoption of more flexible internal agreements.

[118] FAO Communication, above, n 19, Annex 2.
[119] FAO Communication, above, n 19, Annex 2, 2.3.
[120] United Kingdom, Explanatory Memorandum, above, n 108, para 18.
[121] ibid.
[122] Item 20.1 in the 148th session of the FAO Council, 4 December 2013.
[123] Council of the European Union, Joint statement concerning the representation of the EU and its Member States during the 148th session of the FAO Council, Doc No 17679/1/13, 13 December 2013.
[124] Cf I Govaere, J Capiau and A Vermeersch, 'In-Between Seats: The Participation of the European Union in International Organizations' (2004) *European Foreign Affairs Review* 155–87, 165.

B. International Maritime Organization

The IMO, a specialised agency of the UN, is an organisation where the EU may seek to upgrade its status in the near future.[125] It is one of the organisations that have been prioritised for a status upgrade in the Barroso–Ashton Strategy, based on the above-mentioned criteria of interest and prospect.[126] The Union increasingly puts focus on the work of the organisation, especially with regard to working on international environmental issues (such as reduction in CO_2 emissions) and issues of ship safety.[127] While the EU currently has an emissions trading system that covers other fields of transport, including airlines operating in EU Member States,[128] it has not yet implemented a system that regulates emissions from maritime transportation. On 28 June 2013 the Commission set out its plan to integrate maritime emissions into the EU's policy for reducing its domestic greenhouse gas emissions.[129] Despite the slow pace of discussions within the IMO on this issue, the Union still views the IMO as the best international forum to regulate emissions from shipping, which currently constitute around 3 per cent of global greenhouse gas emissions.[130] The EU also plays an active role in other areas relevant to the IMO, such as maritime pollution and maritime safety. Apart from EU legislation in these fields, in 2003 the European Maritime Safety Agency (EMSA) was established to provide specialised technical assistance. Lastly, the EU and the IMO are both becoming active in the field of maritime security and piracy,[131] a topic that is increasingly important to the Union from a security standpoint. Besides, work undertaken by the IMO has led to amendments of the International Convention for the Safety of Life at Sea, 1974 (SOLAS Convention) and the International Ship and Port Facility Security Code (ISPS Code). Thus, interests as well as the significant EU legislation in fields covered by the work of the IMO support an enhanced status of the Union in the work of this organisation.

The European Commission (not the Community or the Union) has been an observer at the IMO since 1974. Although the Commission recommended to the Council to pursue full membership of the then EC in both the IMO and the ICAO

[125] Wouters, de Jong, Marx and De Man, above, n 85.

[126] Barroso–Ashton Strategy, above, n 6, p 3.

[127] European Commission, Press Release, 'Transport: Vice President Kallas in talks with IMO Secretary General—focus on ship safety and reducing emissions', IP/13/409, 7 May 2013.

[128] European Parliament and Council Directive 2008/101/EC of 19 November 2008 amending Directive 2003/87/EC so as to include aviation activities in the scheme for greenhouse gas emission allowance trading within the Community (OJ 2009, L8/3).

[129] Communication from the Commission to the European Parliament, the Council, the European Economic and Social Committee and the Committee of the Regions—Integrating maritime transport emissions in the EU's greenhouse gas reduction policies, COM(2013) 479.

[130] ibid, p 4.

[131] See IMO, Piracy and Armed Robber Against Ships, 'Guidance to shipowners and ship operators, shipmasters and crews on preventing and suppressing acts of piracy and armed robbery against ships', MSC.1/Circ 1334, 23 June 2009; European Commission, Recommendation of 11 March 2010 on measures for self-protection and the prevention of piracy and armed robbery against ships, 2010/159/EU.

back in 2002,[132] this was not supported by the EU Member States.[133] In the face of opposition from EU Member States which are IMO members, the Commission is now seeking instead to change the Commission's representation to that of the 'European Union' in accordance with the Lisbon Treaty. There are also significant external constraints that prevent the EU from becoming a full IMO Member.[134] The IMO Convention is only open to States,[135] and EU membership would require the inclusion of a REIO clause, as was the case with the FAO. There is little incentive, however, to go through the process of treaty modification that would be necessary to amend the Convention, which would require the ratification of two-thirds of the IMO membership.[136]

The IMO therefore represents yet another organisation where, even though the Union has significant competences, legislation and interests in the fields dealt with by this international organisation, its lack of membership means that it must continue to rely on its Member States. This can cause problems within the EU's legal order. When the EU is not a formal member of an international organisation where significant Union competences are concerned, this can create a gap in legal obligations between the EU and its Member States, since only the Member States are formally bound under international law. For instance, in the *ATAA* case the EU's non-membership of the International Civil Aviation Organization (ICAO), another UN specialised agency, meant that the EU was not formally bound by a significant body of international law regulating air transport.[137] EU membership of international organisations such as ICAO and IMO would go a long way to filling this gap. Moreover, the Union's membership of global regulatory bodies such as IMO is important for it to safeguard its own significant regulatory framework. However, the prospects for status upgrade look rather dim, as illustrated by the 2013 information note on the implementation of the Barroso–Ashton Strategy, which states that 'little or no progress could be achieved due to a changed political context' and recommends that '[s]ervices will sustain their efforts in order to unlock the situation'.[138]

[132] European Commission, Recommendation from the Commission to the Council in order to authorise the Commission to open and conduct negotiations with the International Civil Aviation Organization (ICAO) on the conditions and arrangements for accession by the European Community, SEC/2002/0381 final.

[133] Cf De Baere, who observed that 'external sovereignty seems to be regarded as rather more sacred than internal sovereignty: the Member States are quite happy to accept Community-imposed restrictions on their regulatory competences with regard to internal policy areas, while refusing to accept parallel restrictions for the external aspects of the same areas', G De Baere, *Constitutional Principles of EU External Relations* (Oxford, Oxford University Press, 2008) 249–50; see also Govaere, Capiau and Vermeersch, above, n 124, p 164.

[134] For further discussion on these constraints, see L Nengye and F Maes, 'Legal Constraints to the European Union's Accession to the International Maritime Organization' (2012) *Journal of Maritime Law & Commerce* 279–91.

[135] Art 4 IMO Convention.

[136] Art 66 IMO Convention.

[137] ECJ, Case C-366/10 *Air Transport Association of America and Others v Secretary of State for Energy and Climate Change* [2011] nyr.

[138] Information note, above, n 44, p 3.

C. International Atomic Energy Agency

The IAEA, although a separate international organisation, is associated to the UN family, and is also a body where the EU has identified a priority in upgrading its status.[139] The Union is strongly committed to the prevention of proliferation of weapons of mass destruction,[140] and has worked actively in multilateral fora to prevent states such as Iran from acquiring nuclear weapons capabilities[141] and to deal with the nuclear weapons programme of North Korea. Talks with Iran over its nuclear issues have been one of the key priorities of HR/VP Catherine Ashton and Federica Mogherini as part of the E3+3 (EU, France, Germany and the United Kingdom). The Joint Plan of Action[142] on Iran's nuclear activities, concluded in Geneva on 24 November 2013, establishes the IAEA as being responsible for the verification of nuclear-related measures. The EU is also actively involved in issues of nuclear safety, which were brought back to the world's attention after the Fukushima disaster in Japan. While the Union has worked on these issues in other fora, most notably within the UN Security Council, the IAEA also plays a crucial role in these fields.

On 25 January 2013 a meeting was held in Brussels bringing together officials from the EEAS, the European Commission and the IAEA for the first time, to focus on areas of cooperation in the areas of nuclear safety, nuclear security, nuclear applications, technical cooperation, nuclear energy and nuclear safeguards.[143] It is evident that closer cooperation between the EU and IAEA would benefit both organisations. The EU is a major contributor to the IAEA, both in terms of financial aid and technical assistance. The gross overall contribution to the IAEA for the period of 2007–2013 was €111.5 million.[144] On 21 June 2013 the EU and IAEA signed a contribution agreement under the 2012 Annual Action Programme of the Instrument for Nuclear Safety Cooperation (INSC) whereby the EU would contribute €9,260,000 for technical cooperation and nuclear safety. Moreover, many of the issues dealt with by the IAEA are of key importance to EU domestic and foreign policy, most notably the Union's engagement with issues such as nuclear non-proliferation.

The EU itself has no formal observer status at the IAEA although Euratom is an observer. The relationship is based upon an agreement between Euratom and

[139] Barroso–Ashton Strategy, above, n 6, p 3.

[140] Council of the European Union, EU Strategy Against Proliferation of Weapons of Mass Destruction, Doc No 15708/03.

[141] R Gowan, 'The UN and European Strategy' in S Biscop and RG Whitman (eds), *The Routledge Handbook of European Security* (London, Routledge, 2013) 270–80, 279.

[142] Joint Plan of Action agreed by Iran and the E3/EU+3, adopted in Geneva, Switzerland, 24 November 2013, available at http://eeas.europa.eu/statements/docs/2013/131124_03_en.pdf.

[143] Joint Press Statement (2013) of First EU-IAEA Senior Officials Meeting on 25 January 2013, available at http://eeas.europa.eu/250113_press_statement_for_the_first_eu_iaea_som_as_of_25_january.pdf and www.iaea.org/newscenter/mediaadvisory/2013/ma201302.htm.

[144] IAEA, Overview of EU support to the International Atomic Energy Agency (IAEA) in the field of nuclear safety, safeguards, security and technical cooperation financed during the current Multi-annual Financial Framework 2007–2013, available at www.iaea.org/newscenter/pressreleases/2013/eucontribution.pdf.

the IAEA, which has been in force since 1 January 1976 (Cooperation Agreement 1975) and whereby Euratom is invited to the annual sessions of the General Conference of the Agency but does not have the right to vote. There are several options available to the EU for improving its status at the IAEA. The first would require the EU to attain observer status alongside Euratom. This would probably require an agreement between the EU and Euratom concerning competences and clarifying the relationship between the existing IAEA–Euratom Agreement. Another option would be to update the IAEA–Euratom agreement to allow for dual EU–Euratom representation in their respective fields of competence. The 2013 information note on the implementation of the Barroso–Ashton Strategy favourably reported progress made in the internal debates, and stated that 'Commission services and the EEAS are in the process of assessing the most promising approach to obtain an appropriate status for the EU'.[145] Either way, there is still an important requirement for the EU and Euratom 'to ensure consistency between [their] external relations'.[146]

D. United Nations Educational, Scientific and Cultural Organization

UNESCO is an example of a body that is not mentioned in the Barroso–Ashton Strategy although it might arguably fulfil the interest and prospect criteria. It additionally serves as an interesting example of an ad hoc status upgrade strategy, which has the potential for wider application throughout the UN framework.

UNESCO, a UN specialised agency, was founded in 1945 to foster peace 'on the basis of humanity's moral and intellectual solidarity'.[147] Aiming to avoid conflicts by strengthening international cooperation in the fields of culture, education, science and communication, its work focuses on the dissemination of knowledge and ideas, the protection of the world's heritage and cultural diversity, and the promotion of scientific cooperation and quality of education.[148]

Cultural policy was not an obvious competence for a regional integration organisation which was initially primarily economic in nature and consequently it was not part of the EU's portfolio before 1993. The EEC impacted on the Member States' authority in the cultural domain only incidentally, in the context of the freedom of movement of cultural goods, services and people.[149] The Maastricht Treaty introduced a cultural competence into the Union's primary law. Article 3(p) of the

[145] Information note, above, n 44, p 3.

[146] Council Decision 2010/427/EU of 26 July 2010 establishing the organisation and functioning of the EEAS (OJ 2010, L201/3), recital 18.

[147] UNESCO, 'Introducing UNESCO', http://en.unesco.org/about-us/introducing-unesco.

[148] Art I(2) UNESCO Constitution.

[149] E Psychogiopoulou, 'The Convention on the Diversity of Cultural Expressions and the European Union: The Quest for Competence and Implementation' in T Kono, S Van Uytsel (eds), *The UNESCO Convention on the Diversity of Cultural Expressions: A Tale of Fragmentation* (Antwerp, Intersentia, 2012) 365–94, 369.

EC Treaty tasked the Community with 'a contribution … to the flowering of the cultures of the Member States' but its responsibility remained deferential towards the Member States, and did not exceed the competence to encourage cooperation between them and to support and supplement their action. This wording was retained in the current Article 167 TFEU. Article 6(c) TFEU provides that in the area of culture, the Union shall merely 'support, coordinate or supplement the actions of the Member States', and Article 2(5) TFEU stipulates that Union action in the cultural field will neither supersede Member States' competences nor that the adoption of legally binding acts will entail harmonisation of the domestic law. The explicit competence for EU engagement in UNESCO is enshrined in Article 167(3) TFEU,[150] which states that the 'Union … shall foster cooperation with … the competent international organisations in the sphere of culture'. A similar development can be traced for EU policy in the field of education, which found its first basis in a 1976 Action Programme,[151] before being formally introduced into EU primary law with the Maastricht Treaty. EU competences in research, on the other hand, were already included in the ECSC and Euratom treaties, and while the EEC treaty contained only narrow research competences in the field of agriculture, its sweeping Article 235 was used to launch a series of research programmes. The Union's education competence has remained confined to actions that 'support, coordinate or supplement' Member States' initiatives (Article 6(e), 165 TFEU), whereas the Union enjoys a 'parallel' competence in the field of research (Article 4(3), 179 et seq).

Remarkably, formal relations between the EEC and UNESCO were established at a time when the Community enjoyed only limited competences in the research area, and when culture and education still rested exclusively with the Member States. A first exchange of letters between the President of the Commission and the UNESCO Director-General in 1964 established methods for closer cooperation to achieve common goals, including most importantly the reciprocal invitation of observers to participate in the work of the respective bodies.[152] A second exchange of letters in 1972/1973 determined those areas where UNESCO and EEC involvement overlapped, and designated a number of priority areas. In February 1996, the European Commission and UNESCO signed an agreement detailing the methods of their cooperation, particularly focusing on technical assistance and joint projects,[153] followed by an extension of the Financial and Administrative Framework Agreement between the EC and the UN to UNESCO in 2004.[154]

[150] Art 128(3) TEC.

[151] Resolution of the Council and of the Ministers of Education, meeting within the Council, of 9 February 1976 comprising an action programme in the field of education (OJ 1976 C38/1).

[152] L Cavicchioli, 'The European Community at UNESCO: An exceptionally active observer?' in J Wouters, F Hoffmeister and T Ruys (eds), *The United Nations and the European Union: An Ever Stronger Partnership* (The Hague, Asser, 2006) 135–54, 137.

[153] UNESCO, Executive Board, Co-operation between the European Commission and UNESCO, Doc No 147 EX/44, 16 August 1995.

[154] Agreement between UNESCO and European Commission of 23 February 2004, http://ec.europa.eu/europeaid/work/procedures/financing/international_organisations/other_documents_related_united_nations/document/un_specialised_agencies_covered_by_the_fafa_en.xls (7 March 2014); Cavicchioli, above, n 152, p 138.

In 2012 the EU and UNESCO concluded a Memorandum of Understanding in which they laid down principles and objectives for their partnership, identified priorities and made arrangements for cooperation, including provisions on reciprocal invitations to meetings and working groups and on mutual information and consultation.[155]

Despite its long-standing involvement in the work of UNESCO, its financial impact and the increasingly close partnership between both organisations, the EU's status generally remains one of a simple observer, restricting it to a predominantly passive role in the debates held in the framework of UNESCO. While Union representatives may participate in the meetings of the organisation's bodies and make oral interventions, they do not have the right to vote, or to submit proposals or amendments thereto.[156] These limited possibilities for participation were considered to be insufficient by the Commission with regard to the negotiation of the 2005 Convention on the Protection and Promotion of the Diversity of Cultural Expressions.[157] The Commission had supported the initiative since its earliest days, fully endorsing the 2001 UNESCO Universal Declaration on Cultural Diversity and Action Plan and ranking the '[p]reservation and promotion of cultural diversity … among the founding principles of the European model'.[158] In light of its status limitations, the Commission requested a negotiating mandate from the Council,[159] which was supported by the European Parliament and adopted by the Council in November 2004.[160] Thereby the Commission was given the mandate to take part in the negotiations of the Convention on behalf of the Community, as far as EC competences were concerned, and to negotiate alongside the Member States whenever a matter fell in an area of shared competence. A subsequently adopted Code of Conduct detailed the division of work between the Member States and the Commission, according to which the Presidency would represent the common positions of the Member States and the Commission would represent Community positions.[161]

[155] UNESCO/European Union, Memorandum of Understanding concerning the establishment of a partnership between the United Nations Educational, Scientific and Cultural Organisation Secretariat and its subsidiary bodies (hereinafter referred to as 'UNESCO') and the European Union, jointly referred to hereinafter as 'the two Sides', 8 October 2012.

[156] Cavicchioli, above, n 152, p 139 et seq.

[157] Convention on the Protection and Promotion of the Diversity of Cultural Expressions, 20 October 2005, entry into force 18 March 2007, 2440 UNTS.

[158] Communication from the Commission to the Council and the European Parliament—Towards an international instrument on cultural diversity, COM(2003) 520 final.

[159] Recommendation from the Commission to the Council to authorise the Commission to participate, on behalf of the Community, in the negotiations within UNESCO on the convention on the protection of the diversity of cultural contents and artistic expressions, SEC(2004), 1062 final.

[160] Council of the European Union, Press Release, 2616th Council Meeting, Education, Youth and Culture, 15–16 November 2004, Doc No 14380/04; cf Council of the European Union, Draft Council Decision authorising the Commission to participate, on behalf of the Community, in the negotiations within UNESCO on the convention on the protection of the diversity of cultural contents and artistic expressions, Doc No 13840/04, 29 October 2004.

[161] Council of the European Union, Code of Conduct between the Council, the Member States and the Commission on the UNESCO negotiations on the draft Convention on the protection of the diversity of cultural contents and artistic expressions, Doc No 5768/05, 31 January 2005.

While the internal dimension of EC participation in the negotiations was thus quickly and smoothly established, the external dimension caused more difficulties. A first proposal by the Council Presidency in September 2004 to grant the Commission extended rights for the purpose of negotiating the Convention was included in the provisional agenda of the 170th session of UNESCO's Executive Board,[162] where it failed to gain sufficient support. The State Parties were particularly concerned about setting a precedent and endangering the intergovernmental character of the organisation. Additionally, the debate was characterised by a widespread lack of knowledge about the involvement of regional multilateral organisations in the UN framework, in particular through REIO clauses, and the practice of other UN bodies with regard to the EC.[163] The Commission thus remained restricted to its usual observer role for the initial negotiations. In March 2005 the Council Presidency again introduced the matter to the Executive Board's agenda, highlighting the insufficiency of the EC's status to fully participate in the negotiations and to safeguard its interests.[164] A group of eight EU Member States[165] submitted a draft decision, which would grant regional economic integration organisations active participation rights 'in the same manner as full participants', comprising in particular 'the right to speak, to reply, to put forward proposals and amendments at the formal meetings, and to take part in the committees, working groups, formal or informal meetings set up in the course of the work relating to this Convention, the European Community having its own nameplate' but 'excluding the right to vote'.[166] The draft decision proved to be particularly contentious and neither the Special Committee of the Executive Board nor its informal working group could come to an agreement.[167] Finally the Special Committee submitted a revised draft, which had been proposed by the Chairperson of the informal working group, to the Executive Board. The draft contained significantly amended language. In order to appease fears of setting a precedent, the amended draft highlighted that the extended rights were only granted 'on an exceptional basis … while maintaining [the] observer status' of the Community.[168] The draft also omitted the specific list of rights included in the EU Member States' proposal and restricted the scope of the application to the EC alone, not extending it to regional economic integration organisations in general. The decision which was finally adopted by the Executive Board was even narrower. Every comparison to the participation rights of full participants was avoided; instead the EC was granted the right to 'participate actively and as fully as appropriate'.[169] Furthermore, a time limit was introduced, restricting the enhanced rights to no more than the intergovernmental meeting of experts which was held between 25 May and 4 June 2005. The Council Presidency ensured afterwards immediately indication of the list of rights that it deemed to be

[162] UNESCO, Executive Board, 170 EX/37, 29 September 2004.
[163] UNESCO, Executive Board, Summary Records, 170 EX/SR.1-10, 14 January 2005.
[164] UNESCO, Executive Board, 171 EX/47, 17 March 2005.
[165] Czech Republic, France, Germany, Hungary, Italy, Slovakia, Slovenia, and the United Kingdom.
[166] UNESCO, Executive Board, 171 EX/47 Add, 31 March 2005.
[167] UNESCO, Executive Board, 171 EX/62, 27 April 2005.
[168] ibid, p 5.
[169] UNESCO, Executive Board, 171 EX/Decisions, 25 May 2005, p 72.

covered by its 'enhanced observer status' of which the Executive Board took note without objection.[170]

Although the EC draft was thus considerably watered down in the final decision, the 'selective upgrade' of its observer status nevertheless was a significant achievement for the Community. It allowed the Commission to actively participate as a negotiating party in a policy field that held particular internal significance, and to shape the content of the Convention, among others by successfully advocating for the inclusion of a REIO clause.[171] Even though the final decision of the Executive Board and the previous debates expressly stated that the Community's enhanced observer status could not be regarded as setting a precedent, it importantly confirmed a practice that had been launched two years earlier, when the World Health Organization (WHO) granted REIOs active participation rights in the negotiations of the 2003 Framework Convention on Tobacco Control. It also raised awareness among the State Parties of UNESCO for both the particularities of the division of competences between the Community and its Member States, and the participation of REIOs in the UN framework in general. The EC quickly acceded to the Convention, although its implementation record shows symptoms of a 'double standard', with strong results in external affairs and a comparatively weaker approach in the internal dimension.[172] So far, the 'selective enhanced observer status' has not been pursued in other UN bodies and there was no opportunity to repeat the initiative with regard to subsequent UNESCO conventions. Tellingly the Barroso–Ashton Strategy does not even consider this option for upgrading EU status in the UN framework, aiming for general status enhancements instead. It thereby overlooks a very promising and practical option to boost the EU's status ad hoc in those cases which are particularly relevant for the Union and where the Union could make a real difference in the shaping and the subsequent implementation of an international instrument. The process leading towards a temporarily or thematically enhanced observer status requires less time and diplomatic effort and might thus yield a more favourable effort/outcome ratio. At the same time, through setting positive examples of active EU participation in the UN framework, the Union could also pave the way for more permanent status upgrades. The lack of ambition and imagination of the Barroso–Ashton Strategy is therefore also perceptible in its exclusive focus on the traditional goal of general status enhancement, ignoring prominent alternative paths that the recent practice in UNESCO and WHO has demonstrated.

V. CONCLUDING REMARKS

Although cooperation with the UN is a significant political priority for the EU, efforts to enhance the Union's representation in the various UN bodies have

[170] Cavicchioli, above, n 152, p 146 et seq.

[171] Art 27 of the Convention on the Protection and Promotion of the Diversity of Cultural Expressions.

[172] Psychogiopoulou, above, n 149, p 393.

encountered stumbling blocks. The EU continues to deal with problems regarding representation in those fora where the EU Member States remain highly active, due to disagreements concerning the distribution of tasks, in particular with regard to speaking rights and negotiating mandates. Moreover, the EU's efforts to upgrade its status at the UN, as illustrated by the diplomatic saga around the adoption of UNGA Resolution 65/276, did not go as smoothly as planned, and the gaps between the EU's status in most UN bodies and its competences and priorities significantly hinder the effective representation of the Union.

Status enhancements, aligning the Union's internal and external dimensions, thus remain a focal point of the EU's diplomatic activity at the UN. The 2012 Barroso–Ashton Strategy nevertheless reveals a significant decline in ambition, in that it opts for an approach of piecemeal, modest status upgrades, where its predecessor contained a clear commitment to aim for full participation of the Union at the UN level. The Strategy also lacks the precision that would be necessary to effectively guide the Union's diplomatic efforts towards better EU representation in the UN. This concerns in particular the overly broad set of criteria established to identify priority organisations, which provides little explanation, both on the inclusion of the selected bodies and on the omission of other fora. In this regard the Strategy's silence on UNESCO is particularly striking, given that it is an organisation which not only appears to fit the broad selection criteria but also provides a promising example of a 'selective' status upgrade that might inform the strategy for other UN bodies. Moreover, a closer look at the selected priority organisations raises doubts about the plausibility of the Commission's assessment of whether 'an upgrade appears realistic in the short to medium term'.[173] This concerns not only the HRC, where an extension of UNGA Resolution 65/276 to the HRC appears to be neither legally nor politically feasible, but also the FAO and the IMO. The Commission's FAO Communication has already triggered significant internal resistance by the Member States and moreover recommends enhancements of the Union's status at the FAO, for which political support does not appear to be within reach. With regard to the IMO, the Commission itself reverted its positive assessment only a year later in its 2013 information note, reporting 'little or no progress … due to a changed political context'.[174] Of the analysed bodies it is only with regard to the IAEA that a positive assessment of the prospect for status enhancement can cautiously be confirmed.

If the EU is serious about its goal 'to support and work for effective multilateralism, with the United Nations at its core',[175] then this involves the EU's presence and involvement in the UN and the UN system. However, the EU not only remains faced with a series of internal and external obstacles as a participant within the UN and the UN system, barring it from taking up its leading role at the global level; it currently also lacks a convincing strategy to overcome them.

[173] Barroso–Ashton Strategy, above, n 6, p 3.

[174] Information note, above, n 44, p 3.

[175] See European Commission, 'Ashton tells UN Security Council: EU is committed partner for UN in search for international peace', http://ec.europa.eu/commission_2010-2014/ashton/topics/20140219_en.htm.

Part II

The European Union in the International Labour Organization

5

Coordination Between the European Union and its Member States

MARCO FERRI*

THIS CHAPTER PRESENTS how, within existing International Labour Organization (ILO) rules, the European Union (EU) coordinates with its Member States in the ILO to carry out tasks that flow from the EU Treaties after the entry into force of the Lisbon Treaty. The chapter is in four sections. The first analyses the ILO rules and examines the place of the EU within the rules of the organisation. The second gives an overview of the activities of the ILO which are of interest to the EU. The third examines how EU coordination happens and who are the main actors involved. The fourth section contains some concluding remarks.

I. THE EUROPEAN UNION SEEN FROM THE ILO CONSTITUTION

The ILO is an organisation whose creation goes back to the Treaty of Versailles in 1919.[1] It was set up as an independent organisation in the framework of the League of Nations. The preamble underlines the link between social justice within states and international and lasting peace. In 1934 the ILO founding document became independent from the Versailles Peace Treaty and was called henceforth the ILO Constitution. ILO membership was originally composed of 44 states in 1919.[2] In 1946 it became a specialised agency of the newly established United Nations. Today it has 185 Member States. The core function of the ILO is a machinery through which labour standards can be adopted at the international level. The ILO is composed of three categories of actors.

* The views expressed by the author are personal.

[1] It was originally Part XIII of the Peace Treaties.

[2] Among the 29 Founder Members and the 13 other States to whom the designation 'Founder Member' was also granted, the following are today EU Member States (or parts of them): Belgium, British Empire, Czechoslovakia, France, Greece, Italy, Poland, Portugal, Romania, Serbo-Croatian-Slovene State, Denmark, Netherlands, Spain and Sweden.

A. ILO Actors

i. The Three Categories of Actors

According to the ILO Constitution (1919) three categories of 'actors' are involved: States, public international organisations and non-governmental organisations.

The States are the only members.[3] By the same token, ILO Conventions can be ratified only by Member States.[4] Moreover, the ILO is a 'tripartite' organisation. Members must be represented by three types of delegates: government, employers and workers. This is the principle of tripartism, which is unique to the organisation: employers' and workers' organisations have the right to full participation and to vote on an equal footing with governments.

The public international organisations cooperate with the ILO under Article 12 of the ILO Constitution. According to the ILO website, it has entered into cooperation agreements with around 60 other international or regional organisations—including the EU.[5] Representatives of public international organisations may be invited to participate without vote in meetings the ILO convenes.[6]

Finally, the non-governmental international organisations cooperate with the ILO as long as they share the principles and objectives of the ILO.[7] The ILO Special List of Non-Governmental International Organisations was set up in 1956 to establish working relations with them. The length of existence, membership, geographical coverage of the organisation, its practical achievements and the international nature of its activities are the main criteria for such admission. Another requirement is that the organisation has an evident interest in at least one of the fields of activity of the ILO. To participate in meetings the ILO convenes, NGOs have to request an invitation and their requests must be approved by the Governing Body.[8]

B. The EU: A Non-classic International Organisation

In the ILO, from a purely formal point of view, the EU does not fit into the ILO constitutional categories because it is not a classic intergovernmental organisation. It is not a classic international organisation because its Member States have transferred competences to it.[9] The Lisbon Treaty has described the categories of competences for the first time, building on the case law of the European Court of

[3] Art 1(2) and 1(3) ILO Constitution.
[4] Art 19(5)(d) ILO Constitution.
[5] They are published at www.ilo.org/public/english/bureau/leg/rel_org.htm.
[6] Art 12(2) ILO Constitution.
[7] Art 12(3) ILO Constitution.
[8] www.ilo.org/pardev/civil-society/lang--en/index.htm#Statutory_0.
[9] Art 2 TEU; see P Craig and G de Búrca, *EU Law: Text, Cases and Materials* (Oxford, Oxford University Press, 2011) 74–101.

Justice.[10] The EU, unlike other international organisations, it is not a mere functional association (a tool of its Member States), but rather a value-based actor with an autonomous legal order. As an example, the EU is the only international organisation which is a party, alongside States, to a number of international treaties.[11]

C. EU–ILO Cooperation

The cooperation between the European Community and the ILO started in 1958 on the basis of an Agreement concerning Liaison between the International Labour Organisation and the European Economic Community. For the ILO it is based on Article 12 of the ILO Constitution. For the EU, it is today based on Articles 151 and 220 Treaty on the Functioning of the European Union (TFEU).[12] The implementation of the 1958 Agreement takes place on the basis of its Article 13, with a series of exchanges of letters in 1961, 1989 and, lastly, 2001.

In a nutshell, the 2001 exchange of letters establishes a framework for cooperation covering all relevant internal and external EU policies. It also underlines the 'importance of promoting respect for fundamental principles and rights at work, alongside economic development and trade liberalization'. The document identifies the following areas for cooperation: promotion of labour standards, promotion of employment, social dialogue, social and employment aspect of enlargement of the EU, social protection, and development cooperation. The Commission and the ILO committed to hold annual high-level meetings. The tenth of such meetings took place in December 2012.[13]

II. THE ILO ACTIVITIES OF INTEREST TO THE EUROPEAN UNION

A. A Shared Commitment to Social and Economic Progress

The EU in the ILO promotes values and defends interests.[14] The EU supports the values promoted by the ILO[15] as they resound profoundly with the values of the

[10] See J-C Piris, *The Lisbon Treaty, A Legal and Political Analysis* (Cambridge, Cambridge University Press, 2010) pp 74–78; Craig and de Búrca, above, n 9.

[11] The European External Action Service (EEAS) manages a 'Treaties Office Database' available here: http://ec.europa.eu/world/agreements/default.home.do.

[12] The original Articles mentioned in the agreement are 117 and 119 of the TEC (1958).

[13] Exchange of letters between the Commission of the European Communities and the International Labour Organization, OJ C 165, 8.6, May 2001, p 23. On the EU–ILO relations, see R Delarue, 'EU–ILO cooperation on employment and social affairs' in J Wouters, F Hoffmeister and T Ruys (eds), *The United Nations and the European Union: an ever stronger partnership* (The Hague, Asser, 2006) 93–114; R Delarue, 'The EU–ILO partnership and the global identity of the Union's social model' in H de Waele and J-J Kuipers, *The European Union's Emerging International Identity: Views from the Global Arena* (Amsterdam, Martinus Nijhoff, 2013) 135–58.

[14] Art 21(2)(a) TEU.

[15] A Cassese, *International Law*, 2nd edn (Oxford, Oxford University Press, 2005) 16.

EU itself. Promoting the EU values through the ILO gives them greater legitimacy, because they are shared by the international community as a whole (including the social partners). The EU defends interests because countries should not profit from low labour standards to have unfair competitive advantages.

The principles guiding the action of the EU on the international scene are: democracy, rule of law, universality and indivisibility of human rights and fundamental freedoms, respect for human dignity, the principles of equality and solidarity, and respect for the principles of the United Nations charter and international law.[16] Article 21 TEU continues summarising partially the objectives mentioned in the Common Foreign and Security Policy (CFSP), development cooperation, Common Commercial Policy and environment. These principles are applicable to all external action: CFSP, other aspects of external action under Part V TFEU[17] and external aspects of other policies.[18]

The EU supports efforts at global regulation developed by the ILO because the poor labour conditions in developing and emerging countries are a source of concern.[19] Moreover, developing a middle class in emerging economies means creating markets for goods and services in which the EU has a comparative advantage.[20] There are three main areas of activity in the ILO of interest to the EU: technical, policy and political.[21]

i. Technical—Standard Setting

The first is the standard setting area (Conventions and Protocols are legally binding, Recommendations are not). The ILO normative activity presents unique features from an international law point of view because the ILO standards are negotiated with social partners on an equal footing with governments and they are approved by a two-thirds majority in the Conference.[22] It is also worth noting that no reservations can be opposed upon ratification, even if flexibility measures to facilitate ratification are provided for in some ILO Conventions.[23] However, Member States are bound by ILO Conventions only in case of ratification, and ratification is not compulsory.[24]

[16] Art 21(1) TEU.

[17] Art 205 TFEU.

[18] Art 21(3) last sentence.

[19] B De Witte and A Thies, 'Why Choose Europe? The Place of the European Union in the Architecture of International Legal Cooperation' in B Van Vooren, S Blockmans and J Wouters, *The EU's Role in Global Governance. The Legal Dimension* (Oxford, Oxford University Press, 2013) 29.

[20] Communication from the Commission—EUROPE 2020. A strategy for smart, sustainable and inclusive growth, COM(2010) 2020 final, p 22.

[21] See R Kissack, 'The Performance of the European Union in the International Labour Organization' (2011) *Journal of European Integration* 653–54.

[22] Art 19(2) ILO Constitution. H Sauer, 'International Labour Organization (ILO)' in *Max Planck Encyclopedia of Public International Law*, paras 12–16, www.mpepil.com.

[23] International Labour Office, *Manual for drafting ILO instruments*, Online revised version: www.ilo.org/public/english/bureau/leg/, p 46 and appendix 6.

[24] Art 19(5)(e) ILO Constitution.

In its almost 100 years of existence, the ILO has covered a broad range of issues in the social field. It has produced 189 Conventions and 202 Recommendations. This represents a vast international labour code. In creating the ILO, states sought to develop international labour standards and avoid a situation where each state would reduce worker protections to make its exports more competitive.

For EU Member States, some competences in the social field have been transferred to the EU. The main competences of the EU in the fields covered by the ILO are contained in the following provisions of the TFEU: Article 19: anti-discrimination, Articles 45, 46 and 48: free movement of workers; Article 153(1): health and safety at work, working conditions, termination of employment contracts, information and consultation of workers, representation and collective defence of the interests of workers and employers, conditions of employment for third-country nationals, integration of persons excluded from the labour market, equality between men and women, combating social exclusion, modernisation of social protection systems; Article 157(4): equal treatment of men and women in employment an occupation. However, it should be noted that ILO Conventions might engage EU competences that go beyond the social chapters of the TFEU.[25]

It should also be noted that provisions adopted under Article 153 must not affect the right of Member States to define the fundamental principles of their social security systems and must not significantly affect the financial equilibrium thereof and must not prevent any Member State from maintaining or introducing more stringent protective measures compatible with the Treaties.[26] Article 153 does not apply to pay, right of association, right to strike or the right to impose lock-outs.[27]

According to Article 4(2)(b) social policy, for the aspects defined in the TFEU, is a shared competence. EU competence is shared between the EU and the Member States when the EU has competence to legislate and adopt legally binding acts in specific areas, while each Member State remains competent to act as long as the EU has not exercised its competence.[28] The effects of the pre-emption principle are specified by Protocol No 25. This provides that, when the Union has taken action in a certain area of shared competence, the scope of this exercise of competence only covers those elements governed by the Union act in question and therefore does not cover the whole area. Thus, from a legal perspective, EU Member States partly lack the competence for the ratification or for the implementation of ratified ILO conventions.[29]

[25] See, eg, Art 79 TFEU on the treatment of third country nationals residing legally in Member States and on the prevention and eradication of illegal immigration and human trafficking.

[26] Art 153(4) TFEU.

[27] Art 153(5) TFEU.

[28] Art 2(2) TFEU, see also Protocol 25 on the exercise of shared competence, which is only applicable to Art 2(2) TFEU: see Opinion of Advocate-General Kokott, delivered on 27 June 2013, in Case C-137/12 *European Commission v Council of the European Union* [2013] ECR I-441 paras 114–15.

[29] H Sauer, above n 22, para 27, www.mpepil.com.

Since the EU itself cannot ratify ILO Conventions, the EU has authorised its Member States to ratify conventions when they contain issues falling under the competence of the EU. The European Court of Justice in Opinion 2/91 held that the EU, since it is unable to conclude a convention, 'must do so through the medium of the Member States'.[30] The Court added that the adoption of Union legislation in the social field in the form of 'minimum requirements' does not lead to exclusive external competence for the Union.[31] The practice of authorising Member States to ratify ILO Conventions started in 2005. In two Council Decisions the authorisation to ratify mentions that some provisions of Conventions 188 and the Maritime Labour Convention 2006 fall under the exclusive competence of the Union as regards the coordination of social security schemes.[32] The coordination of social security is not a 'minimum standard'. On the other hand, Council Decision 2005/367/EC mentions 'some articles of the Convention [185] fall within the [Union's] competence in the area of visas'.[33] Two other authorisations are currently (December 2013) in the legislative procedure: for Convention 189 concerning decent work for domestic workers[34] and Convention 170 concerning Safety in the Use of Chemicals at Work.[35]

From 1996 to 2000 the European Commission proposed recommendations to Member States on the ratification of ILO Conventions.[36] Recommendations are non-binding in nature and their purpose is merely exhortatory.

EU legislative activity might entail the risk of conflicting legal obligations. Where EU standards are more favourable, the conflict is solved because according to the Constitution ILO instruments are 'minimum standards'. However, when

[30] ECJ, *Opinion 2/91, Convention No 170 of the International Labour Organization concerning safety in the use of chemicals at work* [1993] ECR I-1061, para 37.

[31] ibid, para 21.

[32] Council Decision 2010/321/EU of 7 June 2010 authorising Member States to ratify, in the interests of the European Union, the Work in Fishing Convention, 2007, of the International Labour Organization (Convention No C 188), OJ L 145, 11.6.2010, p 12; Council Decision 2007/431/EC of 7 of June 2007 authorising Member States to ratify, in the interests of the European Community, the Maritime Labour Convention, 2006, of the International Labour Organization, OJ L 161, 22.6.2007, p 63.

[33] Council Decision 2005/367/EC of 14 April 2005 authorising Member States to ratify, in the interests of the European Community, the Seafarers' Identity Documents Convention of the International Labour Organization (Convention 185), OJ L 136, 30.5.2005, p 1.

[34] Proposal for a Council Decision authorising Member States to ratify, in the interests of the European Union, the Convention concerning decent work for domestic workers, 2011, of the International Labour Organization (Convention No 189), COM(2013)152 final.

[35] Proposal for a Council Decision authorising Member States to ratify, in the interests of the European Union, the Convention concerning Safety in the Use of Chemicals at Work, 1990, of the International Labour Organization (Convention No 170), COM(2012) 677 final.

[36] Commission Recommendation of 15 September 2000 on the ratification of the International Labour Organization (ILO) Convention No 182 of 17 June 1999 concerning the prohibition and immediate action for the elimination of worst forms of child labour, OJ L 243, 28.9.2000, p 41; Commission Recommendation of 18 November 1998 on ratification of International Labour Organization (ILO) Convention 180 concerning seafarers' hours of work and the manning of ships, and ratification of the 1996 protocol to the 1976 Merchant Shipping (minimum standards) Convention, OJ L 43, 17.2.1999, p 9; Commission Recommendation of 27 May 1998 on ratification of ILO Convention No 177 on home work of 20 June 1996, OJ L 165, 10.6.1998, p 32.

ILO standards are more favourable, a conflict might arise if EU standards are not 'minimum standards'.[37] For Conventions ratified before the creation of the EU or before a state's membership of the EU, these conflicting obligations have to be solved by the State in question by taking all appropriate steps to eliminate the incompatibilities. Convention 89 on 'Night Work (women)',[38] and Convention 45 on 'Employment of women in underground work in mines of all kind' are a case in point. They have been denounced by almost all EU Member States because they are in conflict with EU rules on equal treatment of men and women.[39] This is an example of the primacy of EU law.[40]

Cooperating with the ILO in this area, it is thus of paramount importance that possible obligations stemming from ILO legal instruments are compatible with EU law and policies. In practice this points to the need to ensure a close coordination between the EU and its Member States during the negotiations of the proposed instrument.[41]

ii. Policy-making

The second area is the ILO 'policy' activity. The ILO adopts action plans, implementation plans, strategies and other documents on various social issues. The October 2013 Governing Body approved three action plans: on social dialogue, on green jobs and on demography. There are many others: on decent work, fundamental principles and rights at work, youth, gender equality, and social protection, just to name a few. These plans instruct the ILO to carry out, upon request, activities in ILO Member States.

For the identification of the priorities to be carried out by the ILO two documents are of particular relevance. The first is the 1998 ILO Declaration on Fundamental Principles and Rights at Work[42] and the 2008 ILO Declaration on Social Justice for a Fair Globalization.[43]

The 1998 Declaration stipulates that ILO Member States which have not ratified the eight fundamental Conventions have an obligation stemming from their membership of the ILO to respect, promote and realise the principles concerning

[37] Art 4 TFEU.

[38] N Wuiame, 'Night Work for Women-Stoeckel revisited' (1994) *Industrial Law Journal* 95–100.

[39] A Seifert, 'The Still Complex Relationship between the ILO and the EU: The Example of Anti-Discrimination Law' (2013) *International Journal of Comparative Labour Law and Industrial Relations* 56–60 gives a summary of the open conflicts in the two cases quoted.

[40] Declaration 17 concerning primacy; P Craig, *The Lisbon Treaty. Law, Politics and Treaty Reform* (Oxford, Oxford University Press, 2013) 146–51.

[41] Conclusion of ECJ Opinion 2/91 at para 37: 'cooperation between the [Union] and its Member States is all the more necessary in view of the fact that the former cannot, as international law stands at present, itself conclude an ILO convention and must do so through the medium of the Member States.'

[42] ILO Declaration on Fundamental Principles and Rights at work and its follow-up, adopted by the International Labour Conference at its Eighty-sixth Session, Geneva, 18 June 1998.

[43] ILO Declaration on Social Justice for a Fair Globalization adopted by the International Labour Conference at its Ninety-seventh Session, Geneva, 10 June 2008.

the four fundamental rights:[44] freedom of association and the effective recognition of the right to collective bargaining; elimination of all forms of forced or compulsory labour; effective abolition of child labour; elimination of discrimination in respect of employment and occupation. The follow-up to the Declaration provides two ways to help Member States, employers and workers achieve the Declaration's objective. First, there is an annual review of reports from countries that have not ratified one or more fundamental Conventions. This reporting process allows governments to inform the ILO on changes which may have taken place in their law and practice, giving representative organisations of employers and workers a chance to express their views.[45] Second, the Global Report on Fundamental Principles and Rights at Work provides a dynamic global picture of the current situation of the principles and rights expressed in the Declaration. The Global Report is an objective view of the global and regional trends on the issues relevant to the Declaration and serves to highlight those areas that require greater attention. It serves as a basis for determining action plans for technical cooperation.[46]

The 2008 Declaration on Social Justice for a Fair Globalization establishes a framework on which the ILO can support the efforts of its Members to promote four strategic objectives of the ILO through the Decent Work Agenda: employment, social protection, social dialogue and tripartism, and fundamental principles and rights at work. The Declaration includes a follow-up mechanism to ensure the means by which the ILO will assist the Members in their efforts to promote the Decent Work Agenda, including a review of the ILO's institutional practices and governance; recurrent discussion by the International Labour Conference responding to realities and needs in Member States and assessing the results of ILO activities; technical assistance and advisory services; and strengthening research capacities, information collection and sharing.[47]

The follow-up to both declarations is important for the EU for two reasons. First, the EU promotes human rights, including labour rights, in all aspects of its external action. The EU makes reference to ILO standards and values in its external action. There is a clear interest in ensuring that these plans are not in contradiction with EU action. In matters relating to employment, social dialogue and social protection as well as any other policy, the external aspects of internal policies need to be taken into account in this context.[48] Second, the EU is a diversified area. It is possible to take inspiration from EU policies and actions in discussing these action plans. This is in the mutual interest of the EU and of the ILO.

[44] ILO Declaration on Fundamental Principles and Rights at work and its follow-up, adopted by the International Labour Conference at its Eighty-sixth Session, Geneva, 18 June 1998, section 2.

[45] ILO Declaration on Fundamental Principles and Rights at work and its follow-up, adopted by the International Labour Conference at its Eighty-sixth Session, Geneva, 18 June 1998, Annex II. Annual Follow-up concerning non-ratified fundamental Conventions.

[46] ILO Declaration on Fundamental Principles and Rights at work and its follow-up, adopted by the International Labour Conference at its Eighty-sixth Session, Geneva, 18 June 1998, Annex III. Global Report on Fundamental Principles and Rights at work.

[47] ILO Declaration on Social Justice for a Fair Globalization, Annex—Follow-up to the Declaration.

[48] Art 18(4) TEU and 21(3) TEU.

iii. Political Issues

The third area is the 'political' one. In the Conference Committee on the Application of Standards and in the Governing Body, some countries are called to explain their non-compliance with ILO Conventions. Since this implies comments on the domestic affairs of third states, it is considered to be political. From an EU perspective, these can be cases of Common Foreign and Security Policy or development policy.[49]

The EU speaks against human rights violations ensuring consistency between positions expressed at the ILO and other human rights fora. The promotion of human rights consideration in all aspects of EU external action can be explained with three interrelated reasons:[50] the EU's commitment to upholding international human rights law, the elevation of the Charter of Fundamental Rights to Treaty-level status and the obligations flowing from the EU's impending accession to the European Convention for the Protection of Human Rights and Fundamental Freedoms. When dealing with country cases at the ILO in Geneva, the Human Rights Strategic Framework and Action Plan[51] adopted in June 2012 is fundamental to the work of the EU. In particular, Action 34 of the Action Plan invites the European External Action Service (EEAS) and EU Member States to develop and agree an annual approach to the identification of priorities at the ILO. Such priorities are the following:

- The EU reaffirms its commitment to the promotion and protection of all human rights, whether civil and political, economic, social and cultural.
- Human rights violations: The EU speaks against human rights violations ensuring consistency between positions expressed at the ILO and other human rights fora, such as the UN General Assembly and the UN Human Rights Council.
- The EU supports the Promotion of universal ratification and implementation of the four ILO core labour standards laid down in eight ILO Conventions:[52]
  - freedom of association and the effective recognition of the right to collective bargaining (Conventions 87 and 98);
  - elimination of all forms of forced or compulsory labour (Conventions 29 and 105);

[49] The ECJ held that EU development cooperation refers also to the respect for human rights and fundamental freedoms, in compliance with commitments in the UN and other international organisations: ECJ, Case C-91/05 *Commission of the European Communities v Council of the European Union (Small arms-ECOWAS)* [2008] ECR I-3651, para 65. The delimitation between CFSP and other policies post-Lisbon is governed by Art 40 TEU. See P Craig, *The Lisbon Treaty. Law, Politics and Treaty Reform* (Oxford, Oxford University Press, 2013) 415–17.

[50] J Kenner, 'Economic Partnership Agreements: Enhancing the Labour Dimension of Global Governance?' in Van Vooren, Blockmans and Wouters, above n 19, 313.

[51] Council of the European Union, EU Strategic Framework and Action Plan on Human Rights and Democracy, 25 June 2012, Doc No 11855/12.

[52] ibid, Action 15.

— effective abolition of child labour (Conventions 138 and 182); and
— elimination of discrimination in respect of employment and occupation (Conventions 100 and 111).

From an EU Member States perspective, all 28 have ratified these eight Conventions. This ensures internal/external coherence. Past practice has also shown that the EU does not speak on EU Member States called before the Committee on the Application of Standards (CAS), to avoid politicisation of the debate.

Third countries have also entered into free trade agreements with the EU. Most of these agreements contain a commitment to labour standards: the sustainable development chapter of EU trade agreements is considered 'the most comprehensive approach':[53] in these cases third countries commit to respect ILO standards.

In the political domain the EU aims at ensuring consistency with CFSP positions and with positions expressed in other fora.

III. HOW EU COORDINATION HAPPENS AND WHO IS DOING ALL THIS?

A. From the Perspective of an EU Member State

For a State, the capacity to participate and play a role in international institutions of all types is crucial today to be an actor on the international scene.[54] Institutions with standard setting powers are of crucial importance, because they lay down obligations for acts performed by contracting states within their jurisdiction. The ILO is such a 'tripartite regulatory agency'.[55] From an EU Member State perspective there are at least four methods to influence or be represented in the ILO.[56] Each of these configurations serves a different purpose.

1) Individually as a government: Member States express their national preferences—sometimes talking to a domestic audience, given that national social partners are in the room. EU Member States also complement EU positions with national statements.
2) As members of the Europe Group, subdivided into the Western (23) and the Eastern European Group (28): The official regional groups of the ILO are the contact points for the International Labour Office in their relations with governments. They deal mainly with elections and nominations.

[53] International Labour Organization—International Institute for Labour Studies, *Social Dimension of Free Trade Agreements* (Geneva, ILO, 2013) 69 ff.

[54] A Chayes and AH Chayes, *The New Sovereignty: compliance with international regulatory agreements* (Cambridge, Mass, Harvard University Press, 1995) 27.

[55] On the ILO as 'the first of the modern international regulatory agencies' see Chayes and Chayes, ibid, 16.

[56] A Johnson, 'EU–ILO relations. Between regional and global governance' in J Orbie and L Tortell (eds), *The European Union and the Social Dimension of Globalization* (Abingdon, Routledge, 2009) 85 ff.

3) As Industrialized Market Economy Countries (IMEC): This group comprises all the EU Member States plus other 11 industrialised economies (Australia, Canada, Iceland, Japan, New Zealand, Norway, Republic of Korea, San Marino, Switzerland, Turkey and USA). IMEC was formed in 1976 by the traditional 'Western Group' in the context of Cold War politics. At the time there was significant politicisation in the ILO from the Soviet Bloc and the Group of 77. IMEC also had the purpose of dissuading the USA from withdrawing from the ILO by using the group's influence to create the necessary conditions to make the USA's withdrawal unnecessary. After the return of the USA in 1978, IMEC continued to function with a focus on structure, reform, programme and budget, building questions, technical cooperation, etc.[57]
4) As the EU: The EU tries to influence the ILO according to its values and interests. A non-exhaustive list of EU statements includes social dialogue, employment, green economy, post-2015 agenda, labour migration, as well as country cases such as Myanmar, Belarus, Iran, Fiji, Uzbekistan, and Bahrain.

From the perspective of the EU Member States, the 'choice of venue' is largely influenced by the evolution of the EU's domestic activities, of a legislative or non-legislative nature. The EU Treaties mention the Member States' room for manoeuvre in a number of areas.[58] The Member States have also declared their retention of responsibilities of 'national representation in … international organisations'.[59] However, the Treaties highlight the necessity to exercise their competences in a 'manner consistent with EU law'.[60] The Lisbon Treaty has clarified the principle of sincere cooperation, which includes a duty of abstention: 'The Member States shall take any appropriate measure, general or particular, to ensure fulfilment of the obligations arising out of the Treaties or resulting from acts of the institutions of the Union. The Member States shall facilitate the achievement of the Union's tasks and refrain from any measure which could jeopardise the attainment of the Union's objectives'.[61]

[57] P Nedergaard, 'Coordination Processes in International Organisations: The EU at the International Labour Conference in 2005', Chapter 6 in (2007) *European Integration online Papers* (EIoP) Vol 12 No 3; http://eiop.or.at/eiop/texte/2008-003a.htm (13 December 2013).

[58] De Witte and Thies, 'Why Choose Europe?', above, n 19, 32–33.

[59] See Declarations 13 and 14 concerning the common foreign and security policy. According to Kaddous their content is 'restrictive'; see C Kaddous, 'Role and position of the High Representative of the Union for Foreign Affairs and Security Policy under the Lisbon Treaty' in S Griller and J Ziller (eds), *The Lisbon Treaty. EU Constitutionalism without a Constitutional Treaty?* (Vienna, Springer, 2008) 205–21, 206. According to Craig, both Declarations 13 and 14 are partly inconsistent with the provisions of the Treaties; see P Craig, *The Lisbon Treaty. Law, Politics and Treaty Reform* (Oxford, Oxford University Press, 2013) 421–22.

[60] ECJ Case C-124/95 *The Queen, ex parte Centro-Com srl v HM Treasury and Bank of England* [1997] ECR I-81, para 25. See, in particular, Art 4(3) TEU 344, 351 TFEU.

[61] Art 4(3) TEU. The content of the principle of sincere cooperation was already set out in Art 10 TEC.

B. EU Coordination in Practice

Our starting point is that since the EU is not a member of the ILO, in principle its external competence can in fact be exercised through the Member States acting jointly in the Union's interest.[62] The principle of sincere cooperation is even more relevant in a complex organisation like the ILO.[63]

Getting an agreement on the list of 'EU statements' is different for the ILC (i) and for the Governing Body (ii). In all cases, EU coordination is a mini-negotiation to reach a common position on issues on the agenda of the ILO. The position can be reflected in a statement or a line to take. First drafts are produced by the EU Delegation, the European Commission or a Member State. The drafts are discussed via an internet platform and in EU coordination meetings. The final version is 'aligned' and delivered on behalf of a maximum of 41 (28 + 13) States. Through the 'alignment procedure' the Candidate Countries, the Countries of the Stabilisation and Association Process and potential candidates, the EFTA/EEA countries and the Eastern European and Central Asian countries are invited to align themselves with EU statements and positions in the field of CFSP and other policies.

i. International Labour Conference: Standard Setting and Other Items

There are five to six stages[64] for the adoption of ILO Conventions and recommendations.[65] The first is the decision taken in the ILO Governing Body to place a standard-setting item on the agenda of the International Labour Conference (ILC). The second is a technical meeting of experts to discuss the content of the instrument. The third consists of a questionnaire sent by the International Labour Office to its members which allows the expression of national preferences. The fourth is the ILC Committee meeting discussing either the draft instrument (single discussion) or proposed conclusions (double discussion). In the case of a single discussion the draft instrument is negotiated in the ILC Committees. This is followed by a vote in the plenary (fifth and final stage for single discussions). In the case of a double discussion, in the first year the ILC Committees discuss the proposed conclusions while in the second year they negotiate the proposed instrument itself (fifth stage of double discussions). This also is followed by a vote in the plenary (sixth and final stage for double discussions).

EU coordination takes place starting from stage four. To gauge the effectiveness of coordination, the final and voting stage of a discussion is worth analysing. Since 2010 three standard-setting items were discussed at the ILC. In 2010 the

[62] ECJ, Case C-45/07 *Commission of the European Communities v Hellenic Republic* [2009] ECR I-701, para 31, building on *Opinion 2/91* [1993] ECR I-1061, para 5.

[63] Art 4(3) TEU.

[64] R Kissack, 'The Performance of the European Union in the International Labour Organization' (2011) *Journal of European Integration* 651–65, 653–54.

[65] International Labour Office, *Manual for drafting ILO instruments*, Online revised version, pp vii–ix explains the stages for adoption of Conventions or Recommendations: www.ilo.org/public/english/bureau/leg/.

ILO Recommendation concerning HIV and AIDS and the World of Work, 2010 (No 200) obtained the support of all EU Member States.[66] In 2011 the Domestic Workers Convention 2011 (No 189) had the support of 25 EU Member States and two abstentions (the United Kingdom and the Czech Republic).[67] In 2012 the Conference adopted the Social Protection Floors Recommendation, 2012 (No 202): all EU Member States voted in favour.[68]

This being said, the ILC also holds general discussions and recurrent discussions which are concluded with the adoption of non binding resolutions. In this case the EU coordinates as for a standard-setting item, since the procedures during the ILC are very similar.

The CAS[69] considers information and reports supplied by governments under Articles 19, 22 and 35 of the ILO Constitution on the effect given to Conventions and Recommendations, together with the Report of the Committee of Experts on the Application of Conventions and Recommendations. In this committee the procedures for coordination are very similar to the other committees. However, the CAS does not produce a final negotiated outcome. For this reason, EU coordination aims to express positions on third countries in the form of statements.

ii. ILO Governing Body

For the Governing Body the process is more time-consuming: once the agenda is published, a list of possible points of interest to the EU is produced. This list is discussed and decided. In terms of content, the EU positions in the ILO Governing Body are focused on a clear formulation of the EU position supporting specific proposals or asking for changes in the decision points.[70]

C. EU Actors in the ILO Context

i. EU Actors and External Representation

The Lisbon Treaty expressly recognised the legal personality of the EU (Article 47 TEU). The idea is that a single legal personality, apart from simplifying

[66] 99th session International Labour Conference Provisional Record 20 (Rev). Final record vote on the adoption of the Recommendation on HIV and AIDS and the world of work, pp 56–60. However, the votes of the Hungarian Government delegates are not recorded. The recommendation obtained 439 votes in favour, 4 against and 11 abstentions.

[67] 100th session International Labour Conference Provisional Record 25 (Rev). The vote records 396 in favour, 16 against and 63 abstentions. The UK explanation of abstention is on page 23.

[68] 101st session International Labour Conference Provisional Record 27. Slovenia is not recorded. The recommendation was adopted with only one abstention (Panama Government delegate).

[69] Officially the 'Committee on the Application of Conventions and Recommendations' according to Art 7 of the Standing Orders of the International Labour Conference.

[70] M Busolin Lucatello, *The role of Union delegations in multilateral contexts. The European Union at the International Labour Organisation and the case of Myanmar* (Bruges, College of Europe, unpublished MA Thesis, 2013) 48–50.

matters, will strengthen the EU's voice as well as its negotiating powers.[71] Along the same lines, the visibility of the EU should be increased by the existence of one single actor. It would be easier for third parties to understand that they deal with one entity, the EU, and not with two separate entities, the EU and the European Community, depending on the subject matter.[72] The Lisbon Treaty has empowered four actors to represent it on the international scene: the President of the European Council,[73] the European Commission,[74] the High Representative/Vice President of the European Commission[75] and the EU Delegations.[76]

The Lisbon Treaty has transformed the former Commission Delegations into EU Delegations. One of the changes brought about by the Treaties is the duty of cooperation between Union Delegations and diplomatic missions of the Member States.[77]

The High Representative, in his/her capacity as Vice President of the Commission, is in charge of coordinating the other aspects of the Union's external action.[78]

ii. Applicable ILO Rules and EU Coordination

According to the 2001 EU–ILO exchange of letters, the EU is regularly invited to meetings of the ILO's International Labour Conference and of the Governing Body.[79] As far as the Governing Body is concerned, its standing orders say that 'representatives of official international organizations which have been invited by the Governing Body to be represented at its meetings shall be entitled to be present at the meetings and may participate without vote in the discussions'. These representatives participate 'under the same conditions as members of the Governing Body'.[80]

Concerning the ILC, the EU is invited to and participates in the ILC as an official international organisation.[81] As far as the Conference committees are concerned, the following rule is applicable to all committees set up by the Conference with the exception of the Finance and the Credentials Committees:[82] 'Representatives of official international organisations which have been invited to be represented

[71] C Kaddous, 'External Action under the Lisbon Treaty' in Ingolf Pernice and Eugeni Tanchev (eds), *Ceci n'est pas une Constitution—Constitutionalisation without a Constitution?* (Baden-Baden, Nomos, 2009) 173–89, 173–75; P Craig, *The Lisbon Treaty. Law, Politics and Treaty Reform* (Oxford, Oxford University Press, 2013) 387.

[72] J-C Piris, above, n 10, 87.

[73] Art 15(6) TEU.

[74] Art 17(1) TEU.

[75] Art 27(2) TEU.

[76] Art 221(1) TFEU.

[77] Art 32 TEU, Art 221(2) TFEU. See P Craig, above, n 71, 405.

[78] Art 18(4) TEU.

[79] Exchange of letters between the Commission of the European Communities and the International Labour Organization, OJ C 165, 8.6.2001, p 23.

[80] Art 1.9, Standing Orders of the Governing Body and Introductory note para 13.

[81] Art 2(3)(b) and Art 14(9) ILC Standing Orders.

[82] Art 55(1) ILC Standing Orders.

at the Conference shall be entitled to be present at the meetings of the committee and may participate, without vote, in the discussion.'[83]

The legal situation and practice are largely different pre-Lisbon and post-Lisbon.

iii. Pre-Lisbon Practice

In the pre-Lisbon era, the way the EU and its Member States behaved in the ILO was dual. On the one hand there were collective positions of the Member States, coordinated and expressed by the Presidency and expressed on behalf of the EU. On the other hand, there was the Commission, representing the European Community, expressing its views on a limited number of issues as an observer.

Looking at the minutes of the Governing Body sessions or the ILC in the period preceding the entry into force of the Lisbon Treaty, one finds that the positions of the EU were expressed 'on behalf of the EU'[84] in the Governing Body. In the conference committees, even if the statements were delivered 'on behalf of the EU', the ILO minutes record 'on behalf of the Governments of Member States of the EU'.[85] However, one also finds that in a limited number of cases the EU Member States were expressing their positions also as members of the IMEC group on the same points on the agenda.[86]

iv. Post-Lisbon Practice

After the entry into force of the Lisbon Treaty, the coordination role was transferred to the EU Delegation. The representation role, in most cases, is performed by a Member State. However, the EU Delegation represented the EU in the Committee on the Application of Standards during the 2013 Conference. Recent practice shows a division of labour between the various EU actors and Member States, in particular the country holding the rotating Presidency of the Council.

The statements of the EU can be prefaced either 'on behalf of the EU' or 'on behalf of the EU and its Member States'. This is provided for in the General Arrangements on EU Statements in multilateral organisations endorsed by the Council in October 2011.[87]

Turning to the practice in the Governing Body and the Conference, one finds that today the ILO minutes reflect exactly how the statement was prefaced. This reflects the legal personality of the EU.

[83] Art 56(7) ILC Standing Orders.

[84] See Minutes of the 306th session Governing Body of the International Labour Office (November 2009) paras 19, 73, 109.

[85] See Record of the discussion in the Committee on the Application of Standards, Myanmar (Convention 29), 2009, www.ilo.org/dyn/normlex/en/f?p=1000:13100:0::NO:13100:P13100_COMMENT_ID,P11110_COUNTRY_ID,P11110_COUNTRY_NAME,P11110_COMMENT_YEAR:2556364,103159,Myanmar,2009.

[86] Minutes of the 303rd session (November 2008) paras 224 (IMEC), 225–26 (EU).

[87] Council Document 15901/11, 24.10.2011.

What has changed in the ILO is that the EU is recognised as a 'hybrid': it is an international organisation but also a group of governments, irrespective of who is the speaker and irrespective of the preface of the particular statement.

In substance, the trend is towards a 'recognizable' voice of the EU. The 'EU venue' can bring about more efficiency and more influence in the ILO. This is also reflected in an informal 'division of labour' between the EU and IMEC. Today it is very rare to find overlapping statements between the two groups.

IV. CONCLUSIONS

Given the particular nature of the ILO, to be effective and influential, the EU relies on two sources of power: the EU itself and its Member States. The EU does not replace the Member States but adds value. The goal is to eliminate unnecessarily procedural complications and expensive duplicative presences.

In the pre-Lisbon era, Member States agreed on the language of statements and negotiating positions. Only the rotating presidency was representing the EU externally. In the post-Lisbon era, we have moved away from the idea that a previous statement was the necessary 'precedent' for another one. The positions of the EU are consistent with its internal and foreign policies. The idea is to agree on a set of objectives and mobilise all EU Member States towards these objectives. In a nutshell, coordination is played by the EU Delegation and negotiation is played by the EU Delegation and its Member States. Burden sharing is essential. The added value is that all 28 Member States should act in the interest of the EU simultaneously (allowing for national differences when this is the case), instead of having one Member State (presidency) representing and negotiating for the EU successively—and only for six months.

6

European Union Participation and Cooperation in ILO Institutions and Activities: An ILO Perspective

GENEVIÈVE PONS-DELADRIÈRE*

Faire travailler les hommes ensemble,
leur montrer qu'au-delà de leurs divergences ou par-dessus les frontières,
ils ont un intérêt commun.[1] (Jean Monnet)

Make people work together,
show them that beyond their differences and dividing borders,
they have a common interest.

THE INTERNATIONAL LABOUR Organization (ILO) and the European Union (EU) share important common goals in relation to social and labour issues, as well as in relation to development. Under their respective constitutions and founding treaties both organisations support lasting peace through social and economic development and cooperation.[2] With these common values as a starting point, the two organisations enjoy a long tradition of working together dating back to the first cooperation agreement between the ILO

* The author's gratitude goes to the legal service team, in particular to Tobias Michels, assisted by Martin Denis and supervised by Susan McCrory.

[1] B Clapier and H Rieben, *Une mémoire vivante* (Lausanne, Fondation Jean Monnet pour l'Europe, 1986) 71 (translation by the author).

[2] See Preamble of the Treaty establishing the European Economic Community (hereafter the Rome Treaty): 'To ensure the economic and social progress of their countries by common action in eliminating the barriers which divide …; constantly improving the living and working conditions of their peoples, strengthen the unity of their economies and to ensure their harmonious development … and strengthen the safeguards of peace and liberty by establishing this combination of resources'; see also Preamble of the ILO Constitution: 'universal and lasting peace can be established only if it is based upon social justice … And whereas conditions of labour exist involving such injustice hardship and privation to large numbers of people as to produce unrest so great that the peace and harmony of the world are imperilled'.

and the European Coal and Steel Community in 1953.[3] Cooperation between the organisations is aimed at contributing to developing employment and raising the standard of living. It is reflected today, inter alia, in their cooperation in the Group of Twenty major economies (G20) aimed at fostering 'sustainable growth, in particular as regards social protection, youth employment and social dialogue'.[4] Recently this cooperation has acquired a particular relevance in the context of the current economic crisis, leading Guy Ryder, the current Director General of the ILO, to declare at the last EU Employment summit: '[our] natural relationship is now married to an urgent need.[5]

The ILO and the EU also share a common inspiration, as they are also linked through Jean Monnet: not only is he known as one of the 'fathers of the European Integration',[6] but he also took part in the Versailles negotiations,[7] which ultimately led to the founding of the ILO.[8] In his function as the President of the High Authority of the European Coal and Steel Community he was the first to sign a cooperation treaty between the ILO and this European Community.[9] Herman van Rompuy, President of the European Council, paying indirect tribute to this common origin, underlined in his address delivered to the International Labour Conference (ILC) in June 2013, that: 'It is … no surprise that, "genetically speaking", the Union and the Organization understand each other very well. And when I say the Union, I mean not just the institutions but also the European Union's 27 member countries. We carry within us the deep conviction that, underlying the economic and social organisation of our societies, lie eminently political goals'.[10]

In very different ways both organisations can be described as *sui generis* due to features making them unique when compared to other public international organisations. The ILO is the only public international organisation with a tripartite structure comprising representatives of the governments of its Member

[3] Published in the Official Bulletin of the ILO, Vol XXXVI, 1953, No 7; available at: www.ilo.org/public/english/bureau/leg/agreements/ceca.htm.

[4] Joint Conclusions of the 10th High Level Meeting between the International Labour Office and the European Commission, Brussels, 4–5 December 2012, p 3, available at www.ilo.org/wcmsp5/groups/public/---europe/---ro-geneva/---ilo-brussels/documents/genericdocument/wcms_212029.pdf.

[5] Closing statement at the EU Employment Conference, Brussels 17 September 2012; available at: www.ilo.org/brussels/key-documents/WCMS_189820/lang--en/index.htm.

[6] CJ Anta, *Les pères de l'Europe* (Bruxelles, PIE Peter Lang, 2007) 37ff.

[7] Regarding Jean Monnet's participation, see A Williams, *Failed Imaginations* (Manchester, Manchester University Press, 1998) 59ff.

[8] For further references, see E Osieke, *Constitutional Law and Practice in the International Labour Organization* (Boston, Martinus Nijhoff Publishers, 1985) 3ff.

[9] Agreement concerning Co-operation between the International Labour Organization and the European Coal and Steel Community, Official Bulletin of the ILO, Vol XXXVI, 1953, No 7.

[10] Speech by the President of the European Council Herman Van Rompuy, International Labour Conference, 14 June 2013, Geneva, available at: www.ilo.org/ilc/ILCSessions/102/media-centre/speeches/WCMS_216042/lang--en/index.htm.

States as well as representatives of the employers and workers of those States.[11] The EU on the other hand is a regional integration organisation that has evolved and expanded from an economic cooperation treaty into a supranational entity[12] that acts for and with its Member States on a very wide range of areas through its institutions and via political cooperation.[13] The two organisations today have 28 Member States in common.

I. AN ACTIVE EU PARTICIPATION IN THE ILO

The special character of each organisation predetermines the institutional relations between them: unlike other international organisations, such as the World Trade Organization (WTO)[14] and the Food and Agriculture Organization (FAO),[15] the ILO Constitution only permits States to become members. Indeed the ILO Constitution explicitly contains provisions on the membership of States in Articles 1(2) and (3) including some special provisions for the compliance of federal States in Article 19(7).

Relations between the ILO and other international organisations are governed by Articles 12(1) and (2), which provide that the ILO 'shall cooperate within the terms of this Constitution with any general international organisation' and that the latter are allowed to participate without a vote in the ILO's deliberations. The EU's relationship with the ILO, including its participation in ILO meetings as well as formal cooperation, is therefore governed by this established ILO constitutional framework and by Article 12(1) and (2) in particular.

A. General Observations

ILO and EU institutional relations are generally governed by agreements and Memoranda of Understanding (MoUs), the first dating from 1953. These are revised and updated from time to time, the most recent examples being the Exchange of Letters of 2001 and the Strategic Partnership of 2004 in the field of

[11] P Sands and P Klein, *Bowett's Law of International Institutions* 6th edn (London, Sweet & Maxwell, 2009) 82–83.

[12] 'Supranationalism' in a legal sense on the EU level is characterised first by the primacy of European law. See ECJ, Case 6/64 *Falminio Costa v ENEL* [1964] ECR 1251, included in the Annex to the Lisbon Treaty, Declaration 17; it is characterised by the direct applicability of European law (see Art 288, sentence 2, 3 TFEU) and by the founding treaties setting up a legal order which is autonomous from its Member States; see ECJ, Case 26/62 *Van Gend & Loos* [1963] ECR 1; U Haltern, *Europarecht: Dogmatik im Kontext* 2nd edn (Tübingen, Mohr Siebeck, 2007) 461–62 and 503; K-K Pease, *International Organizations* 5th edn (Boston, Longman, 2012) 25–26.

[13] See, eg, K Kiljunen, *The European Constitution in the Making* (Brussels, Center for European Policy Studies, 2004) 21–23.

[14] Art II, para 3, FAO Constitution as amended, in force since 18.11.1991.

[15] Art XI, para 1, Marrakesh Agreement Establishing the World Trade Organization.

development.[16] On the standard-setting side the EU as a non-member cannot ratify ILO Conventions, but takes part in the negotiations as a public international organisation and authorises its Member States to ratify ILO Conventions in its fields of competence.[17]

Although the EU is not a member of the ILO, the ILO and the EU have in practice applied a pragmatic approach, so that Member States of the EU may coordinate and express their positions in the ILC and Governing Body according to the topic addressed. Indeed, 'where an agreement has been reached between the Commission and the EC (now EU) Member States upon the existence of the Community's (now Union's) competence, the Community's position has been officially presented at the ILO Conference by the government delegate of the EC Member State holding the Presidency of the Council'.[18] In these circumstances the EU position will be 'officially presented by government delegate … on behalf of the government representatives of the Member States'[19] of the Union. It is to be noted that records of diverse ILO deliberations show that other regional organisations, for example the Mercado Común del Sur (MERCOSUR) and the Association of Southeast Asian Nations (ASEAN) have also taken the floor in a comparable manner.[20]

As only Member States are obliged to contribute to the ILO budget according to Article 13(3) of the ILO Constitution,[21] the EU does not contribute to

[16] Cooperation agreement between the European Commission and the International Labour Organization: Exchange of letters between the ILO and the European Commission in May 2001, 2001/C 165/12, published in the Official Journal of the European Communities C 156, 30.05.2001, available at: www.ilo.org/brussels/key-documents/WCMS_169295/lang--en/index.htm; Memorandum of understanding concerning the establishment of a strategic partnership between the International Labour Organization and the Commission of the European Communities in the field of Development, signed in July 2004, available at: www.ilo.org/brussels/key-documents/WCMS_169299/lang--en/index.htm.

[17] See, eg, Maritime Labour Convention, 2006, Council Decision 2007/431/EC, 07.06.2007; Convention concerning Safety in the Use of Chemicals at Work, Convention No 170, Proposal for a Council Decision authorising Member States to ratify, in the interests of the European Union, 1990, COM/2012/0677 final 2012/0320; available at: http://eur-lex.europa.eu/smartapi/cgi/sga_doc?smartapi!celexplus!prod!DocNumber&lg=EN&type_doc=COMfinal&an_doc=2012&nu_doc=677; Convention concerning decent work for domestic workers, 2011, Convention No 189, Proposal for a Council Decision authorising Member States to ratify, in the interests of the European Union, COM/2013/0152 final—2013/0085, available at: http://eur-lex.europa.eu/LexUriServ/LexUriServ.do?uri=COM:2013:0152:FIN:EN:HTML.

[18] L Cavicchioli, 'The relations between the European Community and the International Labour Organization' in E Cannizaro (ed), *The European Union as an Actor in International Relations* (The Hague, Kluwer Law International, 2002) 261 and 268. For an analysis from the political science point of view see P Nedergaard, 'The European Union at the ILO's International Labour Conferences—A "double" principal–agent analysis' in KE Jørgensen (ed), *The European Union and International Organizations* (London, Routledge, 2009) 149.

[19] Cavicchioli, above n 18, pp 261 and 268.

[20] See for MERCOSUR the discussion in the Convention on Safety and Health, ILC, *Provisional Record*, 93rd Session, 2005, paras 21, 33 and 35; for ASEAN, see Reports of the Selection Committee, ILC, *Provisional Records*, 101st Session, 2012, para 14.

[21] Art 13(3) of the ILO Constitution: 'The expenses of the International Labour Organization shall be borne by the Members in accordance with the arrangements in force in virtue of paragraph 1 or paragraph 2(c) of this article.'

the regular budget of the ILO, but contributes to ILO activities through project funding according to a common vision illustrated notably by the 2004 Strategic Partnership in the field of development.

B. EU Participation in the International Labour Conference (ILC) and ILO Standard-setting Activities

The ILC, held every year, is the representation of all Member States of the ILO (Article 3 ILO Constitution).[22] Each Member State is represented by a delegation consisting of two government delegates, an employer delegate, a worker delegate, and their respective advisers. The ILC's main functions are the drafting and adoption of international labour standards in the form of Conventions and Recommendations, the supervision of those international labour standards and the issue of guidelines for the ILO's general policy and future activities, including its biennial work programme and budget. Under Article 2(3) of the Standing Orders of the ILC, the representatives of international organisations that have been invited to be represented at the ILC are permitted into 'the body of' the conference hall'. The EU is regularly invited to participate in the ILC in accordance with the last Exchange of Letters of 2001.[23]

The EU's right to address the Conference is established under Article 14(9) of the Standing orders of the ILC (possibility to 'participate without vote in the discussions'). Furthermore the EU participates in Committees of the Conference and contributes to the discussions. Its participation is regulated by Article 56(7) of the Standing Orders of the ILC, pursuant to which 'Representatives of official international organisations which have been invited to be represented at the Conference shall be entitled to be present at the meetings of the committee and may participate, without vote, in the discussion'.

As a result of its participation not only in the plenary but also in technical committees, the EU plays a significant role in the drafting, adoption, ratification and implementation of international labour conventions, recommendations and other ILO instruments. The importance ascribed to the ILC by the EU institutions is further reflected by the size and seniority of delegations sent to the ILC in recent years.[24] Records show that the EU has recently actively taken part in the

[22] For further information on the ILC's composition and work see: www.ilo.org/ilc/ILCSessions/102/lang--en/index.htm.

[23] The Exchange of Letters of 2001 reads: 'The Community, represented by the Commission, will continue to be regularly invited to meetings of the ILO's International Labour Conference and of the Governing Body'.

[24] Eg, in June 2013 the EU Delegation was composed of officers of the European External Action Service, the European Commission and of members of the European Economic and Social Committee. A total of 30 members of the delegation included the Commissioner for Employment, the Ambassador leading the Permanent Delegation in Geneva, several Directors and heads of units of the European Commission, and seven members of the European Economic and Social Committee, reflecting the representation of social partners.

negotiations of significant new ILO Conventions, such as the Maritime Labour Convention,[25] Convention 184 on the Promotional Framework for Occupational Safety and Health,[26] Convention 187 on Safety and Health in Agriculture[27] and Convention 189 on Domestic Workers (2011).[28] Further examples of active European participation worth mentioning include the Recommendations on HIV and Aids (2010)[29] and on Social Protection Floors (2012).[30] Through its participation in the Committee on the Application of Standards, the EU, along with its Member States, plays an active role in the implementation and supervision of ILO international labour standards.

The EU as a non-member cannot ratify or accede to the ILO Conventions although recent European practice concerning ILO Conventions has shown that the EU plays an active and important role in the ratification process, by authorising its Member States to ratify certain Conventions 'for the parts falling under Union/Community competence'. This has for example been the case for the Maritime Labour Convention in 2006.[31] A similar process is under way for the Convention concerning Safety in the Use of Chemicals at Work (Convention No 170)[32] and for the Convention concerning Decent Work for Domestic Workers of 2011 (Convention No 189).[33] The close legal connection between ILO standards and EU legislation has been reflected in various explicit references to the ILO and ILO standards in EU legislation, for example in the Directive on Antidiscrimination[34]

[25] See, eg, Discussion on the Report of the Committee of the Whole, ILC, *Provisional Record*, 94th (Maritime) Session, 2006, paras 356 and 372.

[26] See, eg, Discussion on the Report of the Committee on Safety and Health, ILC, *Provisional Record*, 93rd Session, 2005, para. 49.

[27] See for example: Discussion on the Report of the Committee on Safety and Health in Agriculture, ILC, *Provisional Record*, 81st Session, 2001, paras 56 and 61.

[28] Discussion on the Report of the Committee on Domestic Workers, ILC, *Provisional Record*, 100th Session, 2011, para 15.

[29] Discussion on the Report of the Committee on HIV/AIDS, ILC, *Provisional Record*, 98th Session, 2009, paras 17–19.

[30] Discussion on the Report of the Committee on Social Protection Floor, ILC, *Provisional Record*, 101st Session, 2012, para 19.

[31] See Council Decision 2007/431/EC authorising Member States to ratify, in the interests of the European Community, the Maritime Labour Convention, 2006, of the International Labour Organization, 7 June 2007.

[32] Proposal for a Council Decision authorising Member States to ratify, in the interests of the European Union, the Convention concerning Safety in the Use of Chemicals at Work, 1990, of the International Labour Organization (Convention No 170), COM/2012/0677 final—2012/0320, Brussels 22.11.2012; available at: http://eur-lex.europa.eu/smartapi/cgi/sga_doc?smartapi!celexplus!prod!DocNumber&lg=EN&type_doc=COMfinal&an_doc=2012&nu_doc=677.

[33] Proposal for a Council Decision authorising Member States to ratify, in the interests of the European Union, the Convention concerning decent work for domestic workers, 2011, of the International Labour Organization (Convention No 189), COM/2013/0152 final—2013/0085, Brussels, 21 March 2013, available at: http://eur-lex.europa.eu/LexUriServ/LexUriServ.do?uri=COM:2013:0152:FIN:EN:HTML.

[34] Council Directive 2000/78/EC, 20 November 2000, consideration 4: 'Convention No 111 of the International Labour Organization (ILO) prohibits discrimination in the field of employment and occupation.'

and in the Working Time Directive.[35] This illustrates both the sophisticated legal linkages between EU secondary legislation and ILO standards and the general legal status of those standards in European Union law. Even in its external relations, for example in the Cotonou Agreement, the EU has made reference to and asked for application of ILO standards.[36] In this Agreement the EU and its partners have striven to strike a balance between trade on the one hand and labour standards on the other by reaffirming 'their commitment to the internationally recognised core labour standards, as defined by the relevant International Labour Organisation (ILO) Conventions',[37] while mentioning that 'labour standards should not be used for protectionist trade purposes'.[38]

At the same time ILO standards are taken into account in the application and interpretation of EU law by its courts. In various decisions the European Court of Justice (ECJ) has referred to and actually applied ILO labour standards in its judgments.[39] This shows that even though there is no direct link between ILO secondary law and EU law, in general the application of certain core ILO standards can be effectively guaranteed through the legal obligations common to all EU Member States.

In many instances the EU and its institutions have promoted the adoption and ratification of ILO Conventions. The Maritime Labour Convention and the Domestic Labour Convention should be mentioned in this regard.[40] Showing the overlapping interest of EU and ILO, the Union promoted such Conventions, not only by expressing their support in ILO meetings, but also by advocating for it in international fora[41] and by recommending ratification to its Member States.[42] The

[35] Directive 2003/88/EC, 4 November 2003, consideration 6: 'Account should be taken of the principles of the International Labour Organization with regard to the organisation of working time, including those relating to night work.'

[36] Partnership agreement between the members of the African, Caribbean and Pacific Group of States on the one part, and the European Community and its Member States, on the other part, signed in Cotonou on 23 June 2000 (hereafter Cotonou Agreement). The Preamble reads 'Anxious to respect basic labour rights, taking account of the principles laid down in the relevant conventions of the International Labour Organization'.

[37] Coutonou Agreement, Art 50(1).

[38] ibid, Art 50(3).

[39] See, eg, on equal treatment ECJ, Case C-197/96 *Commission v France* [1997] ECR I-01489; see for further references and examples EC Landau and Y Beigbeder, *From ILO Standards to EU Law—The Case of Equality between Men and Woman at Work* (Leiden, Martinus Nijhoff Publishers, 2008).

[40] See above, nn 28, 31, 35 and 37; see also Press release, 18 June 2013, 'ILO and EU-Presidency welcome moves to ensure decent work for domestic workers', available at: www.ilo.org/ilc/ILCSessions/102/media-centre/news/WCMS_216315/lang--en/index.htm.

[41] Joint Conclusions of the 10th High Level Meeting between the International Labour Office and the European Commission, Brussels, 4–5 December 2012, p 3 (see above, n 4).

[42] See Communication from the Commission, Renewed social agenda: Opportunities, access and solidarity in 21st century Europe, COM(2008) 412 final, Brussels 2.07.2008, p 15; available at: http://eur-lex.europa.eu/LexUriServ/LexUriServ.do?uri=COM:2008:0412:FIN:EN:PDF; see also European Parliament Resolution 2010/C 285 E/10, 26 November 2009, Ratification and implementation of updated ILO Conventions; available at: http://eur-lex.europa.eu/LexUriServ/LexUriServ.do?uri=OJ:C:2010:285E:0067:0068:EN:PDF.

coming into force of both Conventions in 2013 can be thus taken as a flagship example of how far the ILO and the EU can get on substantive questions if they pursue a common goal.

C. Participation in the Governing Body

The Governing Body is the executive body of the International Labour Organization, meeting three times a year (Article 7 of the ILO Constitution).[43] It is composed of 56 titular members (28 governments, 14 employers and 14 workers) and 66 deputy members (28 governments, 19 employers and 19 workers). It decides upon the agenda of the ILC, adopts the draft programme and budget of the organisation for submission to the Conference, and elects the Director-General. Of the government seats, 10 are permanently held by States of chief industrial importance decisions on ILO policy.

The EU's participation in the Governing Body is regulated by the Standing Orders of the Governing Body and in particular section 1.9.1 (pursuant to which its Representatives are 'entitled to be present at the meetings … and may participate without vote in the discussion'). Not being a member, the EU participates as a public international organisation and has been represented by the European External Action Service (EEAS) since its establishment in 2010[44] accompanied by other officials.[45]

Of the 10 non-elective Governing Body seats held by Members of chief industrial importance, four are Member States of the EU (France, Germany, Italy and the United Kingdom).[46] There are currently three additional regular government members of the Governing Body (Denmark, Hungary and Lithuania) which are also EU Member States.[47] These EU members of the Governing Body pool their efforts to make common statements 'on behalf of the European Union and its Member States'.[48] This leads back to the statutory framework concerning 'speaking on behalf of' in the Governing Body in general and especially for the European Union. When it comes to voting, it is clear—de facto and de jure—that only regular Members,

[43] For further information on the Governing Body, see www.ilo.org/gb/lang--en/index.htm.

[44] Council Decision establishing the organisation and functioning of the European External Action Service, 2010/427/EU, 26 July 2010; available at: http://eur-lex.europa.eu/LexUriServ/LexUriServ.do?uri=OJ:C:2010:285E:0067:0068:EN:PDF.

[45] See, most recently, Governing Body, Minutes, 319th Session, October 2013, Final list of persons attending the session, p 30.

[46] So-called 'non-elective seats as States of chief industrial importance', see Composition of the Governing Body, 2011–2014 as elected on 6 June 2011; available at: www.ilo.org/gb/about-governing-body/WCMS_083528/lang--en/index.htm.

[47] Results of the elections to the Governing Body of the International Labour Office for the period 2011–14, ILC, *Provisional Record*, 100th Session, 2011, p 8.

[48] See for a most recent example: Governing Body, Minutes, 319th Session, October 2013 (GB.319/LILS/PV/Draft), Draft Minutes on Legal Issues and International Labour Standards Section (LILS), para 64; available at: www.ilo.org/gb/GBSessions/GB319/lils/WCMS_228979/lang--en/index.htm.

whether holding non-elective or elective seats, or their substitutes can vote.[49] However, most decision-making processes in the ILO strive for consensus,[50] and voting is consequently uncommon (apart from votes on the programme and budget and the appointment of the Director-General).

D. EU Participation in Other Meetings

The EU is invited to attend and participates in a wide range of technical meetings and meetings of experts. Notably the EU plays an important role in European regional meetings as was the case in Oslo 2013.[51] These meetings may address issues such as labour statistics[52] and health and safety[53] or discuss other sectorial issues and touch on all aspects of the ILO's activities.

II. A GROWING EU COOPERATION WITH THE ILO

A. Institutional Aspects

The ILO cooperates with a range of EU actors and to this end operates an office in Brussels. Reflecting the growing importance of the relationship to the two organisations, the intensity of this cooperation is rising, and the level of seniority of participants is increasing. This is demonstrated by contacts between the ILO Director-General Ryder and European Council President Herman van Rompuy, European Parliament President Martin Schulz, EU Commission Vice-President Rehn, responsible for economic and euro issues,[54] and 'Development'

[49] Compendium of rules applicable to the Governing Body of the International Labour Office, 2nd edn, Geneva, 2010, introductory note, para 25.

[50] ibid, para 24.

[51] 'Of the official intergovernmental organizations invited to attend the Meeting, in conformity with article 1, paragraph 8, of the Rules for Regional Meetings and in accordance with the relevant agreements or decisions of the Governing Body, the following were represented: … European Union, including the European Commission, the European Parliament, the European Centre for the Development of Vocational Training, the European Training Foundation and the European Foundation for the Improvement of Living and Working Conditions', see Report of the Credentials Committee, ILO, 9th European Regional Meeting, Oslo, Norway, 8–11 April 2013 (ERM-9-D6-2013-Credentials-En.docx), para 11; available at: www.ilo.org/global/meetings-and-events/regional-meetings/europe-and-central-asia/erm-9/WCMS_210357/lang--en/index.htm.

[52] Represented by EUROSTAT, see Report of the Conference, 18th International Conference of Labour Statisticians, Geneva, 24 November–5 December 2008 (ICLS-R-[2008-12-0006-6]-En.doc/v3), p 112; available at: www.ilo.org/global/statistics-and-databases/meetings-and-events/international-conference-of-labour-statisticians/WCMS_101467/lang--en/index.htm.

[53] Final report on the Meeting of Experts to Adopt a Code of Practice on Safety and Health in Agriculture, Geneva, 2010, p 63; available at: www.ilo.org/sector/activities/sectoral-meetings/WCMS_161723/lang--en/index.htm.

[54] See Press release, 9 May 2013, *ILO Director-General urges closer cooperation between IMF, EC and ILO*; available at: www.ilo.org/global/about-the-ilo/media-centre/press-releases/WCMS_210176/lang--en/index.htm.

Commissioner Andris Piebalgs; alongside this there is traditional close cooperation with the Commissioner for Employment and Social Inclusion, currently Laszlo Andor.[55] At the same time, cooperation with the EU through the Member States' rotating presidency and contacts with European Parliament and its committees have become regular (for example, the ILO Deputy Director General Houngbo addressing the European Parliament International Trade Committee (INTA) hearing on Bangladesh).[56] In December 2005, a joint declaration on the strengthening of relations and cooperation was signed between the European Economic and Social Committee (EESC) and the ILO.[57] As a consultative body consisting of representatives of employers, workers and other civil society organisations this committee may be considered as reflecting the notion of tripartism and inclusion of the social partners in the European institutions.

Besides working together on specific issues through projects, the ILO and EU institutions have established various channels of regular communication, of which the annual high level meeting is the most outstanding example. On the occasion of the 2012 high level meeting the EU and ILO expressed 'a joint objective to further strengthen their partnership' and agreed on a common agenda for 2013.[58]

B. Common Agenda

In the common agenda 2013 the ILO and the EU underlined their long-standing cooperation on employment and social affairs and agreed on the promotion of 'decent work in global multilateral fora'.[59] Both organisations committed to reinforce their coordination especially regarding countries where core labour standards are violated. They will notably 'continue working closely together in the context of the G20 to foster policy coherence for strong, balanced and sustainable growth, in particular as regards social protection, youth employment and social dialogue'.[60] By virtue of this common agenda, recent G20 summits have more and more taken into account issues of social protection and labour standards and the G20 has explicitly promoted ratification and implementation of the eight Fundamental [ILO] Conventions and [the ILO's] efforts to support and monitor the follow-up

[55] See (apart from contacts with EC Vice-President Rehn) Newsletter of ILO Office for the European Union and the Benelux countries, No 6, September 2012; available at: www.ilo.org/wcmsp5/groups/public/---europe/---ro-geneva/---ilo-brussels/documents/publication/wcms_189930.pdf.

[56] See www.ilo.org/brussels/information-resources/news/WCMS_222131/lang--en/index.htm.

[57] Déclaration conjointe du Directeur général de l'OIT et de la Présidente du CESE sur le renforcement des relations entre l'OIT et le CESE, 1 January 2005; available at www.ilo.org/brussels/WCMS_216951/lang--en/index.htm.

[58] Joint Conclusions of the 10th High Level Meeting between the International Labour Office and the European Commission, Brussels, 4–5 December 2012 (see above, n 4).

[59] ibid.

[60] ibid.

to the implementation.[61] At the 2013 G20 Leaders Declaration, the G20 Task Force on Employment was explicitly directed to partner with the ILO showing that the ILO and the EU work closely together in this multilateral governance forum.[62] As the promotion of ILO standards is a key issue to the European Union, both organisations pursue the common goal of conciliating free trade, development and the protection of social and labour standards through the 'effective implementation of the ILO fundamental conventions by partner countries in the context of negotiations on and implementation of EU trade and association agreements'.[63] The aforementioned Cotonou Agreement and its provisions referring to social protection and labour standards can be considered a good illustration of this.

C. Practical Aspects of the Cooperation Between the ILO and the EU

Practical aspects of the cooperation between the ILO and the EU can be seen in EU/ILO collaboration concerning research and statistics and in the implementation of projects. The EU is an important donor to the ILO in respect of specific projects and partners with the ILO in several joint activities. The Financial and Administrative Framework Agreement (FAFA) constitutes the basis of this funding relationship as both organisations have strong regulatory requirements in relation to financing.[64]

Cooperation concerning research and statistics takes a prominent role under the EU's 'Europe 2020'[65] strategy and the ILO's 'Strategic Policy framework (2010–2015)',[66] demonstrating that both organisations pursue research projects of mutual interest. Some projects are financed by the EU, with the International Institute for Labour Studies, as part of the ILO, providing its expertise. In 2010 the Institute and the DG Employment of the European Commission embarked on a

[61] G20 Labour and Employment Ministers' Conclusion, Paris 26–27 September 2011, p 8; available at: www.ilo.org/global/about-the-ilo/how-the-ilo-works/multilateral-system/g20/WCMS_164260/lang--nl/index.htm.

[62] G20 Leaders' Declaration, Saint Petersburg 5–6 September 2013, p 10; available at: http://en.g20russia.ru/news/20130906/782776427.html.

[63] Joint Conclusions of the 10th High Level Meeting between the International Labour Office and the European Commission, Brussels, 4–5 December 2012 (see above, n 4).

[64] Financial and Administrative Framework Agreement (FAFA) between the European Community and the United Nations (2003); available at: http://ec.europa.eu/europeaid/work/procedures/implementation/practical_guide/previous_versions/2003/documents/un_ec_fwc_en.pdf. The FAFA has been made applicable to the ILO–EU relation by incorporating it in the Memorandum of understanding concerning the establishment of a strategic partnership between the International Labour Organization and the Commission of the European Communities in the field of Development, signed in July 2004, available at: www.ilo.org/brussels/key-documents/WCMS_169299/lang--en/index.htm.

[65] Communication from the Commission: Europe 2020, A strategy for smart, sustainable and inclusive growth, COM(2010) 2020 final, Brussels, 3.3.2010, pp 27–28; available at: http://eur-lex.europa.eu/LexUriServ/LexUriServ.do?uri=COM:2010:2020:FIN:EN:PDF.

[66] Strategic Policy Framework 2010–15, Making decent work happen, ILO, Governing Body, *Minutes*, 304th Session, March 2009, paras 76–78.

joint research project of particular relevance to both organisations ('Addressing European Labour Market and Social Challenges for a sustainable globalisation').[67] On a more informal basis, the EU and the ILO collaborate on specific research projects, representatives of the European Commission being regularly invited to discuss and comment on the outcomes of research projects carried out by the ILO and the Institute (for instance, in November 2013, the ILO organised an international conference in Brussels launching a study on 'The Social Dimension of Free Trade Agreements').[68]

Technical cooperation between the EU and the ILO in practical projects around the world (those projects often just referred to as 'the field') is designed upon two models, either upon contribution under a joint management or through granting.[69] Under the current FAFA the application of internationally accepted standards regarding accounting, audit, control and procurement procedures standards (the so-called 'four pillar test') is guaranteed.[70] Negotiations are currently ongoing on how to comply with evolving international transparency standards in an amended FAFA for 2014 and the following years. Concerning the second model of technical cooperation by the awarding of grants, the focus in EU–ILO relations is primarily by direct agreement and not through calls for proposals, as the ILO due to its status as 'the' public international organisation concerned with 'the world of work' often holds—de jure and de facto—a monopoly in the area of its activities.[71]

In substance technical cooperation of EU and ILO is regionally based on three pillars, the first pillar being EU accession countries and the EU neighbourhood in eastern Europe and the Mediterranean; the second being the least developed countries, especially the ACP countries (Africa, Caribbean and Pacific); and the third pillar being country programmes focusing on special problems such as decent work, the fight against child labour, social cohesion and social dialogue,

[67] See as an overview: www.ilo.org/inst/research/addressing-crisis-challenges/lang--en/index.htm.

[68] The social dimensions of free trade agreements, International Labour Organization; International Institute for Labour Studies, 2013; available at: www.ilo.org/global/research/publications/WCMS_228965/lang--en/index.htm.

[69] 'Joint management is described by the European Commission as "a specific budget allocation modality applicable to international organisations by which the European Commission entrusts some of its implementing tasks to an international organisation complying with international standards with regard to the four pillars". Despite its name, the EC funds entrusted to an International Organisation under joint management are not jointly managed between the European Commission and the International Organisation. The management of the tasks related to the implementation of these funds is delegated by the European Commission to the International Organisation. The European Commission, however, keeps some prerogatives of control and verification, as required by the Financial Regulation.' See the EU FAQ concerning the cooperation with international organisations as updated in March 2013, question 3, available at: http://ec.europa.eu/europeaid/work/procedures/faq/international_organiszations_en.htm.

[70] Preamble of the Financial and Administrative Framework Agreement (FAFA) between the European Community and the United Nations (2003); see also, EU FAQ, above, n 69.

[71] ibid, question 14.

empowering labour associations, facilitating labour mobility while respecting migrants' rights—objectives which are considered as global public goods by the European Union.[72]

Several core documents of the EU guide technical cooperation and funding by the Union.[73] Common projects have included Monitoring and Assessing Progress on Decent Work (MAP);[74] Technical and Vocational Education and Training (TVET) Reform in Bangladesh,[75] Social protection and employment policies in Burkina Faso, Cambodia and Honduras[76] and Addressing European labour market and social challenges for a sustainable globalisation.[77] The flux of expertise is not only facilitated by regular high-level consultations but also by participation of ILO experts in EU projects and cooperation with the IMF.[78] This shows that technical cooperation in general is not limited to projects in the field but also extends to exchange of technical expertise and assistance in informal ways between the EU and the ILO. This exchange includes a variety of situations such as recent developments in the so-called 'euro crisis'.

III. CONCLUDING REMARKS

Both the EU and the ILO recognise the growing importance of their cooperation. In his speech to the International Labour Conference in June 2013 the President of the European Council, Herman van Rompuy, stated that 'the European Union

[72] For the notion of global public goods see 'The United Nations Development Programme' in I Kaul, I Grunberg and MA Stern (eds), *Global public goods: international co-operation in the 21st century* (New York, Oxford University Press, 1999) 2–19. For the application by European Institutions, see Regulation (EC) No 1905/2006 of the European Parliament and of the Council of 18 December 2006 establishing a financing instrument for development cooperation, Art 11(2)a), Art 12(2)d.ii and Proposal for a Regulation of the European Parliament and of the Council establishing a financing instrument for development cooperation COM(2011) 840 final, Art 7 and Annex V.

[73] First there is the 'agenda of change' setting new priorities on social adjustment and development, infrastructure, food, governance education, social security and agriculture; see Communication from the Commission to the European Parliament, the Council, the European Economic and Social Committee and the Committee of Regions, Increasing the impact of EU Development Policy: an Agenda for Change, COM(2011) 637 final, Brussels, 13 October 2011; Second is the 'strategic partnership', which ideas incorporated therein have also found their way into the Union's development policy, for example by incorporation in the Cotonou Agreement with ACP-countries (n 36), Preamble, Art 1, Art 13(3), Art 13(4) and Art 25.

[74] Project website available at: www.ilo.org/integration/themes/mdw/map/lang--en/index.htm.

[75] Project website available at: www.ilo.org/dhaka/Whatwedo/Projects/WCMS_106485/lang--en/index.htm.

[76] Project website available at: www.ilo.org/brussels/WCMS_194936/lang--en/index.htm.

[77] See: www.ilo.org/inst/research/addressing-crisis-challenges/discussion-paper-series/lang--en/nextRow--10/index.htm.

[78] Report of the ILO 9th European Regional Meeting in Oslo, above, n 51; Joint Statement of the ILO/IMF Conference, Oslo, 13 September 2010; available at: www.imf.org/external/np/sec/pr/2010/pr10339.htm; See also The Oslo Declaration: Restoring confidence in jobs and growth, ERM-9-D7-2013, ILO Ninth European Regional Meeting in Oslo, Norway, 8–11 April 2013, ERM.9/D.7.

believes in the power of universal norms and standards' and stressed that 'the ILO has a fundamental role to play in helping countries to repair the economic and social fabric'.[79] He emphasised that 'it's only by working together that [both organisations] can truly achieve [their] goals'.[80] By recalling the founding values, Guy Ryder, addressing the EU employment conference in September 2012, welcomed the 'opportunity to think together how the ILO and the EU can deepen their positive relationship'.[81]

In order to continue constructive cooperation between both organisations, the observations made by Wilfred C Jenks, then Assistant Director General and later Director General of the ILO, as far back as 1955 on the relation of 'the World organization and European integration', may still hold true: 'the World organization and European integration are not alternative and rival approaches ... but essentially complementary tendencies, each of which can greatly strengthen the other'.[82]

[79] Speech by President of the European Council Herman Van Rompuy, above, n 10.

[80] ibid.

[81] Closing statement at EU Employment Conference, Brussels, 17 September 2012; available at: www.ilo.org/brussels/key-documents/WCMS_189820/lang--en/index.htm.

[82] CW Jenks, 'World Organization and European Integration' in *The European Yearbook* (The Hague, Martinus Nijhoff, 1955) 173 and 185.

Part III

The European Union in the World Trade Organization

7

The European Union in the World Trade Organization Post-Lisbon: No Single Change to the Single Voice?

DETLEV BRAUNS AND TOMAS BAERT*

THE ENTRY INTO force of the Lisbon Treaty and the creation of the European External Action Service (EEAS) have arguably transformed the EU's presence and performance at the global stage. While this is true for many areas of EU external action (as shown in other chapters of this volume), the statement applies less to the EU's role and representation in the World Trade Organization (WTO). Some visible changes occurred in the form of the EU's presence in the WTO, including a newly established 'Mission' in Geneva,[1] the appointment of an EU Ambassador exclusively dedicated to WTO affairs as well as a name change in the WTO from European Communities (EC) to European Union (EU). However, the substantive role and responsibility of the EU in the organisation have been affected less by the latest Treaty change than they have by developments preceding it.

To be sure, the EU's position in the WTO was and still is unique in the landscape of international organisations. We argue in this chapter that this role was and still is well established to the extent that few substantive changes were either feasible or desirable as the Lisbon Treaty took effect. This contrasts with other policy spheres, where the Lisbon Treaty was a welcome and necessary instrument to upgrade the EU's external representation. One could see the strength of the EU's external representation and the pressure for internally reforming that representation to correlate inversely. Where the EU stands comparatively weaker on the international scene, there is arguably more interest in improving that position and representation than in areas where the uniformity and visibility of that

* The views and opinions expressed herein are those of the authors and do not necessarily reflect the views of the European Commission or the European External Action Service.

[1] Communication from the Commission to the Council and the European Parliament—Establishment of an EU Delegation to the UN in Geneva, COM(2010) 287 final.

representation is greater. But what are the factors that gave shape to the EU's role and representation in the WTO?

I. THE EU AS A SINGLE ACTOR IN THE WTO

The EU, and the European Community preceding it, has a long history of working as a single actor and speaking with a single voice on matters that fall within the realm of trade policy in general and the multilateral trading system in particular. This practice, which implies that the European Commission represents the Union and the bundled rights of the Member States who remain silent in the organisation, emerged well before the WTO was created on 1 January 1995. It was foreseen already in the original Treaty of Rome establishing the European Economic Community in 1957 that trade policy or 'common commercial policy' would fall under exclusive Community competence.

The EC exercised the rights and fulfilled the obligations of Member States at a time that the EC was not even a contracting party to the General Agreement on Tariffs and Trade (GATT) but all EC Member States were. The EC participated, for example, in the negotiations of the Kennedy Round (1964–1967). In this sense, the EC acted as a GATT member long before being an actual member of the organisation. This role materialised at a moment that the emergence of the EC itself had become a subject of debate at the multilateral scene. The elimination of barriers between EC Members, combined with the introduction of common policies and a common external tariff, fuelled fears of trade diversion and a deterioration of market access opportunities for US exporters, in particular in the area of agriculture which became subject to a common agricultural policy (CAP).[2] This motivated US President Kennedy to push for a round of negotiations that became the Kennedy Round of negotiations, through which the US could lock in trading opportunities to the newly created European market. As the EC's common market and common policies became the trigger for multilateral negotiations, it is thus not surprising that the EC presented itself as the sole interlocutor in trade negotiations.

Of course, this practice was derived first and foremost from the exclusive character of the EC competence for the common commercial policy. While not entirely codified (for example, the Treaty of Rome did not provide an exhaustive definition of 'common commercial policy'), this exclusivity was well established over time in the case law of the Court of Justice.[3] Indeed, the Court's interpretations have defined but also moved the boundaries of EU common commercial policy over time, as the Union sought to adapt to a changing external as well as internal environment.

[2] C Preston, *Enlargement and integration in the European Union* (London, Routledge, 1997) 168.

[3] The doctrine of implied powers was established by the ECJ in Case 22-70 *Commission v Council (European Agreement on Road Transport)* [1971] ECR 263 and was later followed in other landmark opinions, such as *Opinion 1/94, WTO Agreements* [1994] ECR I-5267.

Initially, the common commercial policy served the primary aim of building Europe by defending the customs union and the tariff preferences it created for Member States. It later extended to other common policies that became the subject of EU legislation, in particular as part of the creation of the EU internal market in the 1980s. In accordance with the doctrine of implied powers, the Court extended the EC's external competence beyond those expressly established in the Treaty and allowed the EC to act externally in matters they regulate(d) internally.

However, while EC competence on trade has been evolutionary and while the scope of EC authority has been subject of debate and tension, this did not fundamentally alter or affect the practice of the single voice followed in the GATT/WTO. Indeed, even in areas where Member States questioned the scope of EC competence, such as after the Uruguay Round of negotiations (1986–1994), Member States still accepted that the EU acted with a single voice in the WTO, along with—in some cases—specific arrangements as regards their presence and participation in meetings where matters of shared or national competence were discussed (for example, aspects of trade in services before the Lisbon Treaty).

As a result, when the Lisbon Treaty codified and confirmed the entire commercial policy as an exclusive EU competence (Article 3(1) Treaty on the Functioning of the European Union (TFEU)), this did not cause a major shift in the EU's role and responsibility in the WTO. Indeed, exclusive competence necessitated legally the EC's single voice, but the single voice in the WTO was not entirely defined by legal competence, as it has its roots also in practical necessity and in the political leverage that was identified with it. In this sense, legal competence is not the most appropriate yardstick for measuring the nature or extent of the EU's role in the WTO, despite the fact that the competence shaped this role in particular in the early years of EU integration.

II. A SINGLE VOICE BUT MULTIPLE MEMBERS

When the WTO was created on 1 January 1995, the EC was long established as an important player in the multilateral trading system. After all, it was a logical development to see the EC become a member of the WTO. This came in clear recognition of the competence and relative weight the EC garnered in international trade diplomacy. It was also a sign of the time. Unlike other international organisations, especially those belonging to the UN family, which were created in the aftermath of the Second World War, the WTO was only created in 1995. Contrary to the post-WWII era, states arguably no longer had the monopoly over international diplomacy at this time. This *zeitgeist* arguably further facilitated the EU's claim to its position and place in the WTO.

It could perhaps be considered surprising that both the EC and all Member States became Members of the WTO in their own right. Without entering here into a specific debate on this question, we would argue that the fact that EU Member States are members of the WTO does not render the membership of the EU less important or effective, for it is the single voice practice that continues to prevail. The membership and presence of Member States in the WTO speaks to the size and importance of the EU and the single voice with which it acts. In practice, it is often a useful reminder to the EU's partners that a single voice reflects a great number of nations.

The single external voice obviously conceals the many voices that shape EU trade policy internally. Here again, a sound and solid practice has been laid well before the entry into force of the Lisbon Treaty, with the European Commission in a central role as representing the Union (as confirmed in Article 17 TEU). The Commission also has the sole right of initiative in this area of exclusive competence. An advisory body was created as a subordinate body of the Council of Ministers. Formerly named after the respective Treaty provisions on the common commercial policy (Art 113, then Art 133), the Trade Policy Committee (TPC), as is it currently called, gathers Member States and advises the Commission on matters of trade policy, including WTO matters. This also implies that coordination with Member States in Geneva is limited, for it is done in Brussels through the TPC. A weekly meeting is held with Member States in Geneva every week and every formal WTO meeting in Geneva is typically preceded by a short meeting with Members. However, these meetings are in general more about exchanging information than they are platforms for coordination and policy discussion which are reserved to the TPC. For these reasons, these practices contrast significantly with the practices in the UN environment where close cooperation with some or all Member States, joint EU teams, burden sharing, and so on have emerged in the post-Lisbon era to increase the uniformity and visibility of the EU's external actions.

III. NEW PLAYERS, OLD PRACTICES?

Among the important innovations of the Lisbon Treaty are an expanded role for the European Parliament on trade policy as well as the foundations for the EEAS.

The European Parliament became the co-legislator, together with the Council, of the common commercial policy (Art 207(2) TFEU). This increased power for the Parliament naturally translated into an increased interest from MEPs in trade policy and WTO matters, as witnessed for example by the frequency of visits of Members of the European Parliament to Geneva or by the regularity of debriefings and consultations of MEPs or the International Trade Committee on WTO matters. Nevertheless, the fact that the European Parliament became an important player in trade policy did not alter the way the EU operated in the WTO. For the WTO Ministerial Conferences, the highest decision-making body of the WTO, Members of the European Parliament are members of the EU Delegation, for example. This was already the case before the entry into force of the Lisbon Treaty and thus not a direct result of the changes brought by the Treaty.

The creation of the EEAS raised some questions on the autonomy of the Commission trade policy circuit led by the responsible Commissioner from the foreign policy circuit presided over by the High Representative of the Union for Foreign Affairs and Security Policy, who is equally one of the vice-presidents of the Commission (Article 18(4) TEU).[4] The HR/VP, currently Federica Mogherini, is responsible for the EEAS and also for coordinating aspects of the Union's external action, beyond her responsibility for the Common Foreign and Security Policy (CFSP) and her responsibilities within the Commission for external relations. Two observations can be made as regards the reach and relationship of the EEAS and the HR/VP. One more organisational and one more substantive observation.

First of all, the newly created Permanent Mission of the EU to the WTO, headed by a dedicated Ambassador (who is also an official of the EEAS and not of the Commission), was formally placed under the authority of the HR/VP, like all other Union delegations. Formally speaking, this increased the role of the foreign policy circuit over the organisation and management of the Union's representation on WTO/trade matters. Indeed, Article 5(3) of the Council Decision of 26 July 2010 establishing the organisation and functioning of the European External Action Service indicates that a Head of Delegation shall receive instructions from the High Representative and the EEAS, and shall be responsible for their execution. However, that same article later recognises that 'the Commission may also issue instructions to delegations in areas where the Commission exercises the powers conferred to it by the Treaty'. For a delegation that deals exclusively with trade policy—an area of exclusive competence—this implies that all its instructions come de facto from the Commission, despite being placed under the authority of the HR/VP, who—through the Head of Delegation—is still in charge of organisational aspects. In private sector jargon, this could be summarised as meaning that the Commission is functionally in charge of the EU representation to the WTO, whereas the EEAS is administratively in charge.

In substantive terms, the common commercial policy has also seen a widening reach of the EEAS and in particular the external action principles and objectives. The specific objectives of the common commercial policy include the harmonious development of world trade, the progressive abolition of trade and investment restrictions and the lowering of customs and other barriers (cf Article 206(1) TFEU), but the Lisbon Treaty—for the first time—explicitly supplemented these specific objectives with the general principles and objectives of the Union's external action (Article 207), as enshrined in Article 21 TEU. Of course, trade policy was never apolitical, certainly not in the Cold War years when trade policy was considered an area of 'low politics' subject to the 'high politics' of national security policy. However, as the oldest and most integrated of the EU's external policies, EU trade policy acquired a status that left it less affected by foreign and security policy considerations than in the case of many sovereign nations. Nevertheless, the Lisbon Treaty granted these political objectives a constitutional weight and it remains to be seen still how this will affect the EU role and representation in the WTO.

[4] Centre for European Policy Studies, *Upgrading the EU's role as global actor. Institutions, law and the restructuring of European diplomacy* (Brussels, CEPS, 2011) 85.

The request in the WTO for a waiver to allow the EU to grant unilateral trade preferences to Pakistan in the wake of 2010 floods is a recent example of this foreign policy impact on trade, for it was to serve a humanitarian goal and originated in a call from the Foreign Affairs Council of the EU. This single example does not allow one to conclude that foreign policy has a greater grip on trade policy, following the new CFSP under the Lisbon Treaty.

IV. CONCLUSION

It is clear that the EU's representation to the WTO remains special and of a *sui generis* nature, in particular compared to the broader Geneva landscape of international organisations which are discussed in other contributions to this volume. Due to the single voice practice and the exclusivity of the EU's competence, the work and relationship between the EU and Member States in Geneva is fundamentally different from that in other areas. Despite the many changes it brought, the Lisbon Treaty was neither necessary nor practical to reshaping the practice of the EU's representation to the WTO. While some changes occurred in the internal set-up of the EU, the external representation through a single voice remained unchanged pre- and post-Lisbon.

Some conclusions or even lessons can be drawn here, in particular in relation to considering the EU role in other organisations. First of all, the EU became an important player in the GATT/WTO well before it became a Member of the organisation. In this sense, membership of an organisation is no prerequisite for an effective representation to that organisation. That said, a clear status for the EU of course helps more than it hinders upgrading EU external and representation.

Competence can be an important starting point here to get the ball rolling. But while competence matters, this will not necessarily determine the limits of external action. Put differently, it is often not so much about *having* the legal competence as a negotiator as about *being* a competent negotiator. Over time, the European Commission has garnered an important negotiating experience and capability in the field of external trade policy, which Member States are also increasingly relying on. In this way, the single voice has reinforced the view in Europe that a unified representation on trade simply garners better results, irrespective of the question as to who has the legal competence over a given area. Few today dispute the position of the Commission as a negotiator, whereas agreement is harder to find in the Council, for example, on the legal basis of negotiated agreements. This logic also surfaced in the selection process for a new WTO Director General in 2013, when EU Member States agreed that a unified position was to be presented through a single voice, that of the EU Ambassador to the WTO, irrespective of the question of who holds the competence for voicing preferences in such a process. Through successive rounds, the EU presented a unified position which did not go unnoticed in Geneva and ultimately shows that a single position is more than just the sum of its constituting parts.

8

The European Union and its Member States' Participation in the World Trade Organization: A WTO Perspective

JÁNOS VOLKAI*

THE WORLD TRADE Organization (WTO) Agreement invited both the European Community (EC) and its Member States to become original members. In 1995 the WTO Agreement entered into force for both the EC and its Member States.

This is a rather peculiar arrangement in at least two ways. First, the European Union (EU) is the only customs union explicitly invited to be a WTO member (otherwise, WTO membership has been reserved only for countries and separate customs territories). Second, the EU's WTO membership alongside that of its own Member States necessarily raises various practical and legal issues in the daily operation of the WTO.

Without speculating on the reasons for this arrangement, it is worth mentioning that even at the time of the Uruguay Round, the EC was a 'giant' of international trade. Since then, the EC's exclusive competence in external trade has grown further with the entry into force of the Lisbon Treaty in 2009.

The WTO participation of the EU (and its Member States) certainly tells an intriguing story about the relations of the EU and its Member States. The present contribution focuses on this joint participation from a WTO perspective.

One of the main questions in that respect relates to the issue of whether the WTO is a predominantly legal or a predominantly pragmatic, political organisation? Or is it both at the same time?

As is well known, the WTO has a strong legal aspect—especially in comparison with other international organisations. It is about WTO 'rights' and 'obligations'; and about 'bindings', 'commitments' and 'concessions'—all contained in

* This chapter follows, as faithfully as possible, the author's speaking notes at the conference on The European Union in International Organizations and Global Governance, which took place in Geneva. The views expressed in this chapter are solely those of the author, and shall under no circumstances be attributed to the WTO, its Secretariat or its Members. Any errors or omissions are, of course, solely the author's.

international treaties. Most of these treaties are so-called 'covered agreements', enforceable in binding dispute settlement procedures. The WTO's dispute settlement mechanism is often described as the 'jewel in the crown' of the Uruguay Round results. It is one of the most—if not the most—binding dispute settlement mechanisms between public entities with international legal personality.

At the same time, the WTO was born of its predecessor organisation, the highly pragmatic General Agreement on Tariffs and Trade (GATT). It is worth noting that, for instance, the creation of the GATT Legal Division some 30 years ago happened despite considerable resistance (interestingly, mainly from the EC at the time). It is at the GATT that a mere decision of the contracting parties, the Enabling Clause, created a long-lasting exception from what is arguably the cornerstone of multilateral trade rules, namely most favoured nation (MFN)—and this without formally amending the GATT 1947. The GATT is also where the European Economic Community (EEC) had a goods schedule and participated in trade disputes—without being a GATT contracting party.

This general pragmatism of the GATT was eloquently summarised by the Chairman of the GATT Council. In the discussion of a procedural matter involving territorial and sovereignty issues, in 1965 the Chairman noted that:

> [I]t had been the policy of the CONTRACTING PARTIES to *avoid unproductive controversies over political questions* which did not bear significantly on the many *substantial* questions with which the CONTRACTING PARTIES were concerned. For this reason the CONTRACTING PARTIES had followed the policy expressed in Article 86 of the Havana Charter, namely to *avoid passing judgment in any way on essentially political matters* and to follow decisions of the United Nations on such questions.[1]

So the question remains: is the WTO a political or a legal organisation?

In order to try to answer this question, this chapter examines how the EU and its Member States participate in the WTO.

I. MEMBERSHIP

As mentioned above, both the EC and its Member States had been invited to become original WTO members, and in fact they became WTO members alongside each other.

This is a basic fact. It is also clear that by inviting both the EU and its Member States, the WTO Agreement makes no distinction between their WTO membership status. So, from the strict viewpoint of the WTO Agreement, the EU and its Member States participate in the WTO with equal rights and obligations. But, how does this principle apply in practice?

[1] SR.22/3, pp 21–22. See also GATT Analytical Index, p 1095 (emphasis added).

II. BUDGETARY CONTRIBUTIONS

Being WTO members with equal obligations, one would expect that both the EU and its members participate in the WTO budget. In fact, the WTO Agreement requires each member to participate in the WTO budget. According to the WTO's Financial Regulations, members' contributions shall be counted as a proportion of their share in international trade.[2]

However, this could lead to double counting and contributions from the EU and its Member States. The practical solution agreed upon is that only the EU Member States contribute to the WTO budget.

III. RIGHT TO SPEAK

Turning to the right to speak, it sounds obvious that equal members should have equal rights.

At the WTO, typically, representatives of each EU Member State and the EU participate in most meetings alongside each other; however, only the EU representative will speak. Some smaller informal meetings and consultations in trade negotiations will involve the EU representative only, even without the presence of its Member States.

This certainly flows from the EU's exclusive external competence in external trade matters. It is nowhere written in the WTO rules, though. Based on its internal constitutional arrangements, the EU consults its Member States on WTO matters in regular and formalised procedures. Is this sufficient guarantee for other WTO members that the EU is a reliable single interlocutor with regard to this part of the world? Apparently, yes, as this practice has not been called into question by other WTO members.

Incidentally, the practice is the opposite in the WTO's Budget and Finance Committee. There, typically only EU Member State representatives would take the floor, not the EU.

IV. DECISION MAKING

Pursuant to Article IX of the WTO Agreement, '[t]he WTO shall continue the practice of decision-making by consensus followed under the GATT 1947'. Consensus decision making is the rule and, importantly, also the practice of the WTO. Consensus is defined as an absence of formal objection by a member present at the meeting when the decision is taken.[3]

[2] Financial Regulations of the World Trade Organization, WT/L/156 and /Rev 1 and /Rev 2, Chapter IV(a).

[3] Footnote 1 to Article IX(1) of the WTO Agreement.

The WTO rules also provide for voting, although in practice the WTO does not have resort to a vote. In any event, it is in the context of voting that the WTO rules explicitly address the participation of the EU and its Member States. A footnote to the WTO Agreement provides that '[t]he number of votes of the European Communities and its Member States shall in no case exceed the number of the Member States of the European Communities'.[4]

V. WTO DISPUTE SETTLEMENT

The EU is often described as one of the 'frequent users' of the WTO dispute settlement system. In fact, the EU has been a party—either as a complainant or as a respondent—to many disputes, and it has been a third party in most other WTO disputes.

The standing of the EU and its Member States emanates from their WTO membership, and WTO adjudicators have been operating on this basis. The practical questions come up when a WTO member brings a dispute against the EU and some of its Member States. Even in such disputes, WTO adjudicators would recognise the parallel standing of both the EU and its Member States.

In practice, however, the EU has litigated for the European side. The EU Delegation in the dispute might include the representatives of relevant Member States but these would not make statements at dispute hearings. And the EU would submit the written pleadings and make the oral statements in these disputes.

A. Schedules

In the WTO, each member is required to have goods and services schedules. These schedules list commitments and exemptions specific to the member in question; they are an integral part of the GATT 1994 and the GATS, respectively.

As previously mentioned, under the GATT 1947 the EEC Member States were covered by a joint EEC goods schedule. This practice continues in the WTO, where there are single goods and services schedules for the EU covering EU Member States.

EU Member States would have separate schedules only in regard to the part of their territories not covered by the EU. For instance, the Netherlands has services schedules with respect to Aruba, a territory not covered by the EU Treaties.[5]

As the goods and services schedules are joined for the EU as a whole, modifications to these schedules involve exclusively the EU—at least at the WTO level. At the WTO, negotiations leading to modified schedules involve only the EU on the European side.

[4] Footnote 2 to Article IX(1) of the WTO Agreement.
[5] GATS/SC/5.

The situation is largely similar in the context of the plurilateral Agreement on Government Procurement. The European procuring entities covered by that agreement, both of the EU and of its Member States, and the commitments of these entities are all contained in a single EU schedule attached to that Agreement. At the WTO level, modifications to this schedule also involve only the EU.

B. EU Enlargements

In external competence matters, the EU is often described as a moving target.

In the WTO, this comes out perhaps most clearly in the context of successive EU enlargements. When a country joins the EU, the EU makes a statement formally withdrawing the goods and services schedules of itself and its acceding Member States. The EU then engages in renegotiating its goods and services schedules, and for the period of these negotiations it unilaterally commits itself to continue respecting its withdrawn schedule with regard to its enlarged territory. Once the modifications are negotiated, the changes to the EU schedules are formally certified.

A similar approach has been followed for the last three waves of EU enlargement in the context of the GPA. In fact, in that context, new EU members have not formally acceded to the GPA; merely, the EU's GPA schedule was modified to add the procuring entities of the new EU Member States.[6]

C. Treaty Making

Before the entry into force of the WTO Agreement, both the EC and its Member States had international legal personality. Thus, both the EC and its Member States signed the WTO Agreement in Marrakesh, and those that signed subject to ratification also deposited an instrument of acceptance to express their consent to be bound by the WTO Agreement on the international plane.

The WTO has had only limited treaty acts since 1995 involving the EU or its Member States. The four Services Protocols were accepted by both the EC and its Member States at the time.[7] Also, following the entry into force of the Lisbon Treaty, the EU deposited an instrument of succession for the EC.[8] In addition, the EU deposited an instrument of acceptance for the TRIPS Amendment Protocol,[9] and for the GPA Amendment Protocol.[10]

[6] GPA/78, GPA/90 and GPA/118.

[7] See Status of WTO Legal Instruments, 2012 edn, www.wto.org/english/res_e/booksp_e/wto_status_legal_inst12_e.pdf.

[8] WT/LET/679.

[9] WT/LET/608.

[10] WT/LET/917.

9

The European Union in the World Trade Organization—A Model for the EU's Status in International Organisations?

FRANK HOFFMEISTER

I. INTRODUCTION

COMPARED WITH THE status of the European Union (EU) in other international organisations,[1] the situation in the World Trade Organization (WTO) seems to be rather comfortable. Next to its Member States the Union is a full member and widely recognised as an important and efficient player in the organisation. For example, during the 9th Ministerial Conference in Bali in December 2013, the EU actively contributed to reach a compromise text on a mini-Doha package, which consisted of a new agreement on trade facilitation and a number of Ministerial Decisions on agriculture and development issues.[2] Sitting in the final session of the Conference with the Commissioners for Trade, Agriculture and Customs plus Ministers from 28 Member States (one of which, Lord Green from the United Kingdom, served as Vice-Chairman of the Conference), the EU was able to join the consensus on a proposal made by the WTO Director-General Azevedo following internal deliberations.

This chapter will review how far the Union's WTO membership can serve as a model for the EU's status in other international organisations. In order to do so, it is important to recall first relevant EU and WTO rules, including the practice of their interaction.

[1] For a comprehensive overview see I Govaere, J Capiau and A Vermeersch, 'In between Seats—The participation of the European Union in international organisations' (2004) *European Foreign Affairs Review* 155–87; and F Hoffmeister, 'Outsider or Frontrunner? Recent Developments under International and European Law on the Status of the European Union in international organizations and treaty bodies' (2007) *CML Rev* 41–68.

[2] See the Bali Ministerial Declaration of 7 December 2013 and accompanying decisions, at https://mc9.wto.org/draft-bali-ministerial-declaration.

II. EU RULES

A. EU Powers

The EU has exclusive competence for the conduct of its common commercial policy (Article 3(1)(e) Treaty on the Functioning of the European Union (TFEU)). As has been described many times, the Member States widened the boundaries thereof in successive treaty changes from Amsterdam, through Nice,[3] to Lisbon.[4] This has direct consequences for WTO matters. Ruling on the basis of the Maastricht Treaty of 1993, the Court held in Opinion 1/94 that only trade in goods and Mode 1 of the General Agreement on Trade in Services (GATS) fell into the EU's exclusive competence, while the treaty-making power for the other GATS modes and the agreement on trade-related aspects of intellectual property rights (TRIPS) was shared.[5] Today, though, the situation is fundamentally different.

In the present version of Article 207(1) TFEU services and the commercial aspects of intellectual property are mentioned as well. Taking into account the will of the Member States to 'complete' the EU's powers in the field, the Court recently confirmed that the TRIPS agreement is now entirely covered by EU competence.[6] This finding applies also to the enforcement chapter of TRIPS. Hence, the idea that 'criminal enforcement of IPR' falls under Member State competence and must be therefore negotiated by the Presidency—as still practised with respect to the Agreement on Counterfeiting (ACTA)[7]—has become obsolete. The same is true for services. Doing away with the unreadable exceptions from Nice and Amsterdam, the Treaty nowadays confirms that all services belong to the common commercial policy, while some of them trigger unanimity in the Council. Again, the Court has clarified that the scope of this power may include enforcement provisions, as long as they are ancillary to the main provisions of an agreement.[8] Accordingly, the Council of Europe Convention on audio-visual services had to be concluded on the basis of Article 207 TFEU rather than Article 114 TFEU (internal market) even though one provision of that Convention on confiscatory measures was described by the Council as a 'criminal law' element allegedly falling outside the scope of Article 207 TFEU.[9] In sum, all covered WTO agreements fall today into

[3] See for a masterly overview of the evolution until 2001 P Eeckhout, 'Competence in matters of commercial policy', chapter 2 in *External Relations of the European Union, Legal and Constitutional Foundations* (Oxford, Oxford University Press, 2004) 9–57.

[4] For an analysis of the new Art 207 TFEU under the Treaty of Lisbon see M Bungenberg, 'The EU Common Commercial Policy after Lisbon' in C Herrmann and J Terhechte (eds) (2010) *European Yearbook of International Economic Law* 125–51.

[5] ECJ, *Opinion 1/94—WTO Agreements* [1994] ECR I-5267.

[6] ECJ, Case C-414/11, *Daiichi Sankyo Co Ltd* [2013] ECR nyr, paras 53–62.

[7] F Hoffmeister, 'The EU's common commercial policy a year after Lisbon—Sea change or business as usual?' in P Koutrakos (ed), *The European Union's external relations a year after Lisbon* (The Hague, Asser Press, CLEER Working Papers 2011/3) 83 et seq.

[8] ECJ, Case C-137/12 *Commission v Council* [2013] ECR, nyr, paras 70–72.

[9] ibid, para 81.

the EU's common commercial policy. For the goods side this relates to the GATT, the TBT Agreement, the SPS Agreement, the TRIMs Agreement, the three Trade Defence agreements (Anti-Dumping, Anti-Subsidy, Safeguards), the Agreement on Agriculture as well as a number of technical agreements (Pre-shipment Inspections, Rules of Origin, Import Licensing Procedures). It also covers the Plurilateral Agreements on Trade in Civil Aircraft and the Government Procurement Agreement, as recently confirmed by the Council decision accepting the revised GPA Agreement on the basis of Article 207(4) TFEU after consent of the European Parliament.[10] The post-Lisbon powers extend to both the GATS (services) and the TRIPS (commercial aspects of intellectual property).

Less clear is EU competence in institutional matters connected with the operation of the organisation. We can derive from the case law of the Court that dispute settlement is a necessary corollary of the substantive provisions and thus also falling under the exclusive EU competence.[11] Moreover, budgetary obligations flowing from WTO membership do not in themselves justify the participation of a Member State in the conclusion of a WTO treaty.[12] However, there is not yet any Luxembourg ruling on whether personnel matters, such as the nomination and appointment of Committee Chairs or even the Director-General of the WTO should be handled as an EU only, a shared or as a national matter.

B. EU Coordination

As explained in greater detail by Brauns and Baert,[13] EU coordination takes place on a weekly basis in the Trade Policy Committee (TPC) in Brussels and on the spot in Geneva. The Foreign Affairs Council may take up this function twice during a half-year Presidency. When there is a WTO Ministerial Conference, such as the one in Bali in 2013 referred to above, the Council usually meets on the spot as well in order to follow the developments on the ground and to update EU positions, where necessary.

In this regard, an important legal distinction must be made. On the one hand, when the EU is negotiating about new agreements or the modification of existing WTO agreements, the Council will issue negotiation directives under Article 218(3) TFEU to the Commission. Those define the broad EU objectives and leave the negotiator a certain margin of appreciation on how to best achieve them in view of the position of other WTO members. Thus, a formal update of such guidelines is only necessary when there are major shifts in the negotiations. Below that level the Council will issue guidance to the Commission through the ministerial

[10] Commission proposal for a Council Decision on the conclusion of the Protocol Amending the Agreement on Government Procurement, 22 March 2013, COM(2013) 143 final. The Parliament gave consent in November 2013 and the Council took the decision in December 2013.

[11] ECJ, *Opinion 1/1991, EEA-Agreement* [1991] ECR I-6079, para 40.

[12] ECJ, above, n 5, paras 19–21.

[13] See D Brauns and T Baert, Chapter 7, this volume.

interventions in the presence of the EU Trade Commissioner who would then take up what he considers to constitute the EU position. Of course, once an agreement is adopted in the WTO, the Council would *afterwards* have to take a formal decision on the signature (Article 218(5) TFEU) and—after the consent of the European Parliament—on the conclusion of the WTO agreement under Article 218(6) TFEU. On the other hand, when the WTO is adopting binding decisions, such as waivers or deciding about the accession of a new member, such decisions need to be prepared in the EU in a different way. Here, the Commission would propose a Council decision right away on the basis of Article 218(9) TFEU. Those Council decisions must be adopted *before* the EU can join the WTO consensus. The European Parliament plays no role for these types of WTO decisions, being only informed of the Council decision after the fact.

For all legally non-binding WTO decisions a formal Council position is not necessary. Rather, the Commission will define the EU position in consultation with the TPC, whose role is purely advisory.[14] After the entry into force of the Lisbon Treaty, the views expressed in the European Parliament's Committee on International Trade (INTA) are also taken increasingly into account to shape non-binding EU positions.

C. Presentation of EU Positions

In the area of trade, it is only the European Commission which represents the EU, according to Article 17(1) 6th sentence TEU. At the level of Heads of State this role falls to the Commission President and to the EU Trade Commissioner at the level of Ministers. The EU ambassador accredited to the WTO is (like all EU ambassadors) an official of the European External Action Service, but he receives his instructions from the Commission headquarters. Lacking any Common Foreign and Security Policy (CFSP) aspect, there is no room for the High Representative or the President of the Council. Accordingly, the 'general arrangement' of the Council of October 2011 on EU positions in the international organisations[15] is irrelevant for EU practice in the WTO.[16] Despite this clear constitutional situation some Member States still invoke a pre-Lisbon arrangement on services. They claim that in this field both the Commission and the Presidency should present the EU position. Such claim has no basis in the Treaty and it can be assumed that over time the Commission will act as sole representative in services negotiations also. In the

[14] ECJ, Case C-61/94 *Commission v Germany* [1996] ECR I-3989, para 14.

[15] Council of the European Union, 'EU Statements in multilateral organisations, General Arrangements, 24.10.2011', reprinted in PJ Kuijper, J Wouters, F Hoffmeister et al (eds), *The Law of EU External Relations: Cases, Materials and Commentary on the EU as an International Legal Actor* (Oxford, Oxford University Press, 2013) 47–48.

[16] 'Commission statement to the minutes of the Council session endorsing the General Arrangements', reprinted in Kuijper, Wouters, Hoffmeister et al (eds), above, n 15, 49.

current negotiations for a plurilateral agreement in Geneva, relevant practices are being revised. Moreover, the language of EU services offers is being changed. The new wording makes clear that the EU is the sole author of the offer, whereas its content may vary with respect to the territory of different Member States in areas where there is not yet any EU internal harmonisation.

Only where a WTO matter was not covered by EU competence but by national competence would the situation be legally different. In such instances, Member States can then choose whether they wish to express themselves individually or entrust the Presidency of the Council to speak on their behalf.

III. WTO RULES AND PRACTICE

A. Membership Rights and Obligations

Under Article XI(1) of the Marrakesh Agreement, the contracting parties to the GATT 1947 and the European Communities shall become original Members of the WTO. This means that both the current 28 EU Member States and the European Union itself are full WTO members. In contrast to many international conventions in the UN system to which the EU acceded together with its Member States, no declaration of competence[17] was made. Hence, under international law, the first presumption is that both the EU and all its Member States took the same rights and obligations irrespective of the fact whether a particular WTO matter falls into EU competence or not.[18] Lacking such a specification non-EU WTO Members cannot be expected to know precisely the demarcation line between EU and national competence.

At second sight, the situation is more complicated, though. Did the EU take any WTO obligation against any of its Member States? This is obviously not the case when it comes to customs tariffs, as the EU schedule clearly only applies in the relationship between the EU and non-EU WTO members. So, no Member State could ever invoke Article II GATT against the EU or vice versa. As arguably the same is true for the other substantive standards from the GATT, including Articles III and XI, one may argue that no WTO rights and obligations exist between the EU and its Member States, unless evidence to the contrary exists in special circumstances. That may be the case when a Member State has kept part of its territory 'out of the EU' by declaring the *acquis* non-applicable there. A prominent example is the Faroe Islands: they form part of Denmark, but are not subject to European law. In so far as it has been made clear in 1994 by Denmark that it has assumed rights and obligations vis-à-vis other WTO members also on behalf of the

[17] An example of such a declaration of competence can be found in the Council Decision 2010/48/EC of 26 November 2009 on the conclusion of the UN Disabilities Convention, OJ L 23, 27.1.2010, p 35, Annex II.

[18] PJ Kuijper, 'International Responsibility for EU Mixed Agreements' in C Hillion and P Koutrakos (eds), *Mixed Agreements Revisited* (Oxford, Hart Publishing, 2010) 208–27, at 210.

Faroe islands, it is not excluded that reciprocal rights and obligations also exist between the EU and the Faroe islands. This question would have come up in the *Herring* dispute,[19] but as the parties settled the case in August 2014 we will not dwell further on it.

When it comes to the relationship between the EU and non-EU WTO members one can also argue that membership rights and obligations need to be interpreted in light of the specific intra-EU arrangements. An important indicator in this direction is the voting rule enshrined in Article IX(1) 4th sentence of the Marrakesh Agreement. Under that provision the European Communities shall exercise their right to vote with a number of votes equal to the number of their Member States. Clearly, the idea behind this is that the EU votes in the realm of EU competence with the weight of currently 28 votes/Member States, but not with 29 votes. If, however, the EU and its Member States had taken the same rights and obligations vis-à-vis non-EU WTO members, it would have been logical to grant every Member also a vote. In other words, the voting rule carries the idea that the EU and its Member States act together as a sort of collective member. It is up to 'the Europeans' to decide when they act as the European Union (with 28 votes) or when they act as individual Member States (each with one vote). In principle, such a decision would then also clarify to non-WTO Members whether the EU or its Member States are competent on the particular WTO topic. Such practice could then serve as an ad hoc declaration of competence with important consequences in the WTO system. We can see examples thereof when turning to specific practical cases.

B. Accessions

The first interesting legal case is the accession of new WTO members. Under Article XII(2) of the Marrakesh Agreement, accessions should be decided by a two-thirds majority of Members in the General Council. But as long ago as 1995 it was agreed to apply consensus in this case too.[20] This also makes it easier for Europe to join the consensus as the difficult question of expressing and counting votes does not appear. Internally, the Council adopts an EU position under Article 218(9) TFEU to join the consensus, which the Commission expresses by sitting silently in the room when the President of the WTO Ministerial Meeting establishes that very consensus. Afterwards, the Commission would also congratulate the new Member on behalf of the EU, as did EU Trade Commissioner De Gucht in Bali with respect to Yemen. However, this is only half of the picture. Next to the EU the Member States also take part in WTO accession decisions. In Brussels, the representatives of

[19] Case DS469 *European Union—Measures on Atlanto-Scandian Herring* (complainant: Denmark).

[20] WTO General Council, Statement by the Chairman as agreed by the General Council on 15 November 1995, WTO doc WT/L/93 of 24 November 1995.

the governments usually take a decision of Member States 'meeting in the Council', adding to the formal EU act. Such a 'double decision' (whose necessity is contested by the Commission)[21] then serves as a background for additional national interventions in the WTO. So, after De Gucht's speech the Ministers of Lithuania, the United Kingdom and Germany also took the floor to basically repeat the same message with other words. The WTO secretariat is flexible enough to let this happen, hereby implicitly accepting that the EU (currently) treats WTO accession decisions as matters falling under the shared competence of the EU and its Member States.

C. Law Making

The EU actively takes part in law making at WTO level. Given that the Commission represents the Union over the entire spectrum of substantive WTO matters these days, its presence can even be described as helping the organisation in bringing about results. Rather than negotiating with 28 WTO members, one can rely on the fact that the Europeans have already agreed on an EU position. Hence, it is sufficient to clinch the deal with the Commission, saving time and resources. This mechanism can again be demonstrated with reference to recent practice. Legally, one should distinguish between the adoption of a new treaty and agreeing on treaty amendments.

i. New Treaties

Since its foundation the WTO was only able to negotiate one additional multinational treaty, namely the Trade Facilitation Agreement of Bali 2013. The Ministers supported a text which had been largely agreed by their Ambassadors in Geneva but finalised in Bali by the Secretary-General. Interestingly, the Members had empowered Mr Azevedo to come up with a final compromise text although that diminished the negotiating power of the 'big' members such as the United States, the EU, India and China. That new method worked as the Director-General aptly consulted with the entire membership before landing. Here again, the EU had internally agreed to support this innovative feature of WTO negotiations. At Bali, the EU Council of Ministers convened twice to follow relevant developments and gave feedback to the Commission on a few salient issues, such as the transit provision in the Agreement. Finally, this issue was also solved, as Article 11(3) 2nd sentence on the freedom of transit in the Trade Facilitation Agreement made clear that Members shall not seek, take or maintain any voluntary restraints

[21] For details see F Hoffmeister, 'Institutional Aspects of Global Trade Governance from an EU Perspective' in B Van Vooren, S Blockmans and J Wouters (eds), *The EU's role in Global Governance—The Legal Dimension* (Oxford, Oxford University Press, 2013) 145–61, 151–52.

'without prejudice to existing and future national regulations, bilateral or multilateral arrangements related to regulating transport consistent with WTO rules'. This was an important clarification for a number of EU Member States which currently operate transport quotas for Turkish vehicles in transit over EU territory.

Once legally rectified, the ministerial text will be adopted by the General Council and become a new Agreement in Annex 1A of the Marrakesh Agreement. On the EU side, the text will have to be ratified by the Council and the Parliament under Article 218(5) and (6)(a) TFEU. As trade facilitation falls under exclusive EU competence, no EU Member State may ratify the text on its own behalf. This means that only the EU will notify its formal acceptance to the Trade Facilitation Agreement to the WTO secretariat, making clear that all EU Member States are bound by EU law to comply with it (Article 216(2) TFEU).

While the EU internal procedures are pretty straightforward, the situation is less clear on the WTO side. Any new agreement needs the acceptance of two-thirds of its Members to enter into force under Article X(3) of the WTO Agreement. But how should one calculate this ratio precisely? The easiest way would be to wait for the acceptance of 107 out of 160 members, with the EU notification counting as one. Such approach overlooks, however, that 28 members (namely all EU Member States after the accession of Croatia) are prevented by EU law from notifying their own acceptance. Putting the bar at 107 out of 160 frustrates the objective of Article X(3) of the WTO agreement, namely to bring about the entry of force of an agreement if two-thirds of the competent Members support it. As argued above, all non-EU WTO Members were clearly already aware in 1994 that the EU had replaced the Member States on trade in goods. Accordingly, the special situation of substitution must also be taken into account when defining the entry into force of an agreement that squarely falls within this category.

A first idea could be to 'take out' the EU Member States from the equation altogether. The quorum would then become two-thirds of 132 'competent' Members, that is 88 out of 132, with the EU notification again counting as one. The drawback of this construction is that it touches directly upon the membership status of the EU Member States. One would have to run a fiction that the membership of the WTO differs depending on the substance of an agreement. That seems to be too far-reaching and unnecessary as a second idea can reconcile the dilemma in a more elegant way. Rather than 'subtracting' the EU Member States from one side of the equation one can 'add' them indirectly on the other side. As seen above, WTO members have already accepted that the 'vote' of the EU in an area of its competence carries the weight of the total number of its Member States under Article IX(1) 3rd sentence of the WTO agreement. This rule can be applied by analogy to a notification made under Article X(3) of the WTO agreement for any agreement that falls under EU-only competence: insofar as the EU makes it clear that its notification has the effect of binding all its Member States, it shall be counted as 28 notifications (out of 107 necessary ones).[22] This would respect the 'substitution effect' on the one hand, and keep the WTO membership figure of 160 stable for counting purposes.

ii. Treaty Amendments

A similar consideration can also be submitted when it comes to treaty amendments. The TRIPS amendment of 6 December 2005[23] equally needs the acceptance of two-thirds of WTO Members, and again the EU notified an EU-only acceptance. The WTO website currently contains a list of 49 instruments of acceptance, including the one from the EU.

A former counsel in the WTO secretariat argued that the EU's instrument shall not receive special treatment, counting as one acceptance as any other.[24] In my view, this does not take the special dimension of EU membership sufficiently into account. True, in the area of services in 2007 it was not obvious to the WTO membership whether ratification of the TRIPS amendment was an EU-only matter or would fall into the shared competence of both the EU and its Member States. However, the EU decided this issue internally and communicated the result to the entire WTO membership. The instrument of acceptance of November 2007[25] indicates the internal EU legal basis (at the time Article 133(5) EC) without any mention of a shared competence of Member States. Accordingly, the instrument made clear that EU ratification would not be complemented by any ratification of its Member States. Moreover, the EU instrument 'confirms, in accordance with Article 300(7) of the Treaty establishing the European Community that the Protocol will be binding on the Member States of the European Union'. This wording, in my view, is another indicator that the EU acceptance carries the weight of all its Member States. In analogy to Article IX(1) 3rd sentence of the WTO agreement, it thus needs to be counted as 27 (at the time Croatia was not yet a member), bringing the current number much closer to the required threshold of 107 out of 160 than the 49 instruments of acceptance listed in the WTO website seems to suggest.

Luckily, for plurilateral agreements, the counting rules for amendments are easier to define. Here, the parties to the amendment can simply take the decision themselves. For example, when the Government Procurement Agreement (GPA)

[22] Similarly U Wölker, 'Die Stellung der Europäischen Organisation in den Organen der Welthandelsorganisation' in W Obwexer (ed), *Die Europäische Union im Völkerrecht, Europarecht, Beiheft 2* (Baden-Baden, Nomos, 2012) 125–36, 128, arguing for a weight of an EU notification of 27. The article was written when the EU comprised 27 Member States.

[23] Decision of the General Council of 6 December 2005, WTO/L/641 of 8 December and the Protocol hereto, introducing a new Art 31bis to the TRIPS agreement.

[24] M Kennedy, 'When will the Protocol Amending the TRIPS Agreement Enter into Force?' (2010) *Journal of International Economic Law* 459–73, 468.

[25] www.wto.org/english/tratop_e/trips_e/amendment_e.htm.

was amended under its Article XXIV(7), the relevant decision of 30 March 2012[26] stipulates in section 2 that:

> the Protocol shall enter into force for those Parties to the 1994 Agreement that have deposited their respective instruments of acceptance thereof, on the 30th day following such deposit by two thirds of the Parties to the 1994 Agreement.

As only the EU had become a Party to the GPA in 1994 on the European side, there was no confusion on the relevant numbers. This time, the EU would only count as one entity on both sides of the equation. Accordingly, Ministers at Bali could greet the EU acceptance done on the day of the meeting as progress, bringing the number closer to the required 10 out of 15. However, as lawyers do not rule protocol, a number of Ministers from EU Member States still put themselves into the Bali photo.[27] The WTO website thus counts 31 Ministers (or their representatives) celebrating progress on GPA revision although there are only 15 parties to the amendment. But since photos do not change the legal analysis either, the amendment entered into force on 16 April 2014 with only three additional instruments of acceptance from Iceland, Singapore and Israel.

D. Dispute Settlement

For the WTO, the dispute settlement pillar constitutes an important asset of the organisation. Widely held as speedy and efficient when compared to other branches of international law, bringing cases in the WTO against another Member has become a routine matter. Standing currently at over 400 disputes since 1994 the question can be asked how the double membership of the EU and its Member States affected this pillar. Has it led to additional complications to identify the right complainant or defendant before a Panel or the Appellate Body? Leaving aside the interesting questions of general international law on liability in WTO case law involving the EU,[28] we can roughly summarise the situation[29] as follows.

i. Offensive Cases

In offensive cases, it is only the EU which becomes active against other WTO Members.[30] Never has a Member State sought to start a case itself, probably for

[26] Decision of the Committee on Government Procurement on Adoption of the text of the 'Protocol amending the Government Procurement Agreement', 30.3.2012, GPA/113, p 5.

[27] www.wto.org/english/news_e/news13_e/gpro_04dec13_e.htm.

[28] On this aspect see F Hoffmeister, 'Litigating against the European Union and its Member States—Who responds under the ILC's Draft Articles on International Responsibility of International Organisations?' (2010) *European Journal of International Law* 723–47, 730–38.

[29] For a detailed analysis see T Cottier, 'Dispute Settlement in the World Trade Organization: Characteristics and Structural Implications for the European Union' (1998) *CML Rev* 325–78.

[30] For details see S Billiet, 'The EC and WTO Dispute Settlement: The initiation of trade disputes by the EC' (2005) *European Foreign Affairs Review* 197–214.

two reasons. First, most of the cases relate to trade in goods, where a Member State is plainly not competent. But second, even where shared competence existed, a Member State hesitated to go alone. Putting the expertise of the Commission and the weight of the entire Union behind a case is obviously more prone to success than being perceived as having an isolated problem with another WTO member. It would thus make more sense to activate the Commission to bring a case in the name of the EU.

And indeed, for bringing an EU case there is a long-standing Brussels practice that the Commission discusses potential WTO cases informally with the Council (and, since 2009 the Parliament). However, neither institution has a formal say on the Commission decision to start a case which is adopted under Article 17(1) TEU. Hence, ideas that starting a WTO case would necessitate the formal agreement of the European Parliament[31] are neither founded in law nor supported in practice. Rather, as at national level, starting an international dispute remains with the foreign policy powers of the executive.

For won cases the EU has the right to retaliate if compliance is not ensured within a reasonable time. In that scenario, it must decide internally in which sector and how precisely to formulate the trade sanction. In the past, this was done by ad hoc legislation of the Council. However, after Lisbon, trade legislation also falls under ordinary legislative procedure. That may prove at times too cumbersome to take quick action. Thus, the Commission proposed receiving the power of adopting delegated acts in the field.[32] After intensive discussions with Council and Parliament, the final compromise was reached in a trilogue at the end of January 2014. This new legislation entered into force in June 2014.[33]

ii. Defensive Cases

In defensive cases, the other WTO members and the Panels may have a different approach. As is widely documented, in the beginning the United States brought a number of cases against EU Member States alone.[34] Today, sometimes cases are

[31] A Serdarevic, *The European Union as a Collective Actor in the World Trade Organization* (London, Cameron and May, 2013), 287.

[32] Commission Proposal of 18 December 2012 for a Regulation of the European Parliament and the Council concerning the exercise of the Union's rights for the application and enforcement of international trade rules, COM (2012) 773 final.

[33] Regulation (EU) No 654/2014 of the European Parliament and the Council concerning the exercise of the Union's rights for the application and enforcement of international trade rules, and amending Council Regulation (EC) No 3286/94 laying down Community procedures in the field of the common commercial policy in order to ensure the exercise of the Community's rights under international trade rules, in particular those established under the auspices of the World Trade Organisation, OJ L 189, 27.6.2014, p 50.

[34] Portugal, Patent Protection under the Industrial Property Act, WT/DS37; Belgium, Measures Affecting Commercial Telephone Directory Services, WT/DS80; Ireland—Measures Affecting the Grant of Copyright and Neighbouring Rights, WT/DS82; Greece—Enforcement of Intellectual Property Rights for Motion Pictures and Television Programs, WT/DS 124.

still levelled against the EU and a few Member States together.[35] But again, the logic of working together to defend better, prevailed in all these cases. In the early cases relating to intellectual property rights, the Commission assumed the defence although the subject matter fell into shared competence of the Community and the Member States. These cases were generally settled. In other cases, the EU did not shy away from its responsibility[36] and Panels did not attach great weight to the fact that certain Member States were also assigned to justice. The rulings are generally directed against the EU, and only the Commission replied both in writing and at the pleadings. While the title of some cases remained 'EU and certain Member States', the practical effect thereof was close to nil. Hence, also in defensive cases the overall practice today is that only the EU acts before the dispute settlement bodies.

In contrast to the offensive scenario, the EU is, however, not equipped with specific horizontal legislation ensuring correct implementation. Rather, there is only a partial internal legal basis in Regulation 1515/2001 when the Union loses a trade defence case before the WTO.[37] In that scenario, the Commission can quickly amend or repeal the disputed measure in accordance with the examination procedure. In all other cases, the EU institutions have to decide how to bring about compliance. This has led to a somewhat mitigated implementation record, in particular when cases touched on fundamental societal choices.[38] Moreover, the EU carries an open flank when it has assumed responsibility for certain action which is basically decided at Member State level. If the Member State does not comply with the WTO decision, it risks triggering liability for the entire Union. However, the Commission does not have any leverage over the Member State (or even companies) to deliver. Here, infringement procedures remain the only tool, which are in themselves cumbersome and not prone to prevent retaliation against the EU quickly.

E. Institutional Issues

As reported above, the scope of EU competence on institutional matters within the WTO is not yet clarified. So let us have a brief look at practice in this field.

[35] European Union and a Member State—Seizure of Generic Drugs in Transit, WT/DS 409 (settled in 2012); European Communities and Certain Member States, Measures Affecting Trade in Large Civil Aircraft, WT/DS 316 (in compliance phase).

[36] F Hoffmeister and P Ondrusek, 'The European Community in International Litigation' (2008) *Revue Hellénique de droit international* 205–24, 221.

[37] Council Regulation No 1515/2001 of 23 July 2001 on the measures that may be taken by the Community following a report adopted by the WTO Dispute Settlement Body concerning anti-dumping and anti-subsidy matters, OJ L201, 26.7.2001, p 10, codified by Regulation (EU) 2015/476 of the European Parliament and the Council, OJ L 83, 27.3.2015, p 6.

[38] See PJ Kuijper and F Hoffmeister, 'WTO Influence on EU Law: Too Close for Comfort?' in RA Wessel and S Blockmans (eds), *Between Autonomy and Dependence, The EU Legal Order Under the Influence of International Organisations* (Berlin, Springer, 2013) 131–58, 148–53 discussing the EU implementation record in the Banana, Biotech and Airbus cases.

i. Budgetary Matters

Taking account of the fact that real budget contributions to the WTO stem from each Member State, whereas the EU pays a lump sum to cover the administrative costs of its presence only, Member States are naturally called upon to look after their contributions. Accordingly, they sit in the budgetary committee and have a say on the contribution key and the structure of the budget. The EU Delegation is present and may take the floor as well, but the level of EU coordination in this body is regretfully low.[39]

ii. Personnel Matters

A real grey zone is personnel matters. In Geneva, this is regarded as another 'Member State turf'. For example, the Council on Services is currently chaired by the Swedish Ambassador, and we have already reported that the British Trade Minister Lord Green was appointed co-chair of the Bali conference. Also in other areas of the WTO we currently find personnel hailing from a Member State. The Appellate Body member van den Bossche comes from Belgium, and the recently appointed Deputy-Director General of the WTO, Mr Brauner, has been the German TPC member before. However, that does not mean that EU Commission officials are excluded from getting an interesting position in the WTO. For example, the first European Appellate Body member, Claus-Dieter Ehlermann, had been senior official in the Commission before his appointment, and there are two cases where EU Commission officials have been appointed to serve as a panellist. However, the current indicative list for panellists contains only four officials from the EU in an entry of over 60 names from the Member States.[40] Whether or not one may find EU personnel in the WTO does not therefore depend on the legal rules in place (they are eligible), but seem to reflect more the interest of qualified Commission officials to apply for such jobs and the policy of the institution to support such applications or not.

A related matter is EU coordination in the selection of high WTO posts. The most recent case in point was the election of the successor of Pascal Lamy as Director-General. The rules on the WTO side were clear: the Chair of the General Council, the Pakistani Ambassador, was entrusted to sound members out, which of the nine original candidates would muster sufficient support in the end. In this endeavour, he had to put aside five candidates first and then reduce the list to two candidates who would compete against each other. On the EU side, the Commission took the initiative to bring about EU coordination. In the first round, there was a large convergence on whom to support among the last four competitors. In this respect, some 'extra' wishes, such as supporting a female candidate or a candidate from Africa, were so clearly in the minority that the EU position was beyond doubt. Narrowing the candidates down to two names was already more

[39] U Wölker, above, n 21, 131.

[40] Indicative List of Governmental and Non-Governmental Panellists, WT/DSB/44/Rev 23 of 10 April 2013.

difficult, but again a clear majority supported the two remaining Latin American candidates (Blanco from Mexico and Azevedo from Brazil). The final choice, however, proved to be very tight. Only after a repeated round of voting at TPC level was the Commission able to discern the EU position. As in all previous rounds, the EU ambassador in Geneva was then tasked to submit the EU's choice to the Pakistani Ambassador.

From a legal point of view, the extent of the EU's coordination was remarkable. Clearly, proponents of the theory that personnel matters fall entirely into Member State competence cannot explain why EU institutions were central to identifying and submitting a common position. Moreover, the coordination process did not fall under the CFSP mechanism for adopting EU positions in international organisations. In none of the rounds was the EEAS present, nor did the High Representative for CFSP act as the spokesman. Rather, both internal co-ordination in TPC and external representation (through the EU's Ambassador in Geneva who receives his instructions from the Commissioner for Trade) followed the familiar pattern of trade policy. While praising this remarkable discipline, one should nevertheless not assume that this Brussels-based process was a result of legal reasoning. Rather, there was a silent agreement between the Commission and the Council to leave competence battles aside and concentrate on the functional necessity to remain united. After all, 28 identical votes of the EU are more influential than the scattered behaviour of the Member States which could be traced back in the pre-Lamy elections between Suchapai and Moore in 2002 (leading to a split of three years each for both candidates). This powerful driver of doing better than last time was probably decisive in bringing about a common EU position in this highly sensitive matter.

IV. ASSESSMENT

What does the present position of the European Union in the WTO tell us for the general theme of this volume, namely the functioning of the EU in international organisations? For a short analytical assessment, it seems useful to distinguish between three issues. First, are there impediments at the level of the WTO which prevent the EU from performing as well as it would like to? Second, we shall inquire whether EU action in the WTO may be hampered from the inside. Are Member States raising unnecessary obstacles in order to keep policy space for themselves? Third, could there be a lack of ambition in the EU institutions shying away from tackling problems with either the WTO or the Member States?

A. The WTO Framework

The full membership of the EU next to its Member States is certainly the best status that the EU can enjoy in an international organisation. When compared to the

Food and Agriculture Organization (FAO),[41] this status is not qualified by a declaration of competence. This has its good and bad sides. On the one hand, there is the freedom that the EU enjoys when taking the floor. Nobody is asking for a clear division of the speaking time between the EU representative and Member States. Hence, time-consuming and sometimes nerve-racking competence discussions to divide the agenda are spared. On the other hand, the lack of a clear statement that only the EU is competent for a certain subject matter may create complications as to the 'substitution effect'. As demonstrated above, that may lead to unwarranted results, such as counting an EU instrument of acceptance for a modified WTO agreement (as for the TRIPS amendment and in the future for the Trade Facilitation Agreement) in an area of EU competence as only one instead of 28. However, even that problem can be resolved via an application of the voting role under Article IX(1) 3rd sentence of the WTO agreement. Whether or not the WTO secretariat is willing to go down that road is still out. In the big order of things, that is, however, a minor issue. The EU has not experienced any difficulty from the WTO framework when it comes to dispute settlement, budgetary or personnel matters. Rather, it seems that the necessary flexibility is given to all European actors to make the EU's contribution to the organisation as beneficial as possible.

B. The Conduct of Member States

In some international organisations Member States may be tempted to keep their status alive to the detriment of the EU. A famous example is the International Maritime Organization, where the Council has refused to allow the Commission to negotiate EU membership. The absence of a formal EU status is then, in turn, used as a means to justify continuing national action even in areas where the EU has legislated internally. Upon application of the Commission the Court has not accepted such conduct, stressing that the Member States are under a duty of loyal cooperation even where the EU is not a formal member of the organisation in question.[42]

In the WTO, the conduct of Member States is much more disciplined and loyal in general. Attempts to jeopardise the speaking right of the Commission are relict of the past. The only remaining bone of contention is that the pre-Lisbon informal arrangement on representation in services between the Council and the Commission has not been revoked so far. Four years after the entry into force of the Lisbon Treaty that cannot be seen as a transitional issue any more. Rather, it points to the political attempt of the coalition Government in London to deny EU external competence where possible. Luckily, this attitude has not spread over to the established WTO working arrangements. Thus, keeping the pre-Lisbon services arrangement nominally in place is less damaging than it may seem, and anyway the entire issue may be revisited over time.

[41] JM Pedersen, 'FAO–EU cooperation—an ever stronger partnership' in J Wouters, F Hoffmeister and T Ruys (eds), *The EU and the UN—an ever closer partnership* (The Hague, Asser, 2007) 63–92.

[42] ECJ, Case C-45/07 *European Commission v Greece* [2009] ECR I-701, paras 14–38.

A potentially more dangerous conflict exists, though, with respect to the competence on accession decisions. So far, there was always unanimity in the Council to support a new WTO State once it had concluded a bilateral deal with the EU beforehand. Hence, a 'parallel' decision of Member States serves only as a legal disclaimer against EU-only competence. However, it may not be excluded that one day a controversy within the Council may arise with respect to a potential new WTO member, such as Iran or Palestine. Here, the insistence on a double decision necessarily triggers the veto right of every Member State, whereas voting in the Council on an EU position under Article 218(9) TFEU may be done by qualified majority if none of the sensitive issues are touched upon that lead to unanimity in trade policy. In this scenario, the position of the Member States on accession decisions may become politically and legally more controversial than it is today.

In return, the successful coordination to find an EU position on the selection of the new Director-General can also be read as an encouraging sign. Apparently, in this matter, considerations of political efficiency trumped legal doubts on competence that one or the other Member State may have had. Together with the good EU performance at the 9th Ministerial Meeting in Bali, one can thus remain optimistic that the conduct of Member States is generally supportive and conducive for effective EU action in the WTO.

C. The Ambition of the EU Institutions

This brings us finally to the ambition of the EU institutions. In some areas, the Commission and/or the EEAS are not very active in striving for further EU action in a given international organisation. One may cite the absence of a Commission proposal for a unified external representation of the Euro-area or the hesitation to submit a recommendation for full OECD membership.

Nothing similar can be said on the Commission's ambitions in the WTO, though. The Commission has been assertive to defend its role as sole EU representative in the WTO. One can even argue that Trade Commissioner De Gucht went a step ahead by bringing about an EU position on the selection of the WTO Secretary-General. Moreover, the Commission is present in all major WTO initiatives—next to playing its part on the successful Bali package, it has backed the plurilateral negotiations on services and contributed to the launch of a similar initiative for green goods in January 2014 in Davos. It can thus be said that the Commission plays a regular and important role in making the EU voice in the WTO heard.

V. CONCLUSION

The present overview has shown that the EU can and does work well in the WTO. Is it thus possible to conclude that the EU's status in the WTO may serve as a model for other international organisations?

In my view, the answer is generally affirmative: yes, there is simply no better model in sight! Nevertheless, a few qualifications are warranted as well. The WTO model has evolved with success because of a number of factors which need to be checked before transposing it to other international organisations.

Among those are evidently the scope and nature of EU competence involved: as the bunch of WTO matters was already covered by EU exclusive competence in 1995, there was a strong basis for giving the EU the necessary status within the organisation as a full member. Anything falling short of membership status would have actually hampered the organisation itself as the EU Member States have lost competence to act in a meaningful way in Geneva on the classical tariff negotiations for goods. Thus, a first prerequisite seems to be that a large part of the organisation's task nowadays falls under exclusive EU competence. That can have happened through treaty norms (as in trade and maritime policy) or through extensive internal legislation (as in numerous fields of the internal market).

Beyond this important legal point, a second qualification relates to the politics involved. The EU may only hope to get a similarly strong status in another organisation if it can promise some improvements for the organisation itself. Having the EU as a full member may be positive in budgetary terms or result in less speaking time for—repetitive—interventions from several EU Member States. This benefit must also be seen by the EU Member States themselves. Clearly, the representatives who are actually representing the Member State in question would not readily give up their present role. But, horizontal or strategic considerations in the capitals may well lead to the conclusion that costly national representations at a great many international organisations can be spared if an effective EU representation takes their place. That, in turn, would speak in favour of asking for full EU membership of the organisation.

This last issue also points to the resources of the EU itself. Striving for full membership status in an international organisation would only be credible if the EU institutions can basically take over the work. In times of financial constraints and reorganisation of the European External Action Service this is not evident. Even in the Commission, the appetite to dedicate more personnel to multilateral business cannot be taken for granted. In conclusion, prudence counsels to regard the EU's status in the WTO as a good model in theory, which, however, may remain exceptional in practice for still quite some time before it can be transposed to other international organisations.

Part IV

The European Union in the World Health Organization

10

Coordination Between the European Union and the Member States: An EU Perspective

LOURDES CHAMORRO*

I. THE EUROPEAN UNION'S TREATY FRAMEWORK ON HEALTH

THE TREATY ON the Functioning of the European Union[1] (TFEU), in Articles 9 and 168, stipulates that a high level of human health protection shall be ensured in the definition and implementation of all the European Union's (EU's) policies and activities. The Charter of the Fundamental Rights of the European Union[2] further stipulates in Article 35 that 'Everyone has the right of access to preventive healthcare and the right to benefit from medical treatment under the conditions established by national law and practices'.

The TFEU states that EU action, which shall complement national policies, shall be directed towards improving public health, preventing physical and mental illness and diseases, and obviating sources of danger to physical and mental health. Such action shall cover the fight against the major health scourges, by promoting research into their causes, their transmission and their prevention, as well as health information and education, and monitoring, early warning of and combating serious cross-border threats to health.

When it comes to the division of competences, Article 6 TFEU stipulates that the EU shall have competence to carry out actions to support, coordinate or supplement the actions of the Member States in the area of protection and improvement of human health, among others. However, according to Article 4 TFEU, common safety concerns in public health matters are an area where competence is shared between the EU and the Member States. In light of this

* The views expressed are personal and do not reflect the views of the European institutions or its actors.

[1] Consolidated Version of the Treaty on the Functioning of the European Union, 2008 OJ C 115/47.

[2] Charter of Fundamental Rights of the European Union, 2010 OJ C 83/02.

framework of division of competences, Article 168 TFEU sets out the different types of measures that the EU can adopt:

— measures setting high standards of quality and safety for organs and substances of human origin, blood and blood derivatives, medicinal products and devices for medical use and also measures in the veterinary and phytosanitary fields;
— incentive measures in other matters pertaining to the protection and improvement of human health, that is, for combating major cross-border health scourges, monitoring, early warning of and combating serious threats to health as well as measures which have as their direct objective the protection of public health regarding tobacco and the abuse of alcohol;
— finally, the EU can encourage and support cooperation between the Member States in the area of public health through the so-called 'open method of coordination'.

EU legislation in this field is enacted by the Council and the European Parliament in accordance with the ordinary legislative procedure (as defined by Article 294 TFEU). The Council may also adopt recommendations on a Commission proposal on the basis of a qualified majority.

Finally, the TFEU acknowledges that the Member States remain responsible for the definition of their health policy and the organisation and delivery of health services and medical care, including the management of health services and medical care and the allocation of resources assigned to them.

On an international scale, Article 168 states, inter alia, that the EU and the Member States shall foster cooperation with third countries and competent international organisations in the sphere of public health.

Apart from the specific references to health in the EU Treaties, other areas are also indirectly linked to public health, such as the free movement of goods (restrictions based on the protection of health and life of humans, animals or plants), the internal market (legislation on tobacco products or tobacco advertising), the environment, agriculture, taxation, development, transport, etc), as they fall within the mandate to ensure a high level of human health protection in the definition and implementation of all EU policies and activities.

II. THE EUROPEAN UNION'S ROLE IN GLOBAL HEALTH

The Treaty of the European Union[3] (TEU) outlines the common values of the EU such as combating social exclusion and discrimination, promoting social justice and protection, fostering equality between women and men, etc and avers that, in its relations with the wider world, the EU shall uphold and promote those values. Furthermore, the EU has agreed on shared solidarity-based values as part of its

[3] Consolidated Version of the Treaty on European Union, 2010 OJ C 83/01.

efforts to achieve equitable and universal coverage of quality health care.[4] And, as mentioned above, Article 168 of the TEU gives a specific mandate to the EU and the Member States to foster cooperation with third countries and the competent international organisations in the sphere of public health.

In addition, Article 21 TEU states, inter alia, that the EU 'shall ensure consistency between the different areas of its external action and between these and its other policies'. Addressing global health issues requires coherence between all the internal and external policies and actions based on agreed principles. This becomes particularly relevant when we consider the extent to which multi-sectoral efforts are needed to tackle the variety of social, economic and environmental determinants of health. The EU systematically endorses the 'Equity and Health in All Policies' approach.[5]

In May 2010, the Council of the European Union adopted its conclusions on the EU role in Global Health[6] (hereafter referred to as the Conclusions) recognising the need to take action to improve health, reduce inequalities and increase protection against global health threats. The Conclusions stress that health is central in people's lives, including as a human right; and a key element for equitable and sustainable growth and development, including poverty reduction.

The Council gives the EU the political mandate to play a central role in accelerating progress on global health challenges, including the health-related Millennium Development Goals and non-communicable diseases, through its commitment to protect and promote the right of everyone to enjoy the highest attainable standard of physical and mental health. The common agreed values of solidarity towards equitable and universal coverage of quality health services serve as a basis for the EU policies in this area.

The plethora of actors and initiatives engaged in global health and the continuing need to mobilise resources call for a clearer and more efficient global leadership. The objective of the Council is to take advantage of the tools provided by the Lisbon Treaty[7] in order to see the role of the EU in the World Health Organization (WHO) included as part of broader considerations of its role in the United Nations (UN). On a global level, the Conclusions seek for the EU to endeavour to defend a single position within the UN agencies. The EU should strive to curtail duplication and fragmentation and to increase coordination and effectiveness within the UN system.

The Council calls on EU Member States and the Commission to support an increased leadership of the WHO at global, regional and country level, in its normative and guidance functions addressing global health challenges as well as in

[4] Council Conclusions on Common values and principles in European Union Health Systems, 2006/C 146/01.

[5] Council Conclusions on Health in All Policies (HiAP) of 30 November 2006 and Council conclusions on Equity and Health in All Policies: Solidarity in Health of 8 June 2010, among others.

[6] Council conclusions on the EU role in Global Health of 10 May 2010.

[7] The Treaty of Lisbon, see above, n 3.

technical support to health systems governance and health policy, given its global mandate. Accordingly, the Council requests Member States to gradually move away from earmarked WHO funding towards funding its general budget.

III. COOPERATION BETWEEN THE EUROPEAN COMMISSION AND THE WHO

The WHO has been the directing and coordinating specialised agency for health within the United Nations system since 1948, the year in which the World Health Assembly approved its Constitution.[8] There are currently 194 member countries of the WHO. It is organised into three different levels: the headquarters in Geneva, six highly autonomous regional offices, and 150 country offices around the world. The WHO's governing bodies are the Health Assembly, where the full membership meets yearly in May, and the Executive Board, which is composed of 34 Members elected for three-year terms coming from the different WHO regions. The Executive Board meets at least twice a year and its main functions are to give effect to the decisions and policies of the Health Assembly, to advise it and generally to facilitate its work.

The WHO is responsible for providing leadership on global health matters, shaping the health research agenda, setting norms and standards, articulating evidence-based policy options, providing technical support to countries, and monitoring and assessing health trends. The WHO's objective, as referred in its Constitution,[9] is 'the attainment by all peoples of the highest possible level of health'. As is often the case in the UN system, the EU shares common values and principles with the WHO and as such, there is a great deal of common ground for mutual collaboration that could be easily identified by both entities.

The EU is an increasingly important actor in global and international affairs beyond Europe and a strong supporter of the UN system, particularly with regard to global security, development and humanitarian assistance. This includes significant support for health and for the WHO's work both globally and within Europe. The European Commission has long-standing bilateral relations with the WHO. Cooperation between the European Commission (the former European Communities) and the WHO dates back to the exchange of letters between the two organisations in 1982. At that time both organisations underlined the importance of effective coordination on matters of common interest. With this objective in mind, they committed to encourage and facilitate reciprocal participation in their meetings and exchange pertinent information and documentation. Some years later, and due to changes in the WHO and in the EU, a revised framework governing cooperation was established through a new exchange of letters in 2000.

[8] Consolidated Version of the Constitution of the World Health Organization, New York, 22 February 1946.

[9] Art 1, WHO Constitution, see above, n 8.

The Memorandum[10] attached to that exchange of letters addressed the principles, objectives, areas of cooperation, priorities and procedures for the conduct of their activities. It identified a number of priority areas—including health information, communicable diseases, tobacco control, environment and health, sustainable health development, health research—and outlined practical procedures for cooperation. It embraced the global dimension of the cooperation, as well as the benefits that an enhanced, focused and coherent EU–WHO cooperation would bring for the common WHO–EU Member States.

Since then, on a political level, regular high-level meetings take place between the EU Health Commissioner and the WHO Director General as well as Senior Official Meetings (SOMs), where high-level and senior officials from the two organisations meet periodically to discuss health and joint cooperation issues. On the Commission side, the SOMs are usually attended by the Directorates-General Health and Consumers, Development Cooperation, Research, Humanitarian Aid and Information Society. The European External Action Service (EEAS) also participates as well as the European Centre for Disease Prevention and Control (ECDC). From the WHO side, the participants usually include the WHO Director General, the Directors of the WHO European and African Regions and the WHO Pan-American Health Organization as well as senior managers and representatives of other regions.

On a regional level, the Commission also maintains working relations with the WHO European regional office in Copenhagen. This collaboration has been in place for many years and it has addressed a number of areas. In this regard, it is worth mentioning the Moscow Declaration[11] that the WHO European office and the Commission agreed to in 2010. It seeks to strengthen the policy dialogue and the technical cooperation on public health between the two parties. It outlines a five-year framework and envisages the development of joint systems for health surveillance, alert and information, and stronger collaboration at country level. The Moscow Declaration aims at achieving a cohesive effort to improve health security and join forces to help improve public health surveillance and strengthen alert and response systems to allow quicker and more efficient responses to disease outbreaks and pandemics, and to tackle existing challenges across the 53 countries in the WHO European Region.

In addition to collaboration, the Commission is also a donor to the WHO. The WHO budget is comprised of assessed contributions from WHO Member States[12] and of voluntary contributions from WHO Member States and third parties, which may or may not be earmarked for specific tasks or projects. The EU and its

[10] Exchange of Letters between the WHO and the Commission of the EC concerning the consolidation and intensification of cooperation and Memorandum concerning the framework and arrangements for cooperation between the WHO and the Commission of the EC, OJ C 1, 4/1/2001.

[11] Joint Declaration of the WHO Regional Office for Europe and European Commission seeking to strengthen policy dialogue and technical cooperation on public health, Moscow, 13 September 2010.

[12] The assessed contributions to the WHO are a type of 'membership fee' based on the latest available United Nations scale of assessments.

Member States, individually and collectively, account for about one third of the total WHO annual income. Most of this financing comes under the category of voluntary contributions. The collective contribution administered by the European Commission on behalf of the EU is not negligible. At about €100 million per biennium, averaged over the last 10 years, the EU ranks high among the major non-state voluntary contributors to the WHO.

As a contributor, the European Commission systematically aims to support the priorities common to both the EU and to the WHO. Some of the main examples are the EC–ACP–WHO Partnership on Pharmaceutical Policies, the EU–WHO Universal Health Coverage Partnership Programme, projects on improving access to medicines and effective health services through innovation and technology transfer, and the major contributions to the humanitarian activities of the WHO. It is also worth mentioning that the EU budget is public and is managed and executed under strict financial rules which only allow for earmarked funds and this often poses some additional administrative challenges. These modalities are based on the Financial and Administrative Framework Agreement that the Commission concluded with the UN system and which is applied across the UN system.

IV. THE EU AND ITS MEMBER STATES' PARTICIPATION IN THE WHO

The EU is not a member of the WHO, yet it holds an observer status in the organisation. According to Article 3 of the WHO Constitution,[13] membership of the organisation is open to all States. That means that only 'States' (and not other types of entities) are and can become members of the WHO. So even though the EU, as a Regional Economic Integration Organisation (REIO), is composed of several sovereign states which have transferred competence over a range of matters to it, including the authority to conclude binding decisions, the EU could still not apply for membership without modifying the requirement set out in the WHO Constitution.

In contrast, the 28 EU Member States are members of WHO (14 per cent of the overall membership), and all of them are part of the WHO EURO region, which is composed of a total of 53 states. Therefore, the EU Member States represent 53 per cent of the membership of the WHO EURO Region.

The WHO Rules of Procedure[14] establish the rights and duties that observers hold within the organisation. Plenary meetings of the Health Assembly are, by default, open to attendance by observer intergovernmental and non-governmental organisations admitted into relationship with the WHO. In addition, on the basis of the exchange of letters in 2000, the EU Delegation to the Health Assembly or to the Executive Board sessions is invited, after prior ad hoc request at the beginning of each Governing Body meeting, to attend and participate (without a vote) in the

[13] See above, n 8.

[14] Arts 19 and 45, Consolidated Version of the WHO Rules of Procedure, adopted by the Eighth World Health Assembly, Res WHA8.26 and WHA8.27.

deliberations of the meetings of sub-committees or other such subdivisions. This invitation significantly facilitates the coordination towards defining EU common positions.

The EU and its Member States attach great importance to the WHO and to its on-going processes: the overall contributions of the EU Member States and the Commission represent one third of the income of the WHO, and the EU and the Member States devote a significant amount of resources, both in their respective capitals and in Geneva, to this specific topic.

The vast majority of EU Member States' Permanent Missions in Geneva follow the WHO processes, with varying degrees of intensity, either through a diplomat from the foreign affairs services, through a representative from the relevant national health services, or sometimes through two representatives coming from both services. In some cases, the representatives focus exclusively on health processes, while in other cases they are responsible for liaising with different organisations based in Geneva.

Additionally, there is often another representative who follows humanitarian activities, including those spearheaded by the WHO in its role as Global Health Cluster leader in the event of a humanitarian crisis, under the auspices of the UN Office for the Coordination of Humanitarian Affairs (OCHA). The Global Health Cluster aims to strengthen system-wide humanitarian preparedness by ensuring sufficient capacity in information management; surge; normative guidance and tools; development of the capacities of national stakeholders; as well as advocacy and resource mobilisation. Over 30 partners are working together in the Global Health Cluster, under the leadership of the WHO. This is a particularly relevant area for the EU and its Member States as collectively they are the most important donor in this field.

Within the EU Delegation in Geneva, there are currently two professionals dedicated to working full-time on health issues, namely the on-going processes in the WHO. Their role is mainly focused on the relations between the Commission/EEAS and the WHO, on the coordination of the EU and its Member States' common positions, on outreach to third countries and parties, and on the representation of the EU when the rules of procedure allow for it.

Without prejudice to the division of competences, the EU and its Member States currently tend to coordinate in order to reach common positions on many of the priority issues discussed in the WHO, both at headquarters in Geneva and at regional level. As we will see later, such positions can then be expressed differently depending on the specific settings and processes.

In addition, and usually only for the sessions of the WHO's governing bodies, a number of countries in special relations with the EU (currently the 14 potential or official candidate countries) are invited to align themselves on an ad hoc basis with the EU and its Member States' agreed positions, expressed in the form of statements during the meetings. This alignment procedure could potentially bring together a total of 42 countries around one common position coordinated by the EU (28 EU Member States plus, currently, the 14 additional countries) representing altogether more than 20 per cent of the WHO membership. Also, in this connection, it is worth highlighting the role that the EU plays, or more accurately, could potentially play, within the 53 countries of the WHO EURO region, considering that 28 EU Members, with the possible additional 14 countries, can act on the basis of a common coordinated position. While such wide representation puts the EU and its Member States in a prominent position, it is worth considering the decision-making dynamics currently in place in the WHO. Unlike other organisations within the UN system, decision-making in the WHO is systematically based on consensus. Voting methods are usually not used (except for the resolution on the health conditions in the occupied Palestinian territory and for the election of the Director General at headquarters level) and, moreover, are considered undesirable and are actively avoided by the WHO's membership. This means that, although it may have a greater influence in decision-making processes, the major advantage of the wide EU representation stems more from its increased capacity for intelligence gathering and outreach to third countries than on its actual majority within the membership. This is particularly true at regional level and, given its awareness of the impact that the common EU positions could have on the governance of the region, the EU and its Member States are politically committed to systematically reach out to the non-EU members in the region when preparing for the sessions of the Regional Committee.

In addition to the governing bodies' sessions and the inter-sessional processes, the EU also participates actively in a number of more informal contacts and consultations to further develop the EU political agenda on global health: meetings with the different departments of the WHO's Secretariat, bilateral contacts with other countries or groups (such as the African Union, like-minded or Western European and Others Group (WEOG)), outreach exercises at Ambassador level, meetings with NGOs and civil society, etc.

Overall, it could be concluded that, while the EU holds an observer status in the WHO, the EU's participation at the different levels, and within the various settings and processes of the organisation, has been recently widely developed and recognised. The EU and its Member States are gradually being recognised within the WHO fora and negotiations as a sound and reliable partner.

V. THE EU REPRESENTATION AT THE WHO

As already mentioned, the EU and its Member States endeavour to speak with a stronger and more coherent voice at a global level and in dialogue with third countries and in relation to global health initiatives.

The Council agreed in 2011 the General Arrangements regarding EU Statements in multilateral organisations[15] as a result of a significant institutional crisis. They

[15] Council of the European Union, EU Statements in multilateral organisations—General Arrangements, 15901/11, 24.10.2011.

recalled that the Treaty of Lisbon[16] enables the EU to achieve coherent, comprehensive and unified external representation and that the EU Treaties[17] provide for close and sincere cooperation between the Member States and the Union. Given the sensitivity of representation and potential expectations of third parties, the Council deemed essential that the preparation of statements relating to the sensitive area of competences of the EU and its Member States remained internal and consensual. Therefore, if an agreed EU position exists, it is for an EU actor (that is, the President of the EU Council, the High Representative, the Commission or the EU Delegations) to represent the EU and its Member States as appropriate, and express it in the international fora, provided that the rules of procedure of the specific setting allow for an effective EU representation.

In the case of the WHO, observers such as the EU may make a statement on the subject under discussion upon the invitation of the President and with the consent of the Health Assembly or committee. The established practice is then that observers are invited to take the floor at the end of the discussion, once all the Member States have intervened. Speaking from the observer seat after the discussion is over was not considered as being an influential voice. Therefore, the EU is represented by an EU Member State who speaks early in the debate during the governing bodies' sessions. During the Executive Board sessions the role is usually given to one of the EU Member States that is a member of the Board, usually to the one next in line to hold the Presidency of the Council, although this is not a strict rule. During the Health Assembly, this role is usually given to the Member State holding the rotating Presidency of the Council. In other words, an almost purely 'pre-Lisbon' arrangement for external representation persists in the WHO governing bodies' settings, due to the constraints imposed by the observer status of the EU in the WHO.

Conversely, for the formal or informal intergovernmental processes that regularly take place between the WHO governing bodies' sessions (intergovernmental meetings, consultations, working groups etc) the EU is normally granted access as an REIO on an equal footing with the members of the WHO. This is now a well-established practice, which is formalised through the systematic addition of a footnote 'and, where applicable, to REIOs' to the relevant references to the 'Member States' in the WHO resolutions that establish these processes. This development was greatly facilitated by the role of the EU during the negotiations of the WHO Framework Convention on Tobacco Control (FCTC) and by virtue of the fact that, as a REIO, the EU became a Party to the convention. The practice of having a REIO as a partner has exposed the WHO international community to a new institutional setting and has, successfully in the case of the FCTC, added a new factor to the already complex multi-actor global health diplomacy.

[16] See above, n 3.

[17] TEU, see above, n 3 and TFEU, see above, n 1.

In these particular processes, the EU Delegation in Geneva can effectively represent the EU and its Member States. This has already been the case for several WHO processes over the last two years, even if decisions in that regard are taken on an ad hoc basis after the EU Delegation and the Member States specifically assess each of the processes.

Overall, the EU's voice in the WHO, represented by an EU Member State or by an EU actor (usually the EU Delegation), can be considered as widely present and as particularly strong in certain global health processes.

Full EU membership or enhanced speaking rights in line with those granted by the UN General Assembly resolution of May 2011 on the participation of the EU in the work of the UN[18] could further contribute to raising the EU's profile and to furthering the EU's agenda on global health issues.

VI. THE EU AND THE WHO FRAMEWORK CONVENTION OF TOBACCO CONTROL (FCTC)

The WHO Framework Convention on Tobacco Control (hereafter FCTC)[19] is the first Treaty under Article 19 of the WHO Constitution[20] and it has given a new legal dimension to international health cooperation. It was adopted by the World Health Assembly in May 2003,[21] came into force in February 2005, and is one of the most quickly ratified and most widely embraced treaties in the history of the United Nations.

The EU (formerly the European Community), as a regional economic integration organisation (REIO), is a contracting party to the convention and the only signatory that is not a nation state. Article 1 of the FCTC on the use of terms defines an REIO as 'an organisation that is composed of several sovereign states, and to which its Member States have transferred competence over a range of matters, including the authority to make decisions binding on its Member States in respect of those matters'.

The status of the EU within the FCTC process differs significantly from the EU's role in the WHO and, taking into consideration the specific voting provisions,[22] the EU operates on an equal footing with all other Member States which are parties to the Convention. It seems probable that this status was obtained through the convergence of several factors, namely: the existing legal basis for tobacco control regulation and substantial on-going legislative processes within the EU;

[18] Assembly resolution on the participation of the EU in the work of the UN, A/RES/65/276.

[19] WHO Framework Convention on Tobacco Control, WHA Resolution 56, WHO Doc WHO/PMA/21/5/2003.

[20] See above, n 8.

[21] See above, n 14.

[22] REIOs, in matters within their competence, shall exercise their right to vote with a number of votes equal to the number of their Member States that are Parties to the Convention. Such an organisation shall not exercise its right to vote if any of its Member States exercises its right, and vice versa. Art 32(2) of the FCTC, see above, n 19.

strong commitment to tobacco control by the Commission, European Parliament, Council and the EU Member States; international political momentum; and a supportive environment from civil society.

The EU and its Member States have been heavily engaged throughout the FCTC process. The convention has been one of the mechanisms through which the EU has been able to contribute to the achievement of its global health objectives. It constitutes an excellent example of a strong and effective EU voice in the global health arena thanks to the joint efforts of the Commission and the EU Member States to work together so that real added value could be achieved. In addition, it has exposed the international community to a new institutional setting, having a REIO as a partner, thus adding a new actor to the already complex multi-actor global diplomacy.

VII. INTERNAL EU COORDINATION PROCESS: A PRACTICAL CASE

While the common EU institutional framework is clearly defined, the local coordination and representation practices are still diverse among the multilateral EU Delegations, or even among the different areas within the same Delegation. This can be explained by several factors, including previous consolidated practices, different momentums towards full implementation of the Lisbon Treaty, or the different status or interests of the EU in the various international organisations.

Locally, the EU coordination in connection with the WHO in Geneva is organised by way of two practical tools: 1) a common web portal used to share information and hold discussions between the EU institutions and the 28 Member States, and 2) face-to-face meetings chaired by the EU Delegation (periodicity according to needs, usually daily during the Governing Bodies' sessions and once or twice a week during the inter-sessional periods, approximately 120 meetings a year).

The European Commission, the representatives in Geneva and the designated focal points in the capitals of the EU Member States have access to the common web portal. The EU Delegation has the role of administrator and is in charge of uploading onto the website the relevant documents for discussion. Member States can then respond and upload their national comments to the proposed document. This portal is also used to send invitations to the EU coordination meetings and set its agenda. This is also under the responsibility of the EU Delegation.

The practical case presented below is not intended to represent any standard practice (probably such a standard cannot yet be defined), but just to illustrate with a practical example some implementation practices in a specific area and at a given moment. By way of such an example, the process for the preparation of the 134th session of the WHO Executive Board (EB) (Geneva, January 2014) is described as follows:

(1) Joint effort in intelligence gathering and information analysis—October and November 2013

The EU and its 28 Member States can constitute, when acting jointly, an extremely powerful force in terms of intelligence gathering and information analysis. EU Member States volunteer to gather information from different sources on the specific topics of the EB agenda and to report back to the group to allow for questions, further contributions and exchange of views. This exercise greatly facilitates a common and informed assessment of each of the topics and provides for an early identification of specific sensitive issues. It allows the EU Member States to work on the basis of similar and common information on each of the topics.

(2) Decision on the topics and the form of the EU's action during the EB—December 2013

The decision on the issues on which the EU and its Member States would take action during the EB session is based on different factors such as the importance of the topic, its strategic relevance for the global discussions, the existence of *acquis communautaire* or guidance from the Council in any of its formats, the added value and effectiveness of a common position at a given time or in a given situation, the need for coherence with other positions, etc. As can be appreciated, while the EU's positions must be defined by the Council, the local coordination in Geneva is well placed to assess other relevant factors.

Such EU action, in the case of the EB, usually takes the form of 1) proposed amendments to the draft resolutions and/or 2) statements on behalf of the EU and its Member States. Generally speaking, it also implies enhanced outreach to partners outside the EU.

The group then agrees on the priority areas on which a statement will be prepared and delivered on behalf of the EU and its Member States. In addition, it is agreed that amendments will be collected and coordinated within the EU for all the draft resolutions on technical issues and some of the decisions.

As for areas where there is no decision for formal EU action, an informal exchange of views among the EU Member States often takes place, which de facto also contributes to an increased shared understanding and coherence among the national actions within the EU.

(3) Distribution of tasks and preparation of a proposed EU position—December 2013

Considering the intense work involved in preparing the final EU positions, some Member States volunteer to 'burden-share' part of the work. 'Burden-sharers' for the statements and for the resolutions are then identified and agreed. They prepare the first draft of the EU statements that are then coordinated within the EU group. Similarly, some Member States volunteer to 'burden-share' on the amendments to the draft resolutions.

(4) Discussion and agreement on the proposed EU positions—January 2014

After the EU Delegation/Commission and the burden-sharers have shared the proposed EU positions, they are discussed within the group and eventually agreed, thus defining the final input from the EU and its Member States to the EB session. Adaptation on the spot during the meeting is often needed and the EU and its Member States hold coordination meetings on a daily basis during the EB sessions.

(5) Alignment procedure with eligible countries

Once the EU statements are agreed, time permitting, they are shared with the 14 countries eligible for alignment.

To illustrate the process with some figures, there were 65 items on the EB agenda in January 2014, and 14 resolutions on technical issues, seven resolutions on non-technical issues and five decisions were presented. The EU and its Member States delivered 10 statements and proposed amendments to 12 of the resolutions on technical issues. Up to 10 countries aligned with the EU statements shared for alignment.

After the EB session, the EU health group carries out an evaluation of the outcomes of the meeting. The EU Delegation debriefs the EU Heads of Mission in Geneva and the Presidency of the Council debriefs the Council as appropriate.

VIII. CONCLUSIONS

The Treaties provide a sound framework for EU action on global health and in multilateral fora, such as the WHO. They define common EU values to be upheld and promoted, and require that a high level of human health protection is ensured in all the EU's policies and activities. In addition, consistency between the different areas of the EU's external action and between these and its other policies also needs to be ensured. It is within this context, and as further developed by several conclusions of the Council, that the EU's mandate to act at the multilateral level in the WHO lies. In addition, the EU and its Member States attach great political importance to the WHO and to its on-going processes, as can be appreciated by the high degree of commitment and resources devoted to them.

Building on a long-standing relationship between the former European Communities and the WHO, the EU is also moving towards implementing the Lisbon Treaty in this particular forum. The 28 EU Member States are members of the WHO, but the EU only holds an observer status. Thanks to the ad hoc request for participation in the sub-committees of the WHO governing bodies, which is usually granted, and to the recognition of the specific nature of REIOs, the role of the EU in the WHO exceeds de facto that of other observers. The EU Delegation, in line with the positions agreed with the EU Member States, participates actively in working/drafting groups and in intersessional formal and informal consultations. Overall, the profile of the EU and its Member States and their effectiveness in the WHO has increased over the last few years.

In the post-Lisbon era, progressive improvement of local coordination methods is allowing the EU and its Member States to maximise the effectiveness of the political and technical resources available within the EU Delegation and the Member States' Missions in Geneva and capitals, fostering synergies and developing a more strategic and effective role in the WHO in a collective manner.

In terms of representation, since the EU holds an observer status in the WHO and does not have enhanced speaking rights, as is the case in the UN General Assembly, the EU is represented by a Member State during the WHO Governing Bodies. In other words, an almost purely 'pre-Lisbon' arrangement for external representation persists in the WHO Governing Bodies' settings.

In contrast, during other intergovernmental processes, which take place between the sessions of the Governing Bodies, the EU Delegation is allowed to effectively participate as a REIO. In these cases it often takes the role of representing the EU and its Member States if so decided depending on the specific process.

Overall, both through the formal and informal channels, the voice of the EU and its Member States in the WHO can be considered to be increasingly present and effective across the range of ongoing discussions and particularly comes to the fore in certain global health processes.

11

The European Union and the World Health Organization: Interactions and Collaboration from a Governance and Policy Perspective

GIAN LUCA BURCI*

I. INTRODUCTION

UNLIKE THE UNITED Nations or other specialised agencies such as the Food and Agriculture Organization, the participation of the European Union (EU) in the work of the World Health Organization (WHO), and more generally the interactions between the two organisations, have remained at a low level of visibility until recently. Even though the then European Community[1] concluded a cooperative arrangement with the WHO in the early 1970s and was invited to attend the meetings of the WHO's governing bodies from the early 1980s, it only started playing an active role as a participant in the WHO's governance and as an actor in global health in the late 1990s. In view of the institutional and policy developments brought about by the entry into force of the Lisbon Treaty in 2009, moreover, it cannot be excluded that such a role will be further enhanced in the future. The considerations contained in this chapter should therefore be considered as a 'work in progress'.

The evolution in question has several causes: first, the competences of the EU in public health and in areas related thereto have been gradually expanding since the Single European Act in 1987 and in particular with the Maastricht Treaty in 1992 and the Lisbon Treaty in 2009, both internally and with regard to the EU's foreign policy; second, public health at the international level has become increasingly

* The views expressed are solely those of the author and do not reflect the views, policies or positions of the World Health Organization.

[1] Even though 'European Union' was only introduced as the name of the organisation by the Lisbon Treaty, it will be used consistently in this chapter for the sake of simplicity even though references to events preceding the entry into force of the Lisbon Treaty in 2010 should be read as referring to the European Community or Communities as the case may be.

politicised and interactions with issues of larger EU competence such as trade, environmental protection and international security have multiplied. These developments have directly affected the agendas of the WHO and the EU; third, the EU has embraced 'effective multilateralism' as a central tool of its foreign and security policy and has consequently identified the United Nations and its funds, programmes and specialised agencies as privileged partners and a crucial pillar of an international system of governance that reflects the 'European model'.[2] In the area of public health, the WHO has consequently been identified as a key counterpart for health policy and standard setting.

This chapter will review from a legal and institutional point of view some features and examples of the EU's participation in, and cooperation with, the WHO as it has been developing since the late 1990s. After an analysis of the legal basis of EU participation in the WHO, two main areas of interaction will be reviewed, namely, the participation of the EU in the WHO's governance with particular regard to its intergovernmental meetings and negotiations (III); and the cooperation between the two organisations at a policy-making level (IV). The EU is also an important donor to the WHO, but the legal issues arising from the EU's role as a provider of financial resources are common to other international organisations within and outside the United Nations system rather than specific to the WHO; they will therefore not be reviewed in this chapter. The overview that follows will reflect the WHO's perspective; the EU perspective on its interactions with the WHO is provided in Chapter 10 of this volume by Lourdes Chamorro.

II. LEGAL BASIS FOR THE EU'S PARTICIPATION AND INTERACTION WITH THE WHO

The legal basis for the EU's participation and interaction with the WHO should, first of all, be seen from the perspective of the constitutional and legal framework of each organisation. Even though, as noted above, the EU's position on this matter is the subject of another chapter in this volume, it can be recalled that the central provision establishing the EU's competence in public health is currently Article 168 of the Treaty on the Functioning of the European Union (TFEU).[3] This Article, which replaced Article 152 of the Treaty on the European Community (TEC), lays out a broad horizontal mandate for the EU to ensure 'a high level of human health protection … in the definition and implementation of all Union

[2] Emblematic in this connection are the considerations contained in the Communication from the Commission to the Council and the European Parliament: The European Union and the United Nations: The choice of multilateralism, COM (2003) 526 final. The first sentence of the communication, in particular, reads as follows: 'The European Union's commitment to multilateralism is a defining principle of its external policy.'

[3] A good historical summary of the place of public health in the various treaties since the 1952 Treaty of Paris is contained in T Emmerling and J Heydemann, 'The EU as an Actor in Global Health Diplomacy' in I Kickbusch, G Lister, M Told and N Drager (eds), *Global Health Diplomacy* (New York, Springer, 2013) 223–41.

policies and activities' (paragraph 1) and to 'foster cooperation with third countries and the competent international organizations in the sphere of public health' (paragraph 3). Article 168 spells out and strengthens the general provision of Article 9 TFEU as well as of Article 35 of the Charter of Fundamental Rights of the European Union.[4] Article 168(3) has in turn to be read in conjunction with Article 220 TFEU, which gives the High Representative for Foreign Affairs and Security Policy a general mandate to 'establish all appropriate forms of cooperation with the organs of the United Nations and its specialised agencies'. EU competence under Article 168 is largely complementary to that of its Member States pursuant to Article 6 TFEU and focuses on encouraging cooperation between Member States as well as incentivising measures to protect and improve human health. Member States retain full competence for their health policies and health services, and the EU has no law-harmonisation authority as stated expressly in paragraph 5 of Article 168. However, the Union may adopt quality and safety standards for human organs and substances including blood as well as for medical products and devices. It can also adopt measures in the veterinary and phytosanitary fields.

The EU's direct competence in the field of public health has also to be seen in the broader and diverse context of the many areas that inextricably form part of the WHO's global health agenda—from access to medicines, international trade and intellectual property rules, prevention and control of international spread of disease, prevention of non-communicable diseases and market regulation, human rights and social protection, international security etc—for which the respective competences of the EU and its Member States have to be assessed on a case-by-case basis. The EU's authority to negotiate international instruments in areas covered by internal legislation, based on the so-called ERTA principle,[5] varies therefore between and within topics dealt with by the WHO with at times a complex situation of 'mixity'.

From the perspective of the WHO, its Constitution refers to cooperation and interaction with other international organisations in three articles: Article 70 provides for the establishment of effective relations and cooperation with intergovernmental organisations through the conclusion of agreements subject to approval by the World Health Assembly, the WHO's plenary organ; Article 18(h) authorises the Assembly to invite international organisations 'with responsibilities related to those of the Organization' to participate in its work without the right to vote; finally, Article 33 authorises the Director-General to 'establish direct relations with international organizations whose activities come within the competence of the Organization'.[6] These provisions are not clearly linked to one another, and

[4] Art 9 TFEU requires the Union to 'take into account' (rather than 'ensure') a high level of protection of human health in defining and implementing its policies and activities. Art 35 reiterates the general statement of Art 168 TFEU about ensuring a high level of human health protection besides providing for an individual right of access to preventive health care and medical treatment.

[5] ECJ, Case 22/70 *Commission v Council (ERTA)* [1971] ECR 263, 274, paras 16–19.

[6] Constitution of the World Health Organization, adopted on 22 July 1946, in UNTS, vol 14, p 185. The text is available on website of the World Health Organization, http://apps.who.int/gb/bd/PDF/bd47/EN/constitution-en.pdf.

they seem to allow the establishment of relations with international organisations through three different channels managed either by the WHO's Member States through the Health Assembly, or by the Director-General directly.

General frameworks for cooperation with intergovernmental organisations, including a reciprocal invitation to participate in the meetings of the other organisation, have in general been concluded by the WHO as formal agreements under Article 70 of the Constitution—for the most part with other specialised agencies but recently also with important partners such as the *Organisation internationale des épizooties* (OIE) and the African Union.[7] At the same time, cooperation agreements have also been concluded by the Director-General without submission to the Health Assembly, either because of their narrower project focus or in order to accommodate specific political concerns.

The main arrangements between the EU and the WHO fall into the latter category and consist of exchanges of letters or memoranda of understanding concluded between the Commissioner responsible for public health and the WHO's Director-General or other senior officials. Interaction between the two organisations was established either at a global level or with specific reference to the European Region, which was obviously of particular importance for the EU. This is without prejudice to the agreements or memoranda of understanding that the EU concludes with regional and country offices in other WHO regions with regard to funding technical cooperation projects. It should be recalled in this respect that the WHO is an unusually decentralised and regionalised specialised agency, with six regional offices headed by regional directors selected in practice by their respective regional committees.[8]

The increasing institutionalisation of the cooperation between the EU and the WHO was also accompanied by the establishment in Brussels in 2000 of a WHO liaison office to the EU. The staff of the office was initially composed of officials from the WHO's Headquarters as well as from the European and American Regional Offices with a direct reporting line to their respective offices; this arrangement led occasionally to representatives of the Office expressing different views in their interaction with EU institutions. In order to overcome the impression of a division within WHO and to increase consistency and synergies, it was decided in 2010–11 that the Regional Office for Europe would ensure the leadership of the Liaison Office on behalf of the entire organisation.

The first exchange of letters, concluded in 1972, focused on the interaction of the EU with the Regional Committee and Regional Office for Europe and was followed by a second exchange of letters in June 1982 between a Member of the Commission and the then Director-General Halfdan Mahler, elevating

[7] The text of most of the agreements in question, including that with the OEI, is reproduced in *WHO Basic Documents* 39th edn (Geneva, WHO, 2009) 38–80. The agreement with the African Union was approved by resolution WHA65.16 of 26 May 2012, in WHA65/2012/REC/1, p 47.

[8] See Constitution of the World Health Organization, above, n 6, Arts 44–54. On the regional structure of the WHO, see also GL Burci and CH Vignes, *World Health Organization* (The Hague, Kluwer, 2004) 53–61.

cooperation to a global level.[9] That arrangement laid down the general procedural channels for consultation, collaboration, and exchange of information without referring to specific substantive areas of common interest or concern. There was no provision for regular meetings or for the establishment of a joint consultation and review mechanism; at the same time, paragraphs 2 and 3 of the memorandum attached to the exchange of letters contained the following mutual invitation to attend governance meetings:

> 2. The Commission of the European Communities shall invite, where appropriate, representatives of the World Health Organization to participate as observer at its meetings with respect to items of the agenda in which the World Health Organization and the European Communities have a common interest.
> 3. The World Health Organization shall invite a representative of the European Communities to participate as observer in sessions of the World Health Assembly, the Executive Board and the Regional Committee for Europe and, where appropriate, in the work of their committees, with respect to items on their agenda in which the European Communities and the World Health Organization have a common interest.

The currently applicable general instrument for cooperation consists of an exchange of letters of December 2000 between the WHO's Director-General GH Brundtland and Health Commissioner D Byrne.[10] The content of the exchange of letters is more elaborate than the previous ones; in particular, it spells out the legal basis for the EU's assumption of new responsibilities in public health (at the time, Article 152 TEC) and the distinct but complementary roles of the two institutions in global health beyond the geographical confines of the EU as such. The exchange of letters lays out a number of principles and objectives as well as of areas and priorities that will orientate cooperation between the WHO and the EU. Importantly, it establishes a formal basis and conditions for EU financing of the WHO's technical cooperation projects as well as regular periodic meetings at a very senior level of the two organisations with the dual purpose of reviewing on-going cooperation and planning for future programmes. The meetings in question, referred to as 'Senior Official Meetings', have become important opportunities for policy consultations and even to facilitate actions to address challenges or points of friction between the two organisations.

From a governance perspective, it is noteworthy that the WHO's invitation to attend meetings of the Commission was eliminated and that participation is now only in one direction, with the 'Commission of the European Communities' enjoying a standing invitation to attend and participate without the right to vote in the Health Assembly, Executive Board and the 'Regional Committees' (and not only

[9] Exchange of letters between the European Commission and the World Health Organization (WHO) laying down the procedure for cooperation between the two organizations, OJ L 300, 28.10.1982, p 20–21.

[10] Exchange of letters between the World Health Organization and the Commission of the European Communities concerning the consolidation and intensification of cooperation, OJ C 1, 4.1.2001, pp 7–11.

the Regional Committee for Europe). Paragraph 1.4 of the arrangement provides furthermore that the Director-General may 'draw the attention of the competent governing body of [the WHO] to the question of participation of the Commission on the work of that body in specific cases, such as, for example, the negotiation of international agreements, and on the status of the European Communities under such agreements.' That provision was a consequence of the request by the Commission to have its competences reflected by the status it was seeking for particular negotiations (the immediate concern at the time was the on-going negotiation of the WHO Framework Convention for Tobacco Control), coupled with its concern at a hostile reaction by third states. The Director-General, pursuant to WHO's rules, could not unilaterally take decisions on the modalities of participation by observers beyond pure attendance at meetings, hence the compromise of the Director-General bringing issues of status and competence to the attention of the governing body concerned.

It is interesting to note that the general invitation in the above-mentioned exchanges of letters to the EU to participate in the work of the WHO's governing bodies was extended by the Director-General within her authority under Article 33 of the WHO Constitution. In other words, the WHO's Member States did not partake of that decision and their acceptance of the EU's participation relies more on acquiescence or silent consent rather than an affirmative decision. This, of course, is without prejudice to the affirmative decisions referred to below on specific forms of participation.

The 2000 exchange of letters is supplemented by a memorandum of understanding of December 2003 establishing a strategic partnership between the WHO and the EU in the field of development.[11] Finally, the central instrument governing the conditions for EU financing of the WHO's technical cooperation projects and activities is, in principle, the Financial and Administrative Framework Agreement (FAFA) concluded with the United Nations on 29 April 2003 and to which the WHO acceded on 11 December 2003. With some notable exceptions, the FAFA forms the basis upon which specific contribution and other similar agreements are concluded and spells out the standard conditions for EU financing.[12]

III. EU'S PARTICIPATION IN THE WHO'S GOVERNANCE

The participation of the EU in the WHO's governing bodies and intergovernmental meetings and negotiations offers an interesting example of institutional

[11] Memorandum of Understanding concerning the establishment of a strategic partnership between the World Health Organization and the Commission of the European Communities in the field of development, 2004, on file with the author.

[12] Financial and administrative framework agreement between the European Communities, represented by the Commission of the European Communities, and the United Nations, 29 April 2003, available on the website of the European Union at http://ec.europa.eu/europeaid/work/procedures/financing/international_organisations/other_documents_related_united_nations/index_en.htm.

adaptation and evolution, brought forth by a combination of pragmatism, sensitivity to the peculiarities of the EU as a supranational organisation, and an increasing familiarity of third states to the role and operating procedures of the EU and its Member States. The importance of a growing familiarity with the EU should not be underestimated. As noted above, the EU is a relatively recent participant in the WHO's governance and many non-EU Member States were either unfamiliar with the unique institutional construct of the EU and/or were wary of the motives of the EU's requests for participation and of a 'mandate creep' and exceptional treatment for an organisation that was associated with strong industrial and commercial interests in the medical field. It is also well known that other regional blocs on the path towards economic and political integration did not want to set a precedent that could jeopardise future recognition of their regional or sub-regional organisations with the same rights and status as the EU.

In terms of representation of the EU the WHO Secretariat, consistent with its constitutional role, has kept a neutral position on questions of status, exercise of rights and designation and has deferred to the decision of the EU and its Member States or those of the governing bodies, as appropriate. It has, for example, honoured requests for a particular denomination of the EU Delegation that, before the entry into force of the Lisbon Treaty, oscillated between 'European Commission' and 'European Community'. The EU's positions are presented either by the EU Delegation or by the Presidency or another EU Member State, depending on the distribution of competence and the procedural circumstances. In view of the constraints faced by the EU explained below, the EU's position is often presented by an EU Member State rather than the EU Delegation. In an organ of limited membership such as the Executive Board, moreover, the EU Presidency is often not a member and another EU delegation is authorised to take the floor on the basis of an internal arrangement between the EU and its Member States.

Finally, the WHO has treated the shift from European Community to European Union as a continuation of the same international legal person subject to a change of name. Even though Article 1 of the Treaty on European Union states that the Union 'shall replace and succeed the European Community', the consultations held between the WHO Secretariat, the then Presidency and the Commission clearly pointed to an understanding that the participation of the EU would just continue and not require a new legal arrangement or some form of admission. This position is confirmed by the communication sent on 8 March 2010 to the Secretary-General in his capacity as depositary of international treaties, whereby the EU Council states, inter alia, that 'the European Union has replaced the European Community … and has taken over all rights and obligations of the European Community'[13] without any reference to succession as a term of art under the law of treaties. It is decisive that the EU has not deposited instruments of succession to

[13] The letter is reproduced on the website of the United Nations at https://treaties.un.org/pages/HistoricalInfo.aspx?#"European%20Union".

the treaties in force for the European Community but that the Secretary-General has simply changed the name of the party to 'European Union' maintaining the date of the treaty action originally effected by the Community.

A. General Legal Status

The rights of participation of the EU in the WHO's governing bodies have not been defined through a general resolution as in the case of the United Nations through General Assembly Resolution 65/276 of 3 May 2011.[14] The complexity of the institutional transition brought about by the Lisbon Treaty, the lesser extent of EU competence in public health compared to other areas, and possibly the reluctance to experience again the hurdles faced by the EU during the negotiation of the General Assembly resolution, may have led to a pragmatic sense of caution for the time being.

Consequently, the status and rights of the EU in the Health Assembly, Executive Board and Regional Committees is by default equated to that of an 'intergovernmental organization with which the Organization has established effective relations under Article 70 of the Constitution'. (The absence of an Article 70 agreement in the case of the EU, and the reliance instead on Article 33, has never been questioned by WHO Member States.) In accordance with Rule 4 of the Rules of Procedure of the Executive Board, Rule 46 of the Rules of Procedure of the Health Assembly and Rule 2 of the Rules of Procedure of the Regional Committee for Europe, such organisations may participate without vote in open meetings of those bodies and their committees and take the floor after Member and non-Member States as well as observers enjoying a special status such as Palestine.[15] Under the WHO's rules and practice, non-members of the governing bodies have very limited opportunities, if any, to exercise sometimes crucial rights of participation such as circulating official documents or submitting proposals.

The aforementioned procedural situation forces EU representatives to take the floor only after Member States and prevents them from submitting formal proposals related to the decision or document under negotiation and, in general, from taking an active part in the work of the bodies concerned. Even though the

[14] United Nations General Assembly, Participation of the European Union in the work of the United Nations, Resolution 65/276, 3 May 2011. The resolution is available on the UN website at www.un.org/depts/dhl/resguide/r65_en.shtml.

[15] The Rules of Procedure of the Health Assembly and Executive Board are reproduced in WHO Basic Documents, above, n 7, pp 121–65. The Rules of Procedure of the Regional Committee for Europe are available on the website of the Regional Office for Europe at www.euro.who.int/en/about-us/governance/standing-committee/rules-of-procedure-of-the-regional-committee-and-the-standing-committee-of-the-regional-committee. For a good summary of the EU's status in the WHO's governing bodies, see B Egger and F Hoffmeister, 'UN-EU Cooperation on Public Health: the Evolving Participation of the European Community in the World Health Organization' in J Wouters, F Hoffmeister and T Ruys (eds), *The United Nations and the European Union: An Ever Stronger Partnership* (The Hague, TMC Asser Press, 2006) 155–68.

position of the EU and its Member States can be also expressed by the state holding the rotating Presidency or another EU Member State, the EU's competence in a growing number of topics within the WHO's agenda made it imperative to find tools enabling the Commission—and the External Action Service since the entry into force of the Lisbon Treaty—to fully participate in the WHO's negotiations. In the absence of a general decision, two pragmatic solutions were found.

B. Ad Hoc Invitations

The first opportunity to address the issue of increased rights of participation for the EU came in 1999 with the launch of the negotiations on the WHO Framework Convention on Tobacco Control (hereafter FCTC) since it became clear that a number of issues related to the internal market as well as international trade would fall within the scope of the Convention. After protracted negotiations, the Health Assembly decided in its Resolution WHA52.18 'that regional economic integration organizations constituted by sovereign States, Members of the World Health Organization, to which their Member States have transferred competence over matters governed by this resolution, including the competence to enter into treaties in respect to these matters, may actively participate, in accordance with Rule 55 of the Rules of Procedure of the Health Assembly, in the drafting and negotiations of the intergovernmental negotiating body'.[16] The reference to 'regional economic integration organizations' (REIOs), an expression borrowed from multilateral environmental agreements to which the EU was a party, avoided the aforementioned sensitivities surrounding a special status for the EU as such. Moreover, active participation was limited to the negotiating body established by the Assembly rather than the Assembly itself.

With regard to the exact scope of the rights of participation of the EU in the FCTC negotiations, the reference to Rule 55 only enabled the EU to take the floor together with Member States; however, it was clear that active participation in negotiations would require more than that, in particular the possibility to present and discuss proposals and amendments. In order to address the ambiguity of the Assembly's decision, the legal services of the WHO and of the Commission consulted informally and agreed to use as a plausible template in case of challenges the rights conferred to the EU in 1995 by the United Nations Economic and Social Council with regard to participation in the Commission on Sustainable Development.[17] Such rights included taking the floor, submitting proposals and amendments, exercising the right of reply, and raising a point of order to the effect that negotiations on matters of EU competence were under way. The EU would not

[16] World Health Assembly, Towards a WHO framework convention on tobacco control, Resolution WHA52.18, 24 May 1999, WHA/52/1999/REC/1, pp 21–24.

[17] Economic and Social Council, Full participation of the European Community in the Commission on Sustainable Development, Decision 1995/201, 8.2.1995, E/1995/5, Supplement No 1, p 65.

have the right to vote or to exercise other rights reserved to Members such as raising procedural motions.

The EU representatives participated fully and took a very active role in the negotiations of the FCTC; that experience was probably the 'ice breaker' that familiarised the WHO's membership with the dynamics between the Commission and its Member States as well as with the requirement for consultations in order to reach a common position. The need to await the outcome of such consultations occasionally delayed the course of the negotiations and tested the patience of other negotiators as much as the occasional rigidity of the common positions that had to be painstakingly negotiated internally. The extent of the EU's rights of participation was, however, never challenged, in large part due to the unspoken agreement that the Negotiating Body would not vote but conduct its negotiations by consensus.

The same 'REIO formula' was used for subsequent negotiations undertaken by special negotiating committees or working groups established by the Health Assembly or the Executive Board, such as those on the revised International Health Regulations[18] and the Global Strategy and Action Plan on Public Health, Innovation and Intellectual Property.[19] The growing familiarity with the EU's participation in WHO negotiation has recently led to a procedural simplification, whereby the formal invitation clause in the relevant resolutions has been replaced by a simple footnote in the operative paragraph launching the negotiation and establishing a negotiating body. The reference to 'Member States' in the resolution is extended through the footnote to 'where applicable, regional economic integration organizations'.[20] The absence of qualifications as to the rights of participation of REIO in the footnote, however, does not mean that the EU can enjoy full rights equivalent to those of Member States; rather, it maintains the rights of participation implicitly included in the previous REIO formula. This simplified REIO formula is also increasingly used to extend to the EU substantive requests addressed by Health Assembly resolutions to WHO Member States and touching on areas of Union competence.[21] It is also significant that the EU has been invited through the device of the aforementioned footnote to participate in negotiations on constitutional matters where its competence can be questioned, such as notably the revision of the process for the election of the Director-General,[22] and that it

[18] World Health Assembly, *Revision of the International Health Regulations*, Resolution WHA56.28, 28.5.2003, available on the WHO website at http://apps.who.int/gb/archive/e/e_wha56.html.

[19] World Health Assembly, *Public health, innovation, essential health research and intellectual property rights: towards a global strategy and plan of action*, Resolution WHA59.24, 27.5.2006, WHA/59/2006/REC/1, p 32.

[20] A recent example was the establishment in 2010 of a Working Group on counterfeit medical products: World Health Assembly, *Substandard/spurious/falsely-labelled/falsified/counterfeit medical products*, Decision WHA63(10), 21.5.2010, A63/DIV/3.

[21] See, eg, Resolution WHA59.24, above, n 19.

[22] *Election of the Director-General of the World Health Organization*, Executive Board Resolution EB128.R14, 24.1.2011, available on the WHO website at http://apps.who.int/gb/ebwha/pdf_files/EB128-REC1/B128_REC1-en.pdf#page=15.

has been included in a standing Member State mechanism established in 2012 to guide and coordinate the WHO's response to the growing problem of falsified and counterfeit medical products.[23] The mechanism held its first two sessions in 2012 and 2013 and the EU played an active and unchallenged role in coordination with its Member States.

An initially sensitive issue concerned the seat of the EU Delegation. Since the negotiations on the FCTC, the EU Delegation has constantly requested to be seated next to the delegation holding the rotating Presidency of the EU Council for purposes of consultations and coordination during the meetings. A request in this sense was addressed by the Commission and the Presidency to the Secretariat before the first negotiating session on the FCTC in 2000 as if it were simply an administrative measure. However, at least within the United Nations system seating arrangements define the status of different categories of participants and in particular visually divide Member States from other entities; moving the EU next to the Presidency and among Member States consequently exceeded the authority of the Secretariat and required an affirmative decision of the negotiating body. A request from the floor by France, as the country holding the rotating Presidency, was accepted by the negotiating body at its first session but reportedly caused a major diplomatic incident with the United States due to the lack of prior consultations. Faced with that precedent a number of countries—notably but not exclusively the United States—refused to entertain the same request in subsequent negotiations, for example those on the revision of the International Health Regulations and on the Global Strategy and Action Plan on Public Health, Innovation and Intellectual Property. Also in this case, however, the initially hostile and suspicious attitude of a number of countries to the elevation of the EU to a status symbolically closer to that of a full member of WHO progressively relaxed and the EU Delegation has sat next to the rotating Presidency without any challenge in recent negotiating bodies.

C. EU Participation in Drafting Groups

Many resolutions or outcome documents are negotiated or finalised in drafting groups convened during the sessions of the Health Assembly and the Executive Board. Their meetings are more or less formal depending on the circumstances of their establishment, but in principle they are only open to Member States and are not covered by the ad hoc invitations to REIO discussed in the previous section. Participation by international organisations in such meetings requires a specific case-by-case invitation by the Board under Rule 4 or by the Assembly under Rule 46 of their respective Rules of Procedure. The EU's exclusion from participating in

[23] *Substandard/spurious/falsely-labelled/falsified/counterfeit medical products*, resolution WHA65.19, 26.5.2012, available on the WHO website at http://apps.who.int/gb/ebwha/pdf_files/WHA65-REC1/A65_REC1-en.pdf#page=25.

drafting groups, enforced by a number of countries when EU delegates attempted to attend them, created growing problems in view of the frequent inclusion in their deliberations of issues of EU competence.

Consequently, after informal consultations between the legal services of the WHO and the Commission, Portugal requested at the opening meeting of the 117th session of the Executive Board in January 2006 that in accordance with Rule of Procedure 4 the EU be allowed to participate in drafting groups convened during that session dealing with technical items falling in whole or in part under EU competence. Australia and the United States subjected their acceptance to a clarification of the EU competence by the Presidency and an understanding that the Commission and EU Member States would not take the floor on the same subject matter and would not set a precedent for other international forums.[24] That arrangement set a pattern which has been successfully followed since 2006 in every session both of the Executive Board and of the technical committee of the Health Assembly. Also in this case, a growing familiarity to an active presence of the EU Delegation has led to a progressive relaxation of the position of third countries so that, for example, a statement on the EU's competence on items on the agenda is no longer requested and neither are there questions or challenges when both the EU and its Member States take the floor on specific points under discussion.

D. EU Status in the WHO's International Legal Instruments

The negotiation of the FCTC and of the revised International Health Regulations (2005) (IHR) can be considered a turning point in the effort of coordinating the negotiating positions of the EU and its Member States, with different degrees of difficulty and success also because of the interests at play.[25]

In terms of the legal status of the EU in the two legal instruments, different solutions were found. In the case of the FCTC, the final text of the Convention followed the model of the multilateral environmental agreements that formed the template used by the negotiators for its institutional and final clauses. In particular, REIOs can sign (Article 34) and formally confirm or accede to the FCTC subject to a declaration of the extent of their competence under the Convention (Article 35); their participation is subject to the principle of alternative exercise of rights with their Member States both in terms of the right to vote in the Conference of the Parties to the Convention (Article 32) as well as in the performance of their obligations (Article 35).[26] The European Union deposited its instrument of formal

[24] See EB117/2006/REC/2, pp 3–4.

[25] A good summary of the status of the EU in those negotiations and of the problems and approaches underlying the search for common positions in each of them is provided in Eggers and Hoffmeister, above, n 15, 162–68.

[26] *WHO Framework Convention on Tobacco Control*, adopted on 21.5.2003, UNTS 2302, p 166. The Convention entered into force on 27 February 2005 and had 177 Parties as of the end of 2014.

confirmation on 30 June 2005 alongside an elaborate declaration of the extent of EU competence and of EU legislation on topics dealt with in the FCTC.

The EU has been a very active participant in the work of the Conference of the Parties to the FCTC, in particular for the development of guidelines providing an authoritative interpretation and guidance on several articles of the Convention touching on areas of EU competence and legislation such as labelling and packaging of tobacco products as well as advertising, sponsorship and promotion thereof. The EU has also taken a leadership role in the negotiation of the first protocol of the FCTC, on the elimination of illicit trade in tobacco products. A representative of the European Anti-Fraud Office chaired all the negotiating sessions and the final text represents to a large extent a confirmation of the approach taken by the EU internally for the prevention and deterrence of contraband and counterfeit of tobacco products. The EU signed the Protocol, which was not yet in force as of June 2015, on 20 December 2013.[27]

The IHR is a legally binding instrument adopted by the Health Assembly under Articles 21 and 22 of the WHO Constitution. Those two articles enable the adoption of regulations within five enumerated areas including the prevention and control of the international spread of disease. Regulations constitute, to use EU terminology, secondary legislation and enter into force for all WHO Member States—except those who either object to them or file a reservation—by a specified deadline.[28] Their legal basis lies in the WHO Constitution rather than general international law and, for this reason, the EU did not seek admission as a party even though it participated very actively in the negotiations and the IHR's approach extensively overlapped on areas of EU competence and legislation such as food safety, phytosanitary measures, personal data protection and international transport of persons and goods. Consequently, a legal difficulty arose at the adoption of the IHR by the Health Assembly, since the Commission could not formally express the EU's position as part of the act of adoption. Pragmatically, the Council authorised EU Member States to accept the final text also in the interest of the EU.[29]

Despite the inability of the EU to join the IHR as a party, its special situation was accommodated by Article 57 paragraph 3, which provides that '[W]ithout prejudice to their obligations under these Regulations, States Parties that are members of a regional economic integration organization shall apply in their mutual relations the common rules in force in that regional economic integration organization.' This compromise solution, while safeguarding the ultimate responsibility and accountability of States Parties under the IHR, introduces a duality of obligations that can potentially lead to difficulties in case of parallel or inconsistent measures and requirements within the EU as compared to the IHR and to WHO's responsibilities thereunder.

[27] *Protocol to Eliminate Illicit Trade in Tobacco Products*, adopted on 12.11.2012. The text is available on the WHO website at http://apps.who.int/iris/bitstream/10665/80873/1/9789241505246_eng.pdf.

[28] On the legal nature and status of WHO regulations, see Burci and Vignes, above, n 8, pp 131–32.

[29] On this point, see Egger and Hoffmeister, above, n 15, 167–68.

Finally, the EU is a member of the Codex Alimentarius Commission by virtue of its full membership of the Food and Agriculture Organization (FAO). The Commission is a joint intergovernmental body of the FAO and the WHO with the mandate of developing harmonised international food standards, guidelines and codes of practice to protect the health of the consumers and ensure fair practices in international food trade. The Codex Commission also promotes coordination of all food standards work undertaken by international governmental and non-governmental organisations.[30] The request by EU Member States to admit the EU to the Codex Commission in its capacity as a 'regional economic integration organization' member of the FAO led to a long and difficult negotiation. This was due to the reluctance of major food exporters such as the United States, Australia, Argentina, Brazil and India to accept a direct presence by the EU and an increased influence of Europe in a body of growing importance for food trade in view of the impact of Codex Alimentarius standard under the WTO agreements on sanitary and phytosanitary standards and on technical barriers to trade, respectively. The negotiations eventually achieved the amendment of the Rules of Procedure of the Codex Alimentarius Commission.[31] The approach followed is based on the FAO's rules and practice; it is based on the alternative exercise of rights depending on competence and requires the EU and/or its Member States to make a written declaration about competence on each item on the agenda of the Commission. At the same time, the EU obtained a small but significant additional right compared to FAO and the strict alternative exercise of rights, namely, that EU Member States may 'develop or support the position of the Member Organization in areas within its competence'.

IV. THE EU AND THE WHO IN POLICY MAKING

Through its participation in the WHO's governance, the EU acts like a discrete entity with its own legal personality and corporate policy, projecting such policy externally through the collective decision-making mechanisms of the WHO. From this point of view, the co-operation between the two organisations is asymmetrical since the WHO does not enjoy a comparable right of participation in the EU's governance. As noted above, the possibility for the WHO to be invited to meetings of the Commission, provided in the 1982 exchange of letters, was not retained in the 2000 revision.

The EU's participation in the WHO is a function of two main aspects of its external policy: its embrace of multilateralism as a pillar of its action as an actor in international policy, and its increasing competence and authority in the various aspects of global health.

[30] More information on the Codex Alimentarius, its structure and activities is available on its website: www.codexalimentarius.net.

[31] *Codex Alimentarius Commission Procedural Manual*, 17th edn (Rome, FAO, WHO, 2007) 6–7.

From the first perspective, the EU seems to have embraced effective multilateralism as 'a defining principle of its external policy' at least since the 2003 European Security Strategy and the Commission's communication to the Council and the Parliament on 'the choice of multilateralism'.[32] The 2003 communication, seen in part as a reaction to the strongly unilateral tendencies of the United States in security and other matters, represents a strong policy statement in support of the rule of law at international level and of the United Nations as the pivot of the multilateral system. The Commission expressed its commitment at having the EU play a 'frontrunner role' in negotiating and implementing UN instruments, including the FCTC, and in increasing its voice and weight in the UN system to better project the European social model externally. The motives for such a strong long-term commitment have been discussed by scholars and range from the ability of multilateralism to turn diverse foreign policy goals into a single, coherent message to the need to compensate the relative weakness of the EU and its Member States as political actors, to the very nature of the EU as a *sui generis* international organisation that would almost instinctively want to use multilateral fora as an end in itself and a principled course of action.[33] While the Lisbon Treaty enhanced the institutional capacity of the EU to be an effective actor in foreign policy, scholars have noted that it does not clarify the long-standing question whether the EU is a 'participant in' or a 'partner to' other international institutions, and this oscillation between the two roles also characterises the EU's participation in the WHO.[34]

Another important statement to understand the policy goals of the EU's participation in the WHO is the 2010 Council Conclusions on the EU role in Global Health.[35] The directions and statements contained in the Conclusions show a strong alignment of the EU's values and its social and economic models with the main policy trends in global health emerging from the WHO. The Council Conclusions reaffirm, in particular, a vision of health as key to equitable and sustainable growth and development, as well as the EU's commitment to protect and promote the 'right to health'. Solidarity towards equitable universal access to health services is seen both as a shared value within the EU and as a basis for EU policies in global health. Other important highlights of the 2010 Conclusions are: 1) the emphasis on strengthening health systems as the central element for addressing most health challenges; 2) a reiteration of the principles of aid effectiveness and reliance on the health strategies of partner countries; 3) a commitment to uphold the WHO's leadership in its normative, guidance and technical support functions; 4) a strong statement on the importance of research and evidence and the regulation of their outcomes as global public goods; and

[32] Communication from the Commission to the Council and the European Parliament—The European Union and the United Nations: the choice of multilateralism, above, n 2.

[33] See R Kissack, 'The European Union and multilateralism' in KE Jorgensen and KV Laatikainen (eds), *Routledge Handbook on the European Union and International Organizations* (London, Routledge, 2013) 405–15.

[34] KE Jorgensen and KV Laatikainen, 'Introduction' in Jorgensen and Laatikainen, above, n 33, 3.

[35] Council Conclusions on the EU role in Global Health of 10 May 2010, 9505/10.

5) a very important affirmation of 'health in all policies' as an effective approach to seek policy coherence and address the impact on health of other areas of the EU's competence or interest such as trade, migration, food security, environmental protection and climate change.

A recent example of a successful exercise of the EU's influence and leadership in the WHO's policy making concerns the FCTC Protocol to Eliminate Illicit Trade in Tobacco Products mentioned above. The Intergovernmental Negotiating Body on the protocol—established by the Conference of the Parties to the FCTC—considered at the beginning of its work which elements should form part of an international instrument addressing the dramatic problem of smuggling, diversion from the supply chain, and counterfeiting of cigarettes and other tobacco products. It also considered a range of pre-existing agreements and other international arrangements relevant for the object of the future protocol.[36] That review showed that the approach followed by the EU to address this phenomenon relies in large part on a number of agreements concluded between the Commission and major tobacco manufacturers such as Philip Morris International, Japan Tobacco and British American Tobacco.[37] The most significant measures introduced by those agreements consist of obligations by the tobacco manufacturers with regard to their sale and distribution practices, an agreed system for the tracking and tracing of tobacco products in the supply chain, and cooperative measures to prevent or reduce the smuggling of tobacco products. Even though a number of States Parties indicated their reluctance to rely on cooperation with the tobacco industry rather than on top-down regulation of its activities, the EU successfully ensured that the Protocol retain several qualifying elements of its own cooperative approach, for example with regard to licensing of the main operators in the supply chain as well as tracking and tracing. As noted above, the commitment of the EU to the negotiations was also shown by its financial support to the process and the fact that all the sessions of the Intergovernmental Negotiating Body were chaired by a representative of the European Anti-Fraud Office.

In terms of the concrete aspects of the EU's interactions with the WHO at policy-making level and development assistance, the general directions mentioned above have found expression in the recent co-operative arrangements concluded between the WHO and the Commission, in particular the exchange of letters of December 2000,[38] the 2003 Memorandum of Understanding on a

[36] WHO Framework Convention on Tobacco Control, Intergovernmental Negotiating Body on a Protocol on Illicit Trade in Tobacco Products, *Existing agreements and arrangements relevant to the objective of the Intergovernmental Negotiating Body*, Noted by the Convention Secretariat, FCTC/COP/INB-IT/1/INF.DOC./1, 12.12.2007.

[37] The text of the agreements is available on the website of the European Anti-Fraud Office, http://ec.europa.eu/anti_fraud/investigations/eu-revenue/cigarette_smuggling_en.htm.

[38] Exchange of letters between the World Health Organization and the Commission of the European Communities concerning the consolidation and intensification of cooperation, above, n 10.

strategic partnership in the field of development,[39] and the 2010 joint declaration between the Commission and the WHO Regional Office for Europe.[40]

The areas for cooperation singled out in the various instruments show, on the one hand, a continuity largely based on the EU's social public health model and, on the other, the development of the EU's priorities in public health over the course of time. Such priorities in turn reflect both the main concerns for health developments within the EU space and the application to health issues of the EU's external policy directions as well as of its position on interrelated areas such as security and the internal market. For example, all three instruments focus on research and generation of authoritative evidence and information as well as protection against communicable diseases as both a focus of joint activities and of EU's financial support to developing countries. However, the 2010 joint declaration reflects more closely the specific health priorities of the whole European region including EU Member States; examples are the recognition of the importance of health for Europe's economy, the importance of investments in health to address increasing health care expenditures, and the growing challenge of non-communicable diseases such as obesity and tobacco-related diseases. At the same time, recurrent themes underscoring the general approach of the EU's external policy also vis-à-vis WHO remain policy coherence, complementarity, coordination and avoidance of duplication.

The overall cohesive and consistent global health agendas of the EU and the WHO are also reflected in the EU's development policy. Health system strengthening and steps towards universal coverage and a right-based approach are important components of the EU's financial support to the WHO's technical cooperation activities. It has been noted that, also in this case, the EU and its Member States deliver consistently on the EU's objectives and principles in public health: the commitment to provide affordable health care and universal coverage within the EU space is coupled with the projection of that model towards third countries through the tools of policy dialogue and development cooperation.[41] This of course is significant given that the EU and its Member States contribute more than half of Official Development Assistance.

As noted above, this contribution will not analyse the details of the EU's financial support of the WHO's activities and the legal issues it raises. Suffice it to note that the EU was the third largest non-state contributor of voluntary funds to the WHO in 2012 (US$ 63.8 million), with the bulk of contributions coming from the Directorates General on Development (DEVCO) and humanitarian assistance (ECHO), with lesser but still significant contributions from the Directorates

[39] Memorandum of Understanding concerning the establishment of a strategic partnership between the World Health Organization and the Commission of the European Communities in the field of development, above, n 11.

[40] EUR/RC60&12 Add.1, 9.10.2010, Annex 2. This joint declaration oddly represents the first formal arrangement between the EU and the WHO's Regional Office for Europe, which naturally holds a prominent place for the EU's cooperation with WHO.

[41] Emmerling and Heydemann, above, n 3, 226–27.

General on research and health and consumers (DG SANCO). The EU mostly follows a project approach rather than funding general programmes, and all its contributions are earmarked. The mutual rights and obligations between the parties, and the conditions for disbursement and administration of the funds, are generally covered by the FAFA.

Finally, the interaction between the EU and WHO at a policy-making level is bidirectional and not only focused on the EU's participation in the shaping of the WHO's policies. The WHO is the sole global public health agency with a unique mandate and an equally unique authority and legitimacy in setting health norms, standards and policies; in advocating for effective health outcomes; and in supporting its Member States through technical and humanitarian cooperation. The WHO would arguably not fully implement its constitutional mandate if it limited itself to providing a forum in its governance to the EU alongside other participants. If the EU participates in the WHO's adoption of norms and policies mostly through its participation in the latter's intergovernmental meetings, however, the WHO discharges its functions mostly through its liaison with the EU's bodies as well as through cooperation at country level with the EU's missions. Interaction and liaison with the main organs of the EU, including the European Parliament and the political parties represented there, is largely ensured by the WHO's liaison office in Brussels, which acts on behalf of the whole Organization including its regional offices. The main goal of the WHO is to seek policy coherence by offering evidence to policy makers and advocating for the incorporation of the WHO's norms and standards into the EU's policies and legislation as well as its development policy. Given the effect of EU legislation on its Member States, the incorporation of the WHO's standards into it is seen as a powerful tool to promote policy coherence at national level within the EU space. A recent example of such cooperation is given by the WHO's role in the revision in 2013 of the Tobacco Products Directive.[42]

V. CONCLUSIONS

Even though the EU is a relative newcomer to global health, its interaction and involvement with the WHO at multiple levels have increased and deepened in a short period of time. All the indications are that they may still evolve and broaden in the context of the implementation of the Lisbon Treaty, the changes it has introduced to the EU's external representation, the increase in EU competence in areas directly or indirectly related to global health, and the evolution of the WHO's agenda. As noted in the introduction, this is still very much a work in progress which will develop in parallel with the WHO's role in global health. The conclusion of a general agreement on the EU's participation in the WHO's governance

[42] See http://ec.europa.eu/health/tobacco/products/revision/.

under Article 70 of the WHO Constitution may be the next step in this direction, together with an increasing integration of the EU into WHO's functions and governance. The perspective of full membership of the WHO, however, advocated by some scholars, seems for the moment a remote possibility.[43]

The status of the EU in the WHO's governance, finally, has to be seen against the background of the increasing economic and political integration among the countries of other regions. The African Union, the Caribbean Community and the Union of South American Nations (UNASUR) are examples of regional or sub-regional organisations expressing the will of their respective Member States to progressively achieve a level of integration not dissimilar to that of the EU. Their stance in other international organisations, including the WHO, with regard to the EU's status has been and continues to be shaped by their intention not to prejudice future claims for a status and recognition comparable to that of the EU.

[43] Egger and Hoffmeister, above, n 15, 154.

12

The European Union's Role and Potential in Research and Innovation for Global Health

ILONA KICKBUSCH, STEPHEN A MATLIN, SAMANTHA BATTAMS AND ALBRECHT JAHN

I. INTRODUCTION

A. Background

i. Research, Development and Innovation

EFFORTS TO PROMOTE European economic growth and competitiveness and ensure a stable, prosperous future for the citizens of the European Union (EU) are central to 'Europe 2020'—the EU's growth strategy for the present decade.[1,2,3,4] Three key drivers for growth are to be implemented through concrete actions at EU and national levels: smart growth, sustainable growth, and inclusive growth. To meet the Europe 2020 targets, the European Commission (EC) has developed a series of flagship initiatives, one of which is the 'Innovation Union'—re-focusing research and development (R&D) and innovation policy on major challenges, while closing the gap between science and the market to turn inventions into products.[5]

The EU's 7th Framework Programme for Research and Technological Development 2007–2013 (FP7) had a total budget of over €50 billion. Then the world's

[1] European Commission, *Europe 2020*. http://ec.europa.eu/europe2020/index_en.htm.

[2] European Commission, Communication from the Commission. *Europe 2020: A strategy for smart, sustainable and inclusive growth*, EC, 3.3.2010, COM(2010) 2020 final. http://eur-lex.europa.eu/LexUriServ/LexUriServ.do?uri=COM:2010:2020:FIN:EN:PDF.

[3] European Commission, *Europe 2020: Commission proposes new economic strategy in Europe*, EC, 3.3.2010. http://europa.eu/rapid/pressReleasesAction.do?reference=IP/10/225&format=HTML&aged=1&language=EN&guiLanguage=fr.

[4] EAMBES, *Bridging technology with therapeutics for innovative therapeutics intervention*: EAMBES, DG RTD Health Proposal, 2010. www.eambes.org/contents/public-repository/DGRT_EAMBES_proposal_062010_final.pdf.

[5] European Commission, Innovation Union. http://ec.europa.eu/research/innovation-union/index_en.cfm.

largest single research programme, FP7 included €6.1 billion for health. FP7 was succeeded in 2014 by Horizon 2020: Framework Programme for Research and Innovation, which incorporates the previous Competitiveness and Innovation Framework Programme and European Institute of Innovation and Technology to create coherence along the whole innovation chain.[5] Horizon 2020 runs from 2014 to 2020, with a budget close to €80 billion.[6] It will focus on strengthening science, innovative industry and technology and tackling societal challenges, whilst aiming to create jobs and growth in Europe.

ii. The Role of Health

Good health is fundamental to the objectives of Europe 2020, the Innovation Union and Horizon 2020:

Health is wealth …

> Good health is essential for a healthy economy[7,8]—'a powerful argument for European governments to invest in the health of their populations, not only because better health is a desirable objective in its own right, but also because it is an important determinant of economic growth and competitiveness'.[9]

… and poor health is a drain on wealth …

- EU countries have ageing populations. As noted by the EC's DG for Economic and Financial Affairs, the EU will require its citizens to work longer and will need to lower the incidence of chronic diseases which reduce healthy working years and which greatly increase the costs of health care in old age.[10]
- Health disparities within and between member countries are large and constitute one of the most profound areas of inequity in the EU. Use of effective measures to tackle health inequities means ensuring that a country's health system is not falling short of its performance potential.[11]

[6] European Commission, *Factsheet: Horizon 2020 budget*, EC, 19.11.2013. http://ec.europa.eu/research/horizon2020/pdf/press/fact_sheet_on_horizon2020_budget.pdf.

[7] Commission on Macroeconomics and Health, *Macroeconomics and health: investing in health for economic development*, Report of the Commission on Macroeconomics and Health. World Health Organization, 2001. http://whqlibdoc.who.int/publications/2001/924154550x.pdf.

[8] WHO Euro: *The Tallinn Charter: Health systems for health and wealth*, Brussels: WHO Regional Office for Europe, 2008. www.euro.who.int/en/what-we-do/conferences/who-european-ministerial-conference-on-health-systems/documentation/conference-documents/the-tallinn-charter-health-systems-for-health-and-wealth.

[9] M Suhrcke, M Mckee, RS Arce, S Tsolova and J Mortensen, *The contribution of health to the economy in the European Union. European Commission*, DG Health and Consumer Protection, 23 August 2005, http://ec.europa.eu/health/ph_overview/Documents/health_economy_en.pdf.

[10] G Carone and D Costello, 'Can Europe Afford to Grow Old?' (2006) *International Monetary Fund Finance and Development* 43(3). www.imf.org/external/pubs/ft/fandd/2006/09/carone.htm.

[11] G Dahlgren and M Whitehead, *European strategies for tackling social inequities in health: Levelling up Part 2* (WHO Regional Office for Europe, 2006). www.euro.who.int/__data/assets/pdf_file/0018/103824/E89384.pdf.

— Costs of prescription medicines are continuously rising. In the last couple of decades the increases have outpaced other categories of health care spending and are projected to continue to exceed the growth rates for hospital care and other professional services throughout the present decade.[12]

— The health workforce accounts for over 8 per cent of GDP and about 10 per cent of the EU's total active workforce, including physicians, nurses, pharmacists, administrative and supportive staff, researchers, teachers and trainees.[13]

... demanding more research and innovation for health and health equity (Box 1)

More effective disease prevention and health promotion are vital—and so are better, cheaper ways of producing drugs, vaccines and diagnostics and more effective ways of delivering health information, products, processes and services to users.[14,15,16,17,18] In addition, we need not only affordable and accessible products and services, but also well organised and accessible health systems in low-and middle-income countries (LMICs) in order to improve global health.

Box 1. The health research and innovation system

Research for health is research in any discipline or combination of disciplines to understand the impact on health of policies, programmes, processes, actions or events originating in any sector—including, but not limited to the health sector itself and encompassing biological, economic, environmental,

[12] E Kimbuende, U Ranji and A Salganicoff, *Prescription Drug Costs*, Kaiser Family Foundation, February 2010. www.kaiseredu.org/Issue-Modules/Prescription-Drug-Costs/Background-Brief.aspx.

[13] W Sermeus, L Bruyneel, *Investing in Europe's health workforce of tomorrow: Scope for innovation and collaboration, Summary report of the three Policy Dialogues*, Leuven, Belgium, 26–30 April 2010, European Observatory on Health Systems and policies, 2010. www.healthworkforce4europe.eu/downloads/Report_PD_Leuven_FINAL.pdf.

[14] SA Matlin, T Evans, J Hasler, C Ijsselmuiden, O Pannenborg and OI Touré, 'Signposts to research for health' (2008) *The Lancet* 372, 1521–22. http://download.thelancet.com/pdfs/journals/lancet/PIIS014067360861630X.pdf?id=e16241398b8eb460:67ac7f42:131dc5efbf3:-4c2e1313662914605.

[15] SA Matlin, 'The scope and potential of innovation for health and health equity' in M Gehner, S Jupp and SA Matlin (eds), *Global Forum Update on Research for Health, Vol 5: Fostering Innovation for Global Health* (London, Pro-Brook Publishing, 2008) 13–20. www.bvsde.paho.org/texcom/cd045364/globalforum5/intro.pdf.

[16] CA Gardner, T Acharya and D Yach, 'Technological and social innovation: a unifying new paradigm for global health' (2007) 26 *Health Affairs* 1052–61. Reprinted in SA Matlin et al (eds), *Health Partnerships Review* (Geneva, Global Forum for Health Research, 2008) 22–27. www.innogen.ac.uk/downloads/HealthPartnershipsReview_Full.pdf .

[17] A Hubert, *Empowering people, driving change: Social innovation in the European Union* (EC Bureau of European Policy Advisers, 2010). http://ec.europa.eu/bepa/pdf/publications_pdf/social_innovation.pdf.

[18] SA Matlin and GMR Samuels, 'The Global Health Research and Innovation System' (2009) *The Lancet* 374 (9702) 1662–63. http://download.thelancet.com/pdfs/journals/lancet/PIIS0140673609619127.pdf?id=e16241398b8eb460:67ac7f42:131dc96470a:-5423131366648971 4 .

political, social and other determinants of health; assist in developing interventions to help prevent or mitigate that impact; and contribute to the achievement of health equity and better health for all (note 14).

Innovation for health and health equity is an initiative in any sector or combination of sectors that takes up novel ideas, inventions or processes and applies them to achieving improved health and greater health equity. It has been stressed that a combination of social and technological innovation is essential and the importance of social innovation (involving new ways to manage people, processes, and information) to the Europe 2020 agenda has been highlighted (notes 15–17).

The global health research and innovation system encompasses all of these activities and requires the development of a comprehensive systems perspective to guide efforts to achieve greater effectiveness, efficiency and impact and respond to innovation failures in science, the market, or public health, as an essential element of reducing health inequities (note 18).

The imperative to reach the highest attainable standard of health for all people, enshrined in the global recognition of health as a human right,[19] demands explicit attention to uncovering and eliminating health inequities. Research has multiple roles to play in detecting health inequities, understanding their causes and developing solutions.[20,21,22] Moreover, research itself must be rigorously constructed to ensure that it is free of biases in conceptualisation, methodology or interpretation that could lead to increasing disadvantage for groups based on factors such as ability, ethnicity, gender, geographic location, poverty or social position.[23]

[19] *Constitution of the World Health Organization*, adopted by the International Health Conference, New York, 19–22 June 1946, entered into force 7 April 1948, amended by the Twenty-sixth, Twenty-ninth, Thirty-ninth and Fifty-first World Health Assemblies. www.who.int/governance/eb/who_constitution_en.pdf.

[20] A Spinakis et al, *Expert review and proposals for measurement of health inequalities in the European Union—Full Report*, Brussels: EC, Directorate General for Health and Consumers. Luxembourg, 2011. http://ec.europa.eu/health/social_determinants/docs/full_quantos_en.pdf.

[21] P Östlin et al, *Priorities for research on equity and health: Implications for global and national priority setting and the role of WHO to take the health equity research agenda forward* (Geneva, WHO, 2010). www.who.int/social_determinants/implementation/Thefinalreportnovember2010.pdf.

[22] R Haber, *Health Equity Impact Assessment: A Primer* (Toronto, The Wellesley Institute, 2011). www.wellesleyinstitute.com/health-care-reform/roadmap-for-health-equity/health-equity-impact-assessment/health-equity-impact-assessment/.

[23] MA Burke and M Eichler, *The Bias Free Framework, A practical tool for identifying and eliminating social biases in health research* (Geneva, Global Forum for Health Research, 2006). www.biasfree.org/full_BF.pdf.

B. The Importance of Global Health

Global health recognises the interdependent relationship between health status within and across countries and policy and legal instruments across diverse sectors, so constituting a distinct field requiring special attention.[24,25]

— As many of the determinants and new challenges for health are global and complex in nature, action on health must transcend national boundaries. The definition of global health[25,26] as 'health issues which transcend national boundaries and governments' includes a range of health challenges operating across the EU, beyond those that can be dealt with nationally, such as health security, social determinants and non-communicable diseases.
— The background paper[27] to the World Conference on the Social Determinants of Health emphasised that due to the 'interconnectedness of the modern world, national action on social determinants is not sufficient. International organizations, nongovernmental agencies, and bilateral cooperation partners need to align their efforts on social determinants broadly with those of national governments'.
— Conceptualised beyond a 'global burden of disease' approach, global health 'emphasises the social, environmental, and economic contexts in which health, disease, and healthcare interventions are embedded'.[28]
— The process of globalisation has created not only threats to health but also many new opportunities that require global frameworks. For example, globalisation has provided significant opportunities for sharing and exchanging knowledge through networks in global research and innovation.

II. THE CASE FOR EXPLICIT EU ENGAGEMENT IN RESEARCH AND INNOVATION FOR GLOBAL HEALTH

Previous experience has shown the gains to be achieved from global, collaborative health research and that some innovations can only occur on a regional/international level.

[24] European Commission, *Communication from the Commission to the Council, the European Parliament, the European Economic and Social Committee and the Committee of the Regions: The EU Role in Global Health*, Brussels: EC, COM(2010)128 final, 31.3.2010. http://ec.europa.eu/development/icenter/repository/COMM_PDF_COM_2010_0128_EN.PDF.

[25] I Kickbusch and G Lister (eds), *European Perspectives on Global Health: A Policy Glossary* (Brussels, European Foundations Centre, 2006). http://global.wisc.edu/development/resources/diprete-brown-european-perspectives.pdf.

[26] S Battams and SA Matlin, *Discussing a definition of global health.* Global Health Diplomacy Briefing. Global Health Programme(Geneva, Graduate Institute of International and Development Studies, 2013). http://graduateinstitute.ch/files/live/sites/iheid/files/sites/globalhealth/shared/1894/Publications/Publications%202013/Definition_Global_Health_v3.pdf.

[27] WHO, *Closing the gap: Policy into practice on social determinants of health: discussion paper for the World Conference on Social Determinants of Health*, October 2011. www.who.int/sdhconference/Discussion-paper-EN.pdf.

[28] R Labonte and J Spiegel, 'Setting global health research priorities—Burden of disease and inherently global health issues should both be considered' (2003) 326 *British Medical Journal* 722.

Justification for attention by the EU to research and innovation for global health includes:

— recognition of health as a human right and promotion of human rights and European values;
— consistency with EU commitments to global health, including global solidarity,[29,30] Millennium development goals (MDGs—some of which are health specific and others health-determining),[31] equity[22] and development;[32]
— benefits to the EU and the world accruing from addressing global health needs and inequities in terms of early control of pandemics, but also through promotion of social cohesion and responsibility;
— fostering innovative models for fair and empowering partnerships with LMICs. Good examples of models include the European and Developing Countries Clinical Trials Partnership (EDCTP)[33] and the Bamako Call to Action on Research for Health;[34]
— adding value to previous investments in joint R&D and capacity building (such as the FP7 funded Call for Africa (Health) (€39 million) capacity-building projects, the EDCTP and the SICAs—see section II.B).

In many European economies, health is the largest industry and is a growing industry. Europe thus has a unique opportunity to take a more prominent role in moving global health research and innovation forward. Support for commercialisation to turn research into products (including medicine and food products) and technological and social innovations, supported by systems and innovative distribution models, will greatly benefit Europe and LMICs. A significant increase in investment for global health is necessary to ensure that Europe is not left behind in terms of global health research and innovation in these areas. Europe also has played a prominent role in research capacity building for global health in LMICs (see section II.B).

[29] JM Barroso, *Statement on behalf of the European Union at the Fourth UN Conference on the Least Developed Countries*, Istanbul 9–13 May 2011, www.un.org/wcm/webdav/site/ldc/shared/ldc4-eu.pdf.

[30] A Piebalgs, *The challenges of meeting the Millennium Development Goals*, Speech at the conference 'Five Years to Go'. http://ec.europa.eu/commission_2010-2014/piebalgs/multimedia/pdf/speeches/challenges_mdg_20100303_en.pdf.

[31] JM Barroso, *State of the Union 2010*, Address to European Parliament, Strasbourg, 7 September 2010. http://europa.eu/rapid/pressReleasesAction.do?reference=SPEECH/10/411&format=HTML&aged=0&language=EN&guiLanguage=en.

[32] European Commission, *EC Development and Cooperation—Europaid, Financing for Development*. http://ec.europa.eu/europeaid/what/development-policies/financing_for_development/index_en.htm.

[33] European and Developing Countries Clinical Trials Partnership (EDCTP). www.edctp.org.

[34] Editorial, 'Bamako Call to Action on Research for Health' (2008) 372 *The Lancet* 1855. doi:10.1016/S0140-6736(08)61789-4. www.who.int/rpc/news/Bamako%20call%20to%20action%20-%20thelancet%20281108.pdf.

A. Recognition of Health as a Human Right and Promotion of Human Rights and European Values

The fundamental right to health is affirmed in the UN Declaration of Human Rights,[35] the WHO Constitution,[36] the International Covenant on Economic, Social and Political Rights,[37] and the Declaration of Alma-Ata.[38] The EU is founded on 'the values of respect for human dignity, liberty, democracy, equality, the rule of law and respect for human rights.' Respect for human rights is also enshrined in the Council of Europe's Convention for the Protection of Human Rights and Fundamental Freedoms.[39] Human rights and health are also interlinked such that the achievement of many human rights, such as social and political rights and freedoms, is dependent upon a good state of physical and mental health.[40] Conversely, achievement of the 'right to health' is also dependent upon other rights being achieved, for example, the 'right to an adequate standard of living'.

The EU cannot credibly sustain human rights within and beyond its borders without explicitly addressing the range of important global health issues discussed here—especially those concerned with equity, access to health services, social determinants of health and effective governance for global health.

Given the shared nature of global health threats and global public goods, global health is a leading field in which Europe can demonstrate and develop its shared values of solidarity, equity, universality and human rights, among the citizens of its own Member States and Associated Countries along with those in other countries. Some EU Member States have experience to share globally when it comes to human rights and health initiatives (for example, the UK Government's Human Rights in Healthcare framework).[41]

B. Consistency with International and EU Commitments to Global Health

Global health has gained increasing prominence through various international forums such as the World Economic Forum (for example, the Global Health Advisory Board, chronic disease and global health activities, and data collection

[35] United Nations, *UN Declaration of Human Rights*, 1948, www.un.org/en/documents/udhr/.

[36] WHO, *Health and human rights* (Geneva, WHO, 2011). www.who.int/hhr/en/.

[37] UN High Commissioner for Human Rights, *International Covenant on Economic, Social and Political Rights*, Geneva. http://www.ohchr.org/EN/ProfessionalInterest/Pages/CESCR.aspx.

[38] WHO, *Declaration of Alma-Ata*, International Conference on Primary Health Care, Alma-Ata, USSR, 6–12 September 1978. http://www.who.int/publications/almaata_declaration_en.pdf?ua=1.

[39] Council of Europe, *Convention for the Protection of Human Rights and Fundamental Freedoms as amended by Protocols No 11 and No 14* (Strasbourg, Council of Europe, 2010). http://conventions.coe.int/treaty/en/treaties/html/005.htm.

[40] L Gostin, 'Human rights of persons with mental disabilities: The European Convention of Human Rights' (2000) *International Journal of Law and Psychiatry* 23, 125–29.

[41] UK Department of Health, *Human rights in health care—a framework for local action* (London, DH Publications, 2008). http://webarchive.nationalarchives.gov.uk/20130107105354/http://www.dh.gov.uk/en/Publicationsandstatistics/Publications/PublicationsPolicyAndGuidance/DH_088970.

and management activities), UN summits (such as the 2001 HIV/AIDS Summit, the 2011 UN Summit on Non-Communicable Diseases) and G-20 and G-8, which committed[42] to promoting research in support of global health in L'Aquila in 2009.

Policy commitments to global health have been made through the EU and through EU Member States' support of international resolutions. They typically require both coherence across a range of sectors and visible action, often in collaboration with international partners. Since many of the global health challenges are testing the limits of current knowledge and tools, research is a vital component of effective response.

One of the European Commission's guiding principles for global health[43] is 'action to make the impact of research more equitable—joint agenda and priority setting for global health research'. One of the sub-areas of the FP7 framework[44] was international public health and health research focused on health policy, systems and services and reproductive and maternal and child health. Research to serve the health-related MDGs was a mandate of this framework. Global research partnerships which have developed research capacity building and global health outcomes have thus been part of previous research frameworks. These and other initiatives for global health include:

— the Call for Africa ('Better Health for Africa') in FP7 (emanating from the EU–Africa Strategic Partnership) which commenced in 2009 and focused on translating research for human health, international public health and health systems and specific topics of malaria control, infectious agents and cancer, human resources for health, maternal and newborn health, capacity building for research and migrants' health;[45]
— the FP7 Specific International Cooperation Actions (SICAs), which developed research capacity in LMICs and research collaboration based around themes, such as health, food, agriculture and fisheries, environment and socioeconomic themes;[46]

[42] *G8 Summit 'Responsible leadership for a sustainable future'*, G8 Aquila Summit, 2009. www.g8italia2009.it/static/G8_Allegato/G8_Declaration_08_07_09_final,0.pdf.

[43] European Commission, *Commission Staff Working Document: Global health—responding to the challenges of globalisation*, Accompanying document to the Communication from the Commission to the Council, the European Parliament, the European Economic and Social Committee and the Committee of the Regions, The EU Role in Global Health, Brussels, 31.3.2010. Sec (2010) 382 final. http://ec.europa.eu/development/icenter/repository/SEC2010_382_EN.pdf.

[44] European Commission, *Public health research in Europe and beyond* new edn (Brussels, EC, 2011). http://ec.europa.eu/research/health/pdf/public-health-research_en.pdf.

[45] European Commission, Call for Africa. FP7-Africa-2010, http://cordis.europa.eu/fp7/dc/index.cfm?fuseaction=UserSite.PeopleDetailsCallPage&call_id=268.

[46] European Commission, *Commission Staff Working Document, A new approach to international scientific and technological co-operation in the 7th Research Framework Programme (2007–2013) and 7th Framework Programme of the European Atomic Energy Community (Euratom) (2007–2011)*, Brussels: EC, 12.1.2007; SEC(2007)47, http://ec.europa.eu/research/iscp/pdf/newapproach_en.pdf.

— the Health Research Programme also funded the EDCTP. The EDCTP was established in 2003 and funded by 16 European countries and the EC. Its main objective is to support the clinical development of new drugs, vaccines and microbicides against HIV/AIDS, malaria and tuberculosis, while also improving the overall environment for carrying out clinical trial activities in Africa;[47]
— capacity building also occurs through the Marie Curie International Research Staff Exchange Scheme,[48] which involves the short-term exchange of researchers between EU/associated countries and 'third countries', most of which are LMICs;
— the Food Security Thematic Programme of the Development Cooperation Instrument,[49] which provided €130 million over 4 years to the Consultative Group on International Agricultural Research (CGIAR).

a. Key examples of related policy documents

The Lisbon Treaty

The Treaty[50] states that the EU will 'support, coordinate or supplement the actions of member states' in a number of areas including 'protection and improvement of human health'. It defines Europe 'as an actor on the global stage' and aims for greater EU visibility and policy coherence in policy development and external policy relations. This necessitates explicit linkages between Horizon 2020 and the EU policies on development and global health.

EC Communication: The EU's Role in Global Health

The Communication[24] recognises that global health 'is about worldwide improvement of health, reduction of disparities, and protection against global health threats. Addressing global health requires coherence of all internal and external policies and actions based on agreed principles'. It is based upon an understanding of the social determinants, and argues that 'public health policies need to go beyond the national level and require strong global institutions and coordinated efforts'. A key aspect of the Communication is a repeated stress on the multi-sectoral

[47] European and Developing Countries Clinical Trials Partnership, n 33, above.

[48] European Commission, *Marie Curie International Research Staff Exchange Scheme*, http://cordis.europa.eu/fp7/mariecurieactions/irses_en.html.

[49] European Commission, *Food Security Thematic Programme*, http://ec.europa.eu/europeaid/how/finance/dci/food_en.htm.

[50] European Commission, *Treaty of Lisbon amending the Treaty on European Union and the Treaty establishing the European Community*, signed at Lisbon, 13 December 2007, Brussels: EC 2007/C 306/01. http://eur-lex.europa.eu/JOHtml.do?uri=OJ:C:2007:306:SOM:en:HTML.

nature of the challenges and the research and capacity building needed to address them, stating the following:

— Progress on the MDGs has been undermined by unbalanced and fragmented attention to health. Special attention needs to be paid by a multi-sectoral approach.
— It is essential that research priorities are geared to making the biggest impact on public health. Access and innovation need to be addressed simultaneously, as highlighted in the Global Strategy and Plan of Action on Public Health, Innovation and Intellectual Property.[51] One requirement is for multidisciplinary research capacity at national level.
— The EU should address the multi-sector nature of health and its close links to gender, nutrition, water, sanitation, environmental quality and education in all relevant policy dialogues.
— On security concerns and global health threats, the EU must pay closer attention to the concept of 'one world, one health'. This[52] promotes 12 'Manhattan Principles', which emphasise the global and multi-sectoral nature of infectious disease challenges and the need to 'better understand the relationships between health and ecosystem integrity to succeed in improving prospects for a healthier planet.'
— The EU should build up a collective expertise on capacity in global health analysis and policy dialogue.
— The Communication calls for a set of specific actions on research, which are further amplified in the accompanying Commission Staff Working Document[53] (Box 2).

Box 2. The EU Role in Global Health

Communication—Section 4.4. Research and evidence-based dialogue and action (note 24)

— The EU should coordinate more effectively research on global health in order to address the highly fragmented landscape and identify shared global priorities for health research. It should promote effective and fair financing of research that benefits the health of all people.

[51] WHO, *Global Strategy and Plan of Action on Public Health, Innovation and Intellectual Property: WHA resolution WHA61.21, 2008*, Geneva: WHO, www.who.int/gb/ebwha/pdf_files/A61/A61_R21-en.pdf.

[52] *One World, One Health*, www.oneworldonehealth.org.

[53] European Commission, *Commission Staff Working Document: European research and knowledge for global health*, Brussels: EC 31.3.2010, SEC(2010)381. http://ec.europa.eu/development/icenter/repository/SEC2010_381_EN.pdf.

- The EU Research Framework Programmes should continue to give priority to actions which tackle global health challenges. These actions should be based on joint priority-setting processes and equitable partnerships, and safeguard access to the knowledge generated.
- The EU should strengthen and balance the complete health research process of innovation, implementation, access, monitoring and evaluation. Such research should provide effective input for health policies, improve health service provision, and include mechanisms for partner countries to build and sustain their national research capacity.
- The EU should enhance its current work 27 with relevant national and international bodies such as the WHO, the OECD and the Health Metrics Network, to improve health information systems and the collection of comparable data and statistics to allow benchmarking and inform global, European and national policies. The EU should promote the use of ICT, including eHealth.
- All global normative action on the safety of food, feed, products, pharmaceuticals, and medical devices must be evidence-based. The EU should promote the dissemination of information on hazards and risks in these areas.

Staff Working Document: European research and knowledge for global health (Ref 52)

- The document emphasises the shared European values of universality, access to good-quality care, equity and solidarity.
- Control/eradication of communicable diseases is a clear example of a global public good benefitting everyone, in poorer and richer countries alike and in present and future generations. Global collaboration could improve health equity.
- EU Framework Programme: European added-value and mutual interest supports an international science and technology policy that has two interdependent objectives:
  - to support and promote European competitiveness by means of strategic research partnerships with non-EU countries, including highly industrialised and emerging economies, by engaging the best scientists to work in and with Europe; and
  - to address specific problems that non-EU countries face or of a global nature, on the basis of mutual interest and mutual benefit.
- The critical area of improving health systems performance is recognised, stressing the need for health policy and systems research, health care services research.

Europe 2020

The strategy states[3] that the EU is a global player and that it needs to take its international responsibilities seriously. It has been developing partnership with LMICs to eradicate poverty, promote growth and fulfil the MDGs. Europe 2020 highlights the need for a research agenda focusing on health challenges, and the need to 'combat poverty and social exclusion and reduce health inequalities' and promote access to health care.

Health in All Policies

The demand for an approach to health that requires attention to policy across a range of sectors (such as planning and development, industry, trade and commerce, environment, finance, agriculture, housing, public works, education, culture and communications)[54] derives its legitimacy from the Ottawa Charter for Health Promotion,[55] from a deepening understanding of the multitude of factors acting as determinants of health[56,57] and from the EU's own charter,[49] which stipulates that 'a high level of health protection shall be ensured in the definition and implementation of all Union policies and activities'. Health in all Policies[58] 'is a horizontal, complementary policy-related strategy contributing to improved population health. The core is to examine determinants of health that can be altered to improve health but are mainly controlled by the policies of sectors other than health'. It was pursued in the 2006 Finnish presidency of the EU[42] and is a central principle of the European Health Strategy.[59] A specific focus on mental health in 'mental health in all policies' approaches have also been recommended.[60]

[54] WHO, *Global Health Strategy for Health for All by the Year 2000* (Geneva, WHO, 1981). http://whqlibdoc.who.int/publications/9241800038.pdf.

[55] WHO, Ottawa Charter for Health Promotion. First international conference on health promotion. Ottawa, 21 November 1986 (Geneva, WHO, 1986), WHO/HPR/HEP/95.1. www.who.int/healthpromotion/conferences/previous/ottawa/en/index.html.

[56] G Dahlgren and M Whitehead, *Policies and strategies to promote social equity in health* (Stockholm, Institute for Future Studies, 1991).

[57] WHO Commission on the Social Determinants of Health, *Closing the gap in a generation: Health equity through action on the social determinants of health* (Geneva, WHO, 2008). http://whqlibdoc.who.int/publications/2008/9789241563703_eng.pdf.

[58] T Ståhl, M Wismar, E Ollila, E Lahtinen and K Leppo, *Health in All Policies: Prospects and potentials* (Helsinki, Ministry of Social Affairs and Health, 2006). http://ec.europa.eu/health/archive/ph_information/documents/health_in_all_policies.pdf.

[59] European Commission: *White Paper, Together for Health: A Strategic Approach for the EU 2008–2013*, Brussels: EC, 23.10.2007, COM(2007) 630. http://ec.europa.eu/health/ph_overview/Documents/strategy_wp_en.pdf.

[60] G Roberts and K Grimes, *Return on Investment: Mental health promotion and mental illness prevention* (Canadian Policy Network at the University of Western Ontario, 2011). https://secure.cihi.ca/free_products/roi_mental_health_report_en.pdf.

The WHO has been tasked[61] to 'work closely with partner agencies in the multilateral system on appropriate measures that address the social determinants of health … and to advocate inclusion of this topic high on global development and research agendas'; and to 'support research on effective policies and interventions to improve health by addressing the social determinants of health that also serve to strengthen research capacities and collaborations'. Institutional mechanisms for working with other sectors are required to achieve these aims.[62]

Implications for the research and innovation agenda: The acknowledgement of the broad-ranging nature of determinants of health creates a need for:

— structuring research that is interdisciplinary, that crosses sectoral boundaries and that is conceived, organised, reported and has its results applied in ways that stand outside the normal frameworks of conventional single-discipline research. Interdisciplinary research, such as that enquiring into the health impacts of various categories of health determinants in different sectors, faces a number of professional, organisational, and cultural obstacles[63] and requires special mechanisms to foster collaborative action;
— organising an innovation environment that bridges sectors and that encompasses social as well as technological aspects of innovation.

Development Policies and Assistance

Europe is the world's largest donor for development assistance.[64] The EU's development policies, encapsulated in the 'European development consensus',[65] have the overarching objective of eradicating poverty in the context of sustainable development and rest on the central pillars of achieving the MDGs[66] and adhering to the Paris Declaration on Aid Effectiveness and Accra Agenda for Action.[67]

— The EU has committed to policy coherence in 12 policy areas to accelerate progress towards the MDGs, including research and innovation.[68] The latest

[61] WHO, *Reducing health inequities through action on the social determinants of health*, 62nd World Health Assembly Resolution WHA62.14, 22 May 2009. http://apps.who.int/gb/ebwha/pdf_files/A62/A62_R14-en.pdf.

[62] W Hein and I Kickbusch, *Global Health, Aid Effectiveness and the Changing Role of the WHO*, GIGA Focus 2010, No 3. http://graduateinstitute.ch/webdav/site/globalhealth/shared/1894/giga%20focus.pdf.

[63] *Interdisciplinarity* (Wikipedia, 2011). http://en.wikipedia.org/wiki/Interdisciplinarity#cite_note-3.

[64] *European Union: Development and Cooperation*, http://europa.eu/pol/dev/.

[65] European Parliament, Council and Commission, *Joint statement, The European Consensus on Development*, Official Journal of the European Union, 24.02.2006, C 46/1–19. http://ec.europa.eu/development/icenter/repository/european_consensus_2005_en.pdf.

[66] United Nations, *Millennium Development Goals* (New York, UN, 2011). www.un.org/millenniumgoals/index.shtml.

[67] European Commission, *EC Development and Cooperation—EuropeAid, Development Policies* (Brussels, EC, 2011). http://ec.europa.eu/europeaid/what/development-policies/index_en.htm.

[68] European Commission, *EC Development and Cooperation—EuropeAid, Policy coherence for development*. http://ec.europa.eu/europeaid/what/development-policies/policy-coherence/index_en.htm.

biennial report[69] notes that research policy provides a good example of positive synergies created between different policies, contributing decisively to development through financing research projects in the health, food security, social sciences and humanities areas. It stresses the need for a 'whole-of-Union' approach and notes that the evolving global financial crisis underlines the importance of development-oriented support in the areas of research and technology. Recognising the need for action beyond 2015, the FP7 work programme for 2012 included[70] a call for proposals to set a new, post-2015 MDG agenda—to include paving the way towards an improved system for global health innovation.

— The EU Strategy for Action on the Crisis in Human Resources for Health in Developing Countries recognised that one obstacle to achieving the MDGs is the dearth of health workers and set out a range of EU actions for the training and retention of health workers in LMICs.[71] One is 'Identifying opportunities to strengthen research capacity', to include supporting research networks and partnerships such as the EDCTP, which is effectively building clinical trials capacity.
— The EU also supports the International Health Partnership Plus (IHP+), within which capacity development for LMICs is a key strategy, along with mobilising donor agencies around country-initiated health strategies and plans.[72]
— Through both its individual Member States and collective action, the EU has a major role to play in the execution of the Global Strategy and Plan of Action on Public Health, Innovation and Intellectual Property which was negotiated by the Intergovernmental Working Group on Public Health, Innovation and Intellectual Property.[73] This will require coherent EU approaches on a range of development, research and global health agendas. In an important further step following adoption of the *Global Strategy*, in 2011 the WHO established a Consultative Expert Working Group on Research and Development[74]

[69] European Commission, *Communication from the Commission to the Council, the European Parliament, the European Economic and Social Committee and the Committee of the Regions, Policy Coherence for Development—Establishing the policy framework for a whole-of-the-Union approach*, Brussels: EC, 15.9.2009, COM(2009) 458, http://ec.europa.eu/development/icenter/repository/COM_2009_458_part1_en.pdf.

[70] European Commission, *FP7 Call for Proposals: HEALTH.2012.4.1-6: Setting health-related development goals beyond 2015*, Brussels: EC NET4SOCIETY, 2011. http://www.2020-horizon.com/Setting-healthrelated-development-goals-beyond-2015-i213.html.

[71] European Commission, *Communication from the Commission to the Council and the European Parliament, EU Strategy for Action on the Crisis in Human Resources for Health in Developing Countries*, Brussels: EC, 12.12.2005, COM(2005) 642. http://eur-lex.europa.eu/LexUriServ/site/en/com/2005/com2005_0642en01.pdf.

[72] *International Health Partnership Plus*. www.internationalhealthpartnership.net/en/home.

[73] WHO, *Public health, innovation, and intellectual property and trade* (Geneva, WHO, 2011). www.who.int/phi/about/en/.

[74] WHO, *Consultative Expert Working Group on Research and Development: Financing and Coordination (CEWG)* (Geneva, WHO, 2011). www.who.int/phi/news/cewg_2011/en/index.html.

(CEWG) to examine mechanisms for financing and coordination. The 2012 report[75] of the CEWG represented a milestone in long-standing international efforts to close a critical gap in the development of drugs and other health technologies to meet the health needs of poor and neglected populations. The report recommended a global framework for R&D including an observatory, coordination mechanisms and financing based on the principle of de-linking the costs of R&D from the prices of products, created through the vehicle of an inter-governmentally negotiated convention. Following discussions of the report at an Open Ended Meeting of WHO Member States[76] in November 2012, the January 2013 WHO Executive Board[77] and the May 2013 World Health Assembly,[78] three key elements of the report are being progressed to different extents through further intergovernmental negotiations: (1) a global health R&D observatory; (2) R&D demonstration projects; and (3) coordination and financing of health R&D. The EU can make a substantial contribution to these processes, both through the coordinated operations of its development, research and global health agendas and through the application of its capacities in science diplomacy (see section II.C.v.a).

It is evident that, as the main instrument through which EU policy and practice in research and innovation are channelled, Horizon 2020 should play a major role in addressing the development aspects of research and innovation in relation to global health and the health aspects of the MDGs. Application of science and technology is indispensable to achieving the MDGs[79] and Horizon 2020 will need to encompass research and innovation that can accommodate the post-2015 global agenda for health and development. Key elements of the research and innovation agenda to support development goals are:

— Within the EU: Funding collaborative research and innovation on new or improved methods for the diagnosis, prevention and treatment of infectious diseases and for non-communicable diseases (NCDs) that pose a significant threat to health in LMICs. While infectious diseases have been specifically

[75] WHO, *Research and Development to Meet Health Needs in Developing Countries: Strengthening Global Financing and Coordination. Report of the Consultative Expert Working Group on Research and Development: Financing and Coordination* (Geneva, WHO, 2012). www.who.int/phi/cewg_report/en/.

[76] WHO, *Open-Ended Meeting on Follow-up of the report of the Consultative Expert Working Group on Research and Development: Financing and Coordination (CEWG, WHO Headquarters, Geneva, 26–28 November 2012* (Geneva, WHO, 2012). www.who.int/phi/cewg/en/.

[77] WHO, *Follow-up of the report of the Consultative Expert Working Group on Research and Development: Financing and Coordination. Report by the Director-General,* WHO Executive Board 132nd session, January 2013 (Geneva, WHO), Paper EB 132/21. http://apps.who.int/gb/ebwha/pdf_files/EB132/B132_21-en.pdf.

[78] WHO, *Follow-up of the report of the Consultative Expert Working Group on Research and Development: Financing and Coordination. Report by the Director-General.* World Health Assembly, May 2013, paper A66/23. http://apps.who.int/gb/ebwha/pdf_files/WHA66/A66_23-en.pdf.

[79] C Juma and Y-C Lee, *Innovation: Applying Knowledge in Development, Report of the UN Millennium Project Task Force on Science, Technology and Innovation* (London, Earthscan, 2005). www.unmillenniumproject.org/documents/Science-complete.pdf.

targeted in the MDGs, 'multiple studies demonstrate a continuing and significant disconnect between aid and the burden of health conditions, including maternal mortality and malaria, and the disability adjusted life years measure'.[80] Little attention has been paid to NCDs in LMICs, although NCDs have now overtaken infectious diseases as the main causes of morbidity and mortality in LMICs.[81] With 70–86 per cent of deaths in Europe now being attributed to NCDs, comparative studies of chronic disease management programmes across countries are providing one important approach to finding effective and affordable solutions.[82] The growing levels of NCDs in LMICs—expected by 2030 to account for three quarters of the disease burden in LMICs, have been described as a 'chronic emergency' by the World Bank,[83] which has argued 'the case for elevating the challenge as a priority item to address on the agenda of decision-makers'.

Research to address issues such as obesity, food security and surveillance, mental health (and associated disability), and developing local research capacity and civil society engagement in these initiatives is required.[84] Furthermore, Public Health Genomics (PHG) is a field of growing importance as it contributes to the better understanding and prevention of growing global health problems, including obesity and mental health.[85]

— Through collaborations between the EU and external actors: Funding collaborative research involving institutions in EU Member States, other high-income countries (HICs) and LMICs on new or improved methods for the diagnosis, prevention and treatment of infectious diseases and NCDs that pose a significant threat to health in LMICs. The UN General Assembly *Political declaration of the High-level meeting of the General Assembly on the Prevention and Control of Non-Communicable Diseases*[86] provides a framework for action and research on NCDs.

[80] H Feldbaum, K Lee and J Michaud, 'Global Health and Foreign Policy' (2010) *Epidemiologic Reviews* 32(1), 82–92. http://epirev.oxfordjournals.org/content/32/1/82.full.pdf.

[81] PZ Zimmet and KGMM Alberti, 'Introduction: Globalization and the Non-communicable Disease Epidemic' (2006) *Obesity* 14, 1–3. http://onlinelibrary.wiley.com/doi/10.1038/oby.2006.1/full.

[82] M Rijken and N Bekkema, *Chronic Disease Management Matrix 2010: Results of a survey in ten European countries* (Utrecht, NIVEL, 2011). www.nivel.nl/sites/default/files/bestanden/Rapport-chronic-disease-management-matrix-2010.pdf.

[83] IA Nikolic, AE Stanciole, M Zaydman, *Chronic Emergency: Why NCDs Matter*, Health, Nutrition, and Population, Human Development Network (Washington DC, The World Bank, 2011). http://siteresources.worldbank.org/HEALTHNUTRITIONANDPOPULATION/Resources/281627-1095698140167/ChronicEmergencyWhyNCDsMatter.pdf.

[84] SL Gortmaker et al, 'Changing the future of obesity: science, policy, and action' (2011) *The Lancet* 378, 838–47. www.thelancet.com/journals/lancet/article/PIIS0140-6736%2811%2960815-5/fulltext?_eventId=login.

[85] *Public Health Genomics European Network (PHGEN)*. www.phgen.eu/typo3/index.php.

[86] United Nations, *Political declaration of the High-level Meeting of the General Assembly on the Prevention and Control of Non-Communicable Diseases*, New York: UN General Assembly A/66/L.1 2001. www.un.org/en/ga/ncdmeeting2011/.

— As a component of empowerment: Supporting LMICs to build national capacities for research and innovation policy development and management, including in all key areas of research and innovation for health:
  — Supporting LMICs to enhance their capacities to conduct research to tackle major health challenges and improve population health—including achieving the specific MDG targets and also such fields as research on NCDs and the very neglected but critical field of health policy and systems research.
  — Supporting LMICs, nationally or regionally, to meet their aspirations for establishing the activities necessary for drug discovery[87] and production.[88] This will include not only clinical trials capacity (for example, the EU-supported EDCTP)[33] but also establishing national or regional capacities for drug innovation and for pharmaceutical production and regulatory agencies and laboratories that can license products and can also conduct high-quality local monitoring of the quality of pharmaceuticals in order to deal with the severe problems associated with substandard and counterfeit drugs that are widely in circulation.[89]
  — Supporting LMICs on research into innovative health financing and creating accessible and equitable health systems, to reduce the burden of health costs for citizens of LMICs and improve health outcomes.[90]

C. Benefits to the EU Itself of Addressing Global Health Needs and Inequities

i. Innovation Union

The EC Communication on the Innovation Union[91] recognises the critical importance for the EU of: (1) strengthening its ability to drive innovation in products, services, business and social processes and models and (2) successfully tackling major societal challenges, such as climate change, energy and resource scarcity,

[87] T Mboya-Okeyo, RG Ridley and S Nwaka, 'The African Network for Drugs and Diagnostics Innovation' (2009) *The Lancet* 373, 1507–08. www.who.int/tdr/news/documents/ANDI_Lancet_2009.pdf.

[88] M Berger et al, *Strengthening pharmaceutical innovation in Africa* (Council on Health Research for Development (COHRED) and New Partnership for Africa's Development (NEPAD), 2010). www.nepad.org/system/files/str.pdf.

[89] WHO, *General information on counterfeit medicines* (Geneva, WHO, 2014). www.who.int/medicines/services/counterfeit/overview/en/.

[90] M-L Escobar et al, *Global health crises* (Brookings global economy and development, 2007). www.brookings.edu/~/media/Files/rc/reports/2007/02globaleconomics/200702_08health.pdf.

[91] European Commission, *Communication from the Commission to the European Parliament, the Council, the European Economic and Social Committee and the Committee of the Regions, Europe 2020 Flagship Initiative—Innovation Union*, Brussels: EC, 6.10.2010, COM(2010) 546 final. http://ec.europa.eu/research/innovation-union/pdf/innovation-union-communication_en.pdf#view=fit&pagemode=none.

health and ageing and social exclusion. Among the weaknesses identified that the Innovation Union aims to tackle are:

- under-investment in the EU's knowledge foundation. Other countries, like the US and Japan, are out-investing the EU, and China is rapidly catching up;
- the need to adopt a much more strategic approach to innovation. An approach whereby:
  - innovation (including 'social innovation') is the overarching policy objective;
  - a medium to longer-term perspective is taken;
  - EU and national/regional policies are closely aligned and mutually reinforcing;
  - new products are addressing priority health needs and are accessible to those in need;
  - international collaboration is based on the principles of fairness and mutuality; and
  - the highest political level sets a strategic agenda; regularly monitors progress; tackles delays.

The EU has endorsed EC proposals to launch a European innovation partnership on active and healthy ageing, the first flagship initiative under the Innovation Union (see section b. below). It must be recognised that innovation *per se* is not an end in itself, but needs to contribute to improving health and reducing inequalities.

Some of the concrete actions that the Innovation Union proposes to achieve its goals are summarised in Box 3.

Box 3. Some concrete actions proposed to achieve the Innovation Union goals

- Protecting and stepping up the investments in education, R&D, innovation and ICTs. For the EU itself, this must include sticking to the target of raising expenditure on R&D to 3 per cent of GDP by 2020.
- EU and national research and innovation systems need to be better linked with each other and their performance improved.
- We need to get more innovation out of our research. Cooperation between the worlds of science and the world of business must be enhanced, obstacles removed and incentives put in place.
- Remaining barriers for entrepreneurs to bring 'ideas to market' must be removed: better access to finance, particularly for SMEs, affordable Intellectual Property Rights, smarter and more ambitious regulation and targets, faster setting of interoperable standards and strategic use

of our massive procurement budgets. As an immediate step, agreement should be reached on the EU patent before the end of the year.

— European Innovation Partnerships should be launched to accelerate research, development and market deployment of innovations to tackle major societal challenges, pool expertise and resources and boost the competitiveness of EU industry, starting with the area of healthy ageing.
— Strengths in design and creativity must be better exploited. We must champion social innovation, develop a better understanding of public sector innovation, identify and give visibility to successful initiatives, and benchmark progress.
— We need to work better with our international partners. That means opening access to our R&D programmes, while ensuring comparable conditions abroad.
— A key concern of the EU is progressing international cooperation with third countries to develop global approaches, address societal challenges and move towards a level playing field by, for example, removing barriers to access.

Communication from the Commission (note 90)

a. Innovation in Healthcare Technologies

There are very few industrial segments whose growth will target the priorities of Europe 2020 and the Innovation Union as effectively as healthcare.[6,92]

The health research and innovation system provides wealth:

— Healthcare technologies promote growth, create wealth and attract investment. They encompass a range of areas including pharmaceutical drugs, vaccines and diagnostics; medical devices, surgical instrumentation, orthopaedics, prosthetics, advanced wound-care, health information technologies, telemedicine, eHealth, mHealth, medical imaging, medical and surgical robotics, and laboratory facilities for a range of R&D and process activities including clinical trials, medical diagnosis and screening, life sciences, toxicology, genetics, drug delivery, medical engineering, information technology, chemical and biochemical analysis.

[92] *The Healthcare Technology Venture Market in Europe* (Cambridge, UK and Yorkshire & Humber LI Group, 2009). http://cymraeg.cardiffmedicentre.co.uk/files/uploaded/files/Healthcare_Technology_Venture_Market.pdf.

— The European medical technology industry invests some €3.8bn in R&D and employs 435,000 people, making a major impact upon Europe's economy. The healthcare technology venture capital market is the second largest sector behind the information and telecommunications sector. Around 24 per cent of all European deals are invested into healthcare technology.[7] Small- and medium-size enterprises (SMEs) comprise the majority (80 per cent) of companies in the medical technology industry. The Lund Declaration under the Swedish Presidency of the EU advocated European leadership in research and called for a focus on grand challenges of our time with the involvement of SMEs.[93] It emphasised the importance of Europe taking a global lead in the development of enabling technologies (including biotechnology). Eucomed (which represents the medical technology industry in Europe) has noted that key barriers to growth in emerging markets include lack of consistent application of EU regulation and lack of easy access to research and development funding.[94]

— The pharmaceutical industry has been one of the major innovative industries in Europe and responsible for a large fraction of economic activity. For example, it is the biggest sector investor in R&D in the UK, accounting for about 25 per cent of total investment by business, valued at £3.3bn. In 2007 the UK had the third-highest share of global pharmaceutical R&D expenditure of any nation, with 9 per cent of the total, behind the USA (49 per cent) and Japan (15 per cent). The UK has the largest pharmaceutical R&D expenditure of any European nation (23 per cent of the total), followed by France (20 per cent), Germany (19 per cent), and Switzerland (11 per cent).[95] Opportunities in emerging pharmaceutical markets such as Brazil, China, India and the Russian Federation are growing rapidly.[96]

But the healthcare industry in general and the pharmaceutical industry in particular provide an example *par excellence* of where the EU is presently losing ground and where an explicit, coherent and comprehensive effort is required if Europe is to sustain its historical leading role. The pharmaceutical industry is now in crisis globally and the European component is in serious decline. Globally, the industry now relies heavily on sales from an aging portfolio of drugs, whilst the proportion of total sales from newer drugs has dropped. There has been a steep decline in the number of new molecular entities registered in the last decade, both in terms

[93] *The Lund Declaration: Europe must focus on the grand challenges of our time*, July 2009. www.nanopartikel.info/files/content/dana/Dokumente/lund_declaration_final_version_9_july.pdf.

[94] Eucomed Medical Technology, *European Health and SMEs: Big Challenges, Small & Medium Sized Solutions*, EUCOMED Position Paper, 22 March 2011, www.eucomed.org/uploads/Modules/Publications/110322_european_health_and_smes2011.pdf.

[95] UK Department For Business, Innovation & Skills, *The Pharmaceutical Sector in the UK*. www.bis.gov.uk/policies/business-sectors/biotechnology-pharmaceuticals-and-healthcare/pharmaceutical.

[96] Association of British Pharmaceutical Industries, *Global Pharmaceutical Industry and Market* (ABPI, 2011). www.abpi.org.uk/industry-info/knowledge-hub/global-industry/Pages/industry-market-.aspx.

of absolute numbers and as a proportion of research spending.[97,98] A combination of factors, including costs of labour and shifting balances between regulation and innovation stimuli, have led to movement of the industry away from Europe and towards the USA and emerging markets,[99],[100] driving companies to invest in emerging economies like India.[101]

Concerted effort within the EU will be essential if it is to retain and revitalise this important sector of its innovation portfolio. This will need to recognise the special features of drug development that distinguish it from other areas of innovation, including the long development lead times (up to 10–15 years) and extremely high costs (hundreds of millions of euros) and high attrition rates, making this a much less attractive area for venture capital and requiring public support at a number of stages of the basic science, drug discovery and development processes; the lack of capacity of SMEs to take products all the way from bench to bedside—as a result of which they tend to get absorbed by large pharmaceutical companies as soon as they have a promising candidate drug, which repeatedly stifles the building of sustainable SME innovation capacity; and the need to develop reward systems that balance returns on investment against access and affordability issues. Consequently, specific measures are required to address this critical area of innovation in the EU. Horizon 2020 should build on the important experience of FP7 in opening access of funding to SMEs for drug development. As observed by one SME, 'EC money could help companies carry their research to higher stages of value without depending on private markets'.[102] The field of public health genomics can also provide examples for innovative business models in health care systems at European and global levels.[103,104]

Furthermore with public intervention, a crucial reform of pharmaceutical innovation can be engineered: re-orientating it towards developing products

[97] *Global Pharmaceutical R&D Productivity Declining According To Thomson Reuters*, CMR International, 1 July 2010. http://thomsonreuters.com/press-releases/072010/RandD-Productivity-Declines.

[98] M Herper, 'The Decline Of Pharmaceutical Research, Measured In New Drugs And Dollars' (2011) *Forbes* 27 June, www.forbes.com/sites/matthewherper/2011/06/27/the-decline-of-pharmaceutical-researchmeasured-in-new-drugs-and-dollars/.

[99] L Davidson and G Greblov, *The Pharmaceutical Industry in the Global Economy* (Indiana University, 2005). www.google.co.uk/url?sa=t&source=web&cd=6&ved=0CEAQFjAF&url=http%3A%2F%2Fwww.bus.indiana.edu%2Fdavidso%2Flifesciences%2Flsresearchpapers%2Fpharmaceutical%2520industryaug12.doc&rct=j&q=pharmaceutical%20industry%20global%20decline&ei=5hBBTrikDcfPhAfyrZzZCQ&usg=AFQjCNET5kK2lpN7T3fahzcaTo3jwLy9LA&cad=rja.

[100] A Daemmrich, *Where is the Pharmacy to the World? International Regulatory Variation and Pharmaceutical Industry Location.* Harvard Business School, Working Paper 2009, 09-118. www.hbs.edu/research/pdf/09-118.pdf.

[101] Boston Consulting Group, *Life Sciences R&D: Changing the Innovation Equation in India* (Boston, BCG, 2011). www.bcg.com/expertise_impact/biopharma_summit.aspx.

[102] G Sinha, 'Money pot for SMEs' (2011) *Nature Biotechnology* 29, 779, doi:10.1038/nbt0911-779a. www.nature.com/nbt/journal/v29/n9/full/nbt0911-779a.html?WT.ec_id=NBT-201109.

[103] *Office of Public Health Genomics, Center for Disease Control and Prevention, USA.* www.cdc.gov/genomics/

[104] AS Daar, K Berndtson, DL Persad and PA Singer, 'How can developing countries harness biotechnology to improve health?' (2007) *BMC Public Health* 7, 346, doi:10.1186/1471-2458-7-346. www.biomedcentral.com/content/pdf/1471-2458-7-346.pdf.

that are intrinsically cheaper and more cost-effective. This will benefit health and health systems globally, enable the EU to re-position itself as a leader in the field and help facilitate health access and products for the 'bottom billion'. For example, a cheaper 'polypill' could be developed, making the treatment of NCDs more accessible in both HICs and LMICs. There are many systems and environmental drivers associated with the food industry contributing to the obesity pandemic.[105] However, the food industry also provides good examples of innovative strategies being used to promote nutritional products for the bottom billion[106] (for example, see Box 4). In addition, EU flagship projects such as IT Future of Medicine (ITFoM)[107] using innovative technologies can serve as a blueprint for the future of medicine and health care.

Box 4. Food industry: Challenges and Opportunities

Important factors in the global obesity pandemic, an issue now prominent across LMICs as well as HICs, include system drivers such as the pursuit of high growth and promotion of consumption, along with environmental drivers such as the food industry's effectively marketed, easily accessible, energy-dense foods (note 104).

Conversely, the company Grameen Danone Foods has developed 'social business' in Bangladesh to tackle malnutrition (provide yogurt to poor populations, contributing to MDG 1 on Nutrition) and providing jobs to many locals, that is, micro-farmers' milk is used for production and the food distribution system used is 'door to door' sales. Similarly, Nestlé Peru has used innovative and inclusive business strategies by developing a food distribution model in order to access new markets in Lima, whilst at the same time developing employment for local women.

World Business Council for Sustainable Development (note 105)

b. Social Innovation

Social innovation has been defined[108] by the EU as 'innovations that are social in both their ends and their means … new ideas (products, services and models) that simultaneously meet social needs (more effectively than alternatives) and create

105 BA Swinburn et al, *The global obesity pandemic: shaped by global drivers and local environments* (2011) *The Lancet* 378, 804–14. www.ncbi.nlm.nih.gov/pubmed/21872749.

106 *Inclusive business for sustainable livelihoods* (World Business Council for Sustainable Development, 2011). www.inclusivebusiness.org/.

107 *IT Future of Medicine (ITFoM)*. www.itfom.eu.

108 European Commission, *Empowering people, driving change: Social innovation in the European Union*, EC, 2010, 131pp, http://ec.europa.eu/bepa/pdf/publications_pdf/social_innovation.pdf.

new social relationships or collaborations. They are innovations that are not only good for society but also enhance society's capacity to act'.

Some key aspects of social innovation that need to be addressed by Horizon 2020 are:

— ***Social exclusion and health:*** One of the five main targets for Europe 2020 requires that at least 20 million fewer people are in or at risk of poverty and social exclusion.[109] Social innovation policies and strategies to tackle these problems are highlighted. The Renewed Social Agenda aims to ensure that all EU policies promote opportunities, access and solidarity (screening new initiatives for social and employment impacts).[110]

  Since poor health is a major cause of poverty and social exclusion, research to understand and address the major causes of ill-health is indispensable. Health itself is not an area of EU competence and Europe 2020 includes a set of national targets covering many areas.[111] However, given that health is a major element of the Framework programmes, there is clearly a need for a research agenda which addresses the determinants of health in relation to the causes of poverty and social exclusion.

  Taking account of the nature of many of the issues that need to be addressed (such as ageing, NCDs, substance abuse, nutrition and diet, transport, work, environment), two elements are essential to the research and innovation agenda on poverty and social exclusion:

  — the research must be ***interdisciplinary*** and cross sectoral boundaries, often taking as its starting point an examination of health impacts of policies, actions and conditions that originate outside the health sector and which influence behaviour and lifestyle;

  — fostering ***social*** innovations to promote and sustain good health must be central to developing solutions.

— ***Migration and health:*** With increasing migration across and into Europe have come new challenges for health, equity and social inclusion.[112] The physical and psychological health of migrants may be affected by a number of factors, including their social and economic circumstances, health history and access to health care prior to arrival in the new country, skills in the language of the new country, along with the circumstances surrounding the migration.[113]

[109] *Europe 2020 targets* (Brussels, EC). http://ec.europa.eu/europe2020/targets/eu-targets/index_en.htm.

[110] *Employment Social Affairs and Inclusion: Renewed Social Agenda* (Brussels, EC, 2 July 2008). http://ec.europa.eu/social/main.jsp?catId=547.

[111] *Europe 2020: National Targets* (Brussels, EC). http://ec.europa.eu/europe2020/pdf/targets_en.pdf.

[112] C Boswell, *Migration in Europe* (Global Commission on International Migration, 2005). http://storage.globalcitizen.net/data/topic/knowledge/uploads/2010072785740705.pdf.

[113] M Carballo and M Mboup, *International migration and health* (Global Commission on International Migration, 2005). www.iom.int/jahia/webdav/site/myjahiasite/shared/shared/mainsite/policy_and_research/gcim/tp/TP13.pdf.

Migrants, refuges and asylum seekers, whose numbers have recently accelerated due to conflict in home countries, are at greater risk for poverty, unemployment and subsequently social exclusion.[114] Access to secure employment and treatment within employment roles is an important issue for migrant populations. The United Nations High Commissioner for Human Rights has made a call for the ratification of the International Convention on the protection of the rights of all migrant workers and members of their families.[115] 'Better integration of migrant workers in the workforce' is a goal of Europe 2020. It has also been recognised[3] that 'Europe needs to make full use of its labour potential to face the challenges of an ageing population and rising global competition'. Fields such as ageing, community care and health care are critical avenues for migrant employment development, social innovation and research. Provision of education, training and language skills will be key to developments in the aged care workforce[116] and other areas. As migration is a cross-country issue, there are many potential benefits of research collaboration in this field.

— ***Ageing, the health care system and informal care:*** Population ageing is a global trend creating many challenges, including increased levels of chronic disease and conditions,[117] increased health and care costs, increasing rates of disability[118] and high levels of informal care. Costs may be exacerbated by over-medication and unnecessary operations occurring in particular regions of Europe.[119] It has been predicted that spending on long-term aged care in OECD nations will double or even triple by 2050.[111] Informal carers also share the burden of care and contribute to GDP; for example it has been estimated that informal care has the same economic value as high-end residential aged care.[120] Carers are also more likely to be unemployed or in part-time paid work than average, and experiencing poverty and health problems, including mental health problems.[111]

[114] B Gushulak, P Pace and J Weekers, 'Migration and health of migrants' in *Poverty and social exclusion in the WHO European Region: health systems respond* (Copenhagen, WHO Regional Office for Europe, 2010) Ch 24, pp 257–81. www.euro.who.int/__data/assets/pdf_file/0006/115485/E94018.pdf.

[115] N Pillay, *Equal rights for all migrants: A call for ratification of the International Convention on the Protection of the Rights of All Migrant Workers and Members of Their Families,* address to the Graduate Institute of International and Development Studies, Geneva, 14 December 2011. www.ohchr.org/en/NewsEvents/Pages/DisplayNews.aspx?NewsID=11723&LangID=E.

[116] INFO-OECD, 'Society: Spending for seniors to double or more by 2050, says OECD' (Paris, OECD, 2011). http://info-oecd.blogspot.co.uk/2011/05/society-spending-on-long-term-care-for.html.

[117] K Christensen G Doblhammer, R Rau and JW Vaupel, *Ageing populations: the challenges ahead* (2009) *The Lancet* 374, 1196–1208. www.demogr.mpg.de/publications%5Cfiles%5C3444_1264435180_1_Christensen%20et%20al%20Lancet%20374%209696%202009.pdf.

[118] WHO, *World Report on Disability* (Geneva, WHO, 2011). www.who.int/disabilities/world_report/2011/en/.

[119] G Leiner, in M Banks, 'EU warned over problem of "unnecessary operations"' (2011). www.theparliament.com/latest-news/article/newsarticle/eu-warned-over-problem-of-unnecessary-operations/.

[120] Access Economics, Carers Australia, *The economic value of informal care in 2010, Report for Carers Australia, 2010.* www.carersaustralia.com.au/storage/Economic-Value-Informal-Care-Oct-2010.pdf.

The European Innovation Partnerships include 'technologies to allow older people to live independently and be active in society'. There are many potential benefits of developing low-cost, low-tech solutions applicable in settings with few resources—for example, IT and other communication technologies (such as eHealth, mHealth) are important innovations in the context of an ageing society. Examples include online and telemedicine services, such as the UK's NHS Direct and NHS 24 providing telephone and online health services, with service goals including reduced hospital admissions, reducing delays in hospital discharge and increasing levels of care provided in the home.[121] Research into such technologies, their access and acceptability and strategies to support their use by older people and informal carers is one area for development.

Ageing is a field where technological and social innovation must go hand-in-hand. The aim of the European innovation partnership on active and healthy ageing[122] is to 'enable EU citizens to lead healthy, active and independent lives while they age, as well as improve the sustainability and efficiency of social welfare and healthcare systems'. The strategy has a research component,[117] 'where possible resulting in new medicines for the elderly, new treatments or diagnostic tools, new institutional or organisational approaches and new solutions allowing for a better quality of life for the elderly'. These resources must be accessible and affordable as inconsistent availability of services (for example, in the diagnostic industry) is evident across Europe. A 'roadmap for ageing research' (launched 18 October 2011) has been developed through the UK-led, European funded Futurage project, which has identified priorities for ageing research across the next 10–15 years.[123]

Some recommendations for ageing research include supporting strategies to promote healthy ageing policies, including early screening through health assessments, 'ageing in place',[124] research to support informal carers, research to support quality of life (QOL) (including defining QOL measures) and quality of care in residential and home care settings to prevent elder abuse, research to explore chronic disease management and health care systems[125] and long-term care insurance policies (such as those available in Japan),[126] and other strategies to promote older people's access to health, residential and

[121] J Turner, *Care and cure, The European Innovation Partnership on Active and Healthy Ageing* (Gastein, European Health Forum, 2011) www.ehfg.org/97.html.

[122] EurActiv, 'Ministers back innovation alliance on "healthy ageing"', *EurActiv*, 10 March 2011. www.euractiv.com/innovation/ministers-back-innovation-alliance-healthy-ageing-news-502972.

[123] Futurage, *A road map for ageing research*. http://futurage.group.shef.ac.uk/.

[124] M Hildebrand and P Neufeld, 'Recruiting older adults into a physical activity promotion program: Active Living Every Day offered in a naturally occurring retirement community' (2009) *Gerontologist* 49, 702–10. www.ncbi.nlm.nih.gov/pubmed/19574541.

[125] P Allotey et al, 'Rethinking health-care systems: a focus on chronicity' (2011) *The Lancet* 377, 450–51. www.thelancet.com/journals/lancet/article/PIIS0140-6736%2810%2961856-9/fulltext .

[126] N Tamiya et al, 'Population ageing and wellbeing: lessons from Japan's long-term care insurance policy' (2011) *The Lancet* 378, 1183–92. www.thelancet.com/journals/lancet/article/PIIS0140-6736%2811%2961176-8/fulltext.

community care. The provision of and research into services such as multidisciplinary care and medication review is also required (Australia's Drug and Therapeutic Information Services (DATIS) is a good example, evaluated by its National Prescribing Service[127]). It should be noted that research focusing on chronic disease management for older people undertaken in LMICs needs to move away from donor-driven and vertical programmes and focus more on primary health care in health system responses.[120]

Research with a health promotion focus may include research into strategies to promote older (over 50s) people's skills and access to the paid workforce as well as flexible employment arrangements, research into lifelong learning approaches (such as the University of the Third Age[128]), research into effective physical activity initiatives and research on strategies to reduce loneliness and social isolation, including intergenerational projects which build bridges across generations (for example, Intergenerational Playgroups,[129] performing and visual arts, radio initiatives or oral history projects).

— Disability: Around 10 per cent of the world's population have a disability (80 per cent are living in LMICs).[130] Disability is strongly associated with social disadvantage and a social gradient of disability.[131] People with disabilities have much lower rates of labour force participation and higher rates of unemployment (up to 80 per cent)[132,133] compared to the general population. Economic losses from excluding people with disabilities from the workplace in LMICs amount to 3 to 7 per cent of GDP.[134] More research into social innovations to enable people with disabilities to function independently or be supported within living and working environments is required (for example, disability access housing/home modifications, supported/supportive housing and employment models where required, web accessibility), especially due to the strong association between ageing and disability. Due to the social nature of disability, participatory action research is particularly recommended in this field. A good example of an organisation which works

[127] Australian National Prescribing Service. www.nps.org.au/health-professionals/professional-development/prescribing-competencies-framework.

[128] University of the Third Age. www.u3a.org.uk.

[129] S Williams et al, 'Evaluation of an intergenerational playgroup in a residential aged care facility' (Australian National Ageing Research Institute, 2010). www.health.vic.gov.au/agedcare/downloads/cui/nari_pg_evaluation40.pdf.

[130] UN Enable, *Factsheet on Persons with Disabilities*. www.un.org/disabilities/default.asp?id=18.

[131] E Emerson, S Einfeld and RJ Stancliffe, 'The mental health of young children with intellectual disabilities or borderline intellectual functioning' (2010) *Social Psychiatry and Psychiatric Epidemiology* 45, 579–87, www.springerlink.com/content/pu9k226888487n2u/.

[132] International Labour Organization, *Disability: A human rights issue* (Geneva, ILO, 2013). www.ilo.org/wcmsp5/groups/public/---ed_emp/---ifp_skills/documents/publication/wcms_229918.pdf.

[133] OECD, *Sickness, Disability and Work Keeping on Track in the Economic Downturn, Background Paper for High-Level Forum, Stockholm, 14–15 May 2009* (Paris, OECD, 2009). www.oecd.org/dataoecd/42/15/42699911.pdf.

[134] International Labour Organization, *The price of excluding people with disabilities from the workplace*. (Geneva, ILO, 2010). www.ilo.org/skills/pubs/WCMS_149529/lang--en/index.htm.

with government, business leaders and people with disabilities to develop disability-inclusive business is Kanchi,[135] an Irish non-governmental organisation (NGO) which promotes the 'business case for disability'. This includes strategies such as 'access to markets' (for example, inclusive design to access markets for people with disabilities), 'access to talent' and 'retention of staff' (equal opportunity policies and the employment and inclusion of people with disabilities) and 'reputation management'.

— Mental health: Mental health is particularly overlooked, although mental health problems affect more than a third of Europeans[136] and are a major contributor to the burden of disease worldwide. Psychosocial factors can affect physical health, just as poor physical health, functional limitations and disability can affect psychological health. The link between mental health and other physical health problems is often misunderstood, such as the relationship between compliance for HIV and tuberculosis treatment and the treatment of depression.[137]

Many countries do not have a stand-alone budget or indicators for mental health funding and outcomes.[138] It has been argued that 'even if policy decisions are to be based on mortality alone, mental illnesses should be considered a priority because mortality both from suicide and from premature death from physical disease among persons with mental illnesses is similar to the global mortality associated with malaria and HIV'.[139]

The Global Challenges in Global Mental Health forum developed 25 priorities for research in global mental health, with future breakthroughs 'likely to depend on discoveries in genomics and neuroscience, in tandem with exploration of the role of socio-cultural and environmental contexts'.[140] Given the shortage of specialists in this area, research is warranted into effective and efficient service delivery models and models of care which consider assessment and treatment in primary care. Such cost-efficient models could also have implications for poorer regions in Europe. Economics-related research into the role of mental health in development is required, and LMICs are likely to be dependent on HICs for such research.[133] Social innovation and models that go beyond a medical model and are better linked to the social

[135] *Kanchi*. www.kanchi.org/.

[136] K Smith, 'Mental disorders affect more than a third of Europeans' (2011) *Nature online* 5 September, doi:10.1038/news.2011.514. www.nature.com/news/2011/110905/full/news.2011.514.html?WT.ec_id=NEWS-20110906.

[137] WHO, *Preventing Chronic Diseases: A Vital Investment* (Geneva, WHO, 2005). http://whqlibdoc.who.int/publications/2005/9241563001_eng.pdf.

[138] R Jenkins et al, 'Mental Health and the Development Agenda in Sub-Saharan Africa' (2010) *Psychiatric Services* 61(3), 229–34. http://ps.psychiatryonline.org/article.aspx?Volume=61&page=229&journalID=18.

[139] ibid, 230.

[140] PY Collins et al, 'Grand challenges in global mental health' (2011) *Nature* 475, 27–30. www.nature.com/nature/journal/v475/n7354/full/475027a.html.

development sector are also required. Mental health promotion and prevention activities particularly require cross-sectoral strategies including areas such as health, education, criminal justice, social services and employment,[59] and housing.

— Violence and conflict mitigation: According to the WHO, violence accounts for 1.5 million deaths per year, with 80 per cent of deaths occurring as a result of suicide and homicide, and 90 per cent of deaths from violence occurring in LMICs.[141] Violence and suicide became important causes of death for young people in the latter half of the 20th century, especially for young men in all regions of the world.[142] War is the eighth leading cause of death for young males (10–24 years) across all regions.[143] Improvements in the mortality rates of young people aged 10–24 years have been half that of children 1–9 years of age. Traffic accidents (14 per cent of young males), violence (12 per cent of young males) and suicide (6 per cent of young people) are prominent causes of death in young people aged 10–24 years, particularly amongst young men in LMICs.[138] For these reasons, it has been recommended[137] that 'future global health targets should include the causes of death in people aged 10–24 years, and should extend beyond HIV infection and maternal mortality to include injury and mental health'. In addition, interpersonal violence (physical, sexual, emotional) against women and children is a significant public health problem with the potential to cause current and intergenerational health problems, particularly drug and alcohol and mental health problems. Research in conflict settings and strategies to mitigate violence (including interpersonal violence) and conflict is required, along with research on the relationships between violence, injury and mental health.

  It has also been noted that cause of death statistics are frequently inaccurate in LMICs, and in terms of research there is a greater need to support monitoring mechanisms and the development of civil registries and quality of certification.[144]

— Maternal Child and Newborn/Infant Health: In 2010 the G8 leaders committed to the Muskoka initiative,[145] furthering MDG goals 4 and 5 on maternal, infant and child health. The G8 leaders at Deauville (2011) reaffirmed their

[141] WHO, *10 facts on violence prevention*. www.who.int/features/factfiles/violence/en/index.html.

[142] RM Viner et al, 50-year mortality trends in children and young people: a study of 50 low-income, middle-income and high-income countries (2011) *The Lancet* 377, 1162–74. www.thelancet.com/journals/lancet/article/PIIS0140-6736%2811%2960106-2/fulltext.

[143] GC Patton et al, 'Global patterns of mortality in young people: a systematic analysis of population health data' (2009) *The Lancet* 374, 881–92. www.thelancet.com/journals/lancet/article/PIIS0140-6736%2809%2960741-8/abstract.

[144] CD Mathers, T Boerma and D Ma Fat, 'Global and regional causes of death' (2009) *British Medical Bulletin* 92, 7–32. www.ncbi.nlm.nih.gov/pubmed/19776034.

[145] *G8 Muskoka Declaration, 2010*. www.whitehouse.gov/the-press-office/g-8-muskoka-declaration.

commitments to achieving the health-related MDGs, including on maternal health and reducing child mortality and sexual and reproductive health.[146] Maternal, child and newborn health should be an ongoing priority for development support and research with low-income countries (LICs). The *Information and Accountability Commission on Women's and Children's Health* was established to support efforts in this area. Again, the report of this Commission observed problems with reporting systems within LICs: of the 49 lowest income countries, only 23 had conducted one national health account in the previous five years, eight had a statistical report with district data online, and only two had coverage of death registration at over 50 per cent of deaths.[147]

ii. Health Security

Whereas security was traditionally seen as related to freedom from armed conflict and other forms of organised violence, human security[148] sees the proper focus for security as the individual rather than only the state. It is broadly defined in terms of secure access to a range of essential human needs, including food, water, shelter, freedom from violence, opportunity to sustain good health and obtain treatment for ill-health; and conditions that minimise the adverse effects of natural and man-made disasters.[149,150] In this people-centred view, human security is necessary for national, regional and global stability[151] and the concept converges with that of human development on a common view that economic growth is insufficient on its own and that areas such as health, education, technology, the environment, and employment should not be neglected. As an important part of people's well-being, human security is therefore an objective of development: both perspectives are people-centred, multidimensional and consider poverty and inequality as the root causes of individual vulnerability.[152]

[146] *G8 Deauville Declaration, 2011.* www.g8.utoronto.ca/summit/2011deauville/2011-declaration-en.html.

[147] Commission on Information and Accountability for Women's and Children's Health, *Keeping Promises, Measuring Results* (Geneva, WHO, 19 May 2011). www.who.int/topics/millennium_development_goals/accountability_commission/PR_Commission_19May2011.pdf .

[148] United Nations Development Programme, *Human Development Report 1994: New dimensions of human security* (New York, UNDP, 1994). http://hdr.undp.org/en/content/human-development-report-1994.

[149] Global Development Research Center, *Definitions of Human Security* (Washington DC, GDRC, 2001) www.gdrc.org/sustdev/husec/Definitions.pdf.

[150] *Report of the Commission on Human Security, 2003.* www.humansecurity-chs.org/finalreport/Outlines/outline.pdf.

[151] 'Human Security', Wikipedia, 2010. http://en.wikipedia.org/wiki/Human_security.

[152] F Stewart, *Development and Security.* Centre for Research on Inequality, Human Security, and Ethnicity (CRISE), Working Paper 3, University of Oxford, 2004. www.crise.ox.ac.uk/pubs/workingpaper3.pdf.

International[153] and global[154] aspects of health security form an important, evolving[155] component of the overall human security picture.

a. Health Security Threats from Infectious Diseases

The Oslo Declaration[156] emphasised the need for preparedness to identify health risks and threats, and global mechanisms to ensure informed and coordinated global responses. Recent global threats to health (such as SARS virus, Avian influenza H5N1), have provided the imperative for Europe to develop its capacity to meet incoming health and health security challenges, prevent problems from developing at the source, prevent the migration of infectious diseases, and support countries' capacities to adhere to the International Health Regulations.

There are also new global challenges for infectious diseases. A research review has shown that, due to migration and weak economies in regions of Europe, 'neglected tropical diseases' (a range of parasitic infections as well as bacterial, fungal and viral infections) that are common in Africa and Asia are appearing more often in Europe.[157] The study recommends increased policy commitments to determine the prevalence and incidence of these neglected infections in Europe, along with R&D for new control tools. In the case of pulmonary TB and the pertussis respiratory infection, research into new antibiotics is required to address drug resistant forms. It appears that protection from pertussis vaccine may be decreasing over time.[158,159] Researchers have proposed the possible negative impact of climate change, and specifically rising sea levels, on vector-borne infectious diseases.[160] Research at the level of vectors is also required following the appearance of vectors in Europe due to migration. The reappearance of malaria in Italy and other

153 WHO, *World Health Day 2007: International health security* (Geneva, WHO, 2007). www.who.int/world-health-day/previous/2007/en/index.html.

154 The Global Health Security Initiative is an international partnership among countries to strengthen health preparedness and response globally to threats of biological, chemical, radio-nuclear terrorism and pandemic influenza. The GHSI Ministerial Forum consists of Ministers/Secretaries/Commissioner of Health from Canada, the European Commission, France, Germany, Italy, Japan, Mexico, the United Kingdom and the United States. The WHO is a technical advisor, www.ghsi.ca/english/index.asp.

155 W Aldis, 'Health security as a public health concept: a critical analysis' (2008) *Health Policy and Planning* 23, 369–75. http://heapol.oxfordjournals.org/content/23/6/369.full.

156 C Amorim et al, 'Oslo Ministerial Declaration on global health: a pressing foreign policy issue of our time' (2007) *The Lancet* 369, 1373–78. www.thelancet.com/journals/lancet/article/PIIS0140-6736(07)60498-X/abstract.

157 P Hotez and M Gurwith, 'Europe's neglected infections of poverty' (2011) *International Journal of Infectious Diseases* 15, e611–e619, www.ijidonline.com/article/S1201-9712(11)00117-2/abstract.

158 HE De Melker et al, 'Re-emergence of Pertussis in the Highly Vaccinated Population of The Netherlands: Observations on Surveillance Data' (2000) *Emerging Infectious Diseases* 6, 348–57. www.ncbi.nlm.nih.gov/pmc/articles/PMC2640897/.

159 Centers for Disease Control and Prevention (CDC), *Whooping Cough (Pertussis)—Fact Sheet for Parents* (CDC, 2013). www.cdc.gov/vaccines/vpd-vac/pertussis/fs-parents.html, .

160 R Ramasamy and Sn Surendran, 'Possible impact of rising sea levels on vector-borne infectious diseases' (2011) *BMC Infectious Diseases* 11, 18. www.ncbi.nlm.nih.gov/pmc/articles/PMC3035583/.

European countries has led to a focus on new treatments[161] and genetic research on mosquitoes which do not produce sperm.[162]

The health and economic impacts of rapidly emerging infectious diseases with pandemic potential, such as SARS[163,164] (Box 5) and avian influenza, as well as re-emerging diseases such as multi-drug resistant TB and antimicrobial resistance,[165] have highlighted the critical importance of global attention to this area. In particular:

- There is a need to develop Europe's capacity to meet emerging challenges and prevent migration of infectious diseases.
- It is vital to prevent problems from developing at the source by building scientific capacities in areas such as surveillance, diagnosis, containment, vaccination and treatment in LMICs—which are often the countries of origin or of onward transmission—and establishing long-term collaborations that create trust and facilitate rapid, coordinated action.
- Capacity building in LMICs for surveillance/response systems (investigation disease and control) and global data and collection systems is another area for research development. At a briefing for the launch of the report of the UN Secretary-General's Commission on Information and Accountability for Women's and Children's Health, Dr Margaret Chan declared that investment in health information systems was largely lacking and appealed for more support in this area which would serve countries well in the longer term.[166]

There are very large economic as well as health benefits accruing from successfully dealing with infectious disease challenges …

- In the 1960s, there were about 10 to 15 million cases of smallpox and 1.5 to 2 million deaths from the disease each year across more than 50 countries, costing their economies at least US$1 billion per year. Eradication of smallpox and cessation of the need for surveillance, containment and global vaccination has brought massive economic benefits to every country. It is

[161] A Bartoloni et al, 'Combined intravenous treatment with artesunate and quinine for severe malaria in Italy' (2010) *American Journal of Tropical Medicine and Hygiene* 83, 274–6. www.ncbi.nlm.nih.gov/pubmed/20682867.

[162] J Thailayil et al, 'Spermless males elicit large-scale female responses to mating in the malaria mosquito *Anopheles gambiae*' (2011) *Proceedings of the National Academy of Sciences USA*, 8 August, doi: 10.1073/pnas.1104738108. www.pnas.org/content/early/2011/08/01/1104738108.abstract.

[163] WHO, *World Health Report, Chapter 5: SARS: lessons from a new disease* (Geneva, WHO, 2003) Ch 5. www.who.int/whr/2003/chapter5/en/index1.html.

[164] MR Keogh-Brown and RD Smith, 'The economic impact of SARS: how does the reality match the predictions?' (2008) *Health Policy* 88(1), 110–20. www.ncbi.nlm.nih.gov/pubmed/18436332.

[165] D Wernli, T Haustein and S Harbarth, 'The European approach to antimicrobial resistance: success stories and challenges' (2011) *Global Health Europe Issue Brief*, February. www.globalhealtheurope.org/images/stories/issues_paper_022011_web.pdf.

[166] WHO, 'WHO appeals for greater investment in information systems to track progress and accountability in women's and children's health' (2011) *WHO Health Metrics Network* 19 May. www.who.int/healthmetrics/news/appeals_for_greater_investment/en/index.html.

Box 5. Severe Acute Respiratory Syndrome (SARS): lessons from a new disease

The fourth lesson concerns international collaboration: the world's scientists, clinicians and public health experts are willing to set aside academic competition and work together for the public health good when the situation so requires. International collaboration greatly advanced understanding of the science of SARS. One month after the laboratory network was established, participating scientists collectively announced conclusive identification of the SARS virus; complete sequencing of its RNA followed shortly afterwards. The network of clinical experts provided a platform for comparison of patient management strategies to indicate to the world which treatments and strategies were effective. In addition, the epidemiology network confirmed the modes of transmission of SARS and began the long-term collaboration needed to understand clearly the clinical spectrum of disease, including its case fatality ratio, while also providing the information needed to regularly reassess and adjust the case definition.

World Health Report (note 162)

calculated that the largest donor, the USA, saves the total of all its contributions to smallpox eradication every 26 days by not having to vaccinate or treat the disease.[167]

— It is estimated that the global initiative to eradicate polio could provide net benefits of at least US$40–50 billion if transmission of wild polioviruses is interrupted within the next few years.[168]

— The costs of anti-retroviral drugs (ARVs) for the treatment of people with HIV/AIDS fell from more than US$10,000 per year in the 1990s to less than US$100 per year by 2008, as a result of innovative work by Indian pharmaceutical companies. This made possible, with support from the international donor community, wide access to ARVs by people with HIV/AIDS in resource-poor countries.[169] It has also demonstrated the potential of generics for massively lowering the costs of drugs globally.

[167] R Levine, *Case Studies in Global Health: Millions Saved. Case Study 1: Eradicating Smallpox* (Washington DC, Center for Global Development, 2007). www.cgdev.org/doc/millions/MS_case_1.pdf.

[168] Polio Global Eradication Initiative, 22 November 2010. http://www.polioeradication.org/tabid/167/iid/82/Default.aspx.

[169] Avert, 'AIDS, drug prices and generic drugs' (2011). www.avert.org/generic.htm.

... while the potential economic and health costs of failure to tackle infectious disease challenges quickly and efficiently are enormous:

— Estimates of economic losses from the Influenza A H1N1 outbreaks in 2009 range from 0.5 per cent to 1.5 per cent of GDP in affected countries[170] and are typical of impacts seen in other cases such as SARS. For the rest of the world, fear of a pandemic leads to emergency measures being taken at both individual and national levels—many of which may be inappropriate in the absence of adequate scientific data and lack of prevention and treatment options of proven effectiveness—causing massive and avoidable economic losses.[171]

— Multi-drug resistant and extremely drug resistant forms of TB present a growing health and economic problem worldwide. Research by the World Bank has emphasised that the economic benefits of effective control programmes will far outweigh the costs of these programmes.[172] It is clear that much more rapidly acting treatment regimes are needed as well as better approaches to diagnosis and case management.[173]

— Antimicrobial resistance to drugs, resulting from evolutionary changes (often exacerbated by the inappropriate use of antibiotics) has become a very serious worldwide problem at a time when there has been falling investment in the development of new antibiotics.[174,175]

— The May 2011 outbreak of enterohemorrhagic *E. coli* food poisoning linked to an organic farm in Germany resulted in about 4,000 cases in several European and North American countries and over 40 deaths. Russia banned the import of all fresh vegetables from the EU for a period of time, highlighting how quickly a public health security issue can become a major economic problem.[176]

[170] 'The cost of swine flu: Swine flu hits public health and the economy in South America' (2009) *The Economist* 27 July. www.economist.com/node/14115951.

[171] Equity-research.com, *Swine Flu: Economic Implications* (2009). http://equity-research.com/swine-flu-economic-implications/.

[172] Who/Stop TB Partnership/World Bank, 'Aggressive TB control can yield big economic gains, says new study' (Geneva, WHO, 2007). www.who.int/mediacentre/news/releases/2007/pr64/en/index.html.

[173] *MDR-TB, XDR-TB*, Global Alliance for TB Drug Development, New York, 2011, www.tballiance.org/why/mdr-xdr.php.

[174] WHO, *Antimicrobial resistance*, Fact sheet No 1 (Geneva, WHO, February 2011). www.who.int/mediacentre/factsheets/fs194/en/.

[175] HW Boucher et al, 'Bad Bugs, No Drugs: No ESKAPE! An Update from the Infectious Diseases Society of America' (2009) *Clinical Infectious Diseases* 48, 1–12, www.idsociety.org/uploadedFiles/IDSA/Policy_and_Advocacy/Current_Topics_and_Issues/Advancing_Product_Research_and_Development/Antimicrobials/Statements/76be6c147e7d4b6a891d7c2b860349fd3.pdf.

[176] '2011 Germany *E. coli* O104:H4 outbreak', Wikipedia, 2011, http://en.wikipedia.org/wiki/2011_E._coli_O104:H4_outbreak.

b. Health Security Threats from Disasters

Natural or man-made disasters can also have sudden and large consequences for both health and economies. These two are often inter-related, with the immediate and longer-term health impacts of physical disasters causing massive economic loss and slowing the pace of economic recovery; and with the economic disruption caused by physical damage to land, buildings and infrastructure and the consequent loss of livelihoods and amenities adversely affecting short-term health recovery and long-term physical and mental health. While the causes, character and predictability of the natural and man-made events are highly variable, they nevertheless share a number of common features that define a research agenda that is designed to underpin:

- risk assessment—including health impacts and emergency health needs for different kinds of events;
- early warning—including, where relevant, devising, testing and implementing health surveillance and reporting systems that can pick up early signs of developing disasters, such as the health consequences of biological, radiological or chemical releases, heatwaves;
- disaster management—including establishing appropriate items of medical and nutritional supplies to be stockpiling and distributed and the training and maintenance of emergency health response teams; and
- recovery—including developing methods to treat the immediate consequences of trauma and injury and to deal with the longer-term physical, mental and psycho-social sequelae.

c. Implications for the Research and Innovation Agenda

The research agenda for health security must operate coherently and consistently across three arenas:

- within the EU:
  - funding research and innovation on new or improved methods for the diagnosis, prevention and treatment of infectious diseases that pose a significant threat to public health in the EU;
  - enhancing capacities at the pan-European level for surveillance, diagnosis and laboratory support for case management and for the collection, sharing, pooling and analysis of relevant data;
- through collaborations between the EU and external countries and agencies:
  - funding collaborative research involving institutions in the EU, other HICs and LMICs on reducing pathogen induction and disease vectors and creating better methods for prevention, diagnosis and treatment of infectious diseases posing significant threats to public health globally;
  - building capacities in LMICs for these research activities and for surveillance, diagnosis and laboratory support for case management and for the containment of pathogens;

 - contributing to enhancing global mechanisms for surveillance and early warning of emerging pandemic threats and global response mechanisms—including research and innovation capacities for rapidly developing new diagnostics, drugs and vaccines;
- as a component of development:
  - supporting governments and institutions in LMICs to build national capacities for surveillance, diagnosis and laboratory support for case management of infectious diseases and for the recognition and safe handling, containment and shipment of pathogens;
  - working with the WHO and the OECD, surveillance/response systems and global data collection systems and collaborating to develop databases and online information and resource tools.

Research and innovation for health security warrants specific attention in Europe because special measures are needed to ensure effective action in this field and the potential costs of neglect, both in health and economic terms, are massive.

iii. Economics, Trade and Health Equity

a. Health Equity and Economic Development

Whilst the health of a country's population is essential for the health of its economy, economic growth does not necessarily translate to the same level of improvements in health. The EU has recently highlighted that 'the long-held belief that economic growth creates employment and wealth that goes on to alleviate poverty has been disproved by recent events' leading to a greater need for social innovation.[177]

An EU-funded Polish study highlighted major gaps in health equity, especially concerning the 10 new EU Member States in Central and Eastern Europe.[178] In connection with Poland's Presidency of the EU in 2011, it pledged to move forward on reducing health inequalities within the EU, and Poland's Minister of Health[179] emphasised the need for continued improvements in public health as crucial for building human capital and achieving economic progress. Poland's call for 'Solidarity for Health' in the EU, which many Member States joined, requires

[177] A Hubert, *Empowering People, Driving Change: Social Innovation in the European Union* (EC Bureau of European Policy Advisers, 2010). https://webgate.ec.europa.eu/socialinnovationeurope/sites/default/files/sites/default/files/Empowering%20People%20BEPA.pdf.

[178] W Zatoński et al (eds), *Closing the health gap in European Union* (Maria Skłodowska-Curie Memorial Cancer Center and Institute of Oncology, Warsaw, 2008). www.hem.home.pl/index.php?idm=87,139&cmd=1.

[179] WHO, *Interview with Polish Minister of Health, Dr Ewa Kopacz, for the World Conference on Social Determinants of Health* (Geneva, WHO, 2011). www.who.int/sdhconference/background/news/InterviewwithPolishMinisterofHealth/en/index.html.

action at national levels and also at the EU level. Elements of the agenda set out by Poland that are relevant to Horizon 2020 include requirements for:

— health impact assessments;
— development of new indicators to take into account the impact of social factors on health;
— creation of standardised methods for the assessment of health status and for data interpretation and comparison;
— joint actions to exchange experiences about closing the health gaps in specific countries and between societal groups, and also with regard to institutional solutions which contribute to improving the health of societies;
— strengthening health literacy to support people in improving their own health through enhanced knowledge;
— building additional capacities for public health.

A key priority in the Agenda for Action arising from the authoritative *Lancet* Series on Trade and Health is to strengthen evidence on trade and health links, supporting the development of research, research capacity and indicators in this field.[180]

b. 'Corporate Social Responsibility' and 'Shared Value' Approaches

Raising 'corporate social responsibility' (CSR) amongst the business community to ensure 'long-term employee and consumer trust' is one objective of Europe 2020. Examples of CSR initiatives in the health field include Areva in Niger, who are tackling HIV/AIDS through a public private partnership,[181] and Chirano Gold Mines' Integrated Malaria Control Programme in Western Ghana.[182] One identified danger of CSR activities is that they are seen as 'sideline' activities not central to the core business of an organisation and it is often difficult to engage the private sector in global health partnerships.[183] It has been argued that we must go beyond the concept of traditional CSR and embrace the concept of 'shared value' defined as 'policies and operating practices that enhance the competitiveness of a company while simultaneously advancing the economic and social conditions in the communities in which it operates'. There is a clear need to research and better understand such initiatives to determine their impact upon health and equity, along with their sustainability.[184]

[180] RD Smith, K Lee and N Drager, 'Trade and health: an agenda for action' (2009) *The Lancet* 373, 768–73. www.thelancet.com/journals/lancet/article/PIIS0140-6736%2808%2961780-8/fulltext?_eventId=login.

[181] S Romieu, *AREVA Niger Case Study* (UN Global Compact, 2006). www.unglobalcompact.org/docs/issues_doc/human_rights/Business_Practices/Areva%20complete_EHRBP%20II.pdf.

[182] B Breiger, 'A goldmine of private sector assistance against malaria'. globalhealthhub.org, www.globalhealthhub.org/2011/08/08/a-goldmine-of-private-sector-assistance-against-malaria/.

[183] K Buse and S Tanaka, 'Global Public-Private Health Partnerships: lessons learned from ten years of experience and evaluation' (2011) *International Dental Journal* 20 July. http://onlinelibrary.wiley.com/doi/10.1111/j.1875-595X.2011.00034.x/full.

[184] ME Porter and MR Kramer, 'The Big Idea: Creating Shared Value' (2011) *Harvard Business Review* 89(1–2), 62–77. http://hbr.org/2011/01/the-big-idea-creating-shared-value.

c. Global Health Governance and Accountability, the Role of Civil Society, Service User and Carers

Governance challenges, international health stakeholders and public-private partnerships: Corporate donations, private foundations and public private partnerships have led to a significant increase in funding for global health initiatives in recent years.[185] With the increasing range of actors within global health, another area for capacity building is global health governance research. United Nations Development Programme (UNDP) principles for good governance include legitimacy and voice, direction and strategic vision, performance (responsiveness, effectiveness and efficiency), accountability and fairness (equity).[186]

Poor governance has been identified as one problem area needing attention,[132,187] particularly in relation to progress on the social determinants of health.[27] One review of governance practices in global public-private partnerships has identified representation, transparency and accountability as three key issues for governance.[186] Clarity regarding transparency in decision making, processes to ensure democratic participation and representation, coherence across policy areas (and coherent representation), clear outcomes and indicators and monitoring and accountability mechanisms are required. Global health governance to achieve action on the social determinants of health and NCDs also requires action and research on intersectoral policy and action and policies and practices that promote equity in health systems.[27]

In particular, the UNDP principles for good governance of 'legitimacy and voice' and 'fairness' correspond with UN Universal Declaration of Human Rights Principles, particularly the participation of groups that have faced discriminatory practices.[185] An important aspect of governance is thus democratic processes, ensuring participation and clarifying roles that different actors play within policy processes. Research into effective processes to ensure increased user involvement and empowerment in planning, decision making, implementation and monitoring and accountability mechanisms for global health governance is required, for example, platforms for engagement and participation (including non-government and private sector participation) and accountability mechanisms. Action research into effective strategies for global health governance and involvement of civil

[185] I Kickbusch, W Hein and G Silberschmidt, 'Addressing Global Health Governance Challenges through a New Mechanism: The Proposal for a Committee C of the World Health Assembly' (2010) *Journal of Law, Medicine and Ethics* 551–63. www.ncbi.nlm.nih.gov/pubmed/20880240.

[186] J Graham, B Amos, T Plumptre, 'Principles for good governance in the 21st Century' (2003) *Institute on Governance, Policy Brief15*. http://unpan1.un.org/intradoc/groups/public/documents/UNPAN/UNPAN011842.pdf.

[187] K Buse, AM Harmer, 'Seven habits of highly effective global public–private health partnerships: Practice and potential' (2007) *Social Science* and *Medicine* 64, 259–71. www.researchgate.net/publication/6739577_Seven_habits_of_highly_effective_global_public-private_health_partnerships_practice_and_potential.

society organisations, local health service users (and carers) and ensuring their feedback and evaluation in research is also important for research and capacity building, in particular for research undertaken with LMICs.

Accountability strategies: Health impact assessments: The Oslo Declaration[151] notes that 'health-impact assessments of all foreign, trade, and defence policies would do much to advance the cause of health across governments'. Haber[188] suggests that a useful tool for building equity into priorities for planning and measuring outcomes is 'Health Equity Impact Assessment'. Specific evaluation and impact assessments to determine the impact of health, educational and social policies on people with disabilities have also been recommended.[189]

iv. Capacity Building in the Health Workforce and Research

Capacity building in the global health workforce is necessary and will lead to potential benefits for Europe.

— One Europe 2020 flagship initiative is 'youth on the move', an objective being 'to explore ways of promoting entrepreneurship through mobility programmes for young professionals'. One strategy would be practice-based research exchange programmes for young health professionals going to LMICs (and vice versa).
— The Commission on Education of Health Professionals for the 21st Century[190] found a dearth of research on the effectiveness of health professional education. They state that 'sharing learning by supporting metrics, evaluation and research should be strengthened to build up the knowledge base about which innovations work under which circumstances'. They also recommend a systems approach to training and research in order to follow an education-care-research continuum, whilst acknowledging the need for capacity building in LMICs in academic systems. Educational systems should be guided by the determinants of health and should include 'social accountability' (to ensure health services address the priorities of the community) and measure competencies and research into meeting them.[191] In addition, the Commission considered the shortage of health professionals in LMICs and the need for 'scaling up' health organisations within LICs.

[188] R Haber, *Health Equity Impact Assessment—A primer* (Wellesley Institute, 2010). www.wellesleyinstitute.com/wp-content/uploads/2011/02/Health_Equity_Impact_Assessment_Haber.pdf.

[189] J Robertson et al, *The Impact of Person Centred Planning* (Institute of Health Research, Lancaster University, 2005). www.lincs.cswebsites.org/Libraries/Local/825/Docs/Planning/PCP/pcpimpactresearch%5B1%5D.pdf.

[190] J Frenk et al, 'Health professionals for a new century: transforming education to strengthen health systems in an interdependent world' (2004) *The Lancet* 376, 1923–58). www.healthprofessionals21.org/docs/HealthProfNewCent.pdf.

[191] C Boelen and R Woollard, 'Social accountability and accreditation: a new frontier for educational institutions' (2009) *Medical Education* 43, 887–94. http://nosm.ca/uploadedFiles/About_Us/Governance/Academic_Council/SocAcc%20and%20Accred%20BoelenWoollard%20Oct09.pdf.

— The international diffusion of new knowledge and 'best practices' is one of the key forces of scaling up—a goal now more readily achieved through low-cost methods available through the internet.[192]
— A European forum[193] by Norad on global health and AIDS has also highlighted the 'need to invest in health services research and in mechanisms for research utilisation. The goal is translation of learning into policy. Sustained and further developed systematic reviews are essential in this respect'.
— The Association of Schools of Public Health in the European Region[194] (ASPHER) has established various initiatives to strengthen the many facets of workforce capacities. These activities play an important role for the effective and sustainable development of the health workforce in Europe.

v. Health as Foreign Policy and Diplomacy

Global health challenges have increasingly manifested themselves as problems in foreign policy and international affairs in the last decade, as evidenced, for example, by their periodic appearance in high-level meetings of the UN[195,196] and G8[197] and by the formation of a Foreign Ministers group[198] specifically to address them. The Oslo Declaration[155] of seven foreign ministers from across Europe, South America, South Africa and Asia agreed to work towards prioritising health in foreign policy and trade issues, asserting that 'in a globalised and interdependent world, the state of global health has a profound impact on all nations—developed and developing'. Foreign policy actions in security, trade, conflict, crisis, environment, and human rights have a strong bearing on whether we can achieve national as well as global health security. Often a public health threat in one country requires a concerted response with many foreign policy makers working together. The important role of research was highlighted at the 2010 UN General Assembly debate[199] on 'Global

[192] WHO, *Report of the WHO Commission on Macroeconomics and Health* (Geneva, WHO, 2001). http://whqlibdoc.who.int/publications/2001/924154550x.pdf.

[193] Norad, *Why bother? Global health and AIDS—fighting for justice and equity*, Report of Norad Seminar, Oslo, 13 Jan 2011. www.norad.no/en/_attachment/380299/binary/187768?download=true.

[194] Association of Schools of Public Health in the European Region (ASPHER). www.aspher.org.

[195] United Nations, UN General Assembly High Level Meeting on AIDS, 8–10 June 2011. www.un.org/en/ga/aidsmeeting2011/.

[196] United Nations, UN General Assembly High Level Meeting on Non-communicable Diseases, 19–20 September 2011. www.un.org/en/ga/president/65/issues/ncdiseases.shtml.

[197] K Takemi, MR Reich, 'The G8 and Global Health: Emerging Architecture from the Toyako Summit' in *Global Action for Health System Strengthening* (Japan Center for International Exchange, Tokyo, 2009) 9–25. www.jcie.org/researchpdfs/takemi/ch1.pdf.

[198] *Foreign Policy and Global Health—Responding to new Challenges and Setting Priorities for the Future: The Oslo Ministerial Declaration Three Years Later and Beyond*, Statement from Meeting of Ministers of Foreign Affairs of Norway, Brazil, France, Indonesia, Senegal, South Africa and Thailand, founding members of the Foreign Policy and Global Health initiative, 22 September 2010. www.regjeringen.no/upload/UD/Temabilder/helse/globa_health101022.pdf.

[199] United Nations, *Consensus Text on 'Global Health and Foreign Policy'* (New York, UN 65th General Assembly, 2010). www.un.org/News/Press/docs/2010/ga11034.doc.htm.

Health and Foreign Policy', when the EU stated:[200] 'we should continue to enhance our collective understanding of how health outcomes are affected by different aspects of foreign policy'.

Health is intertwined with the three key global agendas of security, economic policy and social justice. Foreign policy and health can interact in the following ways:[201] (1) foreign policy endangering health when diplomacy breaks down or when trade considerations trump health; (2) health used as a foreign policy instrument in order to achieve other goals; (3) health as an integral part of foreign policy; and (4) foreign policy promoting health goals. It has been noted[202] that 'research in this area aims to develop policy options for reducing the collective vulnerability to health threats by addressing their politically and economically sensitive determinants. It also examines the political and economic effects of disease threats and efforts to combat them'.

It has been said[203] that 'better global health promotes stability and growth, which can deter the spread of extremism, ease pressure for migration, reduce the need for humanitarian and development assistance and create opportunities for stronger political alliances and economic relations'. Global health diplomacy is a potential source of 'soft power' (or building upon 'common interests and values to attract, persuade and influence')[204] enabling the development of trust between countries.

Creating links between health and other related policy areas in order to ultimately impact upon global health is a key objective. It has been argued that in order to fulfil the expectations of global health diplomacy and build links between health and foreign policy, professional development to create improved skills, understanding and resources are required across both areas; specifically, systematic development of specific skills amongst foreign diplomats or global health professionals are necessary, including technical expertise, legal knowledge and diplomatic skills, along with expansion in countries' overseas workforces. In some

[200] EU, *EU Statement at the UN General Assembly debate on 'Global Health and Foreign Policy', 9 Dec 2010* (Brussels, EC, 2010). www.eu-un.europa.eu/articles/en/article_10642_en.htm.

[201] I Kickbusch, 'Global health diplomacy: how foreign policy can influence health' (2011) *British Medical Journal* 342. www.bmj.com/content/342/bmj.d3154.abstract.

[202] *Disease threats and determinants that transcend borders* (Centre on Global Health Security, Chatham House, 2011). www.chathamhouse.org/research/global-health/current-projects/disease-threats-and-determinants-transcend-borders.

[203] K-A Jones, *Global health diplomacy: Negotiating health in the 21st century. Remarks at Negotiating Health in the 21st Century Conference, 2 November 2009, Washington DC* cited in R Katz et al, 'Defining Health Diplomacy: Changing Demands in the Era of Globalization' (2011) *The Millbank Quarterly* 89(3), 503–23. www.stimson.org/images/uploads/Milbank_Quarterly-Defining_Health_Diplomacy.pdf.

[204] J Nye, *Soft Power: The Means to Success in World Politics*, Public Affairs, New York, 2004, cited in *New frontiers in science diplomacy: Navigating the changing balance of power* (London, Royal Society, 2010). http://royalsociety.org/uploadedFiles/Royal_Society_Content/policy/publications/2010/4294969468.pdf.

areas, specific knowledge and skills may be required, such as in the case of previous WHO negotiations regarding virus sharing, where knowledge of vaccine production, epidemiology, intellectual property rights and the context of emerging economies was called upon.[202] NGOs also increasingly play a role in global health diplomacy. For example, during the development and negotiation of the Framework Convention on Tobacco Control (FCTC), five key areas for NGOs included monitoring, lobbying, offering technical expertise, brokering information and fostering inclusion. NGOs helped to facilitate the role of developing countries in diplomacy processes.[205]

a. Science Diplomacy

Science diplomacy refers to the role of science, technology and innovation in informing foreign policy (science in diplomacy), developing international science cooperation (diplomacy for science) and improving international relations (science for diplomacy).[206] Science diplomacy has a crucial role in facilitating international science cooperation and influencing foreign policy and governance for global health. Global science diplomacy is necessary in order to address many important health-related challenges including pandemic threats, food insecurity, poverty, climate change and energy issues. The EU has made a commitment to science diplomacy through a number of global research projects, many of which are global health projects.[207] Developments in science diplomacy, including developing human resources for science diplomacy in foreign offices (science attachés in embassies)[205] and international organisations, international research and knowledge and data and resource sharing, will contribute to innovative and common solutions to global health challenges (Box 6). One recommendation for developing science diplomacy in the area of global health is through the development of regional and international collaborative research centres in order to support intergovernmental panels with the aim of progressing global health (see III.). In any initiatives in science diplomacy, interdisciplinary collaboration is crucial, particularly with the social sciences;[205] see the example (Box 6) of multidisciplinary research to tackle dengue fever in Asia.[208]

[205] R Lencucha, A Kothari and R Labonté, 'The role of non-governmental organizations in global health diplomacy: negotiating the Framework Convention on Tobacco Control' (2010) *Health Policy and Planning* 1–8. www.ncbi.nlm.nih.gov/pubmed/21051475.

[206] *New frontiers in science diplomacy: Navigating the changing balance of power* (London, Royal Society, 2010). http://royalsociety.org/New-frontiers-in-science-diplomacy/.

[207] European Commission, *International cooperation in EU-funded health research* (Luxembourg: EU DG for Research, 2010). http://ec.europa.eu/research/health/pdf/international-cooperation-in-eu-funded_en.pdf.

[208] WHO, *Dengue Bulletin* (Geneva, WHO, December 2012). www.wpro.who.int/mvp/epidemiology/dengue/Dengue_Bulletin_Vol36.pdf.

Box 6. Science as a global endeavour

Science is a truly global endeavour with scientists sharing their knowledge with their colleagues around the world. Most health and bio-medical challenges are borderless and if research is to help meet those challenges, an international approach is essential.

M Geoghegan-Quinn, EU Commissioner for Research, Innovation and Science (note 206, p 3)

Multi-disciplinary, international research to combat dengue fever

One multidisciplinary research project with the aim of controlling dengue fever in Asia focused on **eco-bio-social strategies** for dengue vector control. The research was conducted by the Special Programme for Research and Training in Tropical Diseases (TDR) and Canada's Ecosystems and Human Health Program of the International Development Research Centre (IDRC), and involved entomologists, epidemiologists and social scientists, along with academic institutions, communities, local governments and NGOs. Following a mapping exercise across six countries, site-specific interventions were introduced which included innovative biological, chemical, mechanical and environmental vector control technologies, or a combination of these tools (note 207).

III. CONCLUSIONS AND RECOMMENDATIONS FOR RESEARCH AND INNOVATION

The final outcome of multi-year negotiations involving the European Commission, Council and Parliament has been the allocation of €80 billion for the operation of Horizon 2020 in 2014–2020, focused on the three pillars of excellent science, industrial leadership and societal challenges (including health).[209]

This chapter has argued that European commitment to research and innovation for global health needs to be addressed through Horizon 2020 and that this will benefit Europe in a range of ways. Key reasons for European investment in this field are:

- combating effectively the major health challenges at the European and global levels, including the rising tide of non-communicable diseases and the widening health equity gap;
- strengthening the EU's economy through support for a key but challenged area of European innovation;

[209] European Commission, 'Horizon 2020 launched with €15 billion over first two years' (Brussels, EC, Press Release, 11.12.2013). http://europa.eu/rapid/press-release_IP-13-1232_en.htm.

— providing competitive advantage for European industry and research (bearing in mind the need for balance with access issues for LICs and the importance of the Doha Declaration);
— improving health for Europeans and globally, with consequent positive effects on health systems, employment and global health security;
— sustaining EU credibility with regard to commitments made across a range of EU policies, including those on health, economic growth, social inclusion and development;
— promoting European goals and values in health;
— facilitating global health and science diplomacy, knowledge sharing and common solutions to problems.

Throughout this paper it is repeatedly emphasised that research and innovation for global health has a number of special features that require specific attention, beyond the factors that would be dealt with generically in a broadly framed policy on research and innovation. There are important implications of this set of characteristics for the operation of Horizon 2020:

— the specific needs of research and innovation for global health should be addressed explicitly;
— special mechanisms are needed to promote and support research that is cross-sectoral and interdisciplinary, involving both technological and social innovation;
— special mechanisms are needed to promote and support research collaboration with LMICs, including capacity building;
— innovation stimuli must take account of the special needs of pharmaceutical development, including long lead times, high intensity of investments, high attrition rates, complex registration processes and the danger of repeatedly eliminating innovative SMEs as they are absorbed by large pharmaceutical companies;
— previous experience has shown the gains to be achieved from global, collaborative health research and that some innovations can only occur on a regional/international level.

The section below outlines some specific initiatives through which the policy goals in research and innovation for global health can be pursued effectively.

A. Recommended Strategies to Progress Research and Innovation for Global Health

1. Policy directives

In the elaboration and implementation of Horizon 2020, clear policy statements should establish global health as a priority; recognise its special characteristics; and define areas for priority attention across such domains as pharmaceutical and social innovation, health security and development.

2. ***Interdisciplinary and cross-sectoral research***

The special challenges of interdisciplinary and cross-sectoral research need to be recognised and mechanisms instituted that create an enabling environment and promote such research, including funding and review mechanisms.

3. ***Focus on health and equity research***

The WHO Commission on Social Determinants of Health called for strengthening research to improve health equity. Recent suggestions[210] on priority areas for research on equity and health include:

— global factors and processes that affect health equity;
— structures and processes differentially affecting people's chances to be healthy in a given society;
— health system factors that affect health equity;
— policies and interventions to reduce health inequity.

4. ***European Grand Challenges in Global Health***

In line with the Lund Declaration[92] a programme of European Grand Challenges should be established to develop collaborative global health research tackling major health challenges, which should be open to 'bottom-up' identification of challenges and approaches to solutions. Models include Canada's Grand Challenges in Global Health programme,[211] funded by the Bill and Melinda Gates Foundation.[212] This programme is a family of grants which focus on addressing 14 key grand challenges (with a focus on infectious diseases and infections).[213]

Another example of a 'grand challenges' approach is the US Grand Challenges in Global Mental Health Initiative, which has focused on developing research priorities for neuropsychiatric disorders including 'depression, anxiety disorders, schizophrenia, bipolar disorders, alcohol and drug use disorders, mental disorders of childhood, migraines, dementias, and epilepsy'.[214] This initiative is led by the US National Institute of Mental Health and the Global Alliance for Chronic Disease, in partnership with the

[210] P Ostlin et al, 'Priorities for research on equity and health: Towards an equity focused health research agenda', (2011) *PLoS Medicine* 8(11): e1001115. doi:10.1371/journal.pmed.1001115. www.plosmedicine.org/article/info%3Adoi%2F10.1371%2Fjournal.pmed.1001115.

[211] *Grand Challenges in Global Health, Canada*. www.grandchallenges.org/about/Pages/Overview.aspx.

[212] *Global Health—Grand Challenges Grants Program*, Bill and Melinda Gates Foundation. www.gatesfoundation.org/What-We-Do/Global-Health/Discovery-and-Translational-Sciences#bodyregion_0_interiorarticle_0_strategysections_3_strategysubsections1e9e85ded3fb4757a1d86dc8508751d9_0_lnkHeader.

[213] Grand Challenges in Global Health, Canada, *Browse the Grand Challenges*. www.grandchallenges.org/Pages/BrowseByGoal.aspx.

[214] US National Institute of Mental Health, *Grand Challenges in Global Mental Health* (Washington DC, NIMH, 2012). http://grandchallengesgmh.nimh.nih.gov/.

Wellcome Trust, the McLaughlin-Rotman Centre for Global Health, and the London School of Hygiene and Tropical Medicine.[209] The process included a Scientific Advisory Board establishing the scope and questions for global mental health, with a Delphi Panel then refining priorities for research.[215] The priority setting process also developed a network of research funders.[216]

A European Grand Challenges in Global Health programme would build upon these initiatives and provide important opportunities for partnerships between the EU, the private sector and foundations; and for creating consortia that include academic and private sector actors, including multinationals and SMEs. They can be built around multi-sectoral and multi-disciplinary teams, with partners from across fields such as engineering, business, statistics and the social, chemical and biological sciences. A European approach should not necessarily specify specific topics, but promote an inclusive, fair, needs-driven and transparent process of priority setting for research.

5. ***European Global Health Chairs***

These provide the opportunity to promote research in a hitherto under-resourced field. The Canadian Global Public Health chairs provide a possible model: funded by the Canadian Research Chair Programme (2000 research professorships in all, with 35 per cent for research in health), they attract outstanding researchers who are world leaders in their field, and whose research corresponds with the strategic research plan of the host university. Renewable chairs are available for either seven years (university receives $200,000 annually) or for five years (university receives $100,000 annually). Chairs are also eligible for infrastructure funding from the Canada Foundation for Innovation. Nominations are peer reviewed through a 'College of Reviewers', with involvement from a Steering Committee in the review process.[217]

6. ***Collaborative global health research centres***

European involvement in global health research could be advanced through the development of collaborative research centres for global health which have strong links to a global health policy forum. Models to draw upon include the German Collaborative Research Centres and the Australian Research Council's Centres of Excellence (which facilitate cross-disciplinary research across institutes, departments and faculties and with external organisations).

The Center for Global Health Research in Toronto[218] is an example of a research collaboration which conducts studies in LMICs. It is an independent,

[215] US National Institute of Mental Health, *Grand Challenges in Global Mental Health: Methodology*, (Washington DC, NIMH, 2012). http://grandchallengesgmh.nimh.nih.gov/about.shtml#overview.

[216] PY Collins et al, 'Grand Challenges in Global Mental Health' (2011) *Nature* 475, 27–30, http://grandchallengesgmh.nimh.nih.gov/Grand%20Challenges%20in%20Global%20Mental%20Health.pdf.

[217] *Canada Research Chairs*, Government of Canada, 2013. http://www.chairs-chaires.gc.ca/chairholders-titulaires/index-eng.aspx.

[218] Center for Global Health Research. www.cghr.org.

non-profit NGO funded through a public-private partnership which includes the Canadian Institutes of Health Research, the US National Institutes of Health, the Bill and Melinda Gates Foundation, St Michael's Hospital and the University of Toronto.

7. ***Capacity building initiatives with LMICs, including the involvement of civil society, and 'people's initiatives'***

Global health research and innovation initiatives should continue to develop research capacity within LMICs and across LMICs/HICs. There are already some examples[33,46,219,220] where this is occurring. One way to develop research capacity in LMICs and ensure that research is relevant and appropriately meeting the needs of local populations, is through the involvement of civil society, which needs to be engaged in the research process through a range of strategies such as citizens' juries and participatory research projects.

[219] Netherlands Organization for Scientific Research, *Global Health Policy and Health Systems Research Programme*. hwww.nwo.nl/en/research-and-results/programmes/Global+Health+Policy+and+Health+Systems.

[220] M Parker et al, *The Ethics of Collaborative Global Health Research* (Oxford, The Ethox Centre, 2011). www.ethox.org.uk/research/global-health-ethics/the-ethics-of-collaborative-global-health-research.

Part V

The European Union in the World Intellectual Property Organization

13

The European Union in the World Intellectual Property Organization: From a Cloudy Complexity towards an Ordered Pluralism

An External Appraisal

JEAN-CHRISTOPHE GALLOUX

THE PURPOSE OF this chapter is to set out the legal framework of the participation of the EU in the World Intellectual Property Organization (WIPO).

To borrow the words used by Professor Kickbusch with regard to the World Health Organization (WHO), the European Union (EU) is something of a 'good global citizen'. It is indisputably a respected player, but the role that its constituencies have written for it comes both from the Treaties and from a particularly complex history, which means that it is unable to play either the young leads or the statue of the Commendatore, or even to appear at the top of the bill. In short, the EU is a minor player in comparison with the roles that certain of its members have played in the past in the creation of a global intellectual property law. It is also true that the casting is more difficult now than at the end of the 19th century.

The fact is that the situation of the EU with regard to WIPO is no less complex than with regard to other international organisations. The EU is no more on the road to simplification here than elsewhere: it still needs distinct treatment of intellectual property on the part of the international organisations. In addition, intellectual property is a disparate set of rights which are fundamentally rooted in the principle of territoriality, subject to different international regimes, and constantly changing. You therefore have all the ingredients of a situation with a rare complexity.

I will start with an explanation of this complexity in an attempt to establish a certain order. After all, we all know that no legal system is spontaneously ordered…

I. A CLOUDY COMPLEXITY

Why cloudy? Cloud is undoubtedly the best description of the immaterial quality of intellectual property. What are the factors of this complexity and the consequences thereof with regard to the EU's actions at the WIPO?

A. The Factors of Complexity

These factors are fourfold—interdependence, discontinuity, interaction and unpredictability—and affect both the field concerned and the internal relations at the EU.

i. The Complexity of the Subject Matter

Intellectual property is neither a unified matter nor a trouble-free area. It comprises multiple rights which are not always recognised at international level, but the treaties which relate thereto, when they are recognised, are administered by the WIPO. Added to this complexity of the subject matter is the complexity relating to the internal operation of the EU.

The perimeter of intellectual property rights has never been precisely defined by international or Community texts. Although everyone agrees on the fact that intellectual property is divided into industrial property and literary and artistic property, this is one of the rare certainties on the matter. The former is defined by Article 1 of the Paris Convention for the protection of industrial property of 20 March 1883 revised at The Hague in 1925 (Hague Treaty)[1] in that it comprises 'patents, utility models, industrial designs, trademarks, service marks,[2] trade names, indications of source or appellations of origin, and the repression of unfair competition'. Unfair competition is not, strictly speaking, an intellectual property right but an action intended to penalise any act of competition contrary to honest industrial or commercial practices; the case law of the Court of Justice sometimes classes it as an intellectual property right.[3]

This list must also include rights which indisputably fall thereunder, such as plant variety protection certificates, organised at international level by the Paris Convention of 2 December 1961 and at Community level by Regulation 2100/94 of 27 July 1994, and the rights regarding layout designs or topographies of semiconductors, created at international level by the WIPO Convention of 26 May 1989 and at Community level by Directive 87/54 of 16 December 1986.

The Stockholm Convention of 4 July 1967 establishing WIPO proposes, for its part, a list of intellectual property rights: 'the rights relating to: literary, artistic

[1] The Hague conference Proceedings, p 332, French proposal 410–12; 534–35: Report of the drafting Committee; 572: adopted in the second round.

[2] Added during the revised Convention of Lisbon in 1958, proposed by Sweden and United States delegations: The Lisbon conference Proceedings, pp 624, 626–27.

[3] ECJ, Joint Cases C-300/98 and 392/98 *Parfums Christian Dior* [2000] ECR I-11307.

and scientific works; performances of performing artists, phonograms, and broadcasts; inventions in all fields of human endeavour; scientific discoveries; industrial designs; trademarks, service marks, and commercial names and designations; protection against unfair competition, and all other rights resulting from intellectual activity in the industrial, scientific, literary or artistic fields'. The list provided by the Stockholm Convention supplements that of the Paris Convention by including commercial designations and scientific works. The latter do not benefit from any privative protection in the majority of countries, as the Geneva treaty of 7 March 1978, which provides solely for the international registration of scientific discoveries, forming recognition of a sort of moral right and the granting of material recompense to their authors, never entered into force due to an insufficient number of ratifications. As specified in the text, literary and artistic property comprises copyright and rights related to copyright: the rights of performing artists, the right of the producers of phonograms, the right of the producers of videograms and the rights of audiovisual communication companies. The interest of the Stockholm text lies in its open nature: intellectual property concerns all rights 'resulting from intellectual activity' in all fields of human endeavour, beyond those which are listed.

The TRIPS annex of the Agreement on the World Trade Organization (WTO) proposes yet another interpretation of intellectual property to which it dedicates its subject. According to paragraph 2 of Article 1: 'For the purposes of this Agreement, the term "intellectual property" refers to all categories of intellectual property that are the subject of Sections 1 through 7 of Part II', namely: copyright and related rights (right of performing artists, producers of phonograms and broadcasting organisations); trademarks; geographical indications and particularly those for wines or spirits; industrial designs; patents; protection *sui generis* of plant varieties;[4] layout designs (topographies) of integrated circuits; undisclosed information. It is important to note that, contrary to the Paris Convention, unfair competition is no longer protected as such but appears as a means of protecting undisclosed information.

Finally, the Directive 48/2004 relating to 'the enforcement of intellectual property rights' of 29 April 2004 only designates as intellectual property rights those falling under the Community acquis, and those protected as such by national legislation so as to 'define the scope of this Directive as widely as possible'.[5] It authorises the Member States to extend 'for internal purposes' the provisions of this Directive to include 'acts involving unfair competition, including parasitic copies, or similar activities'. For its part, the case law of the Court of Justice has recognised copyright[6] and geographical indications[7] in particular as being industrial or commercial property, within the meaning of Article 30 TEC.

[4] Allowed by Art 27(3)(b).

[5] Preamble, point 13.

[6] ECJ, Cases 57/80 and 55/80 *Musik-Vertrieb membran GmbH and K-tel International v GEMA* [1981] ECR 147.

[7] ECJ, Case C-3/91 *Exportur SA v LOR SA and Confiserie du Tech SA* [1992] ECR I-5529.

Since the major Paris Convention on industrial property (1883) and Berne Convention on copyright (1886), the international intellectual property players have changed, as have the purposes of intellectual property. With regard to the act of creation, the first principle of protection, certain contributions now only justify the granting of a privative right, which leads to expansion of the subject matter. Nevertheless, the internationalisation of protection remains an imperative, as stated by Plaisant: 'The convention-based law is a means which makes it possible to place the person [of the creator] and the ideas which emanate therefrom above the network of the nations'.[8]

But Rome is no longer in Rome: intellectual property is no longer entirely contained in texts administered by WIPO, it is also mentioned in other forums. For instance, the Rio Convention on biodiversity, ratified by the European Union,[9] includes in Article 15 ('access to genetic resources') and Article 16 ('access to technology') certain provisions[10] which maintain that they may enter into conflict with intellectual property rights, particularly patents, as they are recognised by the international instruments, the Paris Convention or the TRIPS Agreement.[11] More recently, the second protocol adopted in the scope of the Rio Convention, the Nagoya Protocol on access to genetic resources and the fair and equitable sharing of benefits arising from their utilisation adopted on 29 October 2010, has the objective of allowing fair and equitable sharing of benefits arising from the utilisation of genetic resources; it is aimed in particular at combating 'biopiracy', the unlawful appropriation of genetic resources and traditional indigenous knowledge which may be associated therewith. It has been and will continue to be necessary to carefully handle the monopoly conferred in the field of plants intended for food as undertaken in the International Treaty on plant genetic resources for food and agriculture signed on 3 November 2001 under the aegis of the Food and Agriculture Organization (FAO).[12] Mention may also be made, as diversification of the subject, of the Convention for the safeguarding of intangible cultural heritage which was adopted by the United Nations Educational, Scientific and Cultural Organization (UNESCO) on 17 October 2003 and entered into force in April 2006, the subject of which notably overlaps that of intellectual property.[13]

[8] M Plaisant, *Traité de droit conventionnel international concernant la propriété industrielle* (Paris, Sirey, 1959).

[9] Council Decision 93/626, 25 October 1993, OJ 1993 L 309/1.

[10] Developing countries, essentially: R Vellvé, 'Brevetabilité du vivant: les enjeux Nord-Sud', in *Vers un anti-destin?* (Paris, O Jacob, 1992) 398.

[11] For a summary of the Rio Convention, see M-A Hermitte, 'La Convention sur la diversité biologique' (1992) *Annuaire français de droit international* 844.

[12] www.fao.org/legal/treaties/033t-f.htm; J-C Galloux, Chronique de créations techniques, Propr. intell. October 2002.

[13] 'The "intangible cultural heritage" means the practices, representations, expressions, knowledge, skills—as well as the instruments, objects, artefacts and cultural spaces associated therewith—that communities, groups and, in some cases, individuals recognize as part of their cultural heritage. This intangible cultural heritage, transmitted from generation to generation, is constantly recreated by communities and groups in response to their environment, their interaction with nature and their history,

In a more general manner concerning all industrial property rights, the TRIPS agreement moved the centre of gravity of intellectual property from WIPO to the WTO. The WTO, through its integration and reinforcement of the major conventions on intellectual property, now implements them in the scope of a wider mechanism of management of world trade, in which the WTO is the prime mover. It is therefore necessary to consider that, today, the political initiative with regard to industrial property finds its source more within the WTO than within WIPO. The cooperation between WTO and WIPO is organised by an agreement signed in Geneva on 22 December 1995.

It is therefore no longer just WIPO which deals with global intellectual property policy, but also the WTO, UNESCO and the FAO. It is necessary to keep this background in mind in order to understand the issues of participation within WIPO.

ii. The Complexity of the Relations Between the EU and the Member States

Added to the complexity of the subject matter is the complexity relating to the internal operation of the EU. The question of the division of the internal and external competences of the EU and, before it, the European Communities with regard to intellectual property is still latent.[14] Without going into institutional details, it is important to remember that, from 1958 up to the Lisbon Treaty, the competences of the European institutions were widened to the detriment of those of the Member States. The remaining difficulties result, on the one hand, from the fact that intellectual property, the scale and diversity of which has been noted, extends beyond the field of trade policy and, on the other hand, from the survival, despite the creation of various EU intellectual property rights,[15] of the national rights, harmonised or otherwise.

The Treaty of Rome did not transfer competences between the Member States and the Communities with regard to intellectual property: it therefore did not confer special competences on the European institutions, as judged by the Court of First Instance on 10 July 1991.[16] However, they exercised them by way of harmonisation from the end of the 1980s, with regard to trademarks then patents,[17] then by

and provides them with a sense of identity and continuity, thus promoting respect for cultural diversity and human creativity. For the purposes of this Convention, consideration will be given solely to such intangible cultural heritage as is compatible with existing international human rights instruments, as well as with the requirements of mutual respect among communities, groups and individuals, and of sustainable development.'

[14] See V Ruzek, *L'action extérieure de la Communauté européenne en matière de droits de la propriété intellectuelle: approche institutionnelle* (Apogée, 2007); K Ben Dahmen, *Interactions du droit international et du droit de l'Union européenne: un pluralisme juridique rénové en matière de propriété industrielle* (L'Harmattan, 2013).

[15] See below.

[16] CFI, Case T-76/89 *Independent Television Publications Ltd v Commission* [1991] ECR II-575.

[17] Directive 89/104 of 21 December 1988 on trademarks, OJ 1989 L 40/1; Directive 98/44 of 6 July 1998 on the legal protection of biotechnological inventions, OJ 1998 L 213/13.

way of unification from the 1990s through the creation of Community industrial property rights, valid over the entire territory of the Union and resulting from a unique and centralised granting procedure. This gave rise to the Community trademark,[18] the Community plant variety protection certificate,[19] the Community design[20] and the Community indication of geographical origin.[21] Copyright and patents have notably remained outside of this integration movement, for different reasons.

In its Opinion 1/94 on the accession to the WTO, the Court of Justice confirmed the competence of the European Community with regard to intellectual property, but the competence has been considered as shared with the Member States.

The Lisbon Treaty made great changes in this regard. The EU may still rely on Article 207 TFEU related to the common commercial policy of the EU, in so far as intellectual property rights are related thereto.

As mentioned above, the competence granted to the EU in this regard has not brought an end to the coexistence between Union rights and national rights: this coexistence may even go as far as the accumulation of the two rights on the same subject for trademarks and designs[22] but not for plant variety protection certificates.[23] The survival of the national rights means that the Member States retain their international competence with regard thereto: there is therefore no succession from the EU to the Member States here or, consequently, no complete transfer of competence to the EU in the presence of these national rights. The removal of these national rights in the near future is not and cannot be envisaged. They correspond to a need of industrial and trade circles that the European Union rights do not necessarily meet.

B. The Consequences of this Complexity on EU/WIPO Relations

The complex division of competences between the EU and the Member States, giving the former altered external competences, means that it has varying capacities: it therefore participates in a different manner in the various forums within WIPO.

Article 5 of the Convention establishing WIPO only reserves membership status to States. It is in the scope of Article 13 (concerning relations with other intergovernmental organisations) that the links with WIPO could be established. Here, as elsewhere, the insertion of the EU into international relations troubles traditional legal categories. By its very nature, the EU cannot be classed as a state or a classical international organisation. Its participation in international

[18] Regulation 40/94 of 20 December 1993, OJ 1994 L 11/1.
[19] Regulation 2100/94 of 27 July 1994, OJ 1994 L 227/1.
[20] Regulation 6/2002 of 12 December 2001, OJ 2002 L 3/1.
[21] Regulation 1107/96 of 12 June 1996, OJ 1996 L 148/1.
[22] Arts 94 and 95, Regulation 207/2009 (codified version), OJ 2009 L 78/1; Art 95 Regulation 6/2002.
[23] Art 92 Regulation 2100/94.

conventions concerning intellectual property therefore implies the creation of novel formulations capable of expressing the specific nature of the EU.[24]

The EU's participation is either direct or indirect, according to the circumstances. The forms of participation depend to a large extent on the ratification or otherwise by the EU of the international instrument governing the intellectual right concerned, but such ratification does not always resolve the problems. The accession of the EU to these conventions obviously depends on what is provided for by the text in question.

The oldest texts did not allow the accession of international organisations: this is the case with the Paris Convention (1883) and the Berne Convention (1886). The more modern texts now provide for this.

The Council was thus able to take the following ratification decisions, for texts concerning intellectual property:

— Council Decision of 19 November 2007 on the acceptance, on behalf of the European Community, of the Protocol amending the TRIPS Agreement, done at Geneva on 6 December 2005;
— Council Decision No 2006/954/EC of 18 December 2006 approving the accession of the European Community to the Geneva Act of the Hague Agreement concerning the international registration of industrial designs, adopted in Geneva on 2 July 1999;
— Council Decision of 30 May 2005 approving the accession of the European Community to the International Convention for the Protection of New Varieties of Plants, as revised at Geneva on 19 March 1991;
— Council Decision (EU) No 793 of 27 October 2003 approving the accession of the European Community to the Protocol relating to the Madrid Agreement concerning the international registration of marks, adopted at Madrid on 27 June 1989;
— Council Decision of 16 March 2000 on the approval, on behalf of the European Community, of the WIPO Copyright Treaty and the WIPO Performances and Phonograms Treaty (2000);
— Marrakech Treaty (June 2013) to facilitate Access to Published Works by Visually Impaired Persons and Persons with Print Disabilities.

The following treaties have now entered into force with regard to the EU:

— Beijing Treaty on Audiovisual Performances adopted by the Diplomatic Conference on 24 June 2012;
— Trademark Law Treaty adopted at Geneva on 27 October 1994;

[24] R Kovar, 'La participation des Communautés européennes aux Conventions multilatérales' (1975) *Annuaire Français de droit International* 903. See, more recently, C Flaesch-Mougin, 'Le statut de la Communauté Européenne au sein des organisations internationales' in J-V Louis and M Dony (eds), *Commentaire J Mégret: Le Droit de la CE et de l'Union Européenne*, Vol 12: Relations extérieures (Brussels, Editions de l'Université de Bruxelles, 2005) 369–97; C Kaddous, 'European Union Participation in International Financial Organizations' in I Govaere and S Poli (eds), *EU Governance of Global Emergencies* (Brill book series, Studies in EU External Relations, 2014) 277–95.

- — WIPO Copyright Treaty (14 March 2010);
- — WIPO Performances and Phonograms Treaty (14 March 2010);
- — Hague Agreement Concerning the International Registration of Industrial Designs (1 January 2008);
- — Protocol Relating to the Madrid Agreement Concerning the International Registration of Marks (1 October 2004).

The EU participated in all the diplomatic conferences in respect of the abovementioned instruments. But its status may vary from one conference to the next. The EU appears as a 'Special member delegation' during the diplomatic conference in Marrakech on 17–28 June 2013: the EU was the only party to be given this status, being classed as neither an intergovernmental organisation (such as the AIPO, the ARIPO or the WTO) nor a non-governmental organisation. The rules of procedure of this conference did not provide a voting right for the EU, but authorised the special delegation of the EU to exercise the voting right of the Member States represented at the conference, provided that they did not exercise it themselves and the number of votes expressed was not greater than the number of Member States represented.[25] This 'special delegation' status had already been held during diplomatic conferences in Beijing in November 2012 and in Geneva on 2–20 December 1996 regarding certain questions concerning copyright and related rights. The EU also has 'special delegation' status within the Intergovernmental Committee on intellectual property and genetic resources, traditional knowledge and folklore.

It is possible to notice a discrete presence of the EU in international literary and artistic property law, the (four) ratified texts being quite marginal in this regard. The harmonisation of copyright and related rights started relatively late within the Union,[26] being the victim of a certain reluctance on the part of some Member States to grant the Union's institutions wider powers in a field intimately linked with national cultural interests. Furthermore, a Decision proposal made by the European Commission with a view to accession to the Paris Act (1971) of the Berne Convention and the Rome Convention[27] only resulted in a Resolution.[28]

Besides its 'special delegation' status, the EU's status can be that of 'observer' or 'member' with or without a voting right in the various forums within the WIPO. It is thus an 'observer' at the Permanent Committee on patent law or at the Permanent Committee on copyright and with the Unions of which it cannot become a plenary member through lack of possibility of accession (Union of Paris or Berne, for example). This may lead to strange legal situations: the EU is not a member of the Assembly of Lisbon, not being a member of this Convention relating to the protection of appellations of origin; nevertheless, it has exclusive competence for

[25] Art 33(3).

[26] Green book: Le droit d'auteur et le défi technologique, Problèmes de droit d'auteur appelant une action immédiate, Communication of the Commission, COM(88) 172 final, 1988.

[27] COM(90) 582 final, Syn 318 of 11 January 1991.

[28] Council Resolution of 14 May 1992 concerning the protection of copyright and neighbouring rights, 92/C 138/01, OJ C 138/1, 28 May 1992.

these distinctive signs with regard to the Member States.[29] The EU is a member of the permanent committee on trademark and design law, but does not have a voting right. When the EU is given a voting right, the methods of exercising that right within the assemblies may vary depending on the nature of the questions addressed, and whether they fall within the competence of the Union or that of the Member States: mention is therefore made of cumulative and/or additional status, or alternative status.[30] All combinations exist: convention-based assemblies in which the Member States are represented as well as the EU; in which the Member States are represented but without the presence of the EU; in which the EU is represented but the Member States are not: it is, however, rare for the participation of the EU to be exclusive of that of the Member States.

It is difficult to imagine a more refined casuistry. Can order emerge from what might pass for chaos?

II. TOWARDS AN ORDERED PLURALISM

The reader will understand from the situation set out above that its complexity cannot be overcome without a number of conditions being met. Three come straight to mind.

The first would lie in a complete transfer of competence to the EU in respect of all intellectual property rights. Such a solution cannot be envisaged in the near future or even in the medium term. This is because it would suppose complete and exhaustive harmonisation of all intellectual property rights, which is not the case for the two most important amongst them: copyright and patent rights. Furthermore, with regard to patent rights, the EU has just renounced such harmonisation by approving, through the Agreement on a Unified Patent Court of 17 February 2013,[31] that this (partly) take place outside of the Community framework. A worse political signal could not be given.

The European Institutions' inability to obtain such harmonisation, more than half a century after the signing of the Treaty of Rome and 23 years after the launch of the 'single market', places the EU in a paradoxical situation: how to have credibility for negotiating the harmonisation of intellectual property rights at international level while being incapable of achieving that for itself?

In fact, a complete transfer of competence from the Member States to the EU is not necessarily part of their plans, as shown by the above-mentioned example of the lack of ratification of the Berne and Rome Conventions.[32]

The second condition would involve the removal of the national intellectual property rights: only the Community rights would remain. Such a programme is not on the agenda.

[29] ECJ, Case C-166/078, September 2009.
[30] K Ben Dahmen, above, n 14, p 354.
[31] JC Galloux, RTD Com 2013 No 4.
[32] Cf above.

The third condition would involve the conventions administered by WIPO all providing for the possibility of accession by the EU. This would require revision of all the oldest texts, the Paris Convention in particular. However, everyone knows that this industrial property monument has been left untouched since the Stockholm revision in 1976.

Faced with these insurmountable obstacles, how is it possible to nevertheless improve the situation of the EU within WIPO? The solution may lie in the implementation of an 'ordered pluralism'. This would involve analysis of the successes achieved through the cooperation between the EU and the Member States in their participation in the forums of WIPO and, it has to be admitted, in expressing a number of wishes.

A. Developing European Success within WIPO

The EU and its Member States are and remain key players in the field of intellectual property and their participation within WIPO is essential for the proper operation of that organisation. The success of the EU within WIPO is based on its efficient coordination and the knock-on effect that it produces both in Europe and beyond.

i. The Success of European Coordination

This is a European coordination success which must be credited to the EU. If this coordination had failed, all the most recent conventions which we have mentioned would not have been ratified by the EU and its Member States. If this coordination had failed, these texts would undoubtedly not even have been created, as they are prepared within the different committees in which the Europeans assiduously participate. However, in reality, it must be recognised that the EU does not very often appear as a leader: this is due both to the complexity of the methods of representation and to a lack of vision in the areas concerned. Is there still a political plan and will behind a technical consensus? We need only look at the number of diplomatic conferences held in a country of the Union at the latter's initiative since transfers of competence were granted by the Member States: none. For political reasons, they are held either in emerging countries or on the neutral territory of Switzerland. The EU is a minor player.

In the EU's defence, it must be admitted that the issues relating to the majority of intellectual property rights go beyond the simple framework of trade policy, which also explains the division of competences between it and the Member States. Copyright is linked to the cultural policy of the States; patent rights are linked to the industrial policy and technological independence of the States; geographical indications are linked to agricultural policy; traditional knowledge raises delicate questions relating to North–South relations.

More than an increase in pro-European political will on the part of the Member States, the erosion of the role of the States in these fields will lead to the consideration of greater transfers to the European Union.[33]

ii. The Knock-on Effect[34]

The extent of the success can also be seen in what may be called the knock-on effect of the EU with regard to intellectual property through its action within WIPO. This effect is measured on three levels.

First, in its relations with the Member States: the EU's accession to a number of international instruments in the scope of WIPO automatically leads them to modernise the legal framework of their intellectual property rights. Many would not have done this at all or would have done this later.

Still in relation to the Member States, the direct integration of a number of international standards into the sources of the law of the Union by way of the accessions of the Union, or the changes made to the major intellectual property conventions by the TRIPS, now require a renewed respect for these instruments by the Member States.[35] Ireland was thus found guilty of non-compliance for its failure to recognise the provisions of the Berne Convention.[36] The EU is therefore becoming the watchful guardian of international intellectual property law.

At international level, in its relations with third countries, the knock-on effect is translated in the bilateral agreements concluded by the Union in the field of commercial cooperation, through the imposition of minimum standards with regard to intellectual property right protection, drawn from the Community standards.

Furthermore, the European legislation with regard to intellectual property serves as a model for third countries, particularly those which maintain close commercial relations with the Union. This is the case in particular with the Maghreb countries, Turkey and, to a certain extent, Eastern European countries.

B. Going Further?

The successes of the coordination and the knock-on effect are most certainly not enough to give the EU full capability in the scope of its action within WIPO. From

[33] See our study 'Les propriétés intellectuelles: un exemple du retrait de l'Etat au XXIème siècle', *Mélanges en l'honneur d'André Lucas*, 2014.

[34] R Medhi, Le droit communautaire à l'heure de l'élargissement, GP 2007, p 2239; K Ben Dahmen, above, n 14, p 501.

[35] See, in particular, ECJ, Case C-135/10 *Società Consortile Fonografici (SCF) v Marco Del Corso* [2012] nyr. In that judgment the Court considered that the TRIPS agreement is part of the European legal system, for the matters within its competence; then, the Rome Convention of October 1961 produced indirect effects in Union law.

[36] ECJ, Case 13/00 *Commission v Ireland* [2002] ECR I-2943.

this perspective, and without citing the radical solutions presented above which are not realistic, several improvements could be made.

Speaking with one voice: everyone knows that each voice comes from two vocal cords.[37] Be that as it may, harmonisation of positions in advance of negotiations at WIPO is a necessity. There is also no doubt that such harmonisation is easier to construct around joint projects defended together; from this perspective, it seems a shame that the EU is no longer at the forefront on a number of sensitive subjects such as traditional knowledge. As we have found, the EU has no longer been behind diplomatic conferences and the last attempt to have a new intellectual property right, database protection, adopted at international level failed in 1996. The EU should no longer be content with remaining a minor player.

There would need to be more coherence, from a technical perspective, between national and EU intellectual property rights, for example the possibility of obtaining two international registrations for designs, through the national and international route.[38] In general, better cooperation between the different national and EU rights, from an international perspective, is desirable, as this coexistence situation needs to endure.

Finally, the success of the EU within WIPO also requires more solidarity on the part of the Member States. In all the fields which correspond to the objectives of the Treaty, Article 4(3) TEU obliges the Member States to assist the Union in carrying out its tasks, particularly in the international domain.

[37] C Flaesch-Mougin, 'Les relations avec les organisations internationales et la participation à celles-ci' in *Commentaire J Mégret* 2nd edn (2005) p 341.

[38] Azéma et Galloux, Droit de la propriété industrielle, 7th edn (2012) nos 1354 et seq.

Part VI

The European Union Participation in International Organisations and Its Normative Power

14

How to Evaluate the European Union as a Normative Power in Multilevel Governance of Public Goods?

Methodological Pluralism and its Constitutional Limits in European Governance

ERNST-ULRICH PETERSMANN

IN THE ACADEMIC and policy discussions during the conference on *The EU in International Organizations and Global Governance* at Geneva, the policy conclusions drawn by academics and by practitioners from the European Union (EU), United Nations (UN) and World Trade Organization (WTO) institutions—even though informed by the highest levels of practical knowledge of the relevant legal and policy details—often remained a 'cacophony' due to their diverse methodologies and (sometimes unrevealed) value preferences.[1] If European diplomats and academics wish to promote democratic and civil society support for their multilevel governance of international public goods (PGs) in UN, WTO and EU institutions, they have to explain their 'inter-governmentalism' and diplomatic pragmatism also in terms of principles that citizens can understand and support as protecting the reasonable self-interests of EU citizens. As most citizens remain 'rationally ignorant' of the economic, legal and political complexities of intergovernmental decision-making and political compromises in EU, UN and WTO institutions, they evaluate the EU institutions in terms of the unique promises of EU law that:

— the Union is founded on the values of respect for human dignity, freedom, democracy, equality, the rule of law and respect for human rights

[1] On the need for respecting 'methodological pluralism' in legal and democratic justifications of law, governance and 'public reason' see E-U Petersmann, 'JIEL Debate: Methodological Pluralism and its Critics in International Economic Law Research' (2012) *Journal of International Economic Law* 15, 921–70.

(Article 2 TEU); decisions are taken as openly as possible and as closely as possible to the citizen (Article 1 TEU);

— the Union's action on the international scene shall be guided by the same principles which have inspired its own creation, development and enlargement, and which it seeks to advance in the wider world: democracy, the rule of law, the universality and indivisibility of human rights and fundamental freedoms, respect for human dignity, the principles of equality and solidarity, and respect for the principles of the United Nations and international law (Article 21 TEU).

The EU Charter of Fundamental Rights protects—in conformity with national and international human rights law (HRL) and also WTO law—comprehensive guarantees of 'access to justice' for 'everyone' (cf Article 47) and governmental duties of justifying 'any limitation on the exercise of the rights and freedoms recognized by this Charter' as being legally necessary for protecting the fundamental rights and general interests of EU citizens (cf Article 52).[2] Hence, the EU institutions and EU Member States have to justify also their EU, UN and WTO decision making in terms of 'cosmopolitan principles of justice' that are easier to understand for citizens than intergovernmental decision making in distant UN and WTO institutions. Also the diverse policy proposals by academics for EU, UN and WTO reforms (such as for EU representation in UN institutions, reforming euro governance on the basis of 'the principle of subsidiarity' rather than federalism, supervision of over-indebted euro Member States by the 'troika' of the IMF, the European Commission and the European Central Bank) should more clearly reveal and justify their value premises so that citizens can evaluate and democratically discuss the legal coherence, 'financial risks' and redistributive effects of, for example, EU monetary and financial regulations. This contribution proceeds from the democratic assumptions underlying EU law that:

— in constitutional democracies like the EU Member States, citizens are the 'democratic owners' and 'principals' of all governance institutions (as 'agents' with limited, delegated powers), whose legitimacy derives from respecting, protecting and fulfilling human and constitutional rights of citizens, other 'principles of justice' (cf Article 2 TEU) and democratic 'public reason' recognised in EU law;

— as UN HRL, the WTO dispute settlement system and EU law protect individual rights of 'access to justice' and to public justification of governmental restrictions of equal freedoms and require 'strict observance of international law' (Article 3 TEU) and mutually consistent interpretations, claims by EU

[2] On guarantees of 'access to justice' in UN law, WTO law and EU law see F Francioni (ed), *Access to Justice as a Human Right* (2007); AA Cançado Trindade, *The Access of Individuals to International Justice* (2011); E-U Petersmann, *The GATT/WTO Dispute Settlement System* (1997) 194 ff, 233 ff; *Access to Justice in Europe: An Overview of Challenges and Opportunities* (European Union Agency for Fundamental Rights, 2011). On the human right to justification see R Forst, *The Right to Justification. Elements of a Constructivist Theory of Justice* (2012).

governments to 'freedom of manoeuvre'[3] to violate international UN and WTO agreements ratified by parliaments for the benefit of citizens require justification in terms of fundamental rights of EU citizens, as illustrated by the '*Kadi* jurisprudence' of the EU Court of Justice (CJEU) protecting human rights in the foreign policy area;[4]

— conflicts of interest among EU citizens insisting on 'access to justice' and EU institutions limiting their legal, democratic and judicial accountability vis-à-vis citizens (for example, for welfare-reducing violations of WTO guarantees of non-discriminatory conditions of transnational competition and rule of law) require citizen-oriented public justifications which citizens—as democratic authors and addressees of legitimate law—can accept as 'public reason' rather than mere intergovernmental power politics violating EU law (like disregard for more than a dozen GATT/WTO dispute settlement rulings against the EU in the 'banana dispute' from 1991 to 2012 without effective EU legal remedies of adversely affected EU citizens and EU Member States interested in complying with WTO law and avoiding legal responsibility for EU majority decisions violating international law).

Section I of this chapter argues that respect for legitimate 'methodological pluralism' requires more comprehensive 'balancing' of public and private interests in determining 'public reason', 'rule of law' and legitimate 'Community interests' inside the EU and the common 'principles of justice' justifying UN, WTO and EU law. Section II illustrates this argument by comparing five competing policy approaches to international economic law (IEL) in the light of the EU law requirement to promote 'cosmopolitan constitutionalism' also in the EU's external actions. Section III concludes that the EU's UN and WTO policies should use the EU's 'civilian power' and 'normative power' more actively for exercising 'cosmopolitan leadership' in multilevel governance of international PGs demanded by EU citizens by interpreting the 'constitutional principles' common to UN, WTO and EU law for the benefit of citizens.

I. METHODOLOGICAL PLURALISM AND ITS CONSTITUTIONAL LIMITS IN EUROPEAN GOVERNANCE

Law and governance require justification in order to be supported by citizens as a legitimate exercise of power. Lawyers, economists and political scientists tend

[3] The term 'freedom of manoeuvre' continues to be used by both the political EU institutions and the CJEU (eg in Joined Cases C-120 and C-121/06P *Fiamm*, ECR 2008 I-6513, para 119) as the only justification for their disregard of legally binding WTO rules and WTO dispute settlement rulings.

[4] On failures by the CJEU to protect the EU law requirement of 'strict observance of international law' (Article 3 TEU) vis-à-vis EU violations of UN and WTO obligations to the detriment of EU citizens, without even demanding the EU institutions to prove how violations of international treaties ratified by all parliaments inside the EU are necessary for promoting legitimate 'Community interests' as defined by the Lisbon Treaty, see E-U Petersmann, 'Can the EU's Disregard for "Strict Observance of International Law" (Article 3 TEU) Be Constitutionally Justified?' in M Bronckers, V Hauspiel and R Quick (eds), *Liber Amicorum for J Bourgeois* (2011), 214–25.

to use diverse methodologies for justifying law and governance. In constitutional democracies, reasonable citizens require justification of law and governance not only on deontological grounds (eg in terms of equal freedoms as 'first principle of justice') and consequentialist grounds (such as promotion of general consumer welfare through open markets and non-discriminatory conditions of competition). Successful democracies also depend on 'virtue ethics' of citizens, 'civil servants' and parliamentarians committed to transforming agreed 'principles of justice' (eg in EU constitutional law) into democratic legislation, judicial administration of justice and multilevel protection of transnational PGs. This republican conception of multilevel governance of PGs—as being dependent on 'republican virtues' and a '*démocratie de tous les jours*' struggling for progressive transformation of constitutionally agreed 'principles of justice' into multilevel legislative, administrative, judicial and international protection of 'aggregate PGs' as demanded by citizens that must be recognized as 'constituent powers' entitled to hold all multilevel governance agents and their limited 'constituted powers' legally and democratically accountable[5]—is often absent in intergovernmental UN, WTO or other negotiations prioritising rights of governments over rights of citizens.

A. Competing Legal, Economic and Political Approaches to Multilevel Governance of PGs

Lawyers use the term 'legal methodology' as referring to the respective conceptions of the sources and 'rules of recognition' of law, the methods of interpretation, the functions and systemic nature of legal systems and of their relationships to other areas of law and politics. National courts and the CJEU interpret EU law as a cosmopolitan legal system whose 'primary rules of conduct' (for example, the common market law) and 'secondary rules of recognition, change and adjudication' derive their legitimacy from protecting human and constitutional rights of citizens, transnational rule of law and democratic governance for the benefit of citizens. In the foreign policy area, public and private interests inside the EU often diverge as to how the EU law requirements of promoting 'strict observance of international law' (Article 3 TEU) and the EU's 'cosmopolitan constitutional law' principles (such as in Article 21 TEU) should be reconciled with the fact that UN and WTO law also protect power-oriented conceptions of 'sovereign equality of states' (for example, based on factual governmental control over a population in a recognised territory) without enforcing the legal limitations of 'state sovereignty' by 'popular sovereignty' and 'individual sovereignty' as recognised in UN HRL. As EU law has not conferred any explicit powers on EU institutions to violate international law to the detriment of EU citizen interests in the 'rule

[5] Cf EU Petersmann, *Cosmopolitan Constitutionalism for Multilevel Governance of Global Public Goods* (forthcoming 2015).

of law' and in a rules-based 'social market economy' based on 'strict observance of international law' (Article 3 TEU), the political claims by EU institutions for 'freedom of manoeuvre' to violate international treaties ratified by parliaments—without offering adversely affected citizens and EU Member States effective judicial remedies—remain contested by citizens, national governments and courts of justice[6] and risk undermining the legitimacy of EU law, as illustrated by the persistent violations of the budget, debt and economic convergence disciplines of EU law (cf Article 126 TFEU) by most Member States of the European Monetary Union aggravating the financial, economic, social and democratic crises in the EU since 2008.[7]

Economists are confronted with similar methodological controversies resulting from competing value premises (for example, regarding the relationship between governmental and private interests). Most economists focus on utilitarian 'Pareto efficiency' in the sense of governmental duties to maximise individual preference satisfaction (methodological individualism). 'Welfare utilitarianism' focuses on maximising the aggregate individual welfare levels proceeding from the assumption that promoting welfare interests will lead to higher levels of individual preference satisfaction. Yet, most economists evaluate and interpret UN and WTO agreements on the basis of 'Kaldor-Hicks efficiency' focusing on government preferences justifying governmental policies if the expected social benefits exceed the expected social costs, thus making it possible for agents to whom benefits accrue to compensate those bearing net costs. Yet, there is increasing criticism also by economists (like Nobel Prize economist Amartya Sen) of reductionist conceptions of the utility-maximising *homo economicus* and of neglect (for example, by advocates of 'Kaldor-Hicks efficiency' focusing on potential—rather than actual—compensation of losers by winners) for equal rights and personal autonomy (such as in preference aggregation sacrificing some people for the benefit of all others); 'human development approaches' emphasise that satisfaction of basic needs, 'development as freedom' (for example, to develop one's human capacities) and fulfilment of the human rights obligations of governments are morally and legally more legitimate policy goals than authoritarian governmental preference aggregation to the detriment of general consumer welfare (which would require free trade and non-discriminatory regulation of 'market failures' inside and beyond states).[8] European competition, customs union and common market law and its rights-based interpretation by European courts illustrate the need for reconciling the diverse economic, constitutional and international legal approaches to economic regulation with due respect for the human rights obligations of all governments

[6] On competing claims by national, EU and WTO dispute settlement bodies to define the legal limits and responsibilities of EU institutions for violations of international law see above, nn 3 and 4.

[7] Cf A von Bogdandy and M Ioannidis, 'Systemic Deficiency in the Rule of Law: What it is, What has been done, What can be done' (2014) 51 *CMLRev* 59–96.

[8] Cf A Sen, *Development as Freedom* (2000); MC Nussbaum, *Creating Capabilities. The Human Development Approach* (2011).

to protect equal freedoms as the 'first principle of justice' (Rawls) and general consumer welfare for the benefit of all citizens.[9]

'Realist' political scientists continue to view international relations as dominated by power politics requiring prioritisation of national interests (notably in national security). As the EU institutions lack a common military 'hard power' and are constitutionally committed to promoting 'community interests' rather than state interests, political analyses of the EU's role in international politics tend to focus on the civilian 'soft power' of the EU (for example, in terms of promoting common EU and UN policy objectives through financial assistance, know how, market access opportunities) and its 'normative power' (such as in terms of justifying multilevel governance in terms of 'cosmopolitan constitutionalism') to influence foreign policies through normative justifications and economic assistance (for example, based on the 'human rights clauses' in international agreements of the EU with more than 130 third countries) rather than through physical force.[10] The pro-EU demonstrations by democracy advocates in Ukraine illustrate this 'normative power of attraction' of EU association and accession policies empowering people to enjoy multilevel protection of fundamental rights and rule of law through transformative EU agreements. Yet, just as 'in economics … very little attention is given to the theory of the individual',[11] the diverse foreign policy approaches discussed in Section II—such as 'national political realism' focusing on states and state interests, 'liberal international institutionalism' focusing on reciprocally agreed rules and institutions for intergovernmental supply of international PGs, and alternative cosmopolitan and constitutional approaches to multilevel governance of international PGs—often proceed from diverse political conceptions of individuals, governments and of multilevel 'governance' without clarifying their mutual interrelationships and 'overlapping principles of justice' as recognised in UN, WTO, EU and national legal systems.[12] The disagreement as to what procedural, distributive and corrective 'climate justice' and 'common but differentiated responsibilities' require in restricting greenhouse gas emissions, or the political opposition against liberalising free movements of persons in the EU (for example, so as to restrict perceived 'welfare tourism' by Romanians, Bulgarians or economic migrants from Africa), in free trade agreements with the USA (for

[9] On the need for reconciling the diverse economic and legal approaches in interpreting international economic law see my Chapter IV on 'Need for an Economic Analysis of International Economic Law' in E-U Petersmann, *Constitutional Functions and Constitutional Problems of International Economic Law* (1991) 73–94. On the diverse 'atomistic' and 'socially embedded' conceptions of individuals in economics see JB Davis, *The Theory of the Individual in Economics. Identity and Value* (2003).

[10] Cf E-U Petersmann, 'Integrating Human Rights into EU Trade Relations—The EU as a Global Role Model?' in T Takacs, A Ott and A Dimopoulos (eds), *Linking Trade and Non-Commercial Interests: The EU as a Global Role Model?* CLEER Working Paper 2013/4, 15–26.

[11] Davis, above n 9, at 1.

[12] On the diversity of theories of justice justifying international economic law and their common 'constitutional core principles' see E-U Petersmann, *International Economic Law in the 21st Century. Constitutional Pluralism and Multilevel Governance of Interdependent Public Goods* (2012), chs I and VI.

example, US opposition against immigration from Mexico) and under 'Mode 4' of the WTO's General Agreement on Trade in Services, illustrate the value problems underlying international economic and political regulations. The 'realist chessboard conception' of power-oriented international relations (as illustrated by the exercise of hegemonic veto-powers in UN and WTO institutions) often runs counter to the 'global network conception' applied by transnational corporations (eg in their 'global supply chains' for 'international production' of goods and services) and in citizen-driven 'cosmopolitan governance' of European common markets and free trade agreements.

B. Need for Interdisciplinary Clarification of the 'Principles of Justice' Underlying UN/WTO Law

The tensions between power-oriented and normative approaches to designing, evaluating and justifying EU external actions are reflected in many discussions on EU participation in UN and WTO decision making. At the conference discussions at Geneva, for example, Anglo-Saxon arguments in favour of 'pragmatic ad hoc solutions' for the diverse EU policy objectives in UN institutions (for example, UN Security Council reforms, 'human rights approaches' to reforming international economic regulation as suggested by the UN High Commissioner for Human Rights) and for maximising EU values through 'double memberships' of both the EU as well as of EU Member States (for example, as two complementary sources of legitimacy and power in the FAO, WTO and in other international institutions with 'double membership' of the EU and its Member States) were challenged by EU Commission officials warning of 'too much pragmatism' and 'ad hoc policies' that can cause too many 'bad precedents' exploited by vested interest groups. The contrast between, on the one side, the rights-based '*Kadi* jurisprudence' of the CJEU annulling EU regulations implementing UN Security Council sanctions against alleged terrorists on grounds on violations of fundamental rights[13] and, on the other side, the WTO jurisprudence of the CJEU denying individual rights of EU traders to judicial protection of EU compliance with WTO obligations and WTO dispute settlement rulings, including rights to compensation of injuries caused to EU traders by lawful trade sanctions in response to EU violations of WTO law,[14] appears likewise influenced by constitutional traditions of interpreting constitutionalism as 'constitutional contracts' among institutions (for example, the 'Bill of Rights' enacted by the British Parliament in 1689 and accepted by the new King as a 'constitutional limitation' so as to uphold the nation's 'ancient rights and liberties') rather than as 'social contracts among equal citizens' establishing

[13] Cf Case C-402/05P and C-415/05 *P Kadi and Al Barakaat Foundation v Council and Commission*, ECR 2008 I-6351; Joined Cases C-584/10P, C-593/10P and C-595/10P, judgment of 18 July 2013, para 131 (not yet reported).

[14] Cf A Thies, *International Trade Disputes and EU Liability* (2013).

governments with constitutionally limited powers deriving their legitimacy from protecting fundamental rights of citizens (for example, following the American and French human rights revolutions of the 18th century). EU law defines constitutional democracy in terms of constitutional rights of citizens rather than in terms of English traditions of 'parliamentary freedom to regulate'; it protects also transnational constitutional rights and remedies such as 'the freedom to conduct a business in accordance with Union law' (Article 16 EU Charter of Fundamental Rights). Hence, Anglo-Saxon arguments against judicial protection of EU 'market freedoms' and other fundamental rights in the external trade relations of the EU's customs union (cf Articles 28 TFEU, XXIV GATT) are difficult to reconcile with the comprehensive EU guarantees of fundamental rights and transnational rule of law; as EU law nowhere confers powers on the EU to violate international treaties ratified by parliaments for the benefit of citizens, persistent EU violations of GATT/WTO obligations and of related GATT/WTO dispute settlement rulings require a higher burden of justification as being necessary for protecting legitimate EU community interests than 'political question theories' inside national constitutional democracies like the USA, especially if such EU violations of 'rule of law' undermine consumer welfare, non-discriminatory conditions of competition and equal rights of EU citizens and redistribute 'protection rents' to powerful interest groups. As EU citizens are 'constituent powers' and their national parliaments have delegated only limited foreign policy powers to EU institutions subject to cosmopolitan constitutional restraints (eg in Articles 2, 3 and 21 TEU), the new policy of the EU Commission to exclude rights and effective judicial remedies of citizens under EU free trade agreements (FTAs)—and to conduct such FTA negotiations secretly (eg the EU-Canada FTA negotiations 2009–2014) so as to limit the legal, democratic and judicial accountability of EU politicians—also raises constitutional problems.[15]

Similar to the need for reviewing the spontaneous 'fast thinking' of rational individuals guided by 'basic instincts', traditions and value preferences by more reasonable 'slow thinking' of responsible citizens, as explained by theories of justice and modern brain research,[16] the utility-maximising pursuit of self-interests by rational economic and political actors must remain subject to constitutional 'checks and balances' by legal, democratic and judicial accountability mechanisms protecting the reasonable common interests and constitutional rights of citizens

[15] Cf A Semertzi, 'The Preclusion of Direct Effect in the Recently Concluded EU Free Trade Agreements' (2014) 51 *CMLRev* 1125–58.

[16] On the distinction—as two dialectic thinking processes characteristic of human rationality—of 'unconscious, intuitive fast thinking' from 'conscious slow thinking' based on deductive reasoning double-checking the cognitive biases of human instincts and intuition, see D Kahneman, *Thinking, Fast and Slow* (2011). Modern theories of justice emphasise similarly the dynamic and dialectic nature of constitutional democracies depending on a 'four-stage sequence' (cf J Rawls, *A Theory of Justice*, 1972, at 195 ff) of transforming agreed 'principles of justice' into constitutional and legislative rules and their administrative and judicial enforcement subject to democratic accountability mechanisms and judicial remedies of citizens.

adversely affected by intergovernmental majority politics. The more globalisation transforms national PGs into transnational 'aggregate PGs' (like human rights, rule of law, democratic governance, mutually beneficial monetary, trading, environmental and security systems) that national legal systems can protect only in close cooperation with international law and institutions, the more multilevel governance problems must be resolved in conformity with transnational rule of law protecting the common core of 'human rights and fundamental freedoms for all' (cf Article 1 UN Charter) recognised in UN, WTO, EU and national legal systems with due respect for legitimate 'constitutional pluralism', 'subsidiarity principles' and 'duties to protect' sovereign rights of peoples and individuals to regulate their diverse private and public, national, transnational and international 'contexts of justice' in legitimately diverse ways (for example, by protecting higher standards of human rights at local, national and regional levels of governance than in UN institutions).[17] Just as the American and French human rights advocates in the 'democratic revolutions' of the 18th century had good reasons to interpret constitutionalism as 'social contracts' among citizens on 'principles of justice' (for example, as pronounced in the 1776 US Declaration of Independence rejecting British feudal and colonial disregard for human rights, the 1789 French Declaration on the Rights of Man and the Citizen rejecting also colonial slave trade and other feudal human rights violations), EU citizens have good reason in the 21st century to prioritise their constitutional rights over the limited, delegated powers of all governance agents and to challenge the 'regulatory capture' of intergovernmental decision making in UN and WTO institutions without effective protection of PGs and of constitutional rights and remedies of citizens in mutually beneficial cooperation among citizens across national frontiers.

II. HUMAN RIGHTS LAW AND EU LAW REQUIRE PROTECTING TRANSNATIONAL RULE OF LAW IN MULTILEVEL GOVERNANCE SYSTEMS THROUGH 'CONSISTENT INTERPRETATIONS' AND 'JUDICIAL COMITY'

Democratic self-government of citizens remains an illusion without rule of law at national and international levels of governance. Multilevel governance systems for the collective supply of functionally limited, international PGs demanded by citizens—for example, through UN, WTO and EU law and policies and multilevel legal and judicial protection of common markets at local, national, regional and

[17] On the need for protecting private and public supply of PGs demanded by citizens through 'cosmopolitan constitutionalism' recognising citizens as authors and addressees of constitutional rights (eg rights of access to justice and to public justification of governmental restrictions of equal liberties and social rights) that need to be progressively institutionalised (eg through constitutional, legislative, administrative and also international lawmaking, adjudication, 'participatory' and 'deliberative democracy') in response to the 'public reason' of citizens as 'agents of justice' see E-U Petersmann, 'International Economic Law in the 21st Century: Need for Stronger "Democratic Ownership" and Cosmopolitan Reforms' in (2011) *Polish Yearbook of International Law* XXXI, 9–46.

worldwide levels of governance—tend to be based on the same constitutional principles of popular self-determination, rule of law, access to justice and legal responsibility of states and autonomous customs territories (like the EU, Hong Kong, Macau and Taiwan as independent WTO members).[18] As legal systems of 'primary rules of conduct' and 'secondary rules of recognition, change and adjudication'[19] require clarification and progressive development through legislation, administration, impartial dispute settlement and adjudication, the UN Charter and the WTO Agreement—similar to the Lisbon Treaty—constitute, limit and regulate legislative, administrative and judicial powers and justify their legitimate use by duties to protect human rights (for example, Articles 1, 55 and 56 UN Charter), 'raising standards of living, ensuring full employment and a large and equally growing volume of real income and effective demand', and 'the optimal use of the world's resources in accordance with the objective of sustainable development' (Preamble of the WTO Agreement).[20] Delimiting reciprocal market access commitments enabling a welfare-increasing, global division of labour from sovereign rights and 'duties to protect' non-economic PGs (like human rights, 'sustainable development') remains one of the core 'constitutional problems' of UN and WTO law (for example, in the 'conditionality' of financial assistance from the Bretton Woods institutions). As all agreements use indeterminate legal terms giving rise to disputes over the legal obligations of each member to 'ensure the conformity of its laws, regulations and administrative procedures with its obligations' under the treaties concerned (cf Article XVI(4) WTO Agreement), the UN Charter, the 'dispute settlement system of the WTO' (Article 3 Dispute Settlement Understanding) and EU law also recognise the systemic character of their respective dispute settlement systems and the need for interpreting international treaties—as required by the customary rules of treaty interpretation codified in the Vienna Convention on the Law of Treaties—'in conformity with the principles of justice and international law', including 'human rights and fundamental freedoms for all' (Preamble and Article 31 VCLT). National, regional and worldwide tribunals emphasise that this 'integration principle' of international treaty interpretation requires mutually 'consistent interpretations' of overlapping legal obligations of governments and 'judicial comity' among courts of justice in 'overlapping jurisdictions' so as to administer justice in their common task of impartial dispute settlement aimed at protecting

[18] For inductive proof and deductive justification of this normative claim see Petersmann (n 9); G Anderson (ed), *Internal Markets and Multilevel Governance: The Experience of the EU, Australia, Canada, Switzerland and the US* (Oxford, Oxford University Press, 2012).

[19] On the characteristics of 'legal systems' as a union of 'primary rules of conduct' and 'secondary rules of recognition, change and adjudication' see HLA Hart, *The Concept of Law* (Oxford, Oxford University Press, 1994), ch V.

[20] For a discussion of the different kinds of public goods—eg 'best shot PGs' (like a medical invention), 'weakest link PGs' (like nuclear non-proliferation), and 'aggregate PGs' (like democratic peace)—and their diverse 'production strategies' see S Barret, *Why Cooperate? The Incentive to Supply Gobal Public Goods* (2007); E-U Petersmann (ed), *Multilevel Governance of Interdependent Public Goods. Theories, Rules and Institutions for the Central Policy Challenge in the 21st Century* (Florence, EUI Working Paper RSCAS 2012/23).

transnational rule of law for the benefit of citizens, for instance by 'providing security and predictability to the multilateral trading system' (Article 3 DSU). WTO law—similar to UN human rights law and EU law—provides for legal and judicial remedies not only at intergovernmental levels; it also protects individual access to justice in domestic legal systems, for instance in the field of GATT (cf Article X), the WTO Antidumping Agreement (cf Article 13), the WTO Agreement on Customs Valuation (cf Article 11), the Agreement on Pre-shipment Inspection (cf Article 4), the Agreement on Subsidies and Countervailing Measures (cf Article 23), the General Agreement on Trade in Services (cf Article VI GATS), the Agreement on Trade-Related Intellectual Property Rights (cf Articles 41–50, 59 TRIPS) and the Agreement on Government Procurement (cf Article XX).[21] As multilevel governance and adjudication derive their democratic legitimacy from protecting human and constitutional rights of citizens, national and international dispute settlement bodies must cooperate in their common task of promoting mutually consistent interpretations and transnational rule of law for the benefit of citizens cooperating in the collective supply of international PGs (like the global division of labour based on international trade, global production and 'supply chains').[22]

UN and European HRL, like the multilevel legal and judicial protection of cosmopolitan legal and social rights in international commercial, investment, criminal law and in many regional free trade and customs union agreements based on GATT Article XXIV, proceed from 'individualist conceptions of constitutionalism' based on mutual respect for 'human dignity' and 'reason and conscience' (Article 1 UDHR) of human beings as universally accepted foundations of inalienable human rights. EU constitutional lawyers also rightly interpret the Lisbon Treaty mandate for the EU external relations policies (for example, Articles 3 and 21 TEU) in terms of 'cosmopolitan constitutionalism' (for example, recognising EU citizens as authors and addressees of constitutional democracies entitled to protection of human rights and transnational rule of law also beyond nation states). Diplomats emphasising the need for 'foreign policy discretion' often fail to respond convincingly to constitutional and human rights arguments that legal, democratic and judicial accountability mechanisms holding 'Westphalian intergovernmentalism' accountable to citizens will contribute to 'institutionalizing public reason' beneficial for all (such as protecting diplomats against undue interest group pressures). Arguably, the new policy of the EU Commission to exclude rights and judicial remedies under EU FTAs—eg in Article 14.16 of the EU-Canada FTA—without justification of the necessity of such restrictions (eg of the 'freedom

[21] Cf Petersmann (above, n 2), at 194 ff, 233 ff.

[22] Legal duties of judicial cooperation among national and international courts are increasingly recognised beyond national, regional and functional legal systems (like human rights and economic integration law, international commercial, investment and criminal law), for instance in case of 'overlapping jurisdictions' among international courts (eg in the *Mox Plant* dispute submitted to arbitration under the OSPAR environmental convention, the dispute settlement procedures of the UN Law of the Sea Convention and of EU law; in the *Brazil—retreaded tyres* dispute submitted to both MERCOSUR arbitration and WTO dispute settlement proceedings); cf Petersmann, above, n 12, ch VIII.

to conduct a business in accordance with Union law' pursuant to Article 16 EU Charter of Fundamental Rights) for meeting 'objectives of general interest' or for 'protecting the rights and freedoms of others' (as required by Article 52 EU Charter of Fundamental Rights) violates the constitutional rights and remedies of EU citizens (eg Article 47 EU Charter of Fundamental Rights). The 'executive dominance' in the legal interpretation by diplomats of the five competing paradigms of foreign policies and of multilevel governance of international 'aggregate PGs' (like the horizontally and vertically interdependent monetary, trading, investment, environmental, human rights and rule of law systems) is increasingly challenged by civil society, democratic parliaments and courts of justice in order to limit the intergovernmental disregard for human rights and consumer welfare (which are not explicitly mentioned in WTO law) and the obvious governance failures in collective protection of international PGs through UN law and EU foreign policies.

A. Justice as International Order Protected by Power (for example, GATT 1947)?

National 'political realism' focuses on states as main international actors in a 'billiard ball model' of 'international law among egoist states' driven by power politics so as to maximise national security and other 'state interests'. Realists claim that, as state-centred international law reflects the *status quo* distribution of power rather than 'principles of justice', also 'international adjudication is unable to impose effective restraints upon the struggle for power on the international scene.'[23] International courts can only be effective 'in those spheres which do not affect the security and existence of the state'.[24] 'Political disputes' over the use of force and the distribution of power underlying the applicable rules of international law risk eluding judicial control and being 'non-justiciable', as illustrated by the fact that the Permanent Court of International Justice (PCIJ) considered such an international dispute only once.[25] Similarly, national courts also tended to be ineffective in constraining democratic revolutions challenging power-oriented, authoritarian legal systems (for example, in England in the 17th century, America and France in the 18th century). Colonial and intergovernmental power politics in the context of the General Agreement on Tariffs and Trade (GATT 1947, which was not ratified by the US Congress) prior to the establishment of its Legal Office in 1982/83 illustrated the IEL dimensions of 'political realism'. Many GATT rules and GATT dispute settlement rulings were not effectively implemented inside domestic legal systems (for example, in the context of import restrictions on cotton and

[23] H Morgenthau, *Politics among Nations. The Struggle for Power and Peace* (1951), at 224.

[24] EH Carr, *The Twenty-Years Crisis 1919–1939* (1940), at 249.

[25] Cf Morgenthau, above, n 23, at 224 (discussing the PCIJ advisory opinion on the dispute over the German-Austrian Customs Union, PCIJ Ser A/B, No 41).

textiles from less-developed countries) if domestic interest groups and power-oriented majority politics objected to the adjustment costs resulting from trade liberalisation and trade regulation. As GATT 1947 was applied only on the basis of a 'Protocol on Provisional Application' without ratification by national parliaments and subject to 'grandfather clauses' protecting GATT-inconsistent national legislation, the first and second Directors-General of GATT 1947 (Wyndam White and Olivier Long)—albeit both lawyers by training—deliberately avoided establishing a GATT Office of Legal Affairs up to the 1980s. 'Political realists' conceive IEL as 'international law among sovereign states' (such as GATT 1947) prioritising rights of governments over rights of citizens so as to enable power-oriented, 'pragmatic intergovernmental management' of transnational economic relations. Even though GATT diplomacy aimed at remedying some injustices of colonial politics (for example, by adding Part IV on 'Trade and Development' to GATT 1947), trade diplomats often continue expressing the view of Thrasymachos in Plato's *Republic* that justice is merely whatever the powerful say it is. Realist conceptions of foreign power politics in a 'society of states' fail to protect justice vis-à-vis individuals, including domestic citizens participating in the global division of labour without effective judicial remedies against violations of UN and WTO agreements ratified by national parliaments for the benefit of citizens, yet ignored by most domestic courts at the request of governments interested in limiting their legal, democratic and judicial accountability vis-à-vis citizens for (inter)governmental restrictions of equal liberties and human rights in the foreign policy area.[26] The persistent failures of WTO diplomats to liberalise and regulate world trade through the Doha Development Round negotiations since 2001 illustrate that the prevailing 'chessboard conception' of UN and WTO diplomats insisting on veto powers undermines the decentralised 'network conception' underlying the global division of labour (eg global supply chains) and the increasing reality of unilateral, bilateral and plurilateral trade regulation outside the WTO by governments willing to promote consumer welfare, competition and 'development as freedom' through trade liberalisation and empowerment of citizens.

B. Justice as Republican Democratic Decision Making (for example, the Bretton Woods and 1979 Tokyo Round Agreements)

The foreign policies of liberal states tend to be guided in diverse ways by their domestic 'principles of justice'.[27] 'Wilsonian liberalism' believed that, following World War I, the USA could protect international peace through promoting liberal democratic values and institutions for peaceful resolution of international disputes. But the rejection by the US Congress of US membership of the League of Nations and of US acceptance of the compulsory jurisdiction of the PCIJ

[26] Cf Petersmann, above, n 12, chs V and VI.
[27] Cf FJ Garcia, *Global Justice and International Economic Law. Three Takes* (2013), at 67 ff.

illustrated that democratic people might also refuse to project national democratic and judicial institutions onto international levels of governance in a world including non-liberal and 'outlaw states'. Neither under the League of Nations nor under the UN has it been possible to institute effective 'world parliaments' and 'world courts' with universal compulsory jurisdictions. 'Democratic New Haven approaches' to US foreign policies following World War II succeeded in persuading other states to ratify the UN Charter and other agreements establishing UN Specialized Agencies (like the Bretton Woods institutions) on the basis of drafts prepared by the US Government, and to incorporate explicit references to 'principles of justice' and 'human rights and fundamental freedoms for all' into the UN Charter and other UN agreements (like human rights instruments, the Preamble of the 1969 Vienna Convention on the Law of Treaties (VCLT)). Yet, the policy-oriented 'democratic participant perspective' of the New Haven School was also invoked in order to justify US legal privileges (for example, veto rights in UN and Bretton Woods institutions), unilateral military interventions, US refusals to participate in international PGs regimes (like compulsory jurisdiction of the ICJ, the International Criminal Court, the Kyoto Convention on climate change prevention), and discriminatory economic sanctions (for example, by means of Section 301 of the US Trade Act). Constitutional republicanism (eg definining '*res publica*' in terms of constitutional rights of citizens limiting 'market failures' as well as 'government failures') and economic liberalism require protecting freedom of trade across frontiers and correcting 'market failures' through non-discriminatory internal regulations in order to maximise consumer welfare; yet, due to the 'Lockean dilemma' of inadequate constitutional restraints of foreign policy powers, discretionary trade policy powers tend to be 'captured' by protectionist interest groups also inside constitutional democracies without effective judicial protection of 'equal freedoms' as 'first principle of justice' (Rawls).[28] Rawls' proposals for a Law of Peoples justify the existing principles of UN law for the national pursuit of international justice in an international society of liberal states, non-liberal but 'decent states', outlaw states, and states burdened by unfavourable conditions,[29] without proposing a theory of global justice based on cosmopolitan or communitarian principles limiting the 'justice deficits' of international law. The limited 'duties of international assistance' recognised in Rawls' *Law of Peoples* for a non-ideal 'society of states' confirm that nationalist 'democratic conceptions' of IEL aim to legitimise international economic regulation in terms of parliamentary ratification and control of IEL agreements (for example, US congressional ratification of the Bretton Woods Agreements, congressional control of financial assistance by the Bretton Woods institutions, US 'fast track authority' for negotiating and ratifying the 1979 Tokyo Round Trade Agreements) without effective protection of human rights, justice and international PGs across national borders.

[28] Cf Petersmann, above n 9, and FJ Garcia, *Trade, Inequality and Justice: Toward a Liberal Theory of Just Trade* (2003).
[29] Cf J Rawls, *Law of Peoples* (1999), at 59 ff.

C. 'Constitutional Justice' as Multilevel Constitutional Protection of Constitutional Rights (for example, in European Human Rights and Economic Law)

All UN Member States have adopted national (big C) Constitutions (written or unwritten) that recognise the importance of international law and institutions for the collective supply of international 'aggregate PGs' demanded by citizens, including functionally limited (small c) 'treaty constitutions' (*sic*) establishing UN Specialized Agencies like the International Labour Organization (ILO), the World Health Organization (WHO), the Food and Agriculture Organization (FAO) and the UN Educational, Scientific and Cultural Organization (UNESCO), whose founding treaties were explicitly called 'constitutions'. Such functionally limited treaty constitutions constitute multilevel governance powers (the 'enabling function' of constitutions); subject governments to legal and institutional restraints (the 'limiting function' of constitutions); commit government policies to protecting PGs (like protection of human rights, 'sustainable development') through agreed regulatory instruments (the 'regulatory function' of constitutions); and legitimise law and governance by 'principles of justice' (the 'justificatory function' of constitutions), such as labour rights justifying ILO law, human rights to education and democratic governance justifying UNESCO law, rights to health protection justifying WHO law, and freedom from hunger justifying FAO law. Yet, the inadequate legal, democratic and judicial protection and 'institutionalisation' of such human rights in foreign policies and UN law entails a lack of accountability of governments dominating UN decision-making processes; hence, most UN institutions fail to protect international PGs effectively for the benefit of all citizens (like UN HRL, transnational rule of law). Even though globalisation continues to transform most national PGs into international 'aggregate PGs' and increases transnational interdependencies and global cooperation among citizens, communitarian and cosmopolitan conceptions of IEL have become effective only in regional free trade areas and common markets like the EU. The regional treaties establishing the EU, the European Economic Area (EEA) and the European Convention on Human Rights (ECHR) are interpreted and enforced by national and European courts as 'constitutional instruments' protecting regional PGs—like the European common market, human rights, fundamental freedoms and transnational rule of law for the benefit of citizens—for instance through 'constitutional interpretations' (for example, of 'common market freedoms', parliamentary prerogatives, judicial cooperation) guaranteeing cosmopolitan rights of citizens, democratic and judicial accountability of governments, and 'evolutionary interpretations' adjusting indeterminate rules to 'cosmopolitan public reason'.[30] Such multilevel 'constitutional approaches' suggest that—similar to the experience of 'republican

[30] Cf E-U Petersmann, 'Multilevel Judicial Governance in European and International Economic Law' in S Besson and A Ziegler (eds), *Le juge en droit européen et international* (2013) 45–64.

constitutionalism' (eg since the ancient Athenian and Roman republics 2,500 years ago) that effective protection of *national PGs* depends on participatory rights of citizens and other republican rights to hold government agents legally and democratically accountable—also collective supply of *transnational PGs* depends on republican and 'cosmopolitan rights' of citizens to participate in multilevel governance and hold all multilevel governance agents legally, democratically and judicially accountable.

D. 'Commutative Justice' in Functionally Limited PGs Regimes (for example, WTO Law)

The WTO Agreement establishes multilevel legal, governance and dispute settlement systems outside the UN legal system aimed at promoting reciprocal liberalisation and regulation of a multilateral trading system based on mutually agreed 'commutative justice principles',[31] like reciprocal market access commitments (for example, Articles II and XXVIII GATT) subject to sovereign rights to protect non-economic PGs (for example, Articles XIX–XXI GATT). Yet, similar to UN law, WTO law remains dominated by 'inter-governmental decision-making' and fails to protect its treaty objectives (like 'sustainable development') effectively due to inadequate regulation of 'market failures', 'governance failures' and of legal, democratic and judicial 'accountability mechanisms'. WTO dispute settlement bodies recognise that WTO law does not constitute a 'self-contained regime'; treaty-based IEL systems remain embedded into general and treaty law, as illustrated by the WTO provisions for cooperation with other treaty regimes (for example, IMF law) and regulatory agencies (for example, national and non-governmental risk assessment institutions in the field of technical and sanitary regulation). Yet, even though WTO law provides for a multilevel legal and dispute settlement system protecting also individual 'access to justice' in domestic courts (cf Article X GATT and numerous other WTO provisions), many governments limit their domestic legal and judicial accountability for harmful violations of their WTO obligations by insisting that domestic courts should *not* apply WTO law and WTO dispute settlement rulings for the benefit of citizens. Similarly, many free trade agreements (for example, by the USA) remain dominated by hegemonic power politics rather than liberal and constitutional 'principles of justice'.[32] This defensive

[31] The Latin term 'commutare' means 'to exchange'; 'commutative justice' refers to mutual agreements on functionally limited 'treaty principles of justice' like reciprocal market access commitments and the economic efficiency principles underlying the legal ranking of economically 'optimal trade policy instruments' in GATT/WTO law (eg non-discriminatory domestic regulation and subsidies rather than border discrimination, tariffs rather than non-tariff trade barriers, sanitary regulations on the basis of science-based 'risk-assessments' rather than on the basis of discriminatory protectionism). Due to the absence of universally agreed criteria of just results of economic exchange, IEL provides for more dispute settlement procedures than most other areas of international law.

[32] Cf Garcia, above n 27, eg at 260 ff (describing US abuses of power in NAFTA and CAFTA dispute settlement procedures as illustrating 'how US trade policy is not always consistent with notions of justice', at 257, 324). As to the situation of WTO rules in the EU Legal Order, see notably C Kaddous,

'chessboard mentality' of power-oriented foreign policies—by disconnecting UN and WTO governance from citizens, civil society and domestic courts of justice—undermines the legitimacy and effectiveness of multilevel 'disconnected UN and WTO governance' by unaccountable diplomats.

E. 'Cosmopolitan Justice Regimes' (for example, Commercial and Investment Law)

Cosmopolitan conceptions of IEL and HRL[33] aim at multilevel legal and judicial protection of commercial, property and other rights of citizens and transnational rule of law protecting citizens through institutionalised, citizen-driven networks of national and transnational courts and arbitral tribunals. Cosmopolitan legal regimes—like transnational commercial and investment law and arbitration, rights-based free trade agreements like the EEA, common market and competition law agreements of the EU, international criminal law, consular law and related adjudication—have proved to protect international PGs (like transnational rule of law, fundamental rights) more effectively than 'Westphalian regimes' prioritising rights of governments over rights of citizens without effective legal, democratic and judicial accountability of governments vis-à-vis adversely affected citizens.[34] Similar to defining 'cosmopolitan constitutionalism' by the *trias* of human rights, rule of law and democratic governance, transnational cosmopolitan regimes are characterised by multilevel judicial protection of individual rights, democratic governance and rule of law for the benefit of citizens, for instance through:

— cooperation between national courts and arbitral tribunals in the recognition, surveillance and enforcement of arbitral awards (for example, pursuant to the 1958 New York Convention on Recognition and Enforcement of Foreign Arbitral Awards);
— cooperation among national and regional economic and human rights courts like the European Free Trade Area (EFTA) Court, the CJEU and the European Court of Human Rights (ECtHR);
— the arbitration and annulment procedures of the International Center for the Settlement of Investment Disputes (ICSID) in cooperation with national courts; or
— the more than half a dozen international criminal courts complementing national criminal jurisdictions.

Multilevel cooperation among domestic and international courts in their joint enforcement of transnational legal orders can promote mutually beneficial,

'Le statut du droit de l'OMC dans l'ordre juridique communautaire: développements récents', in *Mélanges en hommage à Jean-Victor Louis* (Editions de l'Université de Bruxelles, 2003) 107–26, 125–26.

[33] The Greek term 'cosmopolite' refers to a 'citizen of the world' recognising all human beings as morally equal and constituting a single world community that should avoid national prejudices.

[34] Cf Petersmann, above n 12, at 145 ff.

transnational cooperation among citizens, governmental and non-governmental actors for the collective supply of PGs (like common markets, human rights, transnational rule of law). But multilevel 'judicial governance' must remain embedded into intergovernmental cooperation and transnational governance networks of regulatory agencies (like central banks, competition authorities, food safety, environmental and other regulatory agencies) subject to legal, democratic and judicial accountability mechanisms promoting legitimacy and domestic political support.[35] Justification of multilevel governance in terms of protecting cosmopolitan rights and transnational cooperation among sub-state actors (for example, in the context of transnational 'supply chains' for 'international production' of goods and services like energy and food security, cooperation among Hong Kong, Macau and Taiwan as sub-state WTO members recreating a common market with China) can reinforce the 'constitutional functions' of multilevel rules and institutions for protecting international PGs demanded by citizens.[36] It requires national, regional and worldwide tribunals to engage not only in more 'judicial comity' in jointly clarifying—through 'dynamic judicial interpretations' with due respect for democratic rule-clarification—the constitutional, legislative, executive and international legal limits of multilevel governance affecting fundamental rights of citizens, such as privacy rights neglected by mass surveillance of personal data by unaccountable security agencies and their private-sector partners; property rights of savers and investors affected by one-sided 'economic justifications' of monetary and financial under-regulation; or secretive 'intergovernmental restrictions' (like unpublished 'voluntary export restrictions') undermining rights of citizens and of parliaments. Multilevel judicial governance in IEL should promote mutually coherent interpretations of the 'principles of justice' underlying UN, WTO, regional and national legal systems and exercise judicial deference vis-à-vis legitimately diverse regulations and 'reasonable disagreements', for instance if—in euro governance adjudication—economists from the European Central Bank invoke 'economic demand side' justifications of using central bank powers broadly for shifting economic adjustment costs on Eurozone countries with current account surpluses (like Germany), and reject 'economic supply side' arguments that the lack of deflationary 'demand side deficits' justifies keeping economic adjustment pressures on over-indebted Eurozone economies persistently violating the EU budget, debt and economic convergence disciplines.

III. EU LAW AND UN HUMAN RIGHTS LAW JUSTIFY EU LEADERSHIP FOR COSMOPOLITAN INTERPRETATIONS OF LAW AND 'RULES OF RECOGNITION'

Just as European HRL has justified cosmopolitan interpretations of European economic law and of the Lisbon Treaty requirement of promoting human rights,

[35] On this emergence of a 'new disaggregated world order' and 'judges constructing a global legal system' see AM Slaughter, *A New World Order* (2004) at 65 ff.

[36] Cf Petersmann, above n 12, chs I to IV.

rule of law and democratic governance in the EU's external actions, so do the universal human rights obligations of all UN Member States justify cosmopolitan interpretations of UN and WTO law for the benefit of citizens. The codification of the 'rules of recognition' in Article 38 ICJ Statute must be interpreted in conformity with the governmental 'duties to protect, respect and fulfill human rights' as limiting Westphalian conceptions of state sovereignty and state consent by the multilevel human rights obligations 'recognized by civilized nations' and supported and clarified through 'judicial decisions and the teachings of the most highly qualified publicists of the various nations, as subsidiary means for the determination of rules of law' in virtually all UN Member States (Article 38(c) and (d)). As recognised by ever more courts of justice, Westphalian traditions of prioritising reciprocal rights and obligations of governments in international treaty provisions do not exclude recognition of corresponding rights of citizens:

> the fact that certain provisions of the Treaty are formally addressed to the Member States does not prevent rights from being conferred at the same time on any individual who has an interest in compliance with the obligations thus laid down (see Case 43/75 *Defrenne v Sabena* [1976] ECR 455, para 31). Such consideration must, *a fortiori*, be applicable to Article 48 of the Treaty, which ... is designed to ensure that there is no discrimination on the labour market.[37]

Also, sociological conceptions of positive law as being based on authoritative issuance and social effectiveness of rules and principles do not run counter to an admission that the incorporation of 'inalienable' human rights and 'principles of justice' into national and international legal systems entails a 'dual nature' and 'constitutional limitation' of modern international law: legitimate authority and *opinio juris* in the 21st century derive from consent of citizens, their democratic representatives and from 'principles of justice' progressively clarified by impartial and independent courts of justice limiting intergovernmental power politics, and protecting human and constitutional rights of citizens. The increasing recognition of limitations of state sovereignty by 'responsibilities to protect' human rights and other internationally recognised 'common concerns' are evidence of the changing nature of international law in the 21st century in response to the universal recognition of the need for protecting international PGs more effectively for the benefit of citizens through multilevel governance and corresponding legal constraints on 'collective action problems' (for example, due to 'prisoners' dilemmas' in preventing terrorism, climate change and economic under-regulation that leave most citizens worse off).

A. Democratic Clarification of 'Principles of Justice' in Conformity with Multilevel HRL

The survey (in Section II) of five competing conceptions of promoting 'justice' in international law illustrates that—in today's non-ideal reality of international

[37] Cf Case C-281/98 *Angonese* [2000] ECR I-4139.

relations—the diverse interpretations of formal, procedural, distributive, corrective, commutative, cosmopolitan justice and equity principles for reforming international law exclude worldwide agreement on one single, comprehensive approach to promoting justice in the global economy. Yet, this need for respecting the legitimate reality of 'constitutional' and 'methodological pluralism' and for 'piecemeal reforms' of unjust state practices does not preclude recognition of the legitimate tasks of civil society struggles and courts of justice to hold governance institutions accountable for their failures to protect human rights and other international PGs more effectively, for instance through judicial clarification of 'principles of justice', multilevel 'judicial dialogues' and protection of fundamental rights across frontiers, and legal promotion of 'participatory' and 'deliberative democracy' through treaty interpretations 'in conformity with principles of justice' and 'human rights and fundamental freedoms for all', as required by the customary rules of treaty interpretation. Just as multilevel HRL emphasises that national and international justice are interdependent and based on principles of subsidiarity (for example, in terms of primary individual and democratic responsibilities inside states and only subsidiary responsibilities of the international community), so are multilevel IEL and its multilevel judicial protection increasingly justified in terms of economic freedoms, private property rights, individual access to justice, rule of law and legal and judicial 'balancing' of economic rights with all other constitutional rights of citizens. The diverse utilitarian, libertarian and egalitarian conceptions of regulating market economies inside states all emphasise governmental duties to protect consumer welfare through liberal trade and non-discriminatory regulation of 'market failures' (like cartel agreements, other abuses of market power, social injustices) so that citizens can accept social outcomes as justifiable in terms of 'principles of justice'. Owing to globalisation, peaceful cooperation and global division of labour beyond state borders likewise require justification of the social distribution of benefits and burdens so that citizens can support and accept international rules and institutions as justifiable. In their current negotiations on a new Transatlantic Trade and Investment Partnership agreement, the EU and the USA should exercise joint leadership for reforming IEL and its human rights dimensions (for example, regarding private data protection) through stronger protection of cosmopolitan rights and transnational rule of law. Similar to the citizen-oriented legal reforms promoted by joint cooperation of the ILO and EU,[38] the 2012 revised WTO Agreement on Government Procurement (for example, its domestic judicial remedies provided for in Article XX) and the 2014 WTO Agreement on Trade Facilitation offer additional opportunities for using EU 'soft' and 'normative powers' for strengthening WTO and UN agreements (for example, on financial assistance by the World Bank for domestic implementation of trade facilitation obligations in less-developed countries) by 'embedding' their rules into domestic legal and institutional reforms empowering citizens and private economic actors.

[38] Cf *The ILO and the EU, Partners for Decent Work and Social Justice* (ILO, 2012).

In conformity with the 'cosmopolitan mandate' in Article 21 TEU for the EU's external policies, the EU Strategic Framework and Action Plan on Human Rights and Democracy adopted by the EU Council in June 2012 emphasises that the 'EU will promote human rights in all areas of its external action without exception … The EU will place human rights at the centre of its relations with all third countries, including its strategic partners'.[39] The explicit exclusion in EU regulations implementing WTO law and recent free trade agreements (such as with Korea, Singapore and Canada) of rights of EU citizens to invoke precise and unconditional WTO and FTA obligations of the EU in domestic courts runs counter to the 'methodological individualism' of HRL and European IEL as well as to the WTO guarantees of individual access to domestic judicial remedies. The protectionist disregard for WTO obligations and WTO dispute settlement rulings by European courts confirms the lack of a coherent concept of EU institutions for protecting transnational rule of law for the benefit of EU citizens in trade relations beyond Europe.[40] Arguably, European 'cosmopolitan constitutionalism' requires 'principled justifications' not only of 'European tolerance' vis-à-vis legitimately diverse national constitutional traditions inside EU and UN Member States. It also requires EU leadership in multilevel governance of international PGs for 'cosmopolitan interpretations' of the common principles and values underlying and justifying UN, WTO and EU law, notwithstanding the often diverse interpretations of these common principles by UN, WTO and EU diplomats representing diverse national peoples and civil societies with diverse traditions of constitutional democracy. 'Cosmopolitan constitutionalism' rightly avoids any dogmatism vis-à-vis the legitimately diverse communitarian forms of constitutional democracies and related multilevel governance of international PGs (such as by remaining agnostic vis-à-vis 'Kantian moral constructivism' and alternative 'Rawlsian contractual' or 'Habermasian democratic discourse' interpretations of 'social contracts' so as to reduce the 'burden of judgment' following from 'Kantian moral imperatives'). HRL protects the normative reality of individual and democratic diversity, 'reasonable disagreement' and 'constitutional pluralism' as 'constitutional values' limiting (inter)governmental lawmaking and justifying the 'constitutional pluralism' characteristic of European law (for example, EU law, EEA law, ECHR, ad hoc solutions for third countries like Switzerland with legitimate democratic preferences to cooperate with the EU as a non-member country). Even though the EU's cosmopolitan constitutionalism (that is, incorporating the national 'constitutional trias' of human rights, democratic governance and rule of law into EU constitutional law) requires respecting legitimate constitutional diversity inside and outside the EU, the 'human rights conditionality' of EU accession, association and economic agreements justifies supporting civil society by interpreting and designing IEL agreements in favour of cosmopolitan rights and more effective

[39] EU Press Release 11855/12 of 25 June 2012, p 2.

[40] Cf Petersmann, above n 12, ch V, and L Pech, *Rule of Law as a Guiding Principle of the EU's External Action* (CLEER Working Paper 2012/3).

judicial remedies of citizens.[41] As the EU's representation and participation in international organisations often involves legal rather than only political and diplomatic issues, recourse to judgments or advisory opinions by the CJEU has proved to be an important option for clarifying the legal cooperation duties of EU Member States and for overcoming political opposition against exercise of EU powers in UN institutions (for example, in view of the limited EU membership status in the FAO), for instance by authoritarian third states resenting 'EU exceptionalism', the 'normative power' of the EU and EU initiatives for stronger democratic accountability mechanisms.[42]

B. Judicial Protection of 'Principles of Justice' and Cosmopolitan Rights

'Transitional justice' advocates emphasise the ancient origins and advantages of judicial administration of justice in conflict situations characterised by social disagreement on 'principles of justice', antagonistic struggles for revenge of past injustices, and the political need for pragmatic 'piecemeal transformations' through restorative and retributive measures aimed at protecting peaceful change and democratic 'public reason'.[43] The role of national and European courts in transforming European legal systems since World War II confirms that the ideas of 'justice' and of change through time—'transition'—are not mutually exclusive in view of the need for progressively adjusting and reforming authoritarian legal systems so as to protect human rights of citizens in concrete disputes through 'judicial administration of justice', notwithstanding continuing disagreement on comprehensive theories of justice for a perfectly just society (such as proposed in Rawls' *Theory of Justice*). The increasing references to human rights and other 'principles of justice' in the jurisprudence of international courts and arbitral tribunals illustrate the increasing recognition that the 'executive dominance' of UN and WTO politics by rulers and diplomats interested in limiting their own legal, democratic

[41] On the EU's promotion of civil society support, social norms and 'corporate social responsibility' in EU trade agreements see the various case studies in Takacs et al, above n 10. In EU investment agreements, the EU's support of investor–state arbitration remains impeded by the non-membership of the EU of the International Center for the Settlement of Investment Disputes (ICSID). In transatlantic relations and FTAs among constitutional democracies, equal protection of effective access of all citizens to domestic courts is also constitutionally more legitimate than investor-state privileges for foreign investors without effective constitutional restraints.

[42] On the EU's representation and participation in international organisations, see C Kaddous, *The European Union in International Organizations and Global Governance*, and the doctrine cited on that topic, in the Introduction to this volume.

[43] 'Transitional justice' is sometimes traced back to Aeschylos' *Oresteia*, where *Athena* saved *Orest* from the revenge of the Furies (the Erinnyes goddesses of revenge in Greek mythology) by submitting the dispute over Orest's killing of his mother (so as to avenge her killing of his father Agamemnon) to the court of Athens and casting the decisive vote for pardoning Orest, thereby inducing the Furies to accept impartial and independent dispute resolution based on 'procedural justice' (similar to the Nuremberg trials following World War II).

and judicial accountabilities vis-à-vis civil societies adversely affected by 'Westphalian power politics' can be constitutionally limited only through 'piecemeal reforms'. As long as the prioritisation of rights of governments in UN and WTO law fails to effectively protect justice vis-à-vis individuals and citizens, case-by-case adjudication and promotion of 'participatory' and 'deliberative democracy' and cosmopolitan accountability mechanisms offer pragmatic 'second-best strategies' in non-ideal multilevel governance and legal systems.[44]

The term 'justice' has been developed in the context of domestic societies for describing principles for justifying rules, institutions, social processes and their distribution of benefits and burdens vis-à-vis the affected people. Globalisation continues to transform national social interactions through transnational and international processes creating new social outcomes requiring new justifications at national, transnational and international levels, with due respect for the diverse 'contexts of justice' and for 'reasonable disagreement' among individuals, people and governments with often conflicting self-interests and comprehensive conceptions of a good life and 'political justice'. The diverse conceptions of IEL discussed in Section II—for example, as 'international law among sovereign states', 'global administrative law', international private and conflicts law, multilevel economic regulation or multilevel constitutional law[45]—require not only respect for legitimate 'constitutional pluralism' as a permanent fact and legitimate, normative claim based on individual and democratic diversity protected by HRL. The need for making multilevel governance of international PGs more effective in order to reduce unnecessary poverty and human rights violations also calls for stronger 'mainstreaming' of the universal human rights obligations accepted by all UN Member States into UN and WTO politics, for instance by stronger legal guarantees of 'access to justice', of national 'margins of regulatory appreciation', and of more comprehensive 'balancing' of civil, political, economic, social and cultural rights with due regard for local democratic preferences and scarcity of resources. The multilevel legal and judicial protection of cosmopolitan rights and transnational rule of law for the benefit of citizens in ever more areas of international law—like international commercial law (for example, multilevel legal and judicial recognition and protection of freedom of contract, freedom of arbitration, supervision of arbitration and enforcement of arbitral awards by national courts), investment law (for example, multilevel legal and judicial recognition and protection of investor rights, judicial remedies, judicial duties of balancing private and public interests pursuant to thousands of investment treaties), international criminal law (for example, multilevel legal and judicial protection of individuals

[44] On this need for promoting non-ideal paradigms of justice, including Kantian 'moral cosmopolitanism' based on individual judgments that remain independent from ideal conditions of justice, see Petersmann, above n 12, chs III, VI–VIII and A Sen, *The Idea of Justice* (2009).

[45] For a discussion of these five different conceptions of IEL, and on the need for their mutually coherent interpretation and integration in order to solve more effectively the 'collective action problems' of multilevel governance of international public goods, see Petersmann, above n 12, ch I.

against, and prosecution of individuals for crimes against humanity), regional integration law and HRL—suggests an emerging 'overlapping consensus'[46] that cosmopolitan legal regimes have:

- protected international PGs more effectively than state-centred 'Westphalian legal regimes' prioritising rights of governments over rights of citizens;
- respected legitimate individual, democratic and constitutional diversity (for example, as illustrated by the diversity of bilateral investment and regional economic and human rights regimes); and
- limited more effectively 'market failures' as well as 'governance failures' through 'countervailing rights' (for example, of individual access to justice and to public justification of all governmental restrictions of individual freedoms) and constitutional 'checks and balances' (such as judicial remedies) compared with the intergovernmental Bretton Woods and GATT/WTO agreements that do not even mention human rights, consumer welfare and the need for limiting abuses of private economic power through competition, environmental and social regulation.

C. EU Leadership for Cosmopolitan International Law?

The EU can rightly claim that its 'Kadi jurisprudence'—rather than 'fragmenting international law'—has contributed to 'constitutionalising' UN law and to reforming UN Security Council policies in conformity with the human rights obligations of all UN Member States, for example by strengthening legal remedies in UN Security Council decision-making procedures and recognising the sovereign rights of UN members to adopt higher levels of human rights protection in national and regional legal systems than have been agreed so far in UN human rights and security regulations. EU leadership for 'cosmopolitan interpretations' of the multilevel legal and dispute settlement system of the WTO—including bilateral, regional and plurilateral free trade agreements building consensus for future global WTO regulation—could, likewise, assist in transforming the ineffective 'Westphalian international law system' for the benefit of citizens by making private and public actors, and their 'interpretative communities', more aware of the common 'constitutional principles' underlying UN, WTO, regional and national legal systems. The former EU High Representative Lady Ashton has rightly emphasised that 'human rights must run like a silver thread' through all EU external relations policies, yet without excluding practical necessities of finding temporary policy compromises; but 'policy pragmatism' should be justified more clearly in terms of practical 'public reason' that citizens can voluntarily support as reflecting 'principles of justice' rather than outdated 'realpolitik models' promoted by authoritarian governments. In contrast to the lamentations by advocates of 'Westphalian international law' of 'fragmentation' and limitation of 'state sovereignty', citizens in constitutional

[46] Cf Petersmann, above n 12, ch VI.

democracies increasingly recognise the legitimacy of 'fragmentation strategies' limiting abuses of veto-powers (for example, in the UN Security Council through 'humanitarian interventions' by democratic 'alliances of the willing', in consensus-based WTO negotiations through regional and plurilateral trade agreements) and reforming international law 'bottom-up' (for example, through the thousands of bilateral investment and double taxation agreements). The pragmatic combination of competing legal and political methodologies must be evaluated from 'dynamic' and result-oriented perspectives: just as theories of justice and constitutional 'contract theories' explain why constitutional democracies must dynamically evolve through constitutional, legislative, administrative and judicial clarification and institutionalisation of 'principles of justice' agreed and supported by citizens, so must multilevel governance of international PGs be constitutionally designed as dynamic, yet pragmatic processes of multilevel constitutional, legislative, administrative and judicial institutionalisation of a new 'cosmopolitan public reason', whose democratic legitimacy depends on justifying imperfect governance practices vis-à-vis citizens through 'deliberative', 'participatory' and representative procedures of democratic governance.

The EU's external relations practices offer numerous successful examples for pragmatic, temporary policy solutions (for example, EC *de facto* membership of GATT since the 1960s) that paved the way for subsequent 'constitutional reforms' (for example, replacement of GATT 1947 by the now almost universal WTO Agreement with de jure EU membership and compulsory dispute settlement systems). The need for legitimising EU governance by 'public reason' and democratic support—also in EU external relations law—requires more attention to justifying the 'methodological pluralism' in EU foreign policy discourses on how the common values underlying UN, WTO and EU law should be interpreted and legally implemented for the benefit of citizens and their human right 'to a social and international order in which the rights and freedoms set forth in this Declaration can be fully realized' (Article 28 of the Universal Declaration of Human Rights of 1948). The online publication—in September 2014—of the EU-Canada draft 'Comprehensive Economic and Trade Agreement' illustrated the potential dangers of allowing EU trade diplomats to negotiate secretly transatlantic FTAs with legislative functions for replacing EU regulatory standards for collective supply of transnational 'aggregate PGs'. EU citizens could find on page 470 of the more than 1630 treaty pages the following Article 14.16 on 'Private Rights':

> Nothing in this Agreement shall be construed as conferring rights or imposing obligations on persons other than those created between the Parties under public international law, nor as permitting this Agreement to be directly invoked in the domestic legal systems of the Parties.
>
> No Party may provide for a right of action under its domestic law against the other Party on the ground that a measure of the other Party is inconsistent with this Agreement.

The EU Commission does not explain why—contrary to the EU Treaty requirement to contribute 'in its relations with the wider world ... to the protection of its citizens' (Article 3:5 TEU) in conformity with the 'principles which have inspired (the EU's) own creation, development and enlargement' (Article 21 TEU) and the transnational rights of citizens under EU constitutional law and under FTAs concluded by the EU up to 2006[47]—it now proposes such an 'anti-citizen clause' excluding legal and judicial accountability of trade politicians vis-à-vis EU citizens for harmful violations of FTA rules and obligations. Informally, EU officials admit that their long-standing arguments against 'direct effect' of GATT/WTO rules—for instance, that GATT/WTO rules are less precise and less unconditional than EU trade rules, or that WTO safeguard, reciprocity and dispute settlement provisions exclude 'direct effect'—were neither legally coherent nor applicable to FTAs. The EU's main argument accepted by the CJEU is its claim of 'political freedom of maneuver' as justification of excluding 'direct effect' of WTO and FTA rules.[48] Yet, isn't the EU constitutional requirement of 'strict observance of international law' (Article 3 TEU) a democratically more legitimate 'principle of justice' for transatlantic FTAs among democracies committed to the 'coherence-' and 'consistent-interpretation' requirements of national and international legal systems (eg Article XVI:4 WTO, Article 3 DSU), the 'network conception' of trading communities (eg interested in reducing transaction costs for global supply chains), multilevel judicial administration of justice (eg judicial comity among national and international courts of justice), and human and cosmopolitan rights of citizens as 'foundation of freedom, justice and peace in the world', as universally emphasised in UN human rights law? Without more 'civilian vigilance' for assuming their cosmopolitan responsibilities for collective supply of transnational PGs and for multilevel protection of cosmopolitan rights, EU citizens, their democratic representatives in national and EU parliaments and civil society will fail to limit the past 'governance failures' and related 'market failures' that have distorted consumer welfare and curtailed rights of citizens in transatlantic relations over the past decades.[49]

[47] Cf Semertzi, above, n 15.

[48] Cf nn 3 and 4 above.

[49] Cf EU Petersmann and M Pollack (eds), *Transatlantic Economic Disputes. The EU, the US and the WTO* (Oxford, Oxford University Press, 2003).

Annex 1

**COUNCIL OF
THE EUROPEAN UNION**

Brussels, 24 October 2011

15901/11

PESC 1328
CONUN 104
COSCE 18
WTO 373
FAO 34
ENV 808
ENER 334
ATO 125
CONOP 67

NOTE

from:	General Secretariat of the Council
to:	Delegations
Subject:	EU Statements in multilateral organisations - General Arrangements

At its meeting on 22 October 2011, the Council endorsed the General Arrangements for EU Statements in multilateral organisations as set out in the Annex.

ANNEX

EU Statements in multilateral organisations
General Arrangements

1. This document offers a number of general arrangements with regard to the delivery of EU Statements in multilateral organisations.

2. The Treaty of Lisbon enables the EU to achieve coherent, comprehensive and unified external representation. The EU Treaties provide for close and sincere cooperation between the Member States and the Union. Given the sensitivity of representation and potential expectations of third parties, it is essential that, in conformity with current practice, the preparation of statements relating to the sensitive area of competences of the EU and its Member States should remain internal and consensual.

3. The following arrangements apply
   - The EU can only make a statement in those cases where it is competent and there is a position which has been agreed in accordance with the relevant Treaty provisions.
   - External representation and internal coordination does not affect the distribution of competences under the Treaties nor can it be invoked to claim new forms of competences.
   - Member States and EU actors[1] will coordinate their action in international organisations to the fullest extent possible as set out in the Treaties.
   - The EU actors and the Member States will ensure the fullest possible transparency by ensuring that there is adequate and timely prior consultation on statements reflecting EU positions to be made in multilateral organisations.

[1] The term EU actor is used to denote those actors competent to represent the Union as provided in the Treaties, i.e. the President of the European Council, the Commission, the High Representative and EU Delegations.

- Member States agree on a case by case basis whether and how to co-ordinate and be represented externally. The Member States may request EU actors or a Member State, notably the Member State holding the rotating Presidency of the Council, to do so on their behalf.
- Member States will seek to ensure and promote possibilities for the EU actors to deliver statements on behalf of the EU.
- Member States may complement statements made on behalf of the EU whilst respecting the principle of sincere cooperation.
- EU representation will be exercised from behind an EU nameplate unless prevented by the rules of procedure of the forum in question.
- EU actors will conduct local coordination and deliver statements on behalf of the EU unless prevented by the rules of procedure of the forum concerned (default setting). Where practical arrangements such as those at the World Trade Organisation, at the Food and Agricultural Organisation and in burden sharing exist for coordination and/or representation, such arrangements will be implemented for the preparation and delivery of the statement on behalf of the EU from behind the EU nameplate.

4. Practical guidelines:

Statements will reflect EU positions agreed in conformity with the decision making procedures as foreseen in the Treaties.

- Should the statement refer exclusively to actions undertaken by or responsibilities of the EU in the subject matter concerned including in the CFSP, it will be prefaced by "on behalf of the European Union".
- Should the statement express a position common to the European Union and its Member States, pursuant to the principle of unity of representation, it will be prefaced by "on behalf some of the EU and its Member States". The introduction "on behalf of the EU and its Member States" does not preclude references to "the EU" or to "the Member States of the EU" later in the text, where such reference accurately reflects the factual situation.

Should the Member States agree to collective representation by an EU actor of issues relating to the exercise of national competences, the statement will be prefaced by "on behalf of the Member States". The introduction "on behalf of the Member States" does not preclude references to the "EU" later in the text, where such reference accurately reflects the factual situation.

5. Disclaimer
The Member States and the Council, the Commission and the EEAS accept the following disclaimer[1]:
"The adoption and presentation of statements does not affect the distribution of competences or the allocation of powers between the institutions under the Treaties. Moreover, it does not affect the decision-making procedures for the adoption of EU positions by the Council as provided in the Treaties".

6. Should a problem arise in the application of these arrangements that cannot be solved through local coordination, the Head of the EU delegation will refer the matter to the EEAS which will, in close consultation with the Commission, submit when appropriate the matter to Coreper for decision.

7. These arrangements, agreed at Coreper level, are forwarded to the Council for its endorsement. The EEAS and the Commission services will present a report on their implementation at the latest by the end of 2012. In light of this Report, the arrangements could, if so decided by Coreper, be reviewed.

---

[1] This disclaimer will be reflected in the minutes of Coreper.

Annex 2

United Nations A/RES/65/276*

General Assembly

Distr.: General
10 May 2011

Sixty-fifth session
Agenda item 120

Resolution adopted by the General Assembly on 3 May 2011

[*without reference to a Main Committee (A/65/L.64/Rev.1)*]

65/276. Participation of the European Union in the work of the United Nations

The General Assembly,

Bearing in mind the role and authority of the General Assembly as a principal organ of the United Nations and the importance of its effectiveness and efficiency in fulfilling its functions under the Charter of the United Nations,

Recognizing that the current interdependent international environment requires the strengthening of the multilateral system in accordance with the purposes and principles of the United Nations and the principles of international law,

Recognizing also the importance of cooperation between the United Nations and regional organizations, as well as the benefits to the United Nations of such cooperation,

Acknowledging that it is for each regional organization to define the modalities of its external representation,

Recalling its resolution 3208 (XXIX) of 11 October 1974, by which it granted observer status to the European Economic Community,

Recalling also that, consistent with the relevant legal provisions, the European Union has replaced the European Community and is a party to many instruments concluded under the auspices of the United Nations and an observer or participant in the work of several specialized agencies and bodies of the United Nations,

Noting that the States members of the European Union have entrusted the external representation of the European Union, previously performed by the representatives of the member State holding the rotating Presidency of the Council of the European Union, to the following institutional representatives: the President of the European Council, the High Representative of the Union for Foreign Affairs and Security Policy, the European Commission, and European Union delegations, which have assumed the role of acting on behalf of the European Union in the exercise of the competences conferred by its member States,

* Reissued for technical reasons on 18 May 2011.

Mindful of the modalities for the participation of observer States and entities, and other observers in the work of the United Nations, as set out in the respective resolutions,

1. *Reaffirms* that the General Assembly is an intergovernmental body whose membership is limited to States that are Members of the United Nations;

2. *Decides* to adopt the modalities set out in the annex to the present resolution for the participation of the representatives of the European Union, in its capacity as observer, in the sessions and work of the General Assembly and its committees and working groups, in international meetings and conferences convened under the auspices of the Assembly and in United Nations conferences;

3. *Recognizes* that, following a request on behalf of a regional organization that has observer status in the General Assembly and whose member States have agreed arrangements that allow that organization's representatives to speak on behalf of the organization and its member States, the Assembly may adopt modalities for the participation of that regional organization's representatives, such as those set out in the annex to the present resolution;

4. *Requests* the Secretary-General to inform the General Assembly during its sixty-fifth session on the implementation of the modalities set out in the annex to the present resolution.

88th plenary meeting
3 May 2011

Annex

Participation of the European Union in the work of the United Nations

1. In accordance with the present resolution, the representatives of the European Union, in order to present positions of the European Union and its member States as agreed by them, shall be:

(*a*) Allowed to be inscribed on the list of speakers among representatives of major groups, in order to make interventions;

(*b*) Invited to participate in the general debate of the General Assembly, in accordance with the order of precedence as established in the practice for participating observers and the level of participation;

(*c*) Permitted to have its communications relating to the sessions and work of the General Assembly and to the sessions and work of all international meetings and conferences convened under the auspices of the Assembly and of United Nations conferences, circulated directly, and without intermediary, as documents of the Assembly, meeting or conference;

(*d*) Also permitted to present proposals and amendments orally as agreed by the States members of the European Union; such proposals and amendments shall be put to a vote only at the request of a Member State;

(*e*) Allowed to exercise the right of reply regarding positions of the European Union as decided by the presiding officer; such right of reply shall be restricted to one intervention per item.

2. The representatives of the European Union shall be ensured seating among the observers.

3. The representatives of the European Union shall not have the right to vote, to co-sponsor draft resolutions or decisions, or to put forward candidates.

4. A precursory explanation or recall of the present resolution shall be made only once by the President of the General Assembly at the start of each session.

Index

CPSIA information can be obtained
at www.ICGtesting.com
Printed in the USA
LVHW072022140623
749768LV00003B/83

9 781509 918379